THE VILLAGE LABOURER

1760-1832

A Study in the Government of England before the Reform Bill

J. L. HAMMOND AND BARBARA HAMMOND

> . . . The men who pay wages ought not to be the political
> masters of those who earn them (because laws should be
> adapted to those who have the heaviest stake in the
> country, for whom misgovernment means not mortified
> pride or stinted luxury, but want and pain, and degradation
> and risk to their own lives and to their children's souls). . . .
>
> LORD ACTON.

ALAN SUTTON
1987

ALAN SUTTON PUBLISHING
BRUNSWICK ROAD · GLOUCESTER

First published 1911
by Longmans, Green, and Co., London

British Library Cataloguing in Publication Data

Hammond, J.L.
The village labourer, 1760–1832 : a study
of the government of England before the
Reform Bill.
1. England—Rural conditions
I. Title II. Hammond, Barbara
942'.009'734   HN398.E5

ISBN 0-86299-345-8

Cover picture: detail from Hampstead Heath
by John Constable; Bury Art Gallery.
Photograph: Bridgeman Art Library

Printed in Great Britain by
The Guernsey Press Company Limited
Guernsey, Channel Islands

TO

GILBERT AND MARY MURRAY

PREFACE

MANY histories have been written of the governing class that ruled England with such absolute power during the last century of the old régime. Those histories have shown how that class conducted war, how it governed its colonies, how it behaved to the continental Powers, how it managed the first critical chapters of our relations with India, how it treated Ireland, how it developed the Parliamentary system, how it saved Europe from Napoleon. One history has only been sketched in outline: it is the history of the way in which this class governed England. The writers of this book have here attempted to describe the life of the poor during this period. It is their object to show what was in fact happening to the working classes under a government in which they had no share. They found, on searching through the material for such a study, that the subject was too large for a single book; they have accordingly confined themselves in this volume to the treatment of the village poor, leaving the town worker for separate treatment. It is necessary to mention this, for it helps to explain certain omissions that may strike the reader. The growth and direction of economic opinion, for example, are an important part of any examination of this question, but the writers have been obliged to reserve the consideration of that subject for their later volume, to which it seems more appropriate. The writers have also found it necessary to leave entirely on one side for the present the movement for Parliamentary Reform which was alive throughout this period, and very active, of course, during its later stages.

Two subjects are discussed fully in this volume, they believe, for the first time. One is the actual method and procedure of Parliamentary Enclosure; the other the labourers' rising of 1830. More than one important book has been written on enclosures during the last few years, but nowhere can the student find a full analysis of the procedure and stages by which the old village was destroyed. The rising of 1830 has only been mentioned incidentally in general histories : it has nowhere been treated as a definite demand for better conditions, and its course, scope, significance, and punishment have received little attention. The writers of this book have treated it fully, using for that purpose the Home Office Papers lately made accessible to students in the Record Office. They wish to express their gratitude to Mr. Hubert Hall for his help and guidance in this part of their work.

The obligations of the writers to the important books published in recent years on eighteenth-century local government are manifest, and they are acknowledged in the text, but the writers desire to mention specially their great debt to Mr. Hobson's *Industrial System,* a work that seems to them to throw a new and most illuminating light on the economic significance of the history of the early years of the last century.

Mr. and Mrs. Arthur Ponsonby and Miss M. K. Bradby have done the writers the great service of reading the entire book and suggesting many important improvements. Mr. and Mrs. C. R. Buxton, Mr. A. Clutton Brock, Professor L. T. Hobhouse, and Mr. H. W. Massingham have given them valuable help and advice on various parts of the work.

Hampstead, *August* 1911

PREFACE TO NEW EDITION

In preparing a new impression of *The Village Labourer*, the authors have corrected certain inaccuracies that have been pointed out by reviewers, to whom they are duly grateful.

They welcome also the opportunity of discussing the more serious criticisms that have been passed on their general treatment of the subject of the enclosures.

These criticisms are three in number :

It is alleged (1) that the writers have drawn an unjust picture, because they deliberately excluded the effect of enclosure in increasing the food supplies of the nation.

(2) That they have not allowed for the decline of domestic industries, though that decline is sometimes represented as a more important cause of the degradation of the labourer than the loss of common rights and the changes in farming.

(3) That the hardships of the poor have been exaggerated, and that though the system of enclosure by Parliamentary Committee lent itself to abuses, there is no evidence that wrong was done in the great mass of enclosures. The references to actual enclosures have been blamed in this connection as misleading.

The writers beg to submit the following considerations :

(1) It has been the accepted view of all modern critics, with the single exception of Dr. Hasbach, that the enclosures of this period, or rather the enclosures that took place after 1795, made the soil of England immediately more productive. That this is the usual view was stated in the text : its correctness was not discussed or questioned. The authors had not set out to examine the general economic effect of enclosures, but the methods by which those enclosures were carried out and their social consequences. It seemed to them no more unreasonable to abstract that aspect for discussion than it would be to treat the exploitation of children in the factories without entering into the general merits of the Industrial

Revolution. Their subject in this volume was the fate of the Village Labourer, and so far as he is concerned the facts which they are accused of neglecting suggest two reflections: (a) the feeding of Manchester and Leeds did not make life cheaper to him; and (b) if agriculture suddenly became a great industry, multiplying as some say England's resources twenty-fold, an equitable readjustment must have increased the prosperity of all classes engaged in that industry. The greater the stress laid on the progress of agriculture, the greater appear the perversity and injustice of the arrangements of a society under which the labourer became impoverished. If it is argued that the misery of the labourer was the price the nation had to pay for that advance, it is worth while to point out that that was not the view of Young, or Davies, or Eden, or Sinclair, or Cobbett, and that the actual revolution that was accomplished was not the only alternative to the old unreformed common field system.

(2) Whatever the effects of the disappearance of domestic industries on the family income of the agricultural labourer in certain districts, the authors cannot agree that the loss of any subsidiary earnings was comparable in importance to the change that alienated the soil from the whole labouring class. If the labourer, by retaining his hold upon the soil, or by receiving a guaranteed and adequate minimum wage, had shared in the expanding prosperity of agriculture, the liberation of his family from domestic manufacture should have been a gain to him, and the process would have resembled any other extension of exchange and division of labour. The subject of these industries they hope to treat in their next volume. With those classes to whom domestic industries were the main source of subsistence the writers were not dealing in *The Village Labourer*. The question how far the loss of spinning was made good by the employment offered by the new domestic industries that grew up in the period, seems to them to demand fuller inquiry than it has yet received.

(3) The authors desire to point out how little they have relied on solitary instances for their general statements.

Complaint has been made of the publishing of the story of the
attempted enclosure of Sedgmoor, but those who read that
account carefully will see that the passages from Selwyn's
letters are important as disclosing the state of mind of a
chairman of an Enclosure Committee ; they will note also
that his letters show that it was a common practice for
Members of Parliament to arrange meetings in order to mani-
pulate Committees in the interest of private persons. Selwyn's
view of the responsibilities of a chairman of one of these
Committees has therefore a special significance. The main
question for the historian is this : Were the poor sacrificed or
not in the enclosures as they were carried out ? The writers
have given their reasons for thinking that they were sacrificed,
and needlessly sacrificed, and no evidence has come under
their notice in the criticisms published to shake that view.
They have set out the actual methods of procedure that were
adopted for converting England from the old to the new
system, and they think it is clear that those methods were
such that the poor were bound to suffer unless Parliament
expressly intervened for their protection. This was apparent,
or became apparent, to observers at the time, and proposals
that would have helped the poor were made by Arthur Young,
by Eden, by Davies, by Suffield, and by the Board of
Agriculture. Those proposals were disregarded, not necessarily
from wickedness or rapacity, but because the atmosphere of
the ruling class was unfavourable. Young referred to his own
proposal six years later in a passage which is worth quoting :
' I have been reading over my *Inquiry into the Propriety
of applying Wastes to the better Maintenance of the Poor.*
I had almost forgotten it, but of all the essays and papers I
have produced, none I think so pardonable as this, so convincing by facts, and so satisfactory to any candid reader. Thank
God I wrote it, for though it never had the smallest effect
except in exciting opposition and ridicule, it will, I trust,
remain a proof of what ought to have been done ; and had
it been executed, would have diffused more comfort among
the poor than any proposition that ever was made ' (*Autobiography*, July 14, 1806).

One further fact of interest and importance in this connection may be mentioned. Michael Sadler, the Factory Reformer, was, unhappily for England, thrown out of Parliament after the passing of the Reform Bill. He was in the House of Commons for only three years. One of the most important speeches that he made in his brief career there was a long speech reviewing the disastrous change that had come over the agricultural labourers in recent times. The chief cause he found in the disappearance of the small farmer, the pulling down of cottages, and the enclosures. He said that the enclosures had inflicted on the poor as a class ' the most irreparable injuries.' Like Thelwall, with whom he would have been slow to recognise any affinity, he argued that enclosure might have benefited the poor, but that in practice it had ruined them. ' Inclosures might indeed have been so conducted as to have benefited all parties ; but now, coupled with other features of the system, they form a part of what Blackstone denominates a " fatal rural policy " ; one which has completed the degradation and ruin of your agricultural poor.'

The conclusion of the writers, based on a careful study of the methods of procedure and a careful reading of the facts they could collect, is thus supported by a great mass of authority, the authority of observers who were in close touch with the population affected by the enclosures, and in general sympathy with the class that made them.

The writers have gone very fully in this volume into the enclosures as the most important social event of the period, but they desire to point out that the subject of the book is the condition of the village labourer, and the way in which the ruling class treated the several problems that were presented by the difficulties of the labourer's position. More than half the book is in fact taken up with other causes of the labourer's degradation than the enclosures themselves. The book is a study in government, a discussion of the lines on which Parliament regulated the lives and fortunes of a class that had no voice in its own destinies.

HEMEL HEMPSTED, *Sept.* 1913.

CONTENTS

CHAPTER I

THE CONCENTRATION OF POWER

'Là l'aristocratie a pris pour elle les charges publiques les plus lourdes afin qu'on lui permît de gouverner ; ici elle a retenu jusqu'à la fin l'immunité d'impôt pour se consoler d'avoir perdu le gouvernement.'

De Tocqueville has set out in this antithesis the main argument that runs through his analysis of the institutions of ancient France. In England the aristocracy had power and no privileges : in France the aristocracy had privileges and no power. The one condition produced, as he read history, the blending of classes, a strong and vigorous public spirit, the calm of liberty and order : the other a society lacking vitality and leadership, classes estranged and isolated, a concentration of power and responsibility that impoverished private effort and initiative without creating public energy or public wealth.

De Tocqueville's description of the actual state of France during the eighteenth century has, of course, been disputed by later French writers, and notably by Babeau. Their differences are important, but for the moment we are concerned to note that in one particular they are in complete agreement. Neither Babeau, nor any other historian, has questioned the accuracy of De Tocqueville's description of the position of the French nobles, from the day when the great cardinals crushed their conspiracies to the day when the Revolution destroyed the monarchy, whose heart and pulse had almost ceased to beat. The great scheme of unity and discipline in which Richelieu had stitched together the discords of France left no place for aristocracy. From that danger, at any rate, the French monarchy was safe. Other dangers were to overwhelm it, for Richelieu, in giving to it its final form, had secured it from the aggressions of nobles but not from the follies of kings. *Tout marche, et le hasard corrige le hasard.* The soliloquy of Don Carlos in *Hernani* contains an element of truth and hope for democracy which is wanting in all systems of personal government, where the chances of recovery all depend on a single caprice. It was the single caprice that Versailles represented. It was the single caprice that destroyed Richelieu's great creation. When Louis XIV. took to piety and to Madame de Maintenon, he rescinded in one hour of fatal zeal the religious settlement that had given her prosperity to France. Her finance and her resources foundered in his hurricanes of temper and of arrogance. Louis XV. was known in boyhood as 'the beloved.' When he fell ill in the campaign of 1744 in Flanders, all France wept and prayed for him. It would have been not less happy for him than it would have been for Pompey if the intercessions of the world had died on the breeze and never ascended to the ear of Heaven. When thirty years later his scarred body passed to the royal peace of St. Denis, amid the brutal jeers and jests of Paris, the history of the French monarchy was the richer for a career as sensual and selfish and gross as that of a Commodus, and the throne which Richelieu had placed absolute and omnipotent above the tempests of faction and civil war had begun to rock in the tempests of two sovereigns' passions.

One half-hearted attempt had indeed been made to change the form and character of the monarchy. When he became regent in 1715, Orleans played with the ideas of St. Simon and substituted for the government of secretaries a series of councils, on which the great nobles sat, with a supreme Council of Regency. As a departure from the Versailles system, the experiment at first excited enthusiasm, but it soon perished of indifference. The bureaucrats, whom Orleans could not afford to put on one side, quarrelled with the nobles : the nobles found the business tedious and uninteresting : the public soon tired of a scheme that left all the abuses untouched : and the regent, at the best a lukewarm friend to his own innovation, had his mind poisoned against it by the artful imagination of Dubois. One by one the councils flickered out; the Council of the Regency itself disappeared in 1723, and the monarchy fell back into its old ways and habits.

As at Versailles, so in France. If the noble had been reduced to a trifling but expensive cypher at the Court, the position of seigneur in the village was not very different. In the sixteenth century he had been a little king. His relations with the peasants, with whom his boyhood was often spent in the village school, were close and not seldom affectionate.

But though he was in many cases a gentle ruler, a ruler he undoubtedly was, and royal ordinances had been found necessary to curb his power. By the eighteenth century his situation had been changed. There were survivals of feudal justice and feudal administration that had escaped the searching eye of Richelieu, but the seigneur had been pushed from the helm, and the government of the village had passed into other hands. It was the middle-class intendant and not the seigneur who was the master. The seigneur who still resided was become a mere rent receiver, and the people called him the ' *Gobereau.*' But the seigneur rarely lived in the village, for the Court, which had destroyed his local power, had drawn him to Paris to keep him out of mischief, and when later the Court wished to change its policy, the seigneur refused to change his habits. The new character of the French nobility found its expression in its new homes. Just as the tedious splendour of Versailles, built out of the lives and substance of an exhausted nation, recorded the decadence and the isolation of the French monarchy, so in the countryside the new palaces of the nobles revealed the tastes and the life of a class that was allowed no duties and forbidden no pleasures. The class that had once found its warlike energy reflected in the castles of Chinon and Loches was now only at home in the agreeable indolence of Azay le Rideau or the delicious extravagance of Chenonceaux. The nobles, unable to feed their pride on an authority no longer theirs, refused no stimulant to their vanity and no sop to their avarice. Their powers had passed to the intendant ; their land was passing to the bourgeois or the peasant ; but their privileges increased. Distinctions of rank were sharper edged. It was harder for a plebeian to become an officer under Louis xvi. than it had been under Louis xiv., and the exemptions from taxation became a more considerable and invidious privilege as the general burdens grew steadily more oppressive. Nature had made the French nobleman less, but circumstances made him more haughty than the English. Arthur Young, accustomed to the bearing of English landlords, was struck by the very distant condescension with which the French seigneur treated the farmer. The seigneur was thus on the eve of the Revolution a privileged member of the community, very jealous of his precedence, quarrelsome about trifles, with none of the responsibilities of a ruler, and with few of the obligations of a citizen. It was an unenviable and an uninspiring position. It is not surprising that Fénelon, living in the frivolous prison of

Versailles, should have inspired the young Duke of Burgundy with his dream of a governing aristocracy, or that Mademoiselle de Lespinasse should have described the public-spirited members of this class as caged lions, or that a nobleman of the fierce energy of the Marquis de Mirabeau should have been driven to divide his time between the public prosecution of his noisy and interminable quarrels with his wife and his sons, and the composition of his feeling treatise on *L'Ami des Hommes*.

For in the France whose king had no thought save for hunting, women and morbid disease, there was endless energy and intellectual life. France sparkled with ideas. The enthusiasms of the economists and philosophers filled the minds of nobles who in England would have been immersed in the practical duties of administration. The atmosphere of social sensibility melted the dry language of official reports, and the intendants themselves dropped a graceful tear over the miseries of the peasants. Amid the decadence of the monarchy and the uncivilised and untamed license of Louis xv., there flourished the emancipating minds of Voltaire, Montesquieu, Diderot and Quesnai, as well as Rousseau, the passion and the spirit of the Revolution. On the one side is Versailles, abandoned to gross and shameless pleasures, on the other a society pursuing here a warm light of reason and science with a noble rage for progress and improvement, bewitched there by the Nouvelle Héloïse and Clarissa, delighting in those storms of the senses that were sweeping over France. The memoirs, the art, the literature of the time are full of these worlds, ruled, one by philosophy and illumination, the other by the gospel of sensibility and tender feeling, the two mingling in a single atmosphere in such a salon as that of Julie de Lespinasse, or in such a mind as that of Diderot. A kind of public life tries, too, to break out of its prison in the zealous, if somewhat mistaken exertions of agricultural societies and benevolent landowners. But amid all this vitality and inspiration and energy of mind and taste, the government and the fortunes of the race depend ultimately on Versailles, who lives apart, her voluptuous sleep undisturbed by the play of thought and hope and eager curiosity, wrapt and isolated in her scarlet sins.

When Louis xvi. called to office Turgot, fresh from his reforms at Limoges, it looked as if the intellect of France might be harnessed to the monarchy. The philosophers believed that their radiant dreams were about to come gloriously true.

Richelieu had planned his system for an energetic minister and a docile king ; Turgot had not less energy than Richelieu, and Turgot's master was not more ambitious than Louis XIII. But the new régime lasted less than two years, for Louis XVI., cowed by courtiers and ruled by a queen who could not sacrifice her pleasures to the peace of France, dismissed his minister, the hopes of the reformers were destroyed, and France settled down to the unrolling of events. The monarchy was almost dead. It went out in a splendid catastrophe, but it was already spent and exhausted before the States-General were summoned. This vast, centralised scheme was run down, exhausted by the extravagance of the Court, unable to discharge its functions, causing widespread misery by its portentous failure. The monarchy that the Revolution destroyed was anarchy. Spenser talks in the *Faerie Queene* of a little sucking-fish called the remora, which collects on the bottom of a ship and slowly and invisibly, but surely, arrests its progress. The last kings were like the remora, fastening themselves on Richelieu's creation and steadily and gradually depriving it of power and life.

It was natural that De Tocqueville, surveying these two centuries of national life, so full of mischief, misdirection and waste, seeing, too, in the new régime the survival of many features that he condemned in the old, should have traced all the calamities of France to the absence of a ruling aristocracy. It was natural that in such a temper and with such preoccupations he should have turned wistfully and not critically to England, for if France was the State in which the nobles had least power, England was the State in which they had most. The Revolution of 1688 established Parliamentary Government. The manners and the blunders of James II. had stripped the Crown of the power that his predecessor had gained by his seductive and unscrupulous politics, and when the great families settled with the sovereign of their choice, their memories of James were too recent and vivid to allow them to concede more than they could help to William. The Revolution put the law of the land over the will of the sovereign : it abolished his suspending and dispensing powers, and it obliged him to summon Parliament every year. It set up a limited monarchy with Parliament controlling the Crown. But though the Revolution gave England a constitutional Parliamentary government, that government had no homogeneous leadership, and it looked as if its effective force might be dissipated in the chaos and confusion of ministries.

In such a situation one observer at least turned his eyes to France. There exists in the British Museum a paper by Daniel Defoe, written apparently for the guidance of Harley, who was Secretary of State in 1704. In this paper Defoe dwelt on the evils of divided and dilatory government, and sketched a scheme by which his patron might contrive to build up for himself a position like that once enjoyed by Richelieu and Mazarin. Defoe saw that the experiment meant a breach with English tradition, but he does not seem to have seen, what was equally true, that success was forbidden by the conditions of Parliamentary government and the strength of the aristocracy. The scheme demanded among other things the destruction of the new Cabinet system. As it happened, this mischievous condition of heterogeneous administration, in which one minister counterworked and counteracted another, came to an end in Defoe's lifetime, and it came to an end by the consolidation of the system which he wished to see destroyed.

This was the work of Walpole, whose career, so uninviting to those who ask for the sublime or the heroic in politics, for it is as unromantic a story as can be desired of perseverance, and coarse method, and art without grace, and fruits without flowers, is one of the capital facts of English history. Walpole took advantage of the fortunate accident that had placed on the throne a foreigner, who took no interest in England and did not speak her language, and laid the foundations of Cabinet government. Walpole saw that if Parliamentary supremacy was to be a reality, it was essential that ministers should be collectively responsible, and that they should severally recognise a common aim and interest; otherwise, by choosing incompatible ministers, the king could make himself stronger than the Cabinet and stronger than Parliament. It is true that George III., disdaining the docility of his predecessors, disputed later the Parliamentary supremacy which Walpole had thus established, and disputed it by Walpole's own methods of corruption and intrigue. But George III., though he assailed the liberal ideas of his time, and assailed them with an unhappy success, did not threaten the power of the aristocracy. He wanted ministers to be eclectic and incoherent, because he wanted them to obey him rather than Parliament, but his impulse was mere love of authority and not any sense or feeling for a State released from this monopoly of class. Self-willed without originality, ambitious without imagination, he wanted to cut the knot that tethered the Crown to the Cabinet, but he had neither the will nor the power to put a knife in the system of aristocracy itself. He wished to set back the clock, but only by half a century, to the days when kings could play minister against minister, and party against party, and not to the days of the more resolute and daring dreams of the Stuart fancy. The large ideas of a sovereign like Henry of Navarre were still further from his petty and dusty vision. He was so far successful in his intrigues as to check and defeat the better mind of his generation, but if he had won outright, England would have been ruled less wisely indeed, but not less deliberately in the interests of the governing families. Thus it comes that though his interventions are an important and demoralising chapter in the history of the century, they do not disturb or qualify the general progress of aristocratic power.

In France there was no institution, central or local, in which the aristocracy held power : in England there was no institution, central or local, which the aristocracy did not control. This is clear from a slight survey of Parliament and of local administration.

The extent to which this is true had probably not been generally grasped before the publication of the studies of Messrs. Redlich and Hirst, and Mr. and Mrs. Webb, on the history of local government or the recent works of Dr. Slater and Professor Hasbach on the great enclosures. Most persons were aware of the enormous power of the aristocracy, but many did not know that that power was greater at the end than at the beginning of the century. England was, in fact, less like a democracy, and more remote from the promise of democracy when the French Revolution broke out, than it had been when the governing families and the governing Church, whose cautions and compromises and restraint Burke solemnly commended to the impatient idealists of 1789, settled their account with the Crown in the Revolution of 1688.

The corruptions that turned Parliamentary representation into the web of picturesque paradoxes that fascinated Burke, were not new in the eighteenth century. As soon as a seat in the House of Commons came to be considered a prize, which was at least as early as the beginning of the sixteenth century, the avarice and ambition of powerful interests began to eat away the democratic simplicity of the old English franchise. Thus, by the time of James i., England had travelled far from the days when there was a uniform franchise, when

every householder who did watch and ward could vote at a
Parliamentary election, and when the practice of throwing
the provision of the Members' wages upon the electorate discouraged the attempt to restrict the franchise, and thereby
increase the burden of the voters. Indeed, when the Whig
families took over the government of England, the case for
Parliamentary Reform was already pressing. It had been
admitted by sovereigns like Elizabeth and James I., and it
had been temporarily and partially achieved by Cromwell.
But the monopolies which had been created and the abuses
which had been introduced had nothing to fear from the great
governing families, and the first acts of the Revolution Parliament, so far from threatening them, tended to give them sanction and permanence. Down to this time there had been a
constant conflict within the boroughs between those who had
been excluded from the franchise and the minorities, consisting
of burgage-holders or corrupt corporations or freemen, who
had appropriated it. These conflicts, which were carried to
Parliament, were extinguished by two Acts, one of 1696, the
other of 1729, which declared that the last determination in
each case was final and irrevocable. No borough whose fate
had been so decided by a Parliamentary committee could ever
hope to recover its stolen franchise, and all these local reform
movements settled down to their undisturbed euthanasia.
These Acts were modified by a later Act of 1784, which allowed
a determination to be disputed within twelve months, but by
that time 127 boroughs had already received their final verdict :
in the others, where the franchise was determined after 1784,
there was some revival of local agitation.

The boroughs that were represented in Parliament in the
eighteenth century have been classified by Mr. Porritt, in
his learned work, in four categories. They were (1) Scot and
lot and potwalloper boroughs, (2) Burgage boroughs, (3) Corporation boroughs, and (4) Freemen boroughs.

The Scot and lot boroughs, of which there were 59, ranged
from Gatton, with 135 inhabitants, to Westminster and
Northampton. On paper they approached most nearly to
the old conditions as to the franchise. A uniform qualification of six months residence was established in 1786. In
other respects the qualifications in these boroughs varied.
In some the franchise depended on the payment of poor rate
or church rate : in others the only condition was that the
voter had not been a charge on the poor rate. The boroughs

of the second of these classes were called potwalloper, because the voter had to prove that he was an inhabitant in the borough, had a family, and boiled a pot there. This potwalloper franchise was a survival from the days when freemen took their meals in public to prove that they did not depend on the table of a lord. In the eighteenth century the potwalloper sometimes put his table in the street to show that he had a vote. But these boroughs, in spite of their wide franchise, fell under the control of the aristocracy almost as completely as the others, for the reason that when the borough itself developed, the Parliamentary borough stood still, and in many cases the inhabitant householders who had the right to vote were the inhabitants of a small and ancient area of the town. All that was necessary in such circumstances in order to acquire the representation of the borough, was to buy the larger part of the property within this area. This was done, for example, at Aldborough and at Steyning.

The Burgage boroughs were 39. They were Parliamentary boroughs in which the right to vote attached exclusively to the possession of burgage properties. The burgage tenants were the owners of land, houses, shops or gardens in certain ancient boroughs. The holders of these sites were originally tenants who discharged their feudal obligations by a money payment, corresponding to the freeholder in the country, who held by soccage. They thus became the men of the township who met in the churchyard or town hall. In many cases residence was unnecessary to the enjoyment of the franchise. The only qualification was the possession of title-deeds to particular parcels of land, or registration in the records of a manor. These title-deeds were called ' snatch papers,' from the celerity with which they were transferred at times of election. The burgage property that enfranchised the elector of Old Sarum was a ploughed field. Lord Radnor explained that at Downton he held 99 out of the 100 burgage tenures, and that one of the properties was in the middle of a watercourse. At Richmond, pigeon-lofts and pig-styes conferred the franchise. In some cases, on the other hand, residence was required; at Haslemere, for example, Lord Lonsdale settled a colony of Cumberland miners in order to satisfy this condition. Sometimes the owner of a burgage property had to show that the house was occupied, and one proof of this was the existence of a chimney. In all of these boroughs the aristocracy and other controllers of boroughs worked hard, through the seventeenth and eighteenth centuries, to restrict the number of properties that carried the right to vote. The holder of burgage property and the borough patron had a common interest in these restrictions. The burgage boroughs provided a great many cases for the decision of Parliamentary committees, and the borough owners mortgaged their estates under the strain of litigation of this kind. Parliamentary committees had to determine for example whether the Widows' Row at Petersfield really stood on the foundation of the house which conferred the franchise in the reign of William III. The most successful borough-monger was the patron who had contrived to exclude first the non-burgage owners, and then the majority of the burgage owners, thus reducing his expenses within the narrowest compass.

The Corporation boroughs, or boroughs in which the corporation had acquired by custom the right to elect, independently of the burgesses, were 43. In days when Parliamentary elections were frequent, the inhabitants of many boroughs waived their right of election and delegated it to the corporations. When seats in the House of Commons became more valuable, the corporations were tenacious of this customary monopoly, and frequently sought to have it established by charter. These claims were contested in the seventeenth century, but without much success, and the charters bestowed at this time restricted the franchise to the corporations in order to prevent ' popular tumult, and to render the elections and other things and the public business of the said borough into certainty and constant order.' It is easy to trace in these transactions, besides the rapacity of the corporations themselves, the influence of the landed aristocracy who were already beginning to finger these boroughs. There was, indeed, an interval during which the popular attacks met with some success. When Eliot and Hampden were on the Committee of Privileges, some towns, including Warwick, Colchester, and Boston, regained their rights. But the Restoration was fatal to the movement for open boroughs, and though it was hoped that the Revolution, which had been in part provoked by the tricks the Stuarts had played with the boroughs, would bring a more favourable atmosphere, this expectation was defeated. All of these boroughs fell under the rule of a patron, who bribed the members of the corporation with money, with livings or clerkships in the state departments, cadetships in the navy and in India. Croker complained that he had further to

dance with the wives and daughters of the corporation at
' tiresome and foolish ' balls.   There was no disguise or mistake about the position.   The patron spoke not of ' my con-
stituents ' but of ' my corporation.'   The inhabitants outside
this little group had no share at all in Parliamentary representation, and neither the patron nor his nominee gave them a single
thought.   The members of the corporation themselves were
often non-resident, and the mayor sometimes never went near
the borough from the first day of his magistracy to the last.
His office was important, not because it made him responsible
for municipal government, but because it made him returning officer.   He had to manage the formalities of an election
for his patron.

The Freemen boroughs, of which there were 62, represent in Mr. Porritt's opinion the extreme divergence from
the old franchise.   In these boroughs restrictions of different
kinds had crept in, a common restriction being that in force
at Carlisle, which limited the franchise to the inhabitants
who belonged to the trade guild.   For some time these restrictions, though they destroyed the ancient significance
of ' freeman ' as a person to be distinguished from the ' villein,'
did not really destroy the representative character of the
electorate.   But these boroughs suffered like the others, and even
more than the others, from the demoralising effects of the appreci-
ation of the value of seats in Parliament, and as soon as votes
commanded money, the corporations had every inducement to
keep down the number of voters.   In many boroughs there
set in a further development that was fatal to the elementary
principles of representation : the practice of selling the freedom
of the borough to non-residents.   There were three classes
of buyers : men who wanted to become patrons, men who
wanted to become members, and men who wanted to become
voters.   The making of honorary freemen became a favourite
process for securing the control of a borough to the corporation or to a patron.   Dunwich, which was a wealthy and
famous seaport in the time of Henry II., gradually crumbled
into the German Ocean, and in 1816 it was described by Old-
field as consisting of forty-two houses and half a church.   This
little borough contained in 1670 forty resident freemen, and in
that year it largessed its freedom on four hundred non-residents.
The same methods were applied at Carlisle, King's Lynn, East
Grinstead, Nottingham, Liverpool, and in many other places.
A particularly flagrant case at Durham in 1762, when 215

freemen were made in order to turn an election, after the issue of the writ, led to a petition which resulted in the unseating of the member and the passing of an Act of Parliament in the following year.   This Act excluded from the franchise honorary freemen who had been admitted within twelve months of the first day of an election, but it did not touch the rights of ordinary freemen admitted by the corporation. Consequently, when a Parliamentary election was impending or proceeding, new freemen used to swarm into the electorate whenever the corporation or the patron had need of them. At Bristol in 1812 seventeen hundred and twenty freemen, and at Maldon in 1826 a thousand freemen, were so admitted and enfranchised.   Generally speaking, corporations seem to have preferred the method of exclusion to that of flooding the electorate with outside creations.   On the eve of the Reform Bill, there were six electors at Rye and fourteen at Dunwich.   At Launceston, early in the eighteenth century, the members of the corporation systematically refused freedom to all but members of their own party, and the same practices were adopted at East Retford, Ludlow, Plympton, Hastings, and other places. Legal remedies were generally out of reach of the excluded freemen. There were some exceptions to the abuses which prevailed in most of these boroughs, notably the case of the City of London. A special Act of Parliament (1774) made it a condition of the enjoyment of the freemen's franchise there, that the freeman had not received alms, and that he had been a freeman for twelve calendar months.   But in most of these boroughs, by the end of the eighteenth century, the electorate was entirely under the influence of the corporations.   Nor was the device of withholding freedom from those qualified by custom, and of bestowing it on those who were only qualified by subservience, the only resource at the command of the borough-mongers. Charities were administered in an electioneering spirit, and recalcitrant voters were sometimes threatened with impressment.

Of the 513 members representing England and Wales in 1832, 415 sat for cities and boroughs. Fifty members were returned by 24 cities, 332 by 166 English boroughs, 5 by single-member boroughs, 16 by the Cinque Ports, and 12 by as many Welsh boroughs.   The twelve Welsh counties returned 12 members, and the forty English counties 82, the remaining 4 members being representatives of the Universities.

The county franchise had a much less chequered history than the various franchises in boroughs. Before the reign of Henry VI., every free inhabitant householder, freeholder or non-freeholder, could vote at elections of Knights of the Shire. The Act of 1430 limited the franchise to forty-shilling freeholders. Many controversies raged round this definition, and by the eighteenth century, men were voting in respect of annuities, rent-charges, the dowries of their wives and pews in church. Mr. Porritt traces the faggot voter to the early days of Charles I. Two changes were made in the county franchise between 1430 and 1832. The residential qualification disappears by 1620 : in 1702 a tax-paying qualification was introduced under which a property did not carry a vote unless it had been taxed for a year. In 1781 the year was cut down to six months. Great difficulties and irregularities occurred with regard to registration, and a Bill was passed into law in 1784 to establish a public system of registration. The Act, however, was repealed in the next year, in consequence of the agitation against the expense. The county franchise had a democratic appearance but the county constituencies were very largely under territorial sway, and by the middle of the fifteenth century Jack Cade had complained of the pressure of the great families on their tenants. Fox declared that down to 1780 one of the members for Yorkshire had always been elected in Lord Rockingham's dining-room, and from that time onwards the representation of that county seems to have been a battle of bribes between the Rockinghams, the Fitzwilliams and the Harewoods.

It is easy to see from this sketch of the manner in which the Parliamentary franchise had been drawn into the hands of patrons and corporations, that the aristocracy had supreme command of Parliament. Control by patrons was growing steadily throughout the eighteenth century. The Society of Friends of the People presented a petition to the House of Commons in 1793, in which it was stated that 157 members were sent to Parliament by 84 individuals, and 150 other members were returned by the recommendation of 70 powerful individuals. The relations of such members to their patrons were described by Fox in 1797, ' When Gentlemen represent populous towns and cities, then it is a disputed point whether they ought to obey their voice or follow the dictates of their own conscience. But if they represent a noble lord or a noble duke then it becomes no longer a question of doubt, and he is not considered a man of honour who does not implicitly obey the orders of a single constituent.'[1] The petition of the Society of Friends of the People contained some interesting information as to the number of electors in certain constituencies : 90 members were returned by 46 places, in none of which the number of voters exceeded 50, 37 'by 19 places in none of which the number of voters exceeds 100, and 52 by 26 in none of which the number of voters exceeded 200. Seventy-five members were returned for 35 places in which it would be to trifle with the patience of your Honourable House to mention any number of voters at all,' the elections at the places alluded to being notoriously a matter of form.

If the qualifications of voters had changed, so had the qualifications of members. A power that reposed on this basis would have seemed reasonably complete, but the aristocracy took further measures to consolidate its monopoly. In 1710 Parliament passed an Act, to which it gave the prepossessing title ' An Act for securing the freedom of Parliament, by further qualifying the Members to sit in the House of Commons,' to exclude all persons who had not a certain estate of land, worth in the case of knights of the shire, £500, and in the case of burgesses, £300. This Act was often evaded by various devices, and the most famous of the statesmen of the eighteenth century sat in Parliament by means of fictitious qualifications, among others Pitt, Burke, Fox and Sheridan. But the Act gave a tone to Parliament, and it was not a dead letter.[2] It had, too, the effect of throwing the ambitious merchant into the landlord class, and of enveloping him in the landlord atmosphere. Selection and assimilation, as De Tocqueville saw, and not exclusion, are the true means of preserving a class monopoly of power. We might, indeed, sum up the contrast between the English and French aristocracy by saying that the English aristocracy understood the advantages of a scientific social frontier, whereas the French were tenacious of a traditional frontier. More effectual in practice than this imposition of a property qualification was the growing practice of throwing on candidates the official expenses

---

[1] House of Commons, May 26, 1797, on Grey's motion for Parliamentary Reform.

[2] The only person who is known to have declined to sit on this account is Southey.

of elections. During the eighteenth century these expenses grew rapidly, and various Acts of Parliament, in particular that of 1745, fixed these charges on candidates.

It followed naturally, from a system which made all municipal government merely one aspect of Parliamentary electioneering, that the English towns fell absolutely into the hands of corrupt oligarchies and the patrons on whom they lived. The Tudor kings had conceived the policy of extinguishing their independent life and energies by committing their government to select bodies with power to perpetuate themselves by co-opting new members. The English aristocracy found in the boroughs—with the mass of inhabitants disinherited and all government and power vested in a small body—a state of things not less convenient and accommodating to the new masters of the machine than it had been to the old. The English towns, which three centuries earlier had enjoyed a brisk and vigorous public life, were now in a state of stagnant misgovernment : as the century advanced, they only sank deeper into the slough, and the Report of the Commission of 1835 showed that the number of inhabitants who were allowed any share in public life or government was infinitesimal. In Plymouth, for example, with a population of 75,000, the number of resident freemen was under 300 : in Ipswich, with more than 20,000 inhabitants, there were 350 freemen of whom more than 100 were not rated, and some forty were paupers. Municipal government throughout the century was a system not of government but of property. It did not matter to the patron whether Winchester or Colchester had any drains or constables : the patron had to humour the corporation or the freemen, the corporation or the freemen had to keep their bargain with the patron. The patron gave the corporation money and other considerations : the corporation gave the patron control over a seat in Parliament. Neither had to consider the interests or the property of the mass of burgesses. Pitt so far recognised the ownership of Parliamentary boroughs as property, that he proposed in 1785 to compensate the patrons of the boroughs he wished to disenfranchise. Every municipal office was regarded in the same spirit. The endowments and the charities that belonged to the town belonged to a small oligarchy which acknowledged no responsibility to the citizens for its proceedings, and conducted its business in secret. The whole system depended on the patron, who for his part represented the absolute supremacy of the territorial aristocracy to which he belonged.　Civic life there was none.

If we turn to local government outside the towns there is the same decay of self-government.

One way of describing the changes that came over English society after the break-up of feudalism would be to say that as in France everything drifted into the hands of the intendant, in England everything drifted into the hands of the Justice of the Peace.　This office, created in the first year of Edward III., had grown during his reign to very great importance and power.　Originally the Justices of the Peace were appointed by the state to carry out certain of its precepts, and generally to keep the peace in the counties in which they served.　In their quarterly sittings they had the assistance of a jury, and exercised a criminal jurisdiction concurrent with that which the king's judges exercised when on circuit.　But from early days they developed an administrative power which gradually drew to itself almost all the functions and properties of government. Its quasi-judicial origin is seen in the judicial form under which it conducted such business as the supervision of roads and bridges.　Delinquencies and deficiencies were 'presented' to the magistrates in court.　It became the habit, very early in the history of the Justices of the Peace, to entrust to them duties that were new, or duties to which existing authorities were conspicuously inadequate.　In the social convulsions that followed the Black Death, it was the Justice of the Peace who was called in to administer the elaborate legislation by which the capitalist classes sought to cage the new ambitions of the labourer.　Under the Elizabethan Poor Law, it was the Justice of the Peace who appointed the parish overseers and approved their poor rate, and it was the Justice of the Peace who held in his hand the meshes of the law of Settlement. In other words, the social order that emerged from mediæval feudalism centred round the Justice of the Peace in England as conspicuously as it centred round the bureaucracy in France.　During the eighteenth century, the power of the Justice of the Peace reached its zenith, whilst his government acquired certain attributes that gave it a special significance.

At the beginning of the eighteenth century there were still many small men taking some part in the affairs of the village. The old manorial civilisation was disappearing, but Mr. and Mrs. Webb have shown that manor courts of one kind or another were far more numerous and had far more to do at the beginning of the eighteenth century than has been commonly supposed. Such records as survive, those, *e.g.* of Godmanchester and Great Tew, prove that the conduct and arrangement of the business of the common fields—and England was still, at the beginning of this period, very largely a country of common fields—required and received very full and careful attention. Those courts crumble away as the common fields vanish, and with them there disappears an institution in which, as Professor Vinogradoff has shown, the small man counted and had recognised rights. By the time of the Reform Bill, a manor court was more or less of a local curiosity. The village vestries again, which represented another successor to the manorial organisation, democratic in form, were losing their vitality and functions, and coming more and more under the shadow of the Justices of the Peace. Parochial government was declining throughout the century, and though Professor Lowell in his recent book speaks of village government as still democratic in 1832, few of those who have examined the history of the vestry believe that much was left of its democratic character. By the end of the eighteenth century, the entire administration of county affairs, as well as the ultimate authority in parish business, was in the hands of the Justice of the Peace, the High Sheriff, and the Lord-Lieutenant.

The significance of this development was increased by the manner in which the administration of the justices was conducted. The transactions of business fell, as the century advanced, into fewer and fewer hands, and became less and less public in form and method. The great administrative court, Quarter Sessions, remained open as a court of justice, but it ceased to conduct its county business in public. Its procedure, too, was gradually transformed. Originally the court received 'presentments' or complaints from many different sources—the grand juries, the juries from the Hundreds, the liberties and the boroughs, and from constable juries. The grand juries presented county bridges, highways or gaols that needed repair : the Hundred juries presented delinquencies in their divisions : constable juries presented such minor anti-social practices as the keeping of pigs. Each of these juries represented some area of public opinion. The Grand Jury, besides giving its verdict on all these presentments, was in other ways a very formidable body, and acted as a kind of consultative committee, and perhaps as a finance committee. Now all this elaborate machinery was simplified in the

eighteenth century, and it was simplified by the aban-
donment of all the quasi-democratic characteristics and
methods.   Presentments by individual justices gradually
superseded presentments by juries.   By 1835 the Hundred
Jury and Jury of Constables had disappeared : the Grand
Jury had almost ceased to concern itself with local government, and the administrative business of Quarter Sessions
was no longer discussed in open court.

Even more significant in some respects was the delegation
of a great part of county business, including the protection
of footpaths, from Quarter Sessions to Petty Sessions or to
single justices out of sessions.   Magistrates could administer
in this uncontrolled capacity a drastic code for the punishment of vagrants and poachers without jury or publicity.
The single justice himself determined all questions of law and
of fact, and could please himself as to the evidence he chose
to hear.   In 1822 the Duke of Buckingham tried and convicted
a man of coursing on his estate.   The trial took place in the
duke's kitchen : the witnesses were the duke's keepers.   The
defendant was in this case not a poacher, who was *fera naturæ*,
but a farmer, who was in comparison a person of substance
and standing.   The office of magistrate possessed a special
importance for the class that preserved game, and readers
of *Rob Roy* will remember that Mr. Justice Inglewood had to
swallow his prejudices against the Hanoverian succession
and take the oaths as a Justice of the Peace, because the
refusal of most of the Northumberland magistrates, being
Jacobites, to serve on the bench, had endangered the strict
administration of the Game Laws.   We know from the novels
of Richardson and Fielding and Smollett how this power
enveloped village life.   Richardson has no venom against
the justices.   In *Pamela* he merely records the fact that Mr.
B. was a magistrate for two counties, and that therefore it was
hopeless for Pamela, whom he wished to seduce, to elude
his pursuit, even if she escaped from her duress in his country
house.

Fielding, who saw the servitude of the poor with less patience
and composure, wrote of country life with knowledge and
experience.   In *Joseph Andrews* he describes the young squire
who forbids the villagers to keep dogs, and kills any dog that
he finds, and the lawyer who assures Lady Booby that ' the
laws of the land are not so vulgar to permit a mean fellow
to contend with one of your ladyship's fortune.   We have

one sure card, which is to carry him before Justice Frolic, who upon hearing your ladyship's name, will commit him without any further question.' Mr. Justice Frolic was as good as his reputation, and at the moment of their rescue Joseph and Fanny were on the point of being sent to Bridewell on the charge of taking a twig from a hedge. Fielding and Richardson wrote in the middle of the eighteenth century. In 1831 Denman, the Attorney-General in Grey's Government, commented on the difference between the punishments administered by judges at Assize and those administered by justices at Quarter Sessions, in the defence of their game preserves, observing that the contrast ' had a very material effect in confusing in the minds of the people the notions of right and wrong.' This territorial power was in fact absolute. In France the peasant was in some cases shielded from the caprice of the seigneur by the Crown, the Parlements and the intendants. Both Henry iv. and Louis xiii. intervened to protect the communities in the possession of their goods from the encroachments of seigneurs, while Louis xiv. published an edict in 1667 restoring to the communities all the property they had alienated since 1620. In England he was at the landlord's mercy : he stood unprotected beneath the canopy of this universal power.

Nor was the actual authority, administrative or judicial, of the magistrates and their surveillance of the village the full measure of their influence. They became, as Mr. and Mrs. Webb have shown, the domestic legislature. The most striking example of their legislation was the Berkshire Bread Act. In 1795 the Berkshire Court of Quarter Sessions summoned justices and 'several discreet persons ' to meet at Speenhamland for the purpose of rating husbandry wages. This meeting passed the famous resolution providing for the supplementing of wages out of the rates, on a certain fixed scale, according to the price of flour. The example of these seven clergymen and eleven squires was quickly followed in other counties, and Quarter Sessions used to have tables drawn up and printed, giving the justices' scale, to be issued by the Clerk of the Peace to every acting magistrate and to the churchwardens and overseers of every parish. It was a handful of magistrates in the different counties, acting on their own initiative, without any direction from Parliament, that set loose this social avalanche in England. Parliament, indeed, had developed the habit of taking the opinion of the magistrates as conclusive on all social questions, and whereas a modern elected local authority has to submit to the control of a department subject to Parliament, in the eighteenth century a non-elected local authority, not content with its own unchecked authority, virtually controlled the decisions of Parliament as well. The opposition of the magistrates to Whitbread's Bill in 1807, for example, was accepted as fatal and final.

Now if the Crown had been more powerful or had followed a different policy, the Justices of the Peace, instead of developing into autonomous local oligarchies, might have become its representatives. When feudal rights disappeared with the Wars of the Roses, the authority of the Justice of the Peace, an officer of the Crown, superseded that of the local lord. Mr. Jenks [1] is therefore justified in saying that ' the governing caste in English country life since the Reformation has not been a feudal but an official caste.' But this official caste is, so to speak, only another aspect of the feudal caste, for though on paper the representatives of the central power, the county magistrates were in practice, by the end of the eighteenth century, simply the local squires putting into force their own ideas and policy. Down to the Rebellion, the Privy Council expected judges of assize to choose suitable persons for appointment as magistrates. Magistrates were made and unmade until the reign of George i., according to the political prepossessions of governments. But by the end of the eighteenth century the Lord Lieutenant's recommendations were virtually decisive for appointment, and dismissal from the bench became unknown. Thus though the system of the magistracy, as Redlich and Hirst pointed out, enabled the English constitution to rid itself of feudalism a century earlier than the continent, it ultimately gave back to the landlords in another form the power that they lost when feudalism disappeared.

Another distinctive feature of the English magistracy contributed to this result. The Justice of the Peace was unpaid. The statutes of Edward iii. and Richard ii. prescribed wages at the handsome rate of four shillings a day, but it seems to be clear, though the actual practice of benches is not very easy to ascertain, that the wages in the rare instances when they were claimed were spent on hospitality, and did not go into the pockets of the individual justices. Lord Eldon gave this as a reason for refusing to strike magistrates off the list in cases of private misconduct. ' As the magistrates gave their services gratis they ought to be protected.' When it

[1] *Outline of English Local Government*, p. 152.

was first proposed in 1785 to establish salaried police commissioners for Middlesex, many Whigs drew a contrast between the magistrates who were under no particular obligation to the executive power and the officials proposed to be appointed who would receive salaries, and might be expected to take their orders from the Government.

The aristocracy was thus paramount both in local government and in Parliament. But to understand the full significance of its absolutism we must notice two important social events—the introduction of family settlements and the abolition of military tenures.

A class that wishes to preserve its special powers and privileges has to discover some way of protecting its corporate interests from the misdemeanours and follies of individual members. The great landlords found such a device in the system of entail which gave to each successive generation merely a life interest in the estates, and kept the estates themselves as the permanent possession of the family. But the lawyers managed to elude this device of the landowners by the invention of sham law-suits, an arrangement by which a stranger brought a claim for the estate against the limited owner in possession, and got a judgment by his connivance. The stranger was in truth the agent of the limited owner, who was converted by this procedure into an absolute owner. The famous case known as Taltarums case in 1472, established the validity of these lawsuits, and for the next two hundred years ' Family Law ' no longer controlled the actions of the landowners and the market for their estates. During this time Courts of Law and Parliament set their faces against all attempts to reintroduce the system of entails. As a consequence estates were sometimes melted down, and the inheritances of ancient families passed into the possession of yeomen and merchants. The landowners had never accepted their defeat. In the reign of Elizabeth they tried to devise family settlements that would answer their purpose as effectually as the old law of entail, but they were foiled by the great judges, Popham and Coke. After the Restoration, unhappily, conditions were more propitious. In the first place, the risks of the Civil War had made it specially important for rich men to save their estates from forfeiture by means of such settlements, and in the second place the landowning class was now all-powerful. Consequently the attempt which Coke had crushed now succeeded, and rich families were enabled to tie up their wealth.[1] Family settlements have ever since been a very important part of our social system. The merchants who became landowners bought up the estates of yeomen, whereas in eighteeenth-century France it was the land of noblemen that passed to the *nouveaux riches*.

The second point to be noticed in the history of this land-lord class is the abolition of the military tenures in 1660. The form and the method of this abolition are both significant. The military dues were the last remaining feudal liability of the landlords to the Crown. They were money payments that had taken the place of old feudal services. The landlords, who found them vexatious and capricious, had been trying to get rid of them ever since the reign of James I. In 1660 they succeeded, and the Restoration Parliament revived the Act of Cromwell's Parliament four years earlier which abolished military tenures. The bargain which the landlords made with the Crown on this occasion was ingenious and characteristic ; it was something like the Concordat between Francis I. and Leo X., which abolished the Pragmatic sanction at the expense of the Gallican Church ; for the landowners simply transferred their liability to the general taxpayer. The Crown forgave the landlords their dues in consideration of receiving a grant from the taxation of the food of the nation. An Excise tax was the substitute.

Now the logical corollary of the abolition of the feudal dues that vexed the large landowners would have been the aboli-tion of the feudal dues that vexed the small landowners. If the great landlords were no longer to be subject to their dues in their relation to the Crown, why should the small copyholder continue to owe feudal dues to the lord ? The injustice of abolishing the one set of liabilities and retain-ing the other struck one observer very forcibly, and he was an observer who knew something, unlike most of the govern-ing class, from intimate experience of the grievances of the small landowner under this feudal survival. This was Francis North (1637-1685), the first Lord Guildford, the famous lawyer and Lord Chancellor. North had begun his career by acting as the steward of various manors, thinking that he would gain an insight into human nature which would be of great value to him in his practice at the bar. His experience in

---

[1] A clear and concise account of these developments is given by Lord Hob-house, *Contemporary Review*, February and March 1886.

this capacity, as we know from Roger North's book *The Lives of the Norths*, disclosed to him an aspect of feudalism which escaped the large landowners—the hardships of their dependants. He used to describe the copyhold exactions, and to say that in many cases that came under his notice small tenements and pieces of land which had been in a poor family for generations were swallowed up in the monstrous fines imposed on copyholders. He said he had often found himself the executioner of the cruelty of the lords and ladies of manors upon poor men, and he remarked the inconsistency that left all these oppressions untouched in emancipating the large landowners. Maine, in discussing this system, pointed out that these signorial dues were of the kind that provoked the French Revolution. There were two reasons why a state of things which produced a revolution in France remained disregarded in England. One was that the English copyholders were a much smaller class: the other that, as small proprietors were disappearing in England, the English copyholder was apt to contrast his position with the status of the landless labourer, and to congratulate himself on the possession of a property, whereas in France the copyholder contrasted his position with the status of the freeholder and complained of his services. The copyholders were thus not in a condition to raise a violent or dangerous discontent, and their grievances were left unredressed. It is sometimes said that England got rid of feudalism a century earlier than the continent. That is true of the English State, but to understand the agrarian history of the eighteenth century we must remember that, as it has been well said, ' whereas the English State is less feudal, the English land law is more feudal than that of any other country in Europe.' [1]

Lastly, the class that is armed with all these social and political powers dominates the universities and the public schools. The story of how the colleges changed from communities of poor men into societies of rich men, and then gradually swallowed up the university, has been told in the Reports of University Commissions. By the eighteenth century the transformation was complete, and both the ancient universities were the universities of the rich. There is a passage in Macaulay describing the state and pomp of Oxford at the end of the seventeenth century, ' when her Chancellor, the venerable Duke of Ormonde, sat in his embroidered mantle on his throne

[1] Holdsworth's *History of English Law.*

under the painted ceiling of the Sheldonian theatre, surrounded by hundreds of graduates robed according to their
rank, while the noblest youths of England were solemnly
presented to him as candidates for academical honours.' The
university was a power, not in the sense in which that could
be said of a university like the old university of Paris,
whose learning could make popes tremble, but in the sense
that the university was part of the recognised machinery
of aristocracy.   What was true of the universities was
true of the public schools.   Education was the nursery not
of a society, but of an order ; not of a state, but of a race
of rulers.

Thus on every side this class is omnipotent.   In Parliament
with its ludicrous representation, in the towns with their
decayed government, in the country, sleeping under the absolute
rule of the Justice of the Peace, there is no rival power.   The
Crown is for all purposes its accomplice rather than its com-
petitor.   It controls the universities, the Church, the law,
and all the springs of life and discussion.   Its own influence is consolidated by the strong social discipline embodied
in the family settlements.   Its supremacy is complete and
unquestioned.   Whereas in France the fermentation of ideas
was an intellectual revolt against the governing system and
all literature spoke treason, in England the existing régime
was accepted, we might say assumed, by the world of letters
and art, by the England that admired Reynolds and Gibbon,
or listened to Johnson and Goldsmith, or laughed with
Sheridan and Sterne.   To the reason of France, the government
under which France lived was an expensive paradox : to the
reason of England, any other government than the government under which England lived was unthinkable.   Hence
De Tocqueville saw only a homogeneous society, a society
revering its institutions in the spirit of Burke in contrast with
a society that mocked at its institutions in the spirit of
Voltaire.

' You people of great families and hereditary trusts and
fortunes,' wrote Burke to the Duke of Richmond in 1772,
' are not like such as I am, who, whatever we may be by
the rapidity of our growth and even by the fruit we bear,
flatter ourselves that, while we creep on the ground, we belly
into melons that are exquisite for size and flavour, yet still
we are but annual plants that perish with our season, and
leave no sort of traces behind us.   You, if you are what you

ought to be, are in my eye the great oaks that shade a country, and perpetuate your benefits from generation to generation.' We propose in this book to examine the social history of England in the days when the great oaks were in the fulness of their vigour and strength, and to see what happened to some of the classes that found shelter in their shade.

CHAPTER II

THE VILLAGE BEFORE ENCLOSURE

To elucidate these chapters, and to supply further information for those who are interested in the subject, we publish an Appendix containing the history, and tolerably full particulars, of twelve separate enclosures. These instances have not been chosen on any plan. They are taken from different parts of the country, and are of various dates; some are enclosures of common fields, some enclosures of commons and waste, and some include enclosures of both kinds.

At the time of the great Whig Revolution, England was in the main a country of commons and of common fields[1]; at the time of the Reform Bill, England was in the main a country of individualist agriculture and of large enclosed farms. There has probably been no change in Europe in the last two centuries comparable to this in importance of which so little is known to-day, or of which so little is to be learnt from the general histories of the time. The accepted view is that this change marks a great national advance, and that the hardships which incidentally followed could not have been avoided : that it meant a vast increase in the food resources of England in comparison with which the sufferings of individuals counted for little : and that the great estates which then came into existence were rather the gift of economic forces than the deliberate acquisitions of powerful men. We are not concerned to corroborate or to dispute the contention that enclosure made England more productive,[2] or to discuss the merits of enclosure itself as a public policy or a means to agricultural progress in the eighteenth century. Our business is with the changes that the enclosures caused in the social structure of

[1] Gregory King and Davenant estimated that the whole of the cultivated land in England in 1685 did not amount to much more than half the total area, and of this cultivated portion three-fifths was still farmed on the old common-field system.

[2] For a full discussion, in which the ordinary view is vigorously combated in an interesting analysis, see Hasbach, *History of the Agricultural Labourer* : on the other side, Levy, *Large and Small Holdings.*

England, from the manner in which they were in practice carried out. We propose, therefore, to describe the actual operations by which society passed through this revolution, the old village vanished, and rural life assumed its modern form and character.

It is difficult for us, who think of a common as a wild sweep of heather and beauty and freedom, saved for the enjoyment of the world in the midst of guarded parks and forbidden meadows, to realise that the commons that disappeared from so many an English village in the eighteenth century belonged to a very elaborate, complex, and ancient economy. The antiquity of that elaborate economy has been the subject of fierce contention, and the controversies that rage round the nursery of the English village recall the controversies that raged round the nursery of Homer. The main subject of contention has been this. Was the manor or the township, or whatever name we like to give to the primitive unit of agricultural life, an organisation imposed by a despotic land-owner on his dependents, or was it created by the co-operation of a group of free tribesmen, afterwards dominated by a military overlord ? Did it owe more to Roman tradition or to Teutonic tendencies ? Professor Vinogradoff, the latest historian, inclines to a compromise between these conflicting theories. He thinks that it is impossible to trace the open-field system of cultivation to any exclusive right of ownership or to the power of coercion, and that the communal organisation of the peasantry, a village community of shareholders who cultivated the land on the open-field system and treated the other requisites of rural life as appendant to it, is more ancient than the manorial order. It derives, in his view, from the old English society. The manor itself, an institution which partakes at once of the character of an estate and of a unit of local government, was produced by the needs of government and the development of individualist husbandry, side by side with this communal village. These conditions lead to the creation of lordships, and after the Conquest they take form in the manor. The manorial element, in fact, is superimposed on the communal, and is not the foundation of it : the mediæval village is a free village gradually feudalised. Fortunately it is not incumbent on us to do more than touch on this fascinating study, as it is enough for our purposes to note that the greater part of England in cultivation at the beginning of the eighteenth century was cultivated on a system which, with certain local variations, belonged to a common type, representing this common ancestry.

The term ' common ' was used of three kinds of land in the eighteenth - century village, and the three were intimately connected with each other. There were (1) the arable fields, (2) the common meadowland, and (3) the common or waste. The arable fields were divided into strips, with different owners, some of whom owned few strips, and some many. The various strips that belonged to a particular owner were scattered among the fields. Strips were divided from each other, sometimes by a grass band called a balk, sometimes by a furrow. They were cultivated on a uniform system by agreement, and after harvest they were thrown open to pasturage. The common meadow land was divided up by lot, pegged out, and distributed among the owners of the strips ; after the hay was carried, these meadows, like the arable fields, were used for pasture. The common or waste, which was used as a common pasture at all times of the year, consisted sometimes of woodland, sometimes of roadside strips, and sometimes of commons in the modern sense.[1]

Such, roughly, was the map of the old English village. What were the classes that lived in it, and what were their several rights ? In a normal village there would be (1) a Lord of the Manor, (2) Freeholders, some of whom might be large proprietors, and many small, both classes going by the general name of Yeomanry, (3) Copyholders, (4) Tenant Farmers, holding by various sorts of tenure, from tenants at will to farmers with leases for three lives, (5) Cottagers, (6) Squatters, and (7) Farm Servants, living in their employers' houses. The proportions of these classes varied greatly, no doubt, in different villages, but we have an estimate of the total agricultural population in the table prepared by Gregory King in 1688, from which it appears that in addition to the Esquires and Gentlemen,

---

[1] This was the general structure of the village that was dissolved in the eighteenth century. It is distinguished from the Keltic type of communal agriculture, known as run-rig, in two important respects. In the run-rig village the soil is periodically redivided, and the tenant's holding is compact. Dr. Slater (*Geographical Journal*, Jan. 1907) has shown that in those parts of England where the Keltic type predominated, *e.g.* in Devon and Cornwall, enclosure took place early, and he argues with good reason that it was easier to enclose by voluntary agreement where the holdings were compact than it was where they were scattered in strips. But gradual enclosure by voluntary agreement had a different effect from the cataclysm-like enclosure of the eighteenth century, as is evident from the large number of small farmers in Devonshire.

there were 40,000 families of freeholders of the better sort,
140,000 families of freeholders of the lesser sort, and 150,000
farmers. Adam Smith, it will be remembered, writing nearly
a century later, said that the large number of yeomen was at
once the strength and the distinction of English agriculture.

Let us now describe rather more fully the different people
represented in these different categories, and the different
rights that they enjoyed. We have seen in the first chapter
that the manorial courts had lost many of their powers by
this time, and that part of the jurisdiction that the Lord of
the Manor had originally exercised had passed to the Justice
of the Peace. No such change had taken place in his relation to the economic life of the village. He might or he might
not still own a demesne land. So far as the common arable
or common meadow was concerned, he was in the same position as any other proprietor : he might own many strips or
few strips or no strips at all. His position with regard to the
waste was different, the difference being expressed by Blackstone ' in those waste grounds, which are usually called commons,
the property of the soil is generally in the Lord of the Manor,
as in the common fields it is in the particular tenant.' The
feudal lawyers had developed a doctrine that the soil of the
waste was vested in the Lord of the Manor, and that originally
it had all belonged to him. But feudal law acknowledged
certain definite limitations to his rights over the waste. The
Statute of Merton, 1235, allowed him to make enclosures on
the waste, but only on certain terms ; he was obliged to leave
enough of the waste for the needs of his tenants. Moreover,
his powers were limited, not only by the concurrent rights of
freeholders and copyholders thus recognised by this ancient
law, but also by certain common rights of pasture and turbary
enjoyed by persons who were neither freeholders nor copyholders, namely cottagers. These rights were explained by
the lawyers of the time as being concessions made by the Lord
of the Manor in remote antiquity. The Lord of the Manor
was regarded as the owner of the waste, subject to these
common rights : that is, he was regarded as owning the minerals
and the surface rights (sand and gravel) as well as sporting
rights.

Every grade of property and status was represented in the
ranks of the freeholders, the copyholders and the tenant
farmers, from the man who employed others to work for him
to the man who was sometimes employed in working for others.

No distinct line, in fact, can be drawn between the small farmer, whether freeholder, copyholder or tenant, and the cottager, for the cottager might either own or rent a few strips ; the best dividing-line can be drawn between those who made their living mainly as farmers, and those who made their living mainly as labourers.

It is important to remember that no farmer, however large his holdings or property, or however important his social position, was at liberty to cultivate his strips as he pleased. The system of cultivation would be settled for him by the Jury of the Manor Court, a court that had different names in different places. By the eighteenth century the various courts of the manorial jurisdiction had been merged in a single court, called indifferently the View of Frankpledge, the Court Leet, the Court Baron, the Great Court or the Little Court, which transacted so much of the business hitherto confided to various courts as had not been assigned to the Justices of the Peace.[1] Most of the men of the village, freeholders, copyholders, leaseholders, or cottagers, attended the court, but the constitution of the Jury or Homage seems to have varied in different manors. Sometimes the tenants of the manor were taken haphazard in rotation : sometimes the steward controlled the choice, sometimes a nominee of the steward or a nominee of the tenants selected the Jury : sometimes the steward took no part in the selection at all. The chief part of the business of these courts in the eighteenth century was the management of the common fields and common pastures, and the appointment of the village officers. These courts decided which seed should be sown in the different fields, and the dates at which they were to be opened and closed to common pasture. Under the most primitive system of rotation the arable land was divided into three fields, of which one was sown with wheat, another with spring corn, and the third lay fallow : but by the end of the eighteenth century there was a great variety of cultivation, and we find a nine years' course at Great Tew in Oxfordshire, a six years' course in Berkshire, while the Battersea common fields were sown with one uniform round of grain without intermission, and consequently without fallowing.[2]

By Sir Richard Sutton's Act [3] for the cultivation of common

[1] See Webb, *Manor and Borough*, vol. i. p. 66 *seq.*
[2] Slater, *The English Peasantry and the Enclosure of Common Fields*, p. 77.
[3] 13 George III. c. 81.

fields, passed in 1773, a majority of three-fourths in number and value of the occupiers, with the consent of the owner and titheholder, was empowered to decide on the course of husbandry, to regulate stinted commons, and, with the consent of the Lord of the Manor, to let off a twelfth of the common, applying the rent to draining or improving the rest of it.[1] Before this Act, a universal consent to any change of system was necessary.[2] The cultivation of strips in the arable fields carried with it rights of common over the waste and also over the common fields when they were thrown open. These rights were known as ' common appendant ' and they are thus defined by Blackstone : ' Common appendant is a right belonging to the owners or occupiers of arable land to put commonable beasts upon the Lord's waste and upon the lands of other persons within the same manor.'

The classes making their living mainly as labourers were the cottagers, farm servants, and squatters. The cottagers either owned or occupied cottages and had rights of common on the waste, and in some cases over the common fields. These rights were of various kinds : they generally included the right to pasture certain animals, to cut turf and to get fuel. The cottagers, as we have already said, often owned or rented land. This is spoken of as a common practice by Addington, who knew the Midland counties well ; Arthur Young gives instances from Lincolnshire and Oxfordshire, and Eden from Leicestershire and Surrey. The squatters or borderers were, by origin, a separate class, though in time they merged into the cottagers. They were settlers who built themselves huts and cleared a piece of land in the commons or woods, at some distance from the village. These encroachments were generally sanctioned. A common rule in one part of the country was that the right was established if the settler could build his cottage in the night and send out smoke from his chimney in the morning.[3] The squatters also often went out as day labourers. The farm servants were usually the children

[1] This was done at Barnes Common ; see for whole subject, *Annals of Agriculture*, vol. xvii. p. 516.

[2] For cases where changes in the system of cultivation of common fields had been made, see *Annals of Agriculture*, vol. xvi. p. 606 : 'To Peterborough, crossing an open field, but sown by agreement with turnips.' Cf. *Report on Bedfordshire* : 'Clover is sown in some of the open clay-fields by common consent (p. 339), and 'Turnips are sometimes cultivated, both on the sands and gravels, by mutual consent' (p. 340).

[3] Slater, p. 119.

of the small farmers or cottagers; they lived in their masters' houses until they had saved enough money to marry and take a cottage of their own.

Were there any day labourers without either land or common rights in the old village? It is difficult to suppose that there were many.[1] Blackstone said of common appurtenant that it was not a general right ' but can only be claimed by special grant or by prescription, which the law esteems sufficient proof of a special grant or agreement for this purpose.' Prescription covers a multitude of encroachments. Indeed, it was only by the ingenuity of the feudal lawyers that these rights did not attach to the inhabitants of the village at large. These lawyers had decided in Gateward's case, 1603, that ' inhabitants ' were too vague a body to enjoy a right, and on this ground they had deprived the inhabitants of the village of Stixswold in Lincolnshire of their customary right of turning out cattle on the waste.[2] From that time a charter of incorporation was necessary to enable the inhabitants at large to prove a legal claim to common rights. But rights that were enjoyed by the occupiers of small holdings or of cottages by long prescription, or by encroachments tacitly sanctioned, must have been very widely scattered.

Such were the classes inhabiting the eighteenth-century village. As the holdings in the common fields could be sold, the property might change hands, though it remained subject to common rights and to the general regulations of the manor court. Consequently the villages exhibited great varieties of character. In one village it might happen that strip after strip had been bought up by the Lord of the Manor or some proprietor, until the greater part of the arable fields had come into the possession of a single owner. In such cases, however, the land so purchased was still let out as a rule to a number of small men, for the engrossing of farms as a practice comes into fashion after enclosure. Sometimes such purchase was a preliminary to enclosure. The Bedfordshire reporter gives an example in the village of Bolnhurst, in that county. Three land speculators bought up as much of the land as they could with a view to enclosing the common fields and then selling at a large profit. But the land turned out to be much less valuable than they had supposed, and they could not get it

---

[1] Dr. Slater's conclusion is that ' in the open field village the entirely landless labourer was scarcely to be found,' p. 130.

[2] See *Commons, Forests, and Footpaths*, by Lord Eversley, p. 11.

off their hands : all improvements were at a standstill, for the speculators only let from year to year, hoping still to find a market.[1] In other villages, land might have changed hands in just the opposite direction. The Lord of the Manor might sell his property in the common fields, and sell it not to some capitalist or merchant, but to a number of small farmers. We learn from the evidence of the Committee of 1844 on enclosures that sometimes the Lord of the Manor sold his property in the waste to the commoners. Thus there were villages with few owners, as there were villages with many owners. The writer of the *Report on Middlesex*, which was published in 1798 says, ' I have known thirty landlords in a field of 200 acres, and the property of each so divided as to lie in ten or twenty places, containing from an acre or two downwards to fifteen perches ; and in a field of 300 acres I have met with patches of arable land, containing eight perches each. In this instance the average size of all the pieces in the field was under an acre. In all cases they lie in long, narrow, winding or worm-like slips.' [2]

The same writer states that at the time his book was written (1798) 20,000 out of the 23,000 arable acres in Middlesex were cultivated on the common-field system.[3] Perhaps the parish of Stanwell, of which we describe the enclosure in detail elsewhere, may be taken as a fair example of an eighteenth-century village. In this parish there were, according to the enclosure award, four large proprietors, twenty-four moderate proprietors, twenty-four small proprietors, and sixty-six cottagers with common rights.

The most important social fact about this system is that it provided opportunities for the humblest and poorest labourer to rise in the village. Population seems to have moved slowly, and thus there was no feverish competition for land. The farm servant could save up his wages and begin his married life by hiring a cottage which carried rights of common, and gradually buy or hire strips of land. Every village, as Hasbach has put it, had its ladder, and nobody was doomed to stay on the lowest rung. This is the distinguishing mark of the old village. It would be easy, looking only at this feature, to idealise the society that we have described, and to paint this age as an age of gold. But no reader of Fielding or of Richardson would fall into this mistake, or persuade himself that this community

---

[1] *Bedfordshire Report*, 1808, p. 223, quoting from Arthur Young.
[2] P. 114.   [3] P. 138.

was a society of free and equal men, in which tyranny was impossible. The old village was under the shadow of the squire and the parson, and there were many ways in which these powers controlled and hampered its pleasures and habits : there were quarrels, too, between farmers and cottagers, and there are many complaints that the farmers tried to take the lion's share of the commons : but, whatever the pressure outside and whatever the bickerings within, it remains true that the common-field system formed a world in which the villagers lived their own lives and cultivated the soil on a basis of independence.

It was this community that now passed under the unqualified rule of the oligarchy. Under that rule it was to disappear. Enclosure was no new menace to the poor. English literature before the eighteenth century echoes the dismay and lamentations of preachers and prophets who witnessed the havoc that it spread. Stubbes had written in 1553 his bitter protest against the enclosures which enabled rich men to eat up poor men, and twenty years later a writer had given a sombre landscape of the new farming : ' We may see many of their houses built alone like ravens' nests, no birds building near them.' The Midlands had been the chief scene of these changes, and there the conversion of arable land into pasture had swallowed up great tracts of common agriculture, provoking in some cases an armed resistance. The enclosures of this century were the second and the greater of two waves.[1] In one respect enclosure was in form more difficult now than in earlier periods, for it was generally understood at this time that an Act of Parliament was necessary. In reality there was less check on the process. For hitherto the enclosing class had had to reckon with the occasional panic or ill-temper of the Crown. No English king, it is true, had intervened in the interests of the poor so dramatically as did the earlier and unspoilt Louis XIV., who restored to the French village assemblies the public lands they had alienated within a certain period. But the Crown had not altogether overlooked the interests of the classes who were ruined by enclosure, and in different ways it had tried to modify the worst consequences of this policy. From 1490 to 1601 there were various Acts and proclamations designed for this purpose. Charles I. had actually annulled the enclosures of two years in certain midland counties, several Commissions had been issued, and the Star Chamber had instituted proceedings against enclosures.

---

[1] See on this point, Levy, *Large and Small Holdings*, p. 1.

on the ground that depopulation was an offence against the Common Law. Mr. Firth holds that Cromwell's influence in the eastern counties was due to his championship of the commoners in the fens. Throughout this time, however ineffectual the intervention of the Crown, the interests of the classes to whom enclosures brought wealth and power were not allowed to obliterate all other considerations.

From the beginning of the eighteenth century the reins are thrown to the enclosure movement, and the policy of enclosure is emancipated from all these checks and after-thoughts. One interest is supreme throughout England, supreme in Parliament, supreme in the country ; the Crown follows, the nation obeys.

The agricultural community which was taken to pieces in the eighteenth century and reconstructed in the manner in which a dictator reconstructs a free government, was threatened from many points. It was not killed by avarice alone. Cobbett used to attribute the enclosure movement entirely to the greed of the landowners, but, if greed was a sufficient motive, greed was in this case clothed and almost enveloped in public spirit. Let us remember what this community looked like to men with the mind of the landlord class. The English landowners have always believed that order would be resolved into its original chaos, if they ceased to control the lives and destinies of their neighbours. ' A great responsibility rests on us landlords ; if we go, the whole thing goes.' So says the landlord in Mr. Galsworthy's novel, and so said the landlords in the eighteenth century. The English aristocracy always thinking of this class as the pillars of society, as the Atlas that bears the burden of the world, very naturally concluded that this old peasant community, with its troublesome rights, was a public encumbrance. This view received a special impetus from all the circumstances of the age. The landlord class was constantly being recruited from the ranks of the manu-facturers, and the new landlords, bringing into this charmed circle an energy of their own, caught at once its taste for power, for direction, for authority, for imposing its will. Readers of *Shirley* will remember that when Robert Moore pictures to himself a future of usefulness and success, he says that he will obtain an Act for enclosing Nunnely Common, that his brother will be put on the bench, and that between them they will dominate the parish. The book ends in this dream of triumph. Signorial position owes its special lustre for English minds to the association of social distinction with power over the life and ways of groups of men and women. When Bagehot sneered at the sudden millionaires of his day, who hoped to disguise their social defects by buying old places and hiding among aristocratic furniture, he was remarking on a feature of English life that was very far from being peculiar to his time. Did not Adam Smith observe that merchants were very commonly ambitious of becoming country gentlemen ? This kind of ambition was the form that public spirit often took in successful Englishmen, and it was a very powerful menace to the old village and its traditions of collective life.

Now this passion received at this time a special momentum from the condition of agriculture. A dictatorship lends itself more readily than any other form of government to the quick introduction of revolutionary ideas, and new ideas were in the air. Thus, in addition to the desire for social power, there was behind the enclosure movement a zeal for economic progress seconding and almost concealing the direct inspiration of self-interest. Many an enclosing landlord thought only of the satisfaction of doubling or trebling his rent : that is unquestionable. If we are to trust so warm a champion of enclosure as William Marshall, this was the state of mind of the great majority. But there were many whose eyes glistened as they thought of the prosperity they were to bring to English agriculture, applying to a wider and wider domain the lessons that were to be learnt from the processes of scientific farming. A man who had caught the large ideas of a Coke, or mastered the discoveries of a Bakewell, chafed under the restraints that the system of common agriculture placed on improvement and experiment. It was maddening to have to set your pace by the slow bucolic temperament of small farmers, nursed in a simple and old-fashioned routine, who looked with suspicion on any proposal that was strange to them. In this tiresome partnership the swift were put between the shafts with the slow, and the temptation to think that what was wanted was to get rid of the partnership altogether, was almost irresistible. From such a state the mind passed rapidly and naturally to the conclusion that the wider the sphere brought into the absolute possession of the enlightened class, the greater would be the public gain. The spirit in which the Board of Agriculture approached the subject found appropriate expression in Sir John Sinclair's high-sounding language. 'The idea of having lands in common, it has been justly remarked, is to be derived from that barbarous state of society, when men were strangers to any higher occupation than those of hunters or shepherds, or had only just tasted the advantages to be reaped from the cultivation of the earth.'[1] Arthur Young[2] compared the open-field system, with its inconveniences ' which the barbarity of their ancestors had neither knowledge to discover nor government to remedy ' to the Tartar policy of the shepherd state.

It is not surprising that men under the influence of these set ideas could find no virtue at all in the old system, and that they soon began to persuade themselves that that system was at the bottom of all the evils of society. It was harmful to the morals and useless to the pockets of the poor. ' The benefit,' wrote Arbuthnot,[3] ' which they are supposed to reap from commons, in their present state, I know to be merely nominal ; nay, indeed, what is worse, I know, that, in many instances, it is an essential injury to them, by being made a plea for their idleness ; for, some few excepted, if you offer them work, they will tell you, that they must go to look up their sheep, cut furzes, get their cow out of the pound, or, perhaps, say they must take their horse to be shod, that he may carry them to a horse-race or cricket-match.' Lord Sheffield, in the course of one of the debates in Parliament, described the commoners as a ' nuisance,' and most people of his class thought of them as something worse. Mr. John Billingsley, who wrote the *Report on Somerset* for the Board of Agriculture in 1795, describes in some detail the enervating atmosphere of the commoners' life. ' Besides, moral effects of an injurious tendency accrue to the cottager, from a reliance on the imaginary benefits of stocking a common. The possession of a cow or two, with a hog, and a few geese, naturally exalts the peasant, in his own conception, above his brethren in the same rank of society. It inspires some degree of confidence in a property, inadequate to his support. In sauntering after his cattle, he acquires a habit of indolence. Quarter, half, and occasionally whole days are imperceptibly lost. Day labour becomes disgusting ; the aversion increases by indulgence ; and at length the sale of a half-fed calf, or hog, furnishes the means of adding intemperance to idleness.'[4]

---

[1] *Report of Select Committee on Waste Lands*, 1795, p. 15, Appendix B.

[2] *Annals of Agriculture*, vol. i. p. 72.

[3] *An Inquiry into the Connection between the present Price of Provisions and the Size of Farms*, 1773, p. 81.

[4] *Report on Somerset*, reprinted 1797, p. 52 ; compare Report on Commons in Brecknock, *Annals of Agriculture*, vol. xxii. p. 632, where commons are denounced as ' hurtful to society by holding forth a temptation to idleness, that fell

Mr. Bishton, who wrote the *Report on Shropshire* in 1794, gives a still more interesting glimpse into the mind of the enclosing class : ' The use of common land by labourers operates upon the mind as a sort of independence.' When the commons are enclosed 'the labourers will work every day in the year, their children will be put out to labour early,' and ' that subordination of the lower ranks of society which in the present times is so much wanted, would be thereby considerably secured.'

A similar view was taken of the moral effects of commons by Middleton, the writer of the *Report on Middlesex*.[1] ' On the other hand, they are, in many instances, of real injury to the public ; by holding out a lure to the poor man—I mean of materials wherewith to build his cottage, and ground to erect it upon : together with firing and the run of his poultry and pigs for nothing. This is of course temptation sufficient to induce a great number of poor persons to settle upon the borders of such commons. But the mischief does not end here: for having gained these trifling advantages, through the neglect or connivance of the lord of the manor, it unfortunately gives their minds an improper bias, and inculcates a desire to live, from that time forward, without labour, or at least with as little as possible.'

One of the witnesses before the Select Committee on Commons Inclosure in 1844 was Mr. Carus Wilson, who is interesting as the original of the character of Mr. Brocklehurst in *Jane Eyre*. We know how that zealous Christian would regard the commoners from the speech in which he reproved Miss Temple for giving the pupils at Lowood a lunch of bread and cheese on one occasion when their meagre breakfast had been uneatable. ' Oh, madam, when you put bread and cheese, instead of burnt porridge, into these children's mouths, you may indeed feed their vile bodies, but you little think how you starve their immortal souls ! ' We are not surprised to learn that Mr. Carus Wilson found the commoners ' hardened and unpromising,' and that he was obliged to inform the committee that the misconduct which the system encouraged ' hardens the heart, and causes a good deal of mischief, and at the same time puts the person in an unfavourable position for the approach of what might be serviceable to him in a moral and religious point of view.'[2]

It is interesting, after reading all these confident gener-

---

parent to vice and immorality ' ; also compare *Ibid.*, vol. xx. p. 145, where they are said to encourage the commoners to be ' hedge breakers, pilferers, nightly trespassers . . . poultry and rabbit stealers, or such like.'

[1] P. 103.   [2] *Committee on Inclosures*, 1844, p. 135.

alisations about the influence of this kind of life upon the character of the poor, to learn what the commoners themselves thought of its moral atmosphere. This we can do from such a petition as that sent by the small proprietors and persons entitled to rights of common at Raunds, in Northamptonshire. These unfortunate people lost their rights by an Enclosure Act in 1797, and during the progress of the Bill they petitioned Parliament against it, in these terms: 'That the Petitioners beg Leave to represent to the House that, under Pretence of improving Lands in the said Parish, the Cottagers and other Persons entitled to Right of Common on the Lands intended to be inclosed, will be deprived of an inestimable Privilege, which they now enjoy, of turning a certain Number of their Cows, Calves, and Sheep, on and over the said Lands; a Privilege that enables them not only to maintain themselves and their Families in the Depth of Winter, when they cannot, even for their Money, obtain from the Occupiers of other Lands the smallest Portion of Milk or Whey for such necessary Purpose, but, in addition to this, they can now supply the Grazier with young or lean Stock at a reasonable Price, to fatten and bring to Market at a more moderate Rate for general Consumption, which they conceive to be the most rational and effectual Way of establishing Public Plenty and Cheapness of Provision; and they further conceive, that a more ruinous Effect of this Inclosure will be the almost total Depopulation of their Town, now filled with bold and hardy Husbandmen, from among whom, and the Inhabitants of other open Parishes, the Nation has hitherto derived its greatest Strength and Glory, in the Supply of its Fleets and Armies, and driving them, from Necessity and Want of Employ, in vast Crowds, into manufacturing Towns, where the very Nature of their Employment, over the Loom or the Forge, soon may waste their Strength, and consequently debilitate their Posterity, and by imperceptible Degrees obliterate that great Principle of Obedience to the Laws of God and their Country, which forms the Character of the simple and artless Villagers, more equally distributed through the Open Countries, and on which so much depends the good Order and Government of the State: These are some of the Injuries to themselves as Individuals, and of the ill Consequences to the Public, which the Petitioners conceive will follow from this, as they have already done from many Inclosures, but which they did not think they were entitled to lay before the House (the Constitutional Patron and Protector of the Poor) until it unhappily came to their own Lot to be exposed to them through the Bill now pending.' [1]

When we remember that the enterprise of the age was under the spell of the most seductive economic teaching of the time, and that the old peasant society, wearing as it did the look of confusion and weakness, had to fear not only the simplifying appetites of the landlords, but the simplifying philosophy, in England of an Adam Smith, in France of the Physiocrats, we can realise that a ruling class has seldom found so plausible an atmosphere for the free play of its interests and ideas. *Des crimes sont flattés d'être présidés par une vertu.* Bentham himself thought the spectacle of an enclosure one of the most reassuring of all the evidences of improvement and happiness. Indeed, all the elements seemed to have conspired against the peasant, for æsthetic taste, which might at other times have restrained, in the eighteenth century encouraged the destruction of the commons and their rough beauty. The rage for order and symmetry and neat cultivation was universal. It found expression in Burnet, who said of the Alps and Appenines that they had neither form nor beauty, neither shape nor order, any more than the clouds of the air : in Johnson, who said of the Highlands that ' the uniformity of barrenness can afford very little amusement to the traveller ' : and in Cobbett, who said of the Cotswolds, ' this is a sort of country having less to please the eye than any other that I have ever seen, always save and except the heaths like those of Bagshot and Hindhead.' The enjoyment of wild nature was a lost sense, to be rediscovered one day by the Romanticists and the Revolution, but too late to help the English village. In France, owing to various causes, part economic, part political, on which we shall touch later, the peasant persisted in his ancient and ridiculous tenure, and survived to become the envy of English observers : it was only in England that he lost his footing, and that his ancient patrimony slipped away from him.

We are not concerned at this juncture to inquire into the truth of the view that the sweeping policy of enclosure increased the productivity and resources of the State : we are concerned only to inquire into the way in which the aristocracy gave shape and effect to it. This movement, assumed by the enlightened opinion of the day to be beneficent and progressive, was none the less a gigantic disturbance ; it broke up the old village life ; it transferred a great body of property ;

[1] *House of Commons Journal*, June 19, 1797.

it touched a vast mass of interests at a hundred points. A governing class that cared for its reputation for justice would clearly regard it as of sovereign importance that this delicate network of rights and claims should not be roughly disentangled by the sheer power of the stronger : a governing class that recognised its responsibility for the happiness and order of the State would clearly regard it as of sovereign importance that this ancient community should not be dissolved in such a manner as to plunge great numbers of contented men into permanent poverty and despair. To decide how far the aristocracy that presided over these changes displayed insight or foresight, sympathy or imagination, and how far it acted with a controlling sense of integrity and public spirit, we must analyse the methods and procedure of Parliamentary enclosure.

Before entering on a discussion of the methods by which Parliamentary enclosure was effected, it is necessary to realise the extent of its operations. Precise statistics, of course, are not to be had, but there are various estimates based on careful study of such evidence as we possess. Mr. Levy says that between 1702 and 1760 there were only 246 Acts, affecting about 400,000 acres, and that in the next fifty years the Acts had reached a total of 2438, affecting almost five million acres.[1] Mr. Johnson gives the following table for the years 1700-1844, founded on Dr. Slater's detailed estimate [2]——

Years.	Common Field and some Waste.		Waste only.	
	Acts.	Acreage.	Acts.	Acreage.
1700–1760	152	237,845	56	74,518
1761–1801	1,479	2,428,721	521	752,150
1802–1844	1,075	1,610,302	803	939,043
Total, .	2,706	4,276,868	1,385	1,765,711

This roughly corresponds with the estimate given before the Select Committee on Enclosures in 1844, that there were some one thousand seven hundred private Acts before 1800,

[1] *Large and Small Holdings*, p. 24.
[2] *Disappearance of Small Landowner*, p. 90 ; Slater's *English Peasantry and the Enclosure of Common Fields*, Appendix B.

and some two thousand between 1800 and 1844. The General Report of the Board of Agriculture on Enclosures gives the acreage enclosed from the time of Queen Anne down to 1805 as 4,187,056. Mr. Johnson's conclusion is that nearly 20 per cent. of the total acreage of England has been enclosed during the eighteenth and nineteenth centuries, though Mr. Prothero puts the percentage still higher. But we should miss the significance of these proportions if we were to look at England at the beginning of the eighteenth century as a map of which a large block was already shaded, and of which another block, say a fifth or a sixth part, was to be shaded by the enclosure of this period. The truth is that the life of the common-field system was still the normal village life of England, and that the land which was already enclosed consisted largely of old enclosures or the lord's demesne land lying side by side with the open fields. This was put quite clearly by the Bishop of St. Davids in the House of Lords in 1781. 'Parishes of any considerable extent consisted partly of old inclosures and partly of common fields.'[1] If a village living on the common-field system contained old enclosures, effected some time or other without Act of Parliament, it suffered just as violent a catastrophe when the common fields or the waste were enclosed, as if there had been no previous enclosure in the parish. The number of Acts passed in this period varies of course with the different counties,[2] but speaking generally, we may say that the events described in the next two chapters are not confined to any one part of the country, and that they mark a national revolution, making sweeping and profound changes in the form and the character of agricultural society throughout England.[3]

---

[1] *Parliamentary Register*, March 30, 1781.

[2] See Dr. Slater's detailed estimate.

[3] There were of course many enclosures without an Act of Parliament. Dr. Slater estimates their extent in the eighteenth century as 8,000,000 acres (*Sociological Review*, Jan. 1912). The evidence of Mr. Carus Wilson upon the committee of 1844 shows that the stronger classes interpreted their rights and powers in a liberal spirit. Mr. Carus Wilson had arranged with the other large proprietors to let out the only common which remained open in the thirteen parishes in which his father was interested as a large landowner, and to pay the rent into the poor rates. Some members of the committee asked whether the minority who dissented from this arrangement could be excluded, and Mr. Wilson explained that he and his confederates believed that the minority were bound by their action, and that by this simple plan they could shut out all cattle from the common, except the cattle of their joint tenants.—*Committee on Inclosures*, 1844, p. 127.

CHAPTER III

ENCLOSURE (1)

AN enclosure, like most Parliamentary operations, began with a petition from a local person or persons, setting forth the inconveniencies of the present system and the advantages of such a measure. Parliament, having received the petition, would give leave for a Bill to be introduced. The Bill would be read a first and a second time, and would then be referred to a Committee, which, after considering such petitions against the enclosure as the House of Commons referred to it, would present its report. The Bill would then be passed, sent to the Lords, and receive the Royal Assent. Finally, the Commissioners named in the Bill would descend on the district and distribute the land. That is, in brief, the history of a successful enclosure agitation. We will now proceed to explore its different stages in detail.

The original petition was often the act of a big landowner, whose solitary signature was enough to set an enclosure process in train.[1] Before 1774 it was not even incumbent on this single individual to let his neighbours know that he was asking Parliament for leave to redistribute their property. In that year the House of Commons made a Standing Order providing that notice of any such petition should be affixed to the church door in each of the parishes affected, for

[1] *E.g.* Laxton enclosed on petition of Lord Carbery in 1772. Total area 1200 acres. Enclosure proceedings completed in the Commons in nineteen days. Also Ashbury, Berks, enclosed on petition of Lord Craven in 1770. There were contrary petitions. Also Nylands, enclosed in 1790 on petition of the lady of the manor. Also Tilsworth, Beds, enclosed on petition of Charles Chester, Esq., 1767, and Westcote, Bucks, on petition of the most noble George, Duke of Marlborough, January 24, 1765. Sometimes the lord of the manor associated the vicar with his petition : thus Waltham, Croxton and Braunston, covering 5600 acres, in Leicestershire, were all enclosed in 1766 by the Duke of Rutland and the local rector or vicar. The relations of Church and State are very happily illustrated by the language of the petitions, 'A petition of the most noble John, Duke of Rutland, and the humble petition' of the Rev. —— Brown or Rastall or Martin.

three Sundays in the month of August or the month of September. This provision was laid down, as we learn from the Report of the Committee that considered the Standing Orders in 1775, because it had often happened that those whose land was to be enclosed knew nothing whatever of transactions in which they were rather intimately concerned, until they were virtually completed.[1]

But the publicity that was secured by this Standing Order, though it prevented the process of enclosure from being completed in the dark, did not in practice give the village any kind of voice in its own destiny. The promoters laid all their plans before they took their neighbours into the secret. When their arrangements were mature, they gave notice to the parish in accordance with the requirements of the Standing Order, or they first took their petition to the various proprietors for signature, or in some cases they called a public meeting. The facts set out in the petition against the Enclosure Bill for Haute Huntre, show that the promoters did not think that they were bound to accept the opinion of a meeting. In that case 'the great majority' were hostile, but the promoters proceeded with their petition notwithstanding.[2] Whatever the precise method, unless some large proprietor stood out against the scheme, the promoters were masters of the situation. This we know from the evidence of witnesses favourable to enclosure. 'The proprietors of large estates,' said Arthur Young, 'generally agree upon the measure, adjust the principal points among themselves, and fix upon their attorney before they appoint any general meeting of the proprietors.'[3] Addington, in his *Inquiry into the Reasons for and against Inclosing*, quoting another writer, says, 'the whole plan is generally settled between the solicitor and two or three principal proprietors without ever letting the rest of them into the secret till they are called upon to sign the petition.'[4] What stand could the small proprietor hope to make against such forces ? The matter was a *chose jugée*, and his assent a mere formality. If he tried to resist, he could be warned

---

[1] This Standing Order does not seem to have been applied universally, for Mr. Bragge on December 1, 1800, made a motion that it should be extended to the counties where it had not hitherto obtained. See *Senator*, vol. xxvii., December 1, 1800.

[2] See particulars in Appendix.

[3] *A Six Months' Tour through the North of England*, 1771, vol. i. p. 122.

[4] Pp. 21 f.

that the success of the enclosure petition was certain, and that those who obstructed it would suffer, as those who assisted it would gain, in the final award. His only prospect of successful opposition to the lord of the manor, the magistrate, the impropriator of the tithes, the powers that enveloped his life, the powers that appointed the commissioner who was to make the ultimate award, lay in his ability to move a dim and distant Parliament of great landlords to come to his rescue. It needs no very penetrating imagination to picture what would have happened in a village in which a landowner of the type of Richardson's hero in *Pamela* was bent on an enclosure, and the inhabitants, being men like Goodman Andrews, knew that enclosure meant their ruin. What, in point of fact, could the poor do to declare their opposition ? They could tear down the notices from the church doors : [1] they could break up a public meeting, if one were held : but the only way in which they could protest was by violent and disorderly proceedings, which made no impression at all upon Parliament, and which the forces of law and order could, if necessary, be summoned to quell.

The scene now shifts to Parliament, the High Court of Justice, the stronghold of the liberties of Englishmen. Parliament hears the petition, and, almost as a matter of course, grants it, giving leave for the introduction of a Bill, and instructing the member who presents the petition to prepare it. This is not a very long business, for the promoters have generally taken the trouble to prepare their Bill in advance. The Bill is submitted, read a first and second time, and then referred to a Committee. Now a modern Parliamentary Private Bill Committee is regarded as a tribunal whose integrity and impartiality are beyond question, and justly, for the most elaborate precautions are taken to secure that it shall deserve this character. The eighteenth-century Parliament treated its Committee with just as much respect, but took no precautions at all to obtain a disinterested court. Indeed, the committee that considered an enclosure was chosen on the very contrary principle. This we know, not from the evidence of unkind and prejudiced outsiders, but from the Report of the Committee of the House of Commons, which inquired in 1825 into the constitution of Committees on Private Bills. ' Under the present system each Bill is

[1] Cf. Otmoor in next chapter.

committed to the Member who is charged with its management and such other Members as he may choose to name in the House, and the Members serving for a particular County (usually the County immediately connected with the object of the Bill) *and the adjoining Counties*, and consequently it has been practically found that the Members to whom Bills have been committed have been generally those who have been most interested in the result.'

During the seventeenth and eighteenth centuries there developed the practice of opening the committees. This was the system of applying to Private Bills the procedure followed in the case of Public Bills, and proposing a resolution in the House of Commons that ' all who attend shall have voices,' *i.e.* that any member of the House who cared to attend the committee should be able to vote. We can see how this arrangement acted. It might happen that some of the county members were hostile to a particular enclosure scheme ; in that case the promoters could call for an open committee and mass their friends upon it. It might happen, on the other hand, that the committee was solid in supporting an enclosure, and that some powerful person in the House considered that his interests, or the interests of his friend, had not been duly consulted in the division of the spoil. In such a case he would call for all to ' have voices ' and so compel the promoters to satisfy his claims. This system then secured some sort of rough justice as between the powerful interests represented in Parliament, but it left the small proprietors and the cottagers, who were unrepresented in this mêlée, absolutely at the mercy of these conflicting forces.

It is difficult, for example, to imagine that a committee in which the small men were represented would have sanctioned the amazing clause in the Ashelworth Act[1] which provided 'that all fields or inclosures containing the Property of Two or more Persons within one fence, and also all inclosures containing the property of one Person only, if the same be held by or under different Tenures or Interests, shall be considered as commonable land and be divided and allotted accordingly.' This clause, taken with the clause that follows, simply meant that some big landowner had his eye on some particular piece of enclosed property, which in the ordinary way would not have gone into the melting-pot at all. The arrangements of the

[1] See Appendix

Wakefield Act would hardly have survived the scrutiny of a committee on which the Duke of Leeds' class was not paramount. Under that Act[1] the duke was to have full power to work mines and get minerals, and those proprietors whose premises suffered in consequence were to have reasonable satisfaction, not from the duke who was enriched by the disturbing cause, but from all the allottees, including presumably those whose property was damaged. Further, to save himself inconvenience, the duke could forbid allottees on Westgate Moor to build a house for sixty years. A different kind of House of Commons would have looked closely at the Act at Moreton Corbet which gave the lord of the manor all enclosures and encroachments more than twenty years old, and also at the not uncommon provision which exempted the tithe-owner from paying for his own fencing.

The Report of the 1825 Committee describes the system as ' inviting all the interested parties in the House to take part in the business of the committee, which necessarily terminates in the prevalence of the strongest part, for they who have no interest of their own to serve will not be prevailed upon to take part in a struggle in which their unbiassed judgment can have no effect.' The chairman of the committee was generally the member who had moved to introduce the Bill. The unreformed Parliament of landowners that passed the excellent Act of 1782, forbidding Members of Parliament to have an interest in Government contracts, never thought until the eve of the Reform Bill that there was anything remarkable in this habit of referring Enclosure Bills to the judgment of the very landowners who were to profit by them. And in 1825 it was not the Enclosure Bills, in which the rich took and the poor suffered, but the Railway Bills, in which rich men were pitted against rich men, that drew the attention of the House of Commons to the disadvantages and risks of this procedure.

The committee so composed sets to work on the Bill, and meanwhile, perhaps, some of the persons affected by the enclosure send petitions against it to the House of Commons. Difficulties of time and space would as a rule deter all but the rich dissentients, unless the enclosure was near London. These petitions are differently treated according to their origin. If they emanate from a lord of the manor, or from a tithe-

[1] See Appendix.

owner, who for some reason or other is dissatisfied with the contemplated arrangements, they receive some attention. In such a case the petitioner probably has some friend in Parliament, and his point of view is understood. He can, if necessary, get this friend to attend the committee and introduce amendments. He is therefore a force to be reckoned with ; the Bill is perhaps altered to suit him ; the petition is at any rate referred to the committee. On the other hand, if the petition comes from cottagers or small proprietors, it is safe, as a rule, to neglect it.

The enclosure histories set out in the Appendix supply some good examples of this differential treatment. Lord Strafford sends a petition against the Bill for enclosing Wakefield with the result that he is allowed to appoint a commissioner, and also that his dispute with the Duke of Leeds is exempted from the jurisdiction of the Enclosure Commissioners. On the other hand, the unfortunate persons who petition against the monstrous provision that forbade them to erect any building for twenty, forty or sixty years, get no kind of redress. In the case of Croydon, James Trecothick, Esq., who is dissatisfied with the Bill, is strong enough to demand special consideration. Accordingly a special provision is made that the commissioners are obliged to sell Mr. Trecothick, by private contract, part of Addington Hills, if he so wishes. But when the various freeholders, copyholders, leaseholders and inhabitant householders of Croydon, who complain that the promoters of the Bill have named commissioners without consulting the persons interested, ask leave to nominate a third commissioner, only four members of the House of Commons support Lord William Russell's proposal to consider this petition, and fifty-one vote the other way. Another example of the spirit in which Parliament received petitions from unimportant persons is furnished by the case of the enclosure of Holy Island. In 1791 (Feb. 23)[1] a petition was presented to Parliament for the enclosure of Holy Island, asking for the division of a stinted pasture, and the extinction of the rights of common or ' eatage ' over certain infield lands. Leave was given, and the Bill was prepared and read a first time on 28th February. The same day Parliament received a petition from freeholders and stallingers, who ask to be heard by themselves or by counsel against the

---

[1] See *House of Commons Journal.*

Bill. From Eden [1] we learn that there were 26 freeholders and 31 stallingers, and that the latter were in the strict sense of the term as much freeholders as the former. Whilst, however, a freeholder had the right to put 30 sheep, 4 black cattle and 3 horses on the stinted common, a stallinger had a right of common for one horse and one cow only. The House ordered that this petition should lie on the table till the second reading, and that the petitioners should then be heard. The second reading, which had been fixed for 2nd April, was deferred till 20th April, a change which probably put the petitioners to considerable expense. On 20th April the Bill was read a second time, and the House was informed that Counsel attended, and a motion was made that Counsel be now called in. But the motion was opposed, and on a division was defeated by 47 votes to 12. The Bill passed the House of Commons on 10th May, and received the Royal Assent on 9th June.[2] In this case the House of Commons broke faith with the petitioners, and refused the hearing it had promised. Such experience was not likely to encourage dissentients to waste their money on an appeal to Parliament against a Bill that was promoted by powerful politicians. It will be observed that at Armley and Ashelworth the petitioners did not think that it was worth the trouble and expense to be heard on Second Reading.

The Report of the Committee followed a stereotyped formula : ' That the Standing Orders had been complied with : and that the Committee had examined the Allegations of the Bill and found the same to be true ; and that the Parties concerned had given their Consent to the Bill, to the Satisfaction of the Committee, except . . .'

Now what did this mean ? What consents were necessary to satisfy the committee ? The Parliamentary Committee that reported on the cost of enclosures in 1800 [3] said that there was no fixed rule, that in some cases the consent of three-fourths was required, in others the consent of four-fifths. This proportion has a look of fairness until we discover that we are dealing in terms, not of persons, but of property, and that the suffrages were not counted but weighed. The method

---

[1] Eden, *The State of the Poor*, vol. ii. p. 157.

[2] Eden, writing a few years later, remarks that since the enclosure 'the property in Holy Island has gotten into fewer hands,' vol. ii. p. 149.

[3] Report of Select Committee on Most Effectual Means of Facilitating Enclosure, 1800.

by which the proportions were reckoned varied, as a glance
at the cases described in the Appendix will show. Value is
calculated sometimes in acres, sometimes in annual value,
sometimes in assessment to the land tax, sometimes in assessment to the poor rate. It is important to remember that
it was the property interested that counted, and that in a case
where there was common or waste to be divided as well as
open fields, one large proprietor, who owned a considerable
property in old enclosures, could swamp the entire community
of smaller proprietors and cottagers. If Squire Western
owned an enclosed estate with parks, gardens and farms of
800 acres, and the rest of the parish consisted of a common or
waste of 1000 acres and open fields of 200 acres, and the village
population consisted of 100 cottagers and small farmers, each
with a strip of land in the common fields, and a right of
common on the waste, Squire Western would have a four-fifths
majority in determining whether the open fields and the waste
should be enclosed or not, and the whole matter would be
in his hands. This is an extreme example of the way in which
the system worked. The case of Ashelworth shows that a
common might be cut up, on the votes of persons holding
enclosed property, against the wishes of the great majority
of the commoners. At Laleham the petitioners against the Bill
claimed that they were ' a great majority of the real Owners
and Proprietors of or Persons interested in, the Lands and
Grounds intended to be enclosed.' At Simpson, where common
fields were to be enclosed, the Major Part of the Owners and Proprietors petitioned against the Bill, stating that they were ' very
well satisfied with the Situation and Convenience of their respective Lands and Properties in their present uninclosed State.' [1]

Even a majority of three-fourths in value was not always
required; for example, the Report of the Committee on the
enclosure of Cartmel in Lancashire in 1796 gave particulars
showing that the whole property belonging to persons interested in the enclosure was assessed at £150, and that
the property of those actually consenting to the enclosure
was just under £110.[2] Yet the enclosure was recommended

---

[1] Cf. also Wraisbury in Bucks, *House of Commons Journal*, June 17, 1799,
where the petitioners against the Bill claimed that they spoke on behalf of
' by much the greatest Part of the Proprietors of the said Lands and Grounds,'
yet in the enumeration of consents the committee state that the owners of
property assessed at £6, 18s. are hostile out of a total value of £295, 14s.

[2] *House of Commons Journal*, March 21, 1796.

and carried. Another illustration is supplied by the Report of the Committee on the enclosure of Histon and Impington in 1801, where the parties concerned are reported to have consented except the proprietors of 1020 acres, out of a total acreage of 3680.[1] In this case the Bill was recommitted, and on its next appearance the committee gave the consents in terms of assessment to the Land Tax instead, putting the total figure at £304, and the assessment of the consenting parties at £188. This seems to have satisfied the House of Commons.[2] Further, the particulars given in the case of the enclosure of Bishopstone in Wilts (enclosed in 1809) show that the votes of copyholders were heavily discounted. In this case the copyholders who dissented held 1079 acres, the copyholders who were neuter 81 acres, and the total area to be divided was 2602 acres. But by some ingenious actuarial calcula- tion of the reversionary interest of the lord of the manor and the interest of the tithe-owner, the 1079 acres held by copyholders are written down to 474 acres.[3] In the cases of Simpson and Louth, as readers who consult the Appendix will see, the committees were satisfied with majorities just above three-fifths in value. At Raunds (see p. 39), where 4963 acres were 'interested,' the owners of 570 are stated to be against, and of 721 neuter.'[4] An interesting illustration of the lax practice of the committees is provided in the history of an attempted enclosure at Quainton (1801).[5] In any case the signatures were a doubtful evidence of consent. 'It is easy,' wrote an acute observer, 'for the large proprietors to overcome opposition. Coaxing, bribing, threatening, together with many other acts which superiors will make use of, often induce the inferiors to consent to things which they think will be to their future disadvantage.'[6] We hear echoes of such proceedings in the petition from various owners and proprietors at Armley, who 'at the instance of several other owners of land,' signed a petition for enclosure and wish to be heard against it, and also in the un- availing petition of some of the proprietors and freeholders of Winfrith Newburgh in Dorsetshire, in 1768,[7] who declared that if the Bill passed into law, their ' Estates must be totally ruined

---

[1] *House of Commons Journal*, June 10, 1801 ; cf. also case of Laleham. See Appendix.   [2] *Ibid.*, June 15, 1801.

[3] *Ibid.*, May 3, 1809.   [4] *Ibid.*, June 29, 1797.

[5] See Appendix A (13).

[6] *A Political Enquiry into the Consequences of enclosing Waste Lands*, 1785, p. 108.   [7] See Appendix A (12).

thereby, and that some of the Petitioners by Threats and Menaces were prevailed upon to sign the Petition for the said Bill : but upon Recollection, and considering the impending Ruin,' they prayed to ' have Liberty to retract from their seeming Acquiescence.' From the same case we learn that it was the practice sometimes to grant copyholds on the condition that the tenant would undertake not to oppose enclosure. Sometimes, as in the case of the Sedgmoor Enclosure, which we shall discuss later, actual fraud was employed. But even if the promoters employed no unfair methods they had one argument powerful enough to be a deterrent in many minds. For an opposed Enclosure Bill was much more expensive than an unopposed Bill, and as the small men felt the burden of the costs much more than the large proprietors, they would naturally be shy of adding to the very heavy expenses unless they stood a very good chance of defeating the scheme.

It is of capital importance to remember in this connection that the enumeration of ' consents ' took account only of proprietors. It ignored entirely two large classes to whom enclosure meant, not a greater or less degree of wealth, but actual ruin. These were such cottagers as enjoyed their rights of common in virtue of renting cottages to which such rights were attached, and those cottagers and squatters who either had no strict legal right, or whose rights were difficult of proof. Neither of these classes was treated even outwardly and formally as having any claim to be consulted before an enclosure was sanctioned.

It is clear, then, that it was only the pressure of the powerful interests that decided whether a committee should approve or disapprove of an Enclosure Bill. It was the same pressure that determined the form in which a Bill became law. For a procedure that enabled rich men to fight out their rival claims at Westminster left the classes that could not send counsel to Parliament without a weapon or a voice. And if there was no lawyer there to put his case, what prospect was there that the obscure cottager, who was to be turned adrift with his family by an Enclosure Bill promoted by a Member or group of Members, would ever trouble the conscience of a committee of landowners ? We have seen already how this class was regarded by the landowners and the champions of enclosure. No cottagers had votes or the means of influencing a single vote at a single election. To Parliament, if they had

any existence at all, they were merely dim shadows in the
very background of the enclosure scheme. It would require
a considerable effort of the imagination to suppose that the
Parliamentary Committee spent very much time or energy
on the attempt to give body and form to this hazy and remote
society, and to treat these shadows as living men and women,
about to be tossed by this revolution from their ancestral homes.
As it happens, we need not put ourselves to the trouble of such
speculation, for we have the evidence of a witness who will
not be suspected of injustice to his class. ' This I know,'
said Lord Lincoln [1] introducing the General Enclosure Bill of
1845, ' that in nineteen cases out of twenty, Committees of
this House sitting on private Bills neglected the rights of the
poor. I do not say that they wilfully neglected those rights
—far from it : but this I affirm, that they were neglected
in consequence of the Committees being permitted to remain
in ignorance of the claims of the poor man, because by reason
of his very poverty he is unable to come up to London for
counsel, to produce witnesses, and to urge his claims before
a Committee of this House.' Another Member [2] had described
a year earlier the character of this private Bill procedure.
' Inclosure Bills had been introduced heretofore and passed
without discussion, and no one could tell how many persons
had suffered in their interests and rights by the interference
of these Bills. Certainly these Bills had been referred to
Committees upstairs, but everyone knew how these Committees were generally conducted. They were attended only
by honourable Members who were interested in them, being
Lords of Manor, and the rights of the poor, though they might
be talked about, had frequently been taken away under that
system.'

These statements were made by politicians who remembered well the system they were describing. There is
another witness whose authority is even greater. In 1781
Lord Thurlow, then at the beginning of his long life of office as
Lord Chancellor,[3] spoke for an hour and three quarters in favour
of recommitting the Bill for enclosing Ilmington in Warwickshire. If the speech had been fully reported it would be a
contribution of infinite value to students of the social history

---

[1] House of Commons, May 1, 1845.

[2] Aglionby, House of Commons, June 5, 1844.

[3] Thurlow was Chancellor from 1778 to 1783 (when Fox contrived to get rid
of him) and from 1783 to 1792.

of eighteenth-century England, for we are told that 'he proceeded to examine, paragraph by paragraph, every provision of the Bill, animadverting and pointing out some acts of injustice, partiality, obscurity or cause of confusion in each.' [1] Unfortunately this part of his speech was omitted in the report as being 'irrelative to the debate,' which was concerned with the question of the propriety of commuting tithes.   But the report, incomplete as it is, contains an illuminating passage on the conduct of Private Bill Committees. 'His Lordship ... next turned his attention to the mode in which private bills were permitted to make their way through both Houses, and that in matters in which property was concerned, to the great injury of many, if not the total ruin of some private families : many proofs of this evil had come to his knowledge as a member of the other House, not a few in his professional character, before he had the honour of a seat in that House, nor had he been a total stranger to such evils since he was called upon to preside in another place.' Going on to speak of the committees of the House of Commons and 'the rapidity with which private Bills were hurried through,' he declared that 'it was not unfrequent to decide upon the merits of a Bill which would affect the property and interests of persons inhabiting a district of several miles in extent, in less time than it took him to determine upon the propriety of issuing an order for a few pounds, by which no man's property could be injured.'   He concluded by telling the House of Lords a story of how Sir George Savile once noticed a man 'rather meanly habited' watching the proceedings of a committee with anxious interest.   When the committee had agreed on its report, the agitated spectator was seen to be in great distress.   Sir George Savile asked him what was the matter, and he found that the man would be ruined by a clause that had been passed by the committee, and that, having heard that the Bill was to be introduced, he had made his way to London on foot, too poor to come in any other way or to fee counsel.   Savile then made inquiries and learnt that these statements were correct, whereupon he secured the amendment of the Bill, 'by which means an innocent, indigent man and his family were rescued from destruction.'   It would not have been very easy for a 'meanly habited man' to make the journey to London from

<hr>

[1] *Parliamentary Register*, House of Lords, March 30, 1781.

Wakefield or Knaresborough or Haute Huntre, even if he knew when a Bill was coming on, and to stay in London until it went into committee ; and if he did, he would not always be so lucky as to find a Sir George Savile on the committee—the public man who was regarded by his contemporaries, to whatever party they belonged, as the Bayard of politics.[1]

We get very few glimpses into the underworld of the common and obscure people, whose homes and fortunes trembled on the chance that a quarrel over tithes and the conflicting claims of squire and parson might disturb the unanimity of a score of gentlemen sitting round a table. London was far away, and the Olympian peace of Parliament was rarely broken by the protests of its victims. But we get one such glimpse in a passage in the *Annual Register* for 1767.

' On Tuesday evening a great number of farmers were observed going along Pall Mall with cockades in their hats. On enquiring the reason, it appeared they all lived in or near the parish of Stanwell in the county of Middlesex, and they were returning to their wives and families to carry them the agreeable news of a Bill being rejected for inclosing the said common, which if carried into execution, might have been the ruin of a great number of families.' [2]

When the Committee on the Enclosure Bill had reported to the House of Commons, the rest of the proceedings were generally formal. The Bill was read a third time, engrossed, sent up to the Lords, where petitions might be presented as in the Commons, and received the Royal Assent.

A study of the pages of Hansard and Debrett tells us little about transactions that fill the *Journals* of the Houses of Parliament. Three debates in the House of Lords are fully reported,[3] and they illustrate the play of forces at Westminster. The Bishop of St. Davids [4] moved to recommit an Enclosure

---

[1] Sir George Savile (1726-1784), M.P. for Yorkshire, 1759-1783 ; carried the Catholic Relief Bill, which provoked the Gordon Riots, and presented the great Yorkshire Petition for Economical Reform.

[2] *Annual Register*, 1867, p. 68. For a detailed history of the Stanwell Enclosure, see Appendix A (10). Unhappily the farmers were only reprieved ; Stanwell was enclosed at the second attempt.

[3] See *Parliamentary Register*, House of Lords, March 30, 1781 ; April 6, 1781 ; June 14, 1781.

[4] John Warren (1730-1800).

Bill in 1781 on the ground that, like many other Enclosure
Bills, it provided for the commutation of tithes—an arrangement which he thought open to many objections. Here was
an issue that was vital, for it concerned the interests of the
classes represented in Parliament. Did the Church stand
to gain or to lose by taking land instead of tithe ? Was it a
bad thing or a good thing that the parson should be put into
the position of a farmer, that he should be under the temptation to enter into an arrangement with the landlord which
might prejudice his successor, that he should be relieved from
a system which often caused bad blood between him and
his parishioners ? Would it ' make him neglect the sacred
functions of his ministry ' as the Bishop of St. Davids feared,
or would it improve his usefulness by rescuing him from a
situation in which ' the pastor was totally sunk in the tithe-
collector ' as the Bishop of Peterborough[1] hoped, and was a man
a better parson on the Sunday for being a farmer the rest of
the week as Lord Coventry believed ? The bishops and the
peers had in this discussion a subject that touched very nearly
the lives and interests of themselves and their friends, and there
was a considerable and animated debate,[2] at the end of which
the House of Lords approved the principle of commuting tithes
in Enclosure Bills. This debate was followed by another on
6th April, when Lord Bathurst (President of the Council) as a
counterblast to his colleague on the Woolsack, moved, but
afterwards withdrew, a series of resolutions on the same subject.
In the course of this debate Thurlow, who thought perhaps that
his zeal for the Church had surprised and irritated his fellow-
peers, among whom he was not conspicuous in life as a prac-
tising Christian, explained that though he was zealous for the
Church, ' his zeal was not partial or confined to the Church,
further than it was connected with the other great national
establishments, of which it formed a part, and no inconsiderable one.' The Bishop of St. Davids returned to the subject
on the 14th June, moving to recommit the Bill for enclosing
Kington in Worcestershire. He read a string of resolutions
which he wished to see applied to all future Enclosure Bills, in
order to defend the interests of the clergy from ' the oppressions of the Lord of the Manor, landowners, etc.' Thurlow
spoke for him, but he was defeated by 24 votes to 4, his only

[1] John Hinchcliffe (1731-1794), at one time Master of Trinity College,
Cambridge.
[2] *Parliamentary Register*, March 30, 1781.

other supporters being Lord Galloway and the Bishop of Lincoln.

Thurlow's story of Sir George Savile's ' meanly habited man ' did not disturb the confidence of the House of Lords in the justice of the existing procedure towards the poor : the enclosure debates revolve solely round the question of the relative claims of the lord of the manor and the tithe-owner. The House of Commons was equally free from scruple or misgiving. One petitioner in 1800 commented on the extraordinary haste with which a New Forest Bill was pushed through Parliament, and suggested that if it were passed into law in this rapid manner at the end of a session, some injustice might unconsciously be done. The Speaker replied with a grave and dignified rebuke : ' The House was always competent to give every subject the consideration due to its importance, and could not therefore be truly said to be incapable at any time of discussing any question gravely, dispassionately, and with strict regard to justice.' [1] He recommended that the petition should be passed over as if it had never been presented. The member who had presented the petition pleaded that he had not read it. Such were the plausibilities and decorum in which the House of Commons wrapped up its abuses. We can imagine that some of the members must have smiled to each other like the Roman augurs, when they exchanged these solemn hypocrisies.

We have a sidelight on the vigilance of the House of Commons, when an Enclosure Bill came down from a committee, in a speech of Windham's in defence of bull-baiting. Windham attacked the politicians who had introduced the Bill to abolish bull-baiting, for raising such a question at a time of national crisis when Parliament ought to be thinking of other things. He then went on to compare the subject to local subjects that ' contained nothing of public or general interest. To procure the discussion of such subjects it was necessary to resort to canvass and intrigue. Members whose attendance was induced by local considerations in most cases of this description, were present : the discussion, if any took place, was managed by the friends of the measure : and the decision of the House was ultimately, perhaps, a matter of mere chance.' From Sheridan's speech in answer, we learn that this is a description of the passing of Enclosure Bills. ' Another honourable gentleman who had opposed this Bill with peculiar vehe-

[1] *Senator*, vol. xxvi., July 2, 1800.

mence, considered it as one of those light and trivial subjects, which was not worthy to occupy the deliberations of Parliament : and he compared it to certain other subjects of Bills : that is to say, bills of a local nature, respecting inclosures and other disposal of property, which merely passed by chance, as Members could not be got to attend their progress by dint of canvassing,' [1] Doubtless most Members of the House of Commons shared the sentiments of Lord Sandwich, who told the House of Lords that he was so satisfied ' that the more inclosures the better, that as far as his poor abilities would enable him, he would support every inclosure bill that should be brought into the House.' [2]

For the last act of an enclosure drama the scene shifts back to the parish.   The commissioners arrive, receive and determine claims, and publish an award, mapping out the new village.   The life and business of the village are now in suspense, and the commissioners are often authorised to prescribe the course of husbandry during the transition.[3]   The Act which they administer provides that a certain proportion of the land is to be assigned to the lord of the manor, in virtue of his rights, and a certain proportion to the owner of the tithes.   An occasional Act provides that some small allotment shall be made to the poor : otherwise the commissioners have a free hand : their powers are virtually absolute.   This is the impression left by all contemporary writers.   Arthur Young, for example, writes emphatically in this sense.   ' Thus is the property of proprietors, and especially of the poor ones, entirely at their mercy : every passion of resentment and prejudice may be gratified without control, for they are vested with a despotic power known in no other branch of business in this free country.' [4]   Similar testimony is found in the Report of the Select Committee (1800) on the Expense and Mode of Obtaining Bills of Enclosure : ' the expediency of despatch, without the additional expense of multiplied litigation, has suggested the necessity of investing them with a summary, and in most cases uncontrollable jurisdiction.' [5]   In the General Report of the Board of Agriculture on Enclosures, published in 1808, though any more careful procedure is deprecated as likely to

---

[1] For both speeches see *Parliamentary Register*, May 24, 1802.

[2] *Ibid.*, June 14, 1781.

[3] See Cheshunt, Louth, Simpson, and Stanwell in Appendix.

[4] *Six Months' Tour through the North of England*, 1771, vol. i. p. 122.

[5] See *Annual Register*, 1800, Appendix to Chronicle, p. 87.

cause delay, it is stated that the adjusting of property worth £50,000 was left to the arbitration of a majority of five, ' often persons of mean education.' The author of *An Inquiry into the Advantages and Disadvantages resulting from Bills of Inclosure,* published in 1781, writes as if it was the practice to allow an appeal to Quarter Sessions ; such an appeal he characterised as useless to a poor man, and we can well believe that most of the squires who sat on such a tribunal to punish vagrants or poachers had had a hand in an enclosure in the past or had their eyes on an enclosure in the future. Thurlow considered such an appeal quite inadequate, giving the more polite reason that Quarter Sessions had not the necessary time.[1] The Act of 1801 is silent on the subject, but Sinclair's draft of a General Inclosure Bill, published in the *Annals of Agriculture* in 1796,[2] provided for an appeal to Quarter Sessions. It will be seen that in five of the cases analysed in the Appendix (Haute Huntre, Simpson, Stanwell, Wakefield and Winfrith Newburgh), the decision of the commissioners on claims was final, except that at Wakefield an objector might oblige the commissioners to take the opinion of a counsel chosen by themselves. In five cases (Ashelworth, Croydon, Cheshunt, Laleham and Louth), a disappointed claimant might bring a suit on a feigned issue against a proprietor. At Armley and Knaresborough the final decision was left to arbitrators, but whereas at Armley the arbitrator was to be chosen by a neutral authority, the Recorder of Leeds, the arbitrators at Knaresborough were named in the Act, and were presumably as much the nominees of the promoters as the commissioners themselves.

The statements of contemporaries already quoted go to show that none of these arrangements were regarded as seriously fettering the power of the commissioners, and it is easy to understand that a lawsuit, which might of course overwhelm him, was not a remedy for the use of a small proprietor or a cottager, though it might be of some advantage to a large proprietor who had not been fortunate enough to secure adequate representation of his interests on the Board of Commissioners. But the decision as to claims was only part of the business. A man's claim might be allowed, and yet gross injustice might be done him in the redistribution. He might be given inferior land, or land in an inconvenient position. In

---

[1] *Parliamentary Register,* June 14, 1781.
[2] *Annals of Agriculture,* vol. xxvi. p. 111.

ten of the cases in the Appendix the award of the commissioners is stated to be final, and there is no appeal from it.   The two exceptions are Knaresborough and Armley.   The Knaresborough Act is silent on the point, and the Armley Act allows an appeal to the Recorder of Leeds.   So far therefore as the claims and allotments of the poor were concerned, the commissioners were in no danger of being overruled.   Their freedom in other ways was restricted by the Standing Orders of 1774, which obliged them to give an account of their expenses.

It would seem to be obvious that any society which had an elementary notion of the meaning and importance of justice would have taken the utmost pains to see that the men appointed to this extraordinary office had no motive for showing partiality.   This might not unreasonably have been expected of the society about which Pitt declared in the House of Commons, that it was the boast of the law of England that it afforded equal security and protection to the high and low, the rich and poor.[1]   How were these commissioners appointed at the time that Pitt was Prime Minister ?   They were appointed in each case before the Bill was presented to Parliament, and generally, as Young tells us, they were appointed by the promoters of the enclosure before the petition was submitted for local signatures, so that in fact they were nominated by the persons of influence who agreed on the measure.   In one case (Moreton Corbet in Shropshire ; 1950 acres enclosed in 1797) the Act appointed one commissioner only, and he was to name his successor.   Sometimes, as in the case of Otmoor,[2] it might happen that the commissioners were changed while the Bill was passing through Committee, if some powerful persons were able to secure better representation of their own interests.   In the case of Wakefield again, the House of Commons Committee placated Lord Strafford by giving him a commissioner.

Now, who was supposed to have a voice in the appointment of the commissioners ?   There is to be found in the *Annals of Agriculture*[3] an extremely interesting paper by Sir John Sinclair, preliminary to a memorandum of the General Enclosure Bill which he promoted in 1796.   Sinclair explains that he had had eighteen hundred Enclosure Acts (taken indiscriminately) examined in order to ascertain what was the usual procedure and what stipulations were made with regard to particular interests ;

[1] February 1, 1793.   [2] See Chapter iv.   [3] Vol. xxvi. p. 70.

this with the intention of incorporating the recognised practice in his General Bill. In the course of these remarks he says, 'the probable result will be the appointment of one Commissioner by the Lord of the Manor, of another by the tithe-owner, and of a third by the major part in value of the proprietors.'[1] It will be observed that the third commissioner is not appointed by a majority of the commoners, nor even by the majority of the proprietors, but by the votes of those who own the greater part of the village. This enables us to assess the value of what might have seemed a safeguard to the poor—the provision that the names of the commissioners should appear in the Bill presented to Parliament. The lord of the manor, the impropriator of tithes, and the majority in value of the owners are a small minority of the persons affected by an enclosure, and all that they have to do is to meet round a table and name the commissioners who are to represent them.[2] Thus we find that the powerful persons who carried an enclosure against the will of the poor nominated the tribunal before which the poor had to make good their several claims. This was the way in which the constitution that Pitt was defending afforded equal security and protection to the rich and to the poor.

It will be noticed further that two interests are chosen out for special representation. They are the lord of the manor and the impropriator of tithes : in other words, the very persons who are formally assigned a certain minimum in the distribution by the Act of Parliament. Every Act after 1774 declares that the lord of the manor is to have a certain proportion, and the tithe-owner a certain proportion of the land divided : scarcely any Act stipulates that any share at all is to go to the cottager or the small proprietor. Yet in the appointment of commissioners the interests that are protected by the Act have a preponderating voice, and the interests that are left to the caprice of the commissioners have no voice at all. Thurlow, speaking in the House of Lords in 1781,[3] said that it was grossly unjust to the parson that his property should be at the disposal of these commissioners,

---

[1] Sinclair's language shows that this was the general arrangement. Of course there are exceptions. See *e.g.* Haute Huntre and other cases in Appendix.

[2] Cf. Billingsley's *Report on Somerset*, p. 59, where the arrangements are described as 'a *little system of patronage.* The lord of the soil, the rector, and a few of the principal commoners, monopolize and distribute the appointments.'

[3] *Parliamentary Register*, June 14, 1781.

of whom he only nominated one. 'He thanked God that the property of an Englishman depended not on so loose a tribunal in any other instance whatever.' What, then, was the position of the poor and the small farmers who were not represented at all among the commissioners? In the paper already quoted, Sinclair mentions that in some cases the commissioners were peers, gentlemen and clergymen, residing in the neighbourhood, who acted without fees or emolument. He spoke of this as undertaking a useful duty, and it does not seem to have occurred to him that there was any objection to such a practice. 'To lay down the principle that men are to serve for nothing,' said Cobbett, in criticising the system of unpaid magistrates, 'puts me in mind of the servant who went on hire, who being asked what wages he demanded, said he wanted no wages : for that he always found about the house little things to pick up.'

There is a curious passage in the General Report of the Board of Agriculture [1] on the subject of the appointment of commissioners. The writer, after dwelling on the unexampled powers that the commissioners enjoy, remarks that they are not likely to be abused, because a commissioner's prospect of future employment in this profitable capacity depends on his character for integrity and justice. This is a reassuring reflection for the classes that promoted enclosures and appointed commissioners, but it rings with a very different sound in other ears. It would clearly have been much better for the poor if the commissioners had not had any prospect of future employment at all. We can obtain some idea of the kind of men whom the landowners considered to be competent and satisfactory commissioners from the Standing Orders of 1801, which forbade the employment in this capacity of the bailiff of the lord of the manor. It would be interesting to know how much of England was appropriated on the initiative of the lord of the manor, by his bailiff, acting under the authority given to him by the High Court of Parliament. It is significant, too, that down to 1801 a commissioner was only debarred from buying land in a parish in which he had acted in this capacity, until his award was made,   The Act of 1801 debarred him from buying land under such circumstances for the following five years.

The share of the small man in these transactions from first to last can be estimated from the language of Arthur Young in 1770. 'The small proprietor whose property in the town-

---

[1] *General Report on Enclosures,* 1808.

ship is perhaps his all, has little or no weight in regulating the clauses of the Act of Parliament, has seldom, if ever, an opportunity of putting a single one in the Bill favourable to his rights, and has as little influence in the choice of Commissioners.'[1] But even this description does less than justice to his helplessness. There remains to be considered the procedure before the commissioners themselves. Most Enclosure Acts specified a date before which all claims had to be presented. It is obvious that there must have been very many small proprietors who had neither the courage nor the knowledge necessary to put and defend their case, and that vast numbers of claims must have been disregarded because they were not presented, or because they were presented too late, or because they were irregular in form. The Croydon Act, for example, prescribes that claimants must send in their claims 'in Writing under their Hands, or the Hands of their Agents, distinguishing in such Claims the Tenure of the Estates in respect whereof such Claims are made, and stating therein such further Particulars as shall be necessary to describe such Claims with Precision.' And if this was a difficult fence for the small proprietor, unaccustomed to legal forms and documents, or to forms and documents of any kind, what was the plight of the cottager ? Let us imagine the cottager, unable to read or write, enjoying certain customary rights of common without any idea of their origin or history or legal basis : knowing only that as long as he can remember he has kept a cow, driven geese across the waste, pulled his fuel out of the neighbouring brushwood, and cut turf from the common, and that his father did all these things before him. The cottager learns that before a certain day he has to present to his landlord's bailiff, or to the parson, or to one of the magistrates into whose hands perhaps he has fallen before now over a little matter of a hare or a partridge, or to some solicitor from the country town, a clear and correct statement of his rights and his claim to a share in the award. Let us remember at the same time all that we know from Fielding and Smollett of the reputation of lawyers for cruelty to the poor. Is a cottager to be trusted to face the ordeal, or to be in time with his statement, or to have that statement in proper legal form ? The commissioners can reject his claim on the ground of any technical irregularity, as we learn from a petition presented to Parliament in 1774 by several persons interested in the

[1] *Six Months' Tour through the North of England,* vol. i. p. 122.

enclosure of Knaresborough Forest, whose claims had been disallowed by the commissioners because of certain ' mistakes made in the description of such tenements . . . notwithstanding the said errors were merely from inadvertency, and in no way altered the merits of the petitioners' claims.' A Bill was before Parliament to amend the previous Act for enclosing Knaresborough Forest, in respect of the method of payment of expenses, and hence these petitioners had an opportunity of making their treatment public.[1] It is easy to guess what was the fate of many a small proprietor or cottager, who had to describe his tenement or common right to an unsympathetic tribunal. We are not surprised that one of the witnesses told the Enclosure Committee of 1844 that the poor often did not know what their claims were, or how to present them. It is significant that in the case of Sedgmoor, out of 4063 claims sent in, only 1798 were allowed.[2]

We have now given an account of the procedure by which Parliamentary enclosures were carried out. We give elsewhere a detailed analysis, disentangled from the *Journals* of Parliament and other sources, of particular enclosures. We propose to give here two illustrations of the temper of the Parliamentary Committees. One illustration is provided by a speech made by Sir William Meredith, one of the Rockingham Whigs, in 1772, a speech that needs no comment. ' Sir William Meredith moved, That it might be a general order, that no Bill, or clause in a Bill, making any offence capital, should be agreed to but in a Committee of the whole House. He observed, that at present the facility of passing such clauses was shameful : that he once passing a Committee-room, when only one Member was holding a Committee, with a clerk's boy, he happened to hear something of hanging ; he immediately had the curiosity to ask what was going forward in that small Committee that could merit such a punishment ? He was answered, that it was an Inclosing Bill, in which a great many poor people were concerned, who opposed the Bill ; that they feared those people would obstruct the execution of the Act, and therefore this clause was to make it capital felony in anyone who did so. This resolution was unanimously agreed to.' [3]

The other illustration is provided by the history of an

---

[1] See Appendix A (6).   [2] *Report on Somerset*, p. 192.
[3] *Parliamentary Register*, January 21, 1772.

attempted enclosure in which we can watch the minds of the chief actors without screen or disguise of any kind : in this case we have very fortunately a vivid revelation of the spirit and manner in which Committees conducted their business, from the pen of the chairman himself. George Selwyn gives us in his letters, published in the *Carlisle Papers*, a view of the proceedings from the inside. It is worth while to set out in some detail the passages from these letters published in the *Carlisle Papers*, by way of supplementing and explaining the official records of the House of Commons.

We learn from the *Journals* of the House of Commons that, on 10th November, 1775, a petition was presented to the House of Commons for the enclosure of King's Sedgmoor, in the County of Somerset, the petitioners urging that this land was of very little value in its present state, and that it was capable of great improvement by enclosure and drainage. Leave was given to bring in a Bill, to be prepared by Mr. St. John and Mr. Coxe. Mr. St. John was brother of Lord Bolingbroke. On 13th November, the Bill was presented and read a first time. Four days later it received a second reading, and was sent to a Committee of Mr. St. John and others. At this point, those who objected to the enclosure began to take action. First of all there is a petition from William Waller, Esq., who says that under a grant of Charles I. he is entitled to the soil of the moor : it is agreed that he shall be heard by counsel before the Committee. The next day there arrives a petition from owners and occupiers in thirty-five ' parishes, hamlets and places,' who state that all these parishes have enjoyed rights of common without discrimination over the 18,000 acres of pasture on Sedgmoor : that these rights of pasture and cutting turf and rushes and sedges have existed from time immemorial, and that no Enclosure Act is wanted for the draining of Sedgmoor, because an Act of the reign of William III. had conferred all the necessary powers for this purpose on the Justices of the Peace. The petitioners prayed to be heard by themselves and counsel against the application for enclosure on Committee and on Report. The House of Commons ordered that the petition should lie on the Table, and that the petitioners should be heard when the Report had been received from Committee. Five days later three lords of manors (Sir Charles Kemys Tynte, Baronet, Copleston Warre Bampfylde, Esq., and William Hawker, Esq.) petition against the Bill and complain of the haste with which the promoters are pushing the Bill through Parliament. This petition is taken more seriously : a motion is made and defeated to defer the Bill for two months, but the House orders that the petitioners shall be heard before the Committee. Two of these three lords of manor present a further petition early in December, stating that they and their tenants are more than a majority in number and value of the persons interested, and a second petition is also presented by the thirty-seven parishes and hamlets already mentioned, in which it is contended that, in spite of the difficulties of collecting signatures in a scattered district in a very short time, 749 persons interested had already signed the petition against the Bill, that the effect of the Bill had been misrepresented to many of the tenants, that the facts as to the different interests affected had been misrepresented to the Committee, that the number and rights of the persons supporting the Bill had been exaggerated (only 213 having signed their names as consenting), and that if justice was to be done to the various parties concerned, it was essential that time should be given for the hearing of complaints and the circulation of the Bill in the district.   This petition was presented on 11th December, and the House of Commons ordered that the petitioners should be heard when the Report was received. Next day Mr. Selwyn, as Chairman of the Committee, presented a Report in favour of the Bill, mentioning among other things that the number of tenements concerned was 1269, and that 303 refused to sign; but attention was drawn to the fact that there were several variations between the Bill as it was presented to the House, and the Bill as it was presented to the parties concerned for their consent, and on this ground the Bill was defeated by 59 to 35 votes.

This is the cold impersonal account of the proceedings given in the official journals, but the letters of Selwyn take us behind the scenes and supply a far livelier picture.[1]   His account begins with a letter to Lord Carlisle in November :

' Bully has a scheme of enclosure, which, if it succeeds, I am told will free him from all his difficulties.   It is to come into our House immediately.   If I had this from a better judgment than that of our sanguine counsellors, I should have more hopes from it.   I am ready to allow that he has been very faulty, but I cannot help wishing to see him once more on his legs. . . .'

(Bully, of course, is Bolingbroke, brother of St. John, called

[1] *Carlisle MSS. ; Historical MSS. Commission*, pp. 301 ff.

the counsellor, author of the Bill.) We learn from this letter that there are other motives than a passion to drain Sedgmoor in the promotion of this great improvement scheme. We learn from the next letter that it is not only Bully's friends and creditors who have some reason for wishing it well:

'Stavordale is returning to Redlinch; I believe that he sets out to-morrow. He is also deeply engaged in this Sedgmoor Bill, and it is supposed that he or Lord Ilchester, which you please, will get 2000*l*. a year by it. He will get more, or save more at least, by going away and leaving the Moor in my hands, for he told me himself the other night that this last trip to town had cost him 4000*l*.'

Another letter warns Lord Carlisle that the only way to get his creditors to pay their debts to him, when they come into their money through the enclosure, is to press for payment, and goes on to describe the unexpected opposition the Bill had encountered. Selwyn had been made chairman of the Committee.

'. . . My dear Lord, if your delicacy is such that you will not be pressing with him about it, you may be assured that you will never receive a farthing. I have spoke to Hare about it, who [was] kept in it till half an hour after 4; as I was also to-day, and shall be to-morrow. I thought that it was a matter of form only, but had no sooner begun to read the preamble to the Bill, but I found myself in a nest of hornets. The room was full, and an opposition made to it, and disputes upon every word, which kept me in the Chair, as I have told you. I have gained it seems great reputation, and am at this minute reputed one of the best Chairmen upon this stand. Bully and Harry came home and dined with me. . . .'

The next letter, written on 9th December, shows that Selwyn is afraid that Stavordale may not get his money out of his father, and also that he is becoming still more anxious about the fate of the Enclosure Bill, on which of course the whole pack of cards depends:

'. . . I have taken the liberty to talk a good deal to Lord Stavordale, partly for his own sake and partly for yours, and pressed him much to get out of town as soon as possible, and not quit Lord I. [Ilchester] any more. His attention there cannot be of long duration, and his absence may be fatal to us all. I painted it in very strong colours, and he has promised me to go, as soon as this Sedgmoor Bill is reported. I moved to have Tuesday fixed for it. We had a debate and division upon my motion, and this Bill will at last not go down so glibly as Bully hoped that it would. It will meet with more opposition in the H. of Lords, and Lord North being adverse to it, does us no good. Lord Ilchester gets, it is said, £5000 a year by it, and amongst others Sir C. Tynte something, who, for what reason I cannot yet comprehend, opposes it. . . .'

The next letter describes the final catastrophe :

'December 12. Tuesday night. . . . Bully has lost his Bill. I reported it to-day, and the Question was to withdraw it. There were 59 against us, and we were 35. It was worse managed by the agents, supposing no treachery, than ever business was. Lord North, Robinson, and Keene divided against. Charles[1] said all that could be said on our side. But as the business was managed, it was the worst Question that I ever voted for. We were a Committee absolutely of Almack's,[2] so if the Bill is not resumed, and better conducted and supported, this phantom of 30,000l. clear in Bully's pocket to pay off his annuities vanishes.

' It is surprising what a fatality attends some people's proceedings. I begged last night as for alms, that they would meet me to settle the Votes. I have, since I have been in Parliament, been of twenty at least of these meetings, and always brought numbers down by those means. But my advice was slighted, and twenty people were walking about the streets who could have carried this point.

' The cause was not bad, but the Question was totally indigestible. The most conscientious man in the House in Questions of this nature, Sir F. Drake, a very old acquaintance of mine, told me that nothing could be so right as the enclosure. But they sent one Bill into the country for the assent of the people interested, and brought me another, differing in twenty particulars, to carry through the Committee, without once mentioning to me that the two Bills differed. This they thought was cunning, and I believe a happy composition of Bully's cunning and John's idea of his own parts. I had no idea, or could have, of this difference. The adverse party said nothing of it, _comme de raison_, reserving the objection till the Report, and it was insurmountable. If one of the Clerks only had hinted it to me, inexperienced as I am in these sort of Bills, I would have stopped it, and by that means have given them a better chance by a new Bill than they can have now, that people will have a pretence for not altering their opinion. . . .'

These letters compensate for the silence of Hansard, so real and instructive a picture do they present of the methods and motives of enclosure. ' Bully has a scheme of enclosure

---

[1] Charles James Fox.   [2] The earlier name of Brooks's Club.

which, if it succeeds, I am told will free him from all his difficulties.' The journals may talk of the undrained fertility
of Sedgmoor, but we have in this sentence the aspect of the
enclosure that interests Selwyn, the Chairman of the Committee, and from beginning to end of the proceedings no other
aspect ever enters his head. And it interests a great many
other people besides Selwyn, for Bully owes money; so too
does Stavordale, another prospective beneficiary: he owes
money to Fox, and Fox owes money to Carlisle. Now Bully
and Stavordale are not the only eighteenth-century aristocrats
who are in difficulties; the waiters at Brooks's and at White's
know that well enough, as Selwyn felt when, on hearing that
one of them had been arrested for felony, he exclaimed, ' What
an idea of us he will give in Newgate.' Nor is Bully the only
aristocrat in difficulties whose thoughts turn to enclosure;
Selwyn's letters alone, with their reference to previous suc-
cesses, would make that clear. It is here that we begin to
appreciate the effect of our system of family settlements in
keeping the aristocracy together. These young men, whose
fortunes come and go in the hurricanes of the faro table, would
soon have dissipated their estates if they had been free to
do it; as they were restrained by settlements, they could
only mortgage them. But there is a limit to this process,
and after a time their debts begin to overwhelm them; perhaps also too many of their fellow gamblers are their creditors
to make Brooks's or White's quite as comfortable a place as
it used to be, for we may doubt whether all of these creditors
were troubled with Lord Carlisle's morbid delicacy of feeling.
Happily there is an escape from this painful situation: a
scheme of enclosure which will put him ' once more on his
legs.' The other parties concerned are generally poor men,
and there is not much danger of failure. Thus if we trace
the adventures of the gaming table to their bitter end, we
begin to understand that these wild revellers are gambling
not with their own estates but with the estates of their neighbours. This is the only property they can realise. *Quidquid
delirant reges plectuntur Achivi.*

The particular obstacle on which the scheme split was a
fraudulent irregularity the Bill submitted for signature to
the inhabitants differing seriously (in twenty particulars)
from the Bill presented to Parliament. Selwyn clearly attached
no importance at all to the Petitions that were received against
the Bill, or to the evidence of its local unpopularity. It is

clear too, that it was very rare for a scheme like this to miscarry, for, speaking of his becoming Chairman of the Committee, he adds, ' I thought it was a matter of form only.' Further with a little care this project would have weathered the discovery of the fraud of which the authors were guilty. ' I begged last night as for alms that they would meet us to settle the Votes. I have, since I have been in Parliament, been of twenty at least of these meetings, and always brought numbers down by these means. But my advice was slighted, and twenty people were walking about the streets who could have carried this point.' In other words, the Bill would have been carried, all its iniquities notwithstanding, if only Bully's friends had taken Selwyn's advice and put themselves out to go down to Westminster. So little impression did this piece of trickery make on the mind of the Chairman of the Committee, that he intended to the last, by collecting his friends, to carry the Bill, for the fairness and good order of which he was responsible, through the House of Commons. This glimpse into the operations of the Committee enables us to picture the groups of comrades who sauntered down from Almack's of an afternoon to carve up a manor in Committee of the House of Commons. We can see Bully's friends meeting round the table in their solemn character of judges and legislators, to give a score of villages to Bully, and a dozen to Stavordale, much as Artaxerxes gave Magnesia to Themistocles for his bread, Myus for his meat and Lampsacus for his wine. And if those friends happened to be Bully's creditors as well, it would perhaps not be unjust to suppose that their action was not altogether free from the kind of gratitude that inspired the bounty of the great king.[1]

[1] For the subsequent history of King's Sedgmoor, see Appendix A (14).

CHAPTER IV

ENCLOSURE (2)

In the year 1774, Lord North's Government, which had already received a bad bruise or two in the course of its quarrels with printers and authors, got very much the worst of it in an encounter that a little prudence would have sufficed to avert altogether. The affair has become famous on account of the actors, and because it was the turning point in a very important career. The cause of the quarrel has passed into the background, but students of the enclosure movement will find more to interest them in its beginning than in its circumstances and development.

Mr. De Grey, Member for Norfolk, and Lord of the Manor of Tollington in that county, had a dispute of long standing with Mr. William Tooke of Purley, a landowner in Tollington, who had resisted Mr. De Grey's encroachments on the common. An action on this subject was impending, but Mr. De Grey, who held, as Sir George Trevelyan puts it, 'that the law's delay was not intended for Members of Parliament' got another Member of Parliament to introduce a petition for a Bill for the enclosure of Tollington. As it happened, Mr. Tooke was a friend of one of the clerks in the House of Commons, and this friend told him on 6th January that a petition from De Grey was about to be presented. A fortnight later Mr. Tooke received from this clerk a copy of Mr. De Grey's petition, in which the Lord Chief Justice, brother of Mr. De Grey was included. Mr. Tooke hurried to London and prepared a counter petition, and Sir Edward Astley, the member for the constituency, undertook to present that petition together with the petition from Mr. De Grey. There were some further negotiations, with the result that both sides revised their respective petitions, and it was arranged that they should be presented on 4th February. On that day the Speaker said the House was not full enough, and the petitions must be presented on the 7th. Accordingly Sir Edward Astley brought up both petitions on the 7th, but the Speaker said it was very extraordinary to present two contrary petitions at the same time. ' Bring the first petition first.' When members began to say ' Hear, hear,' the Speaker remarked, ' It is only a common petition for a common enclosure,' and the Members fell into general conversation, paying no heed to the proceedings at the Table. In the midst of this the petition was read, and the Speaker asked for ' Ayes and Noes,' and declared that the Ayes had it. The petition asking for the Bill had thus been surreptitiously carried without the House being made aware that there was a contrary petition to be presented, the contrary petition asking for delay. The second petition was then read and ordered to lie on the Table.

In ordinary circumstances nothing more would have been heard of the opposition to Mr. De Grey's Bill. Hundreds of petitions may have been so stifled without the world being any the wiser. But Mr. Tooke, who would never have known of Mr. De Grey's intention if he had not had a friend among the clerks of the House of Commons, happened to have another friend who was able to help him in a very different way in his predicament. This was Horne, who was now living in a cottage at Purley, reading law, on the desperate chance that a man, who was a clergyman against his will, would be admitted to the bar. Flushed rather than spent by his public quarrel with Wilkes, which was just dying down, Horne saw in Mr. Tooke's wrongs an admirable opportunity for a champion of freedom, whose earlier exploits had been a little tarnished by his subsequent feuds with his comrades. Accordingly he responded very promptly, and published in the *Public Advertiser* of 11th February, an anonymous indictment of the Speaker, Sir Fletcher Norton, based on his unjust treatment of these petitions. This letter scandalised the House of Commons and drew the unwary Government into a quarrel from which Horne emerged triumphant ; for the Government, having been led on to proceed against Horne, was unable to prove his authorship of the letter. The incident had consequences of great importance for many persons. It was the making of Horne, for he became Horne Tooke, with £8000 from his friend and a reputation as an intrepid and vigilant champion of popular liberty that he retained to the day of his death. It was also the making of Fox, for it was this youth of twenty-five who had led the Government into its scrape, and the king could not forgive him. His temerity on this occasion provoked the famous letter from North. ' Sir, His Majesty has thought proper to order a new Commission of the Treasury to be made out, in which I do not see your name.' Fox left the court party to lend his impetuous courage henceforth to very different causes. But for social students the incident is chiefly interesting because it was the cause of the introduction of Standing Orders on Enclosure Bills. It had shown what might happen to rich men under the existing system. Accordingly the House of Commons set to work to construct a series of Standing Orders to regulate the proceedings on Enclosure Bills.

Most of these Standing Orders have already been mentioned in the previous chapter, but we propose to recapitulate their main provisions in order to show that the gross unfairness of the procedure, described in the last chapter, as between the rich and the poor, made no impression at all upon Parliament. The first Standing Orders dealing with Enclosure Bills were passed in 1774, and they were revised in 1775, 1781, 1799, 1800 and 1801. These Standing Orders prevented a secret application to Parliament by obliging promoters to publish a notice on the church door; they introduced some control over the extortions of commissioners, and laid down that the Bill presented to Parliament should contain the names of the commissioners and a description of the compensation to be given to the lord of the manor and the impropriator of tithes. But they contained no safeguard at all against robbery of the small proprietors or the commoners. Until 1801 there was no restriction on the choice of a commissioner, and it was only in that year that Parliament adopted the Standing Order providing that no lord of the manor, or steward, or bailiff of any lord or lady or proprietor should be allowed to act as commissioner in an enclosure in which he was an interested party.[1] In one respect Parliament deliberately withdrew a rule introduced to give greater regularity and publicity to the proceedings of committees. Under the Standing Orders of 1774, the Chairman of a Committee had to report not only whether the Standing Orders had been complied with, but also what evidence had been submitted to show that all the necessary formalities had been observed; but in the following year the House of Commons struck out this second provision. A Committee of the House of Commons suggested in

---

[1] Most private Enclosure Acts provided that if a commissioner died his successor was to be somebody not interested in the property.

1799 that no petition should be admitted for a Parliamentary
Bill unless a fourth part of the proprietors in number and
value signed the application, but this suggestion was rejected.

The poor then found no kind of shelter in the Standing
Orders. The legislation of this period, from first to last,
shows just as great an indifference to the injustice to which
they were exposed. The first public Act of the time deals
not with enclosures for growing corn, but with enclosures for
growing wood. The Act of 1756 states in its preamble that
the Acts of Henry viii., Charles ii. and William iii. for encouraging the growth of timber had been obstructed by the resistance of the commoners, and Parliament therefore found it
necessary to enact that any owner of waste could enclose for
the purpose of growing timber with the approval of the majority
in number and value of those who had common rights, and
any majority of those who had common rights could enclose
with the approval of the owner of the waste. Any person
or persons who thought themselves aggrieved could appeal
to Quarter Sessions, within six months after the agreement
had been registered. We hear very little of this Act, and the
enclosures that concern us are enclosures of a different kind. In
the final years of the century there was a succession of General
Enclosure Bills introduced and debated in Parliament, under
the stimulus of the fear of famine. These Bills were promoted by the Board of Agriculture, established in 1793 with
Sir John Sinclair as President, and Arthur Young as secretary.
This Board of Agriculture was not a State department in the
modern sense, but a kind of Royal Society receiving, not too
regularly, a subsidy from Parliament.[1] As a result of its efforts
two Parliamentary Committees were appointed to report on the
enclosure of waste lands, and the Reports of these Committees,
which agreed in recommending a General Enclosure Bill, were
presented in 1795 and 1799. Bills were introduced in 1795,
1796, 1797 and 1800, but it was not until 1801 that any Act
was passed.

The first Bills presented to Parliament were General Enclosure Bills, that is to say, they were Bills for prescribing conditions on which enclosure could be carried out without application
to Parliament. The Board of Agriculture was set on this policy
partly, as we have seen, in the interest of agricultural expan-
sion, partly as the only way of guaranteeing a supply of food

[1] Sir John Sinclair complained in 1796 that the Board had not even the
privilege of franking its letters.—*Annals of Agriculture*, vol. xxvi. p. 506.

during the French war. But these were not the only considerations in the mind of Parliament, and we are able in this case to
see what happened to a disinterested proposal when it had to
pass through the sieve of a Parliament of owners of land and
tithes. For we have in the *Annals of Agriculture* [1] the form of
the General Enclosure Bill of 1796 as it was presented to the
Government by that expert body, the Board of Agriculture, and
we have among the Parliamentary Bills in the British Museum
(1) the form in which this Bill left a Select Committee, and (2)
the form in which it left a second Select Committee of Knights
of the Shire and Gentlemen of the Long Robe. We are thus
able to see in what spirit the lords of the manor who sat in
Parliament regarded, in a moment of great national urgency,
the policy put before it by the Board of Agriculture. We
come at once upon a fact of great importance. In the first
version it is recognised that Parliament has to consider the
future as well as the present, that it is dealing not only with
the claims of a certain number of living cottagers, whose
rights and property may be valued by the commissioners
at a five pound note, but with the necessities of generations
still to be born, and that the most liberal recognition of the
right to pasture a cow, in the form of a cash payment to an
individual, cannot compensate for the calamities that a society
suffers in the permanent alienation of all its soil. The Bill
as drafted in the Board of Agriculture enacted that in view
of the probable increase of population, a portion of the waste
should be set aside, and vested in a corporate body (composed
of the lord of the manor, the rector, the vicar, the churchwardens and the overseers), for allotments for ever. Any
labourer over twenty-one, with a settlement in the parish, could
claim a portion and hold it for fifty years, rent free, on condition of building a cottage and fencing it. When the fifty years
were over, the cottages, with their parcels of land, were to
be let on leases of twenty-one years and over at reasonable
rents, half the rent to go to the owner of the soil, and half to
the poor rates. The land was never to be alienated from the
cottage. All these far-sighted clauses vanish absolutely under
the sifting statesmanship of the Parliament, of which Burke
said in all sincerity, in his *Reflections on the Revolution in
France,* that ' our representation has been found perfectly
adequate to all the purposes for which a representation of
the people can be desired or devised.'

[1] Vol. xxvi. p. 85.

There was another respect in which the Board of Agriculture was considered to be too generous to the poor by the lords of the manor, who made the laws of England. In version 1 of the Bill, not only those entitled to such right but also those who have enjoyed or exercised the right of getting fuel are to have special and inalienable fuel allotments made to them : in version 2 only those who are entitled to such rights are to have a fuel allotment, and in version 3, this compensation is restricted to those who have possessed fuel rights for ten years. Again in version 1, the cost of enclosing and fencing small allotments, where the owners are unable to pay, is to be borne by the other owners : in version 2, the small owners are to be allowed to mortgage their allotments in order to cover the cost. The importance of the proposal thus rejected by the Parliamentary Committee will appear when we come to consider the practical effects of Enclosure Acts. The only people who got their fencing done for them under most Acts were the tithe-owners, a class neither so poor nor so powerless in Parliament.

However this Bill shared the fate of all other General Enclosure Bills at this time. There were many obstacles to a General Enclosure Bill. Certain Members of Parliament resisted them on the ground that if it were made legal for a majority to coerce a minority into enclosure without coming to Parliament, such protection as the smaller commoners derived from the possibility of Parliamentary discussion would disappear. Powis quarrelled with the Bill of 1796 on this ground, and he was supported by Fox and Grey, but his objections were overruled. However a more formidable opposition came from other quarters. Enclosure Acts furnished Parliamentary officials with a harvest of fees,[1] and the Church thought it dangerous that enclosure, affecting tithe-owners, should be carried through without the bishops being given an opportunity of interfering. These and other forces were powerful enough to destroy this and all General

---

[1] From the Select Committee on the Means of Facilitating Enclosures in 1800, reprinted in *Annual Register*, 1800, Appendix to Chronicle, p. 85 ff., we learn that the fees received alone in the House of Commons (Bill fees, small fees, committee fees, housekeepers' and messengers' fees, and engrossing fees) for 707 Bills during the fourteen years from 1786 to 1799 inclusive amounted to no less tha £59,867, 6s. 4d. As the scale of fees in the House of Lords was about the same (Bill fees, yeoman, usher, door-keepers' fees, order of committee, and committee fees) during these years about £120,000 must have gone into the pockets of Parliamentary officials.

Enclosure Bills, intended to make application to Parliament unnecessary.

The Board of Agriculture accordingly changed its plans. In 1800 the Board abandoned its design of a General Enclosure Bill, and presented instead a consolidating Bill, which was to cheapen procedure. Hitherto there had been great diversities of form and every Bill was an expensive little work of art of its own. The Act of 1801 was designed to save promoters of enclosure some of this trouble and expense. It took some forty clauses that were commonly found in Enclosure Bills and provided that they could be incorporated by reference in private Bills, thus cheapening legal procedure. Further, it allowed affidavits to be accepted as evidence, thus relieving the promoters from the obligation of bringing witnesses before the Committee to swear to every signature. All the recognition that was given to the difficulties and the claims of the poor was comprised in sections 12 and 13, which allow small allotments to be laid together and depastured in common, and instruct the commissioners to have particular regard to the convenience of the owners or proprietors of the smallest estates. In 1813, the idea of a General Bill was revived once more, and a Bill passed the House of Commons which gave a majority of three-fifths in value the right to petition Quarter Sessions for an enclosure. The Bill was rejected in the Lords. In 1836 a General Enclosure Bill was passed, permitting enclosure when two-thirds in number and value desired it, and in 1845 Parliament appointed central Commissioners with a view to preventing local injustice.

It is unfortunate that the Parliamentary Reports of the debates on General Enclosure Bills in the unreformed Parliament are almost as meagre as the debates on particular Enclosure Bills. We can gather from various indications that the rights of the clergy received a good deal of notice, and Lord Grenville made an indignant speech to vindicate his zeal in the cause of the Church, which had been questioned by opponents. The cause of the poor does not often ruffle the surface of discussion. This we can collect not only from negative evidence but also from a statement by Mr. Lechmere, Member for Worcester. Lechmere, whose loss of his seat in 1796 deprived the poor of one of their very few champions in Parliament, drew attention more than once during the discussions on scarcity and the high price of corn to the lamentable consequences of the disappearances of the small farms, and recommended drastic steps to arrest the process. Philip Francis gave him some support. The general temper of Parliament can be divined from his complaint that when these subjects were under discussion it was very difficult to make a House.

It must not be supposed that the apathy of the aristocracy was part of a universal blindness or anæsthesia, and that the method and procedure of enclosure were accepted as just and inevitable, without challenge or protest from any quarter. The poor were of course bitterly hostile. This appears not only from the petitions presented to Parliament, but from the echoes that have reached us of actual violence. It was naturally easier for the threatened commoners to riot in places where a single enclosure scheme affected a wide district, and most of the records of popular disturbances that have come down to us are connected with attempts to enclose moors that were common to several parishes. An interesting example is afforded by the history of the enclosure of Haute Huntre Fen in Lincolnshire. This enclosure, which affected eleven parishes, was sanctioned by Parliament in 1767, but three years later the Enclosure Commissioners had to come to Parliament to explain that the posts and rails that they had set up had been destroyed ' by malicious persons, in order to hinder the execution of the said Act,' and to ask for permisson to make ditches instead of fences.[1] An example of disturbances in a single village is given by the Bedfordshire reporter for the Board of Agriculture, who says that when Maulden was enclosed it was found necessary to send for troops from Coventry to quell the riots : [2] and another in the *Annual Register* for 1799 [3] describing the resistance of the commoners at Wilbarston in Northamptonshire, and the employment of two troops of yeomanry to coerce them. The general hatred of the poor for enclosures is evident from the language of Eden, and from statements of contributors to the *Annals of Agriculture*. Eden had included a question about commons and enclosures in the questions he put to his correspondents, and he says in his preface that he had been disappointed that so few of his correspondents had given an answer to this question. He then proceeds to give this explanation : ' This question, like most others, that can now be touched upon, has its popular and

[1] See Appendix A (5).   [2] *Bedford Report*, 1808, p. 235.
[3] *Annual Register*, 1799, Chron., p. 27.

its unpopular sides : and where no immediate self-interest, or other partial leaning, interferes to bias the judgment, a good-natured man cannot but wish to think with the multitudes ; stunned as his ears must daily be, with the oft-repeated assertion, that, to condemn commons, is to determine on depopulating the country.' [1] The writer of the *Bedfordshire Report* in 1808 says that ' it appears that the poor have invariably been inimical to enclosures, as they certainly remain to the present day.' [2] Dr. Wilkinson, writing in the *Annals of Agriculture* [3] in favour of a General Enclosure Bill says, ' the grand objection to the inclosure of commons arises from the unpopularity which gentlemen who are active in the cause expose themselves to in their own neighbourhood, from the discontent of the poor when any such question is agitated.' Arthur Young makes a similar statement. [4] ' A general inclosure has been long ago proposed to administration, but particular ones have been so unpopular in some cases that government were afraid of the measure.'

The popular feeling, though quite unrepresented in Parliament, was not unrepresented in contemporary literature. During the last years of the eighteenth century there was a sharp war of pamphlets on the merits of enclosure, and it is noticeable that both supporters and opponents denounced the methods on which the governing class acted. There is, among others, a very interesting anonymous pamphlet, published in 1781 under the title of *An Inquiry into the Advantages and Disadvantages resulting from Bills of Inclosure*, in which the existing practice is reviewed and some excellent suggestions are made for reform. The writer proposed that the preliminary to a Bill should be not the fixing of a notice

[1] Eden, i. Preface, p. xviii.

[2] *Bedford Report*, p. 249. Cf. writer in Appendix of *Report on Middlesex*, pp. 507-15, ' a gentleman of the least sensibility would rather suffer his residence to continue surrounded by marshes and bogs, than take the lead in what may be deemed an obnoxious measure.' This same writer urges, that the unpopularity of enclosures would be overcome were care taken ' to place the inferior orders of mankind—the cottager and industrious poor—in such a situation, with regard to inclosures, that they should certainly have some share secured to them, and be treated with a gentle hand. Keep all in temper—let no rights be now disputed. . . . It is far more easy to prevent a clamour than to stop it when once it is raised. Those who are acquainted with the business of inclosure must know that there are more than four-fifths of the inhabitants in most neighbourhoods who are generally left out of the bill for want of property, and therefore cannot possibly claim any part thereof.'

[3] Vol. xx. p. 456.   [4] Vol. xxiv. p. 543.

to the church door, but the holding of a public meeting, that
there should be six commissioners, that they should be elected
by the commoners by ballot, that no decision should be valid
that was not unanimous, and that an appeal from that decision
should lie not to Quarter Sessions, but to Judges of Assize.
The same writer proposed that no enclosure should be sanctioned which did not allot one acre to each cottage.

These proposals came from an opponent of enclosure, but
the most distinguished supporters of enclosure were also discontented with the procedure. Who are the writers on
eighteenth-century agriculture whose names and publications
are known and remembered ? They are, first of all, Arthur
Young (1741-1820), who, though he failed as a merchant and
failed as a farmer, and never ceased to regret his father's
mistake in neglecting to put him into the soft lap of a living in
the Church, made for himself, by the simple process of observing and recording, a European reputation as an expert adviser
in the art which he had practised with so little success. A
scarcely less important authority was William Marshall (1745-
1818), who began by trading in the West Indies, afterwards
farmed in Surrey, and then became agent in Norfolk to Sir
Harbord Harbord. It was Marshall who suggested the creation
of a Board of Rural Affairs, and the preparation of Surveys and
Minutes. Though he never held an official position, it was
from his own choice, for he preferred to publish his own Minutes
and Surveys rather than to write them for the Board. He
was interested in philology as well as in agriculture ; he published a vocabulary of the Yorkshire dialect and he was a friend
of Johnson, whom he rather scandalised by condoning Sunday
labour in agriculture under special circumstances. Nathaniel
Kent (1737-1810) studied husbandry in the Austrian Nether-
lands, where he had been secretary to an ambassador, and on
his return to England in 1766 he was employed as an estate
agent and land valuer. He wrote a well-known book *Hints
to Gentlemen of Landed Property*, and he had considerable
influence in improving the management of various estates.
He was, for a short time, bailiff of George III.'s farm at Windsor.

All of these writers, though they are very far from taking
the view which found expression in the riots in the Lincolnshire
fens, or in the anonymous pamphlet already mentioned,
addressed some very important criticisms and recommendations to the class that was enclosing the English commons.
Both Marshall and Young complained of the injustice of the

method of choosing commissioners. Marshall, ardent champion of enclosure as he was, and no sentimentalist on the subject of the commoners, wrote a most bitter account of the motives of the enclosers. ' At this juncture, it is true, the owners of manors and tithes, whether clergy or laity, men of ministry or men of opposition, are equally on the alert : not however pressing forward with offerings and sacrifices to relieve the present distresses of the country, but searching for vantage ground to aid them in the scramble.' [1] Holding this view, he was not unnaturally ill-content with the plan of letting the big landlords nominate the commissioners, and proposed that the lord of the soil and the owner or owners of tithes should choose one commissioner each, that the owner or owners of pasturage should choose two, and that the four should choose a fifth. Arthur Young proposed that the small proprietors should have a share in the nomination of commissioners either by a union of votes or otherwise, as might be determined.

The general engrossing of farms was arraigned by Thomas Stone, the author of an important pamphlet, *Suggestions for rendering the inclosure of common fields and waste lands a source of population and of riches,* 1787, who proposed that in future enclosures farms should be let out in different sizes from £40 to £200 a year. He thought further that Parliament should consider the advisability of forbidding the alienation of cottagers' property, in order to stop the frittering away of cottagers' estates which was general under enclosure. Kent, a passionate enthusiast for enclosing, was not less critical of the practice of throwing farms together, a practice which had raised the price of provisions to the labourer, and he appealed to landlords to aid the distressed poor by reducing the size of their farms, as well as by raising wages. Arbuthnot, the author of a pamphlet on *An Inquiry into the Connection between the present Price of Provisions and the Size of Farms,* by a Farmer, 1773, who had defended the large-farm system against Dr. Price, wrote, ' My plan is to allot to each cottage three or four acres which should be annexed to it without power or alienation and without rent while under the covenant of being kept in grass.'

So much for writers on agriculture. But the eighteenth century produced two authoritative writers on social conditions. Any student of social history who wishes to understand

[1] *The Appropriation and Enclosure of Commonable and Intermixed Lands,* 1801.

this period would first turn to the three great volumes of Eden's
State of the Poor, published in 1797, as a storehouse of cold facts.
Davies, who wrote *The Case of Labourers in Husbandry*, published in 1795, is less famous than he deserves to be, if we are to
judge from the fact that the *Dictionary of National Biography*
only knows about him that he was Rector of Barkham in Berkshire, and a graduate of Jesus College, Oxford, that he received
a D.D. degree in 1800, that he is the author of this book, and
that he died, perhaps, in the year 1809. But Davies' book,
which contains the result of most careful and patient investigation, made a profound impression on contemporary observers.
Howlett called it ' incomparable,' and it is impossible for the
modern reader to resist its atmosphere of reality and truth.
This country parson gives us a simple, faithful and sincere
picture of the facts, seen without illusion or prejudice, and
free from all the conventional affectations of the time : a
priceless legacy to those who are impatient of the generalisations with which the rich dismiss the poor. Now both of
these writers warned their contemporaries of the danger of the
uncontrolled tendencies of the age. Eden proposed that in
every enclosure a certain quantity of land should be reserved
for cottagers and labourers, to be vested in the whole district.
He spoke in favour of the crofters in Scotland, and declared
that provision of this kind was made for the labouring classes
in the first settled townships of New England. Davies was
still more emphatic in calling upon England to settle cottagers
and to arrest the process of engrossing farms.[1]

Thus of all the remembered writers of the period who had
any practical knowledge of agriculture or of the poor, there is
not one who did not try to teach the governing class the need
for reform, and the dangers of the state into which they were
allowing rural society to drift. Parliament was assailed on
all sides with criticisms and recommendations, and its refusal
to alter its ways was deliberate.

Of the protests of the time the most important and significant came from Arthur Young. No man had been so
impatient of objections to enclosure : no man had taken so

---

[1] ' Allow to the cottager a little land about his dwelling for keeping a cow,
for planting potatoes, for raising flax or hemp. 2ndly, Convert the waste lands
of the kingdom into *small* arable farms, a certain quantity every year, to be let
on favourable terms to industrious families. 3rdly, Restrain the engrossment and
over-enlargement of farms. The propriety of those measures cannot, I think, be
questioned.'—*The Case of Labourers in Husbandry*, p. 103.

severe and disciplinary a view of the labourer : no man had dismissed so lightly the appeals for the preservation of the fragmentary possessions of the poor. He had taught a very simple philosophy, that the more the landowner pressed the farmer, and the more the farmer pressed the labourer, the better it was for agriculture. He had believed as implicitly as Sinclair himself, and with apparently as little effort to master the facts, that the cottagers were certain to benefit by enclosure. All this gives pathos, as well as force, to his remarkable paper, published under the title *An Inquiry into the Propriety of applying Wastes to the better Maintenance and Support of the Poor.*

The origin of this document is interesting. It was written in 1801, a few years after the Speenhamland system had begun to fix itself on the villages. The growth of the poor rates was troubling the minds of the upper and middle classes. Arthur Young, in the course of his travels at this time, stumbled on the discovery that in those parishes where the cottagers had been able to keep together a tiny patch of property, they had shown a Spartan determination to refuse the refuge of the Poor Law. When once he had observed this, he made further investigations which only confirmed his first impressions. This opened his eyes to the consequences of enclosure as it had been carried out, and he began to examine the history of these operations in a new spirit. He then found that enclosure had destroyed with the property of the poor one of the great incentives to industry and self-respect, and that his view that the benefit of the commons to the poor was ' perfectly contemptible,' and ' when it tempts them to become owners of cattle or sheep usually ruinous,'[1] was fundamentally wrong. Before the enclosures, the despised commons had enabled the cottager to keep a cow, and this, so far from bringing ruin, had meant in very many cases all the difference between independence and pauperism. His scrutiny of the Acts convinced him that in respect of this they had been unjust. 'By nineteen out of twenty Inclosure Bills the poor are injured, and some grossly injured. . . . Mr. Forster of Norwich, after giving me an account of twenty inclosures in which he had acted as Commissioner, stated his opinion on their general effect on the poor, and lamented that he had been accessory to the injuring of 2000 poor people, at the rate of twenty families per parish. . . . The poor in these parishes may say, and with truth, " Parliament may be tender of property : all

[1] *Annals of Agriculture,* vol. i. p. 52.

I know is that I had a cow and an Act of Parliament has taken it from me." '

This paper appeared on the eve of the Enclosure Act of 1801, the Act to facilitate and cheapen procedure, which Young and Sinclair had worked hard to secure. It was therefore an opportune moment for trying to temper enclosure to the difficulties of the poor. Arthur Young made a passionate appeal to the upper classes to remember these difficulties. ' To pass Acts beneficial to every other class in the State and hurtful to the lowest class only, when the smallest alteration would prevent it, is a conduct against which reason, justice and humanity equally plead.' He then proceeded to outline a constructive scheme. He proposed that twenty millions should be spent in setting up half a million families with allotments and cottages : the fee-simple of the cottage and land to be vested in the parish, and possession granted under an Act of Parliament, on condition that if the father or his family became chargeable to the rates, the cottage and land should revert to the parish. The parishes were to carry out the scheme, borrowing the necessary money on the security of the rates.[1] ' A man,' he told the landlords, in a passage touched perhaps with remorse as well as with compassion, ' will love his country the better even for a pig.' ' At a moment,' so he concludes, ' when a General Inclosure of Wastes is before Parliament, to allow such a measure to be carried into execution in conformity with the practice hitherto, without entering one voice, however feeble, in defence of the interests of the poor, would have been a wound to the feelings of any man not lost to humanity who had viewed the scenes which I have visited.'

The appeal broke against a dense mass of class prejudice, and so far as any effect on the Consolidating Act of 1801 is concerned, Arthur Young might never have written a line. This is perhaps not surprising, for we know from Young's autobiography (p. 350) that he did not even carry the Board of Agriculture with him, and that Lord Carrington, who was then President, only allowed him to print his appeal on the understanding that it was not published as an official docu-

---

[1] This scheme marks a great advance on an earlier scheme which Young published in the first volume of the *Annals of Agriculture*. He then proposed that public money should be spent in settling cottagers or soldiers on the waste, giving them their holding free of rent and tithes for three lives, at the end of which time the land they had redeemed was to revert to its original owners.

ment, and that the Board was in no way identified with it. Sinclair, who shared Young's conversion, had ceased to be President in 1798. The compunction he tried to awaken did affect an Act here and there. A witness before the Allotments Committee of 1843 described the arrangements he contrived to introduce into an Enclosure Act. The witness was Mr. Demainbray, an admirable and most public-spirited parson, Rector of Broad Somerford in Wiltshire. Mr. Demainbray explained that when the Enclosure Act for his parish was prepared in 1806, he had been pressed to accept land in lieu of tithes, and that he took the opportunity to stipulate for some provision for the poor. As a consequence of his efforts, half an acre was attached to each cottage on the waste, the land being vested in the rector, churchwardens and overseers for the time being, and eight acres were reserved for the villagers for allotment and reallotment every Easter. This arrangement, which had excellent results, ' every man looking forward to becoming a man of property,' was copied in several of the neighbouring parishes. Dr. Slater has collected some other examples. One Act, passed in 1824 for Pottern in Wiltshire, vested the ownership of the enclosed common in the Bishop of Salisbury, who was lord of the manor, the vicar, and the churchwardens, in trust for the parish. The trustees were required to lease it in small holdings to poor, honest and industrious persons, who had not, except in cases of accident or sickness, availed themselves of Poor Law Relief.[1] Thomas Stone's proposal for making inalienable allotments to cottagers was adopted in two or three Acts in the eastern counties, but the Acts that made some provision for the poor do not amount, in Dr. Slater's opinion, to more than one per cent. of the Enclosure Acts passed before 1845,[2] and this view is corroborated by the great stress laid in the Reports of the Society for Bettering the Condition of the Poor, upon a few cases where the poor were considered, and by a statement made by Mr. Demainbray in a pamphlet published in 1831.[3] In this pamphlet Mr. Demainbray quotes what Davies had said nearly forty years earlier about the effect of enclosures in robbing the poor, and then adds : ' Since that time many hundred enclosures have taken place, but in how few of them

---

[1] Slater, pp. 126-7.   [2] Ibid., p. 128.
[3] *The Poor Man's Best Friend, or Land to cultivate for his own Benefit.* Letter to the Marquis of Salisbury, by the Rev. S. Demainbray, B.D. 1831.

has any reserve been made for the privileges which the poor man and his ancestors had for centuries enjoyed ? '

Some interesting provisions are contained in certain of the Acts analysed in the Appendix. At Stanwell the commissioners were to set aside such parcel as they thought proper not exceeding thirty acres, to be let out and the rents and profits were to be given for the benefit of such occupiers and inhabitants as did not receive parochial relief or occupy lands and tenements of more than £5 a year, and had not received any allotment under the Act. Middleton, the writer of the *Report on Middlesex*, says that the land produced £30 a year,[1] and he remarks that this is a much better way of helping the poor than leaving them land for their use. We may doubt whether the arrangement seemed equally attractive to the poor. It could not have been much compensation to John Carter, who owned a cottage, to receive three roods, twenty-six perches in lieu of his rights of common, which is his allotment in the award, for three-quarters of an acre is obviously insufficient for the pasture of a cow, but it was perhaps still less satisfactory for James Carter to know that one acre and seven perches were allotted to the ' lawful owner or owners ' of the cottage and land which he occupied, and that his own compensation for the loss of his cow or sheep or geese was the cold hope that if he kept off the rates, Sir William Gibbons, the vicar, and the parish officers might give him a dole. The Laleham Commissioners were evidently men of a rather grim humour, for, in setting aside thirteen acres for the poor, they authorised the churchwardens and overseers to encourage the poor, if they were so minded, by letting this plot for sixty years and using the money so received to build a workhouse. A much more liberal provision was made at Cheshunt, where the poor were allowed 100 acres. At Knaresborough and Louth, the poor got nothing at all.

Before we proceed to describe the results of enclosure on village life, we may remark one curious fact. In 1795 and 1796 there was some discussion in the House of Commons of the condition of the agricultural labourers, arising out of the proposal of Whitbread's to enable the magistrates to fix a minimum wage. Pitt made a long speech in reply, and promised to introduce a scheme of his own for correcting evils that were too conspicuous to be ignored. This promise he kept next year in the ill-fated Poor Law Bill, which died,

[1] P. 126.

almost at its birth, of general hostility. That Bill will be considered elsewhere. All that we are concerned to notice here is that neither speech nor Bill, though they cover a wide range of topics, and though Pitt said that they represented the results of long and careful inquiry, hint at this cause of social disturbance, or at the importance of safe-guarding the interests of the poor in future enclosure schemes : this in spite of the fact that, as we have seen, there was scarcely any contemporary writer or observer who had not pointed out that the way in which the governing class was conducting these revolutions was not only unjust to the poor but perilous to the State.

It is interesting, in the light of the failure to grasp and retrieve an error in national policy which marks the progress of these transactions, to glance at the contemporary history of France. The Legislative Assembly, under the influence of the ideas of the economists, decreed the division of the land of the communes in 1792. The following year this decree was modified. Certain provincial assemblies had asked for division, but many of the villages were inexorably hostile. The new decree of June 1793 tried to do justice to these conflicting wishes by making division optional. At the same time it insisted on an equitable division in cases where partition took place. But this policy of division was found to have done such damage to the interests of the poor that there was strenuous opposition, with the result that in 1796 the process was suspended, and in the following year it was forbidden.[1] Can any one suppose that if the English legislature had had as swift and ready a sense for things going wrong, the policy of enclosure would have been pursued after 1801 with the same reckless disregard for its social consequences ?

We have given in the last chapter the history of an enclosure project for the light it throws on the play of motive in the enclosing class. We propose now to give in some detail the history of an enclosure project that succeeded for the light it throws on the attention which Parliament paid to local opinion, and on the generally received views as to the rights of the small commoners. Our readers will observe that this enclosure

[1] See for this subject *Cambridge Modern History*, vol. viii. chap. 24, and P. Sagnac, *La Législation Civile de la Révolution Française*.

took place after the criticisms and appeals which we have described had all been published.

Otmoor is described in Dunkin's *History of Oxfordshire*,[1] as a 'dreary and extensive common.' Tradition said that the tract of land was the gift of some mysterious lady ' who gave as much ground as she could ride round while an oat-sheaf was burning, to the inhabitants of its vicinity for a public common,' and hence came its name of Oatmoor, corrupted into Otmoor. Whatever the real origin of the name, which more prosaic persons connected with ' *Oc*,' a Celtic word for ' water,' this tract of land had been used as a ' public common without stint . . . from remote antiquity.' Lord Abingdon, indeed, as Lord of the Manor of Beckley, claimed and exercised the right of appointing a moor-driver, who at certain seasons drove all the cattle into Beckley, where those which were unidentified became Lord Abingdon's property. Lord Abingdon also claimed rights of soil and of sport : these, like his other claim, were founded on prescription only, as there was no trace of any grant from the Crown.

The use to which Otmoor, in its original state, was put, is thus described by Dunkin. ' Whilst this extensive piece of land remained unenclosed, the farmers of the several adjoining townships estimated the profits of a summer's pasturage at 20s. per head, subject to the occasional loss of a beast by a peculiar distemper called the moor-evil. But the greatest benefit was reaped by the cottagers, many of whom turned out large numbers of geese, to which the coarse aquatic sward was well suited, and thereby brought up their families in comparative plenty.[2]

' Of late years, however, this dreary waste was surveyed with longing eyes by the surrounding landowners, most of whom wished to annex a portion of it to their estates, and in consequence spared no pains to recommend the enclosure as a measure beneficial to the country.'

The promoters of the enclosure credited themselves with far loftier motives : prominent among them being a desire to improve the morals of the poor. An advocate of the enclosure afterwards described the pitiable state of the poor in pre-enclosure days in these words : ' In looking after a brood of goslings, a few rotten sheep, a skeleton of a cow

---

[1] Vol. i. p. 119 ff.

[2] Jackson's *Oxford Journal*, September 11, 1830, said that a single cottager sometimes cleared as much as £20 a year by geese.

or a mangy horse, they lost more than they might have gained by their day's work, and acquired habits of idleness and dissipation and a dislike to honest labour, which has rendered them the riotous and lawless set of men which they have now shown themselves to be.' A pious wish to second the intention of Providence was also a strong incentive : ' God did not create the earth to lie waste for feeding a few geese, but to be cultivated by man, in the sweat of his brow.' [1]

The first proposal for enclosure came to Parliament from George, Duke of Marlborough, and others on 11th March, 1801. The duke petitioned for the drainage and the allotment of the 4000 acres of Otmoor among the parishes concerned, namely Beckley (with Horton and Studley), Noke, Oddington, and Charlton (with Fencott and Moorcott). This petition was referred to a Committee, to consider amongst other things, whether the Standing Orders with reference to Drainage Bills had been duly complied with. The Committee reported in favour of allowing the introduction of the Bill, but made this remarkable admission, that though the Standing Orders with respect to the affixing of notices on church doors had been complied with on Sunday, 3rd August, ' it appeared to the Committee that on the following Sunday, the 10th of August, the Person employed to affix the like Notices was prevented from so doing at Beckley, Oddington and Charlton, by a Mob at each Place, but that he read the Notices to the Persons assembled, and afterwards threw them amongst them into the Church Yards of those Parishes.' Notice was duly affixed that Sunday at Noke. The next Sunday matters were even worse, for no notices were allowed to be fixed in any parish.

The Bill that was introduced in spite of this local protest, was shipwrecked during its Committee stage by a petition from Alexander Croke, LL.D., Lord of the Manor of Studley with Whitecross Green, and from John Mackaness, Esq., who stated that as proprietors in the parish of Beckley, their interests had not been sufficiently considered.

The next application to Parliament was not made till 1814. In the interval various plans were propounded, and Arthur Young, in his *Survey of Oxfordshire for the Board of Agriculture,* published in 1809 (a work which Dunkin describes as supported by the farmers and their landlords and as having caught their strain), lamented the wretched state of the land. ' I made various inquiries into the present value of it by rights of com-

[1] *Oxford University and City Herald*, September 25, 1830.

monage ; but could ascertain no more than the general fact, of its being to a very beggarly amount. . . . Upon the whole, the present produce must be quite contemptible, when compared with the benefit which would result from enclosing it. And I cannot but remark, that such a tract of waste land in summer, and covered the winter through with water, to remain in such a state, within five miles of Oxford and the Thames, in a kingdom that regularly imports to the amount of a million sterling in corn, and is almost periodically visited with apprehensions of want—is a scandal to the national policy. . . . If drained and enclosed, it is said that no difficulty would occur in letting it at 30s. per acre, and some assert even 40s.' (p. 228).

When the new application was made in November 1814, it was again referred to a Committee, who again had to report turbulent behaviour in the district concerned. Notices had been fixed on all the church doors on 7th August, and on three doors on 14th August, ' but it was found impracticable to affix the Notices on the Church doors of the other two Parishes on that day, owing to large Mobs, armed with every description of offensive weapons, having assembled for the purpose of obstructing the persons who went to affix the Notices, and who were prevented by violence, and threats of immediate death, from approaching the Churches.' [1] From the same cause no notices could be affixed on these two church doors on 21st or 28th August.

These local disturbances were not allowed to check the career of the Bill. It was read a first time on 21st February, and a second time on 7th March. But meanwhile some serious flaws had been discovered. The Duke of Marlborough and the Earl of Abingdon both petitioned against it. The Committee, however, were able to introduce amendments that satisfied both these powerful personages, and on 1st May Mr. Fane reported from the Committee that no persons had appeared for the said petitions, and that the parties concerned had consented to the satisfaction of the Committee, and had also consented ' to the changing the Commissioners therein named.' Before the Report had been passed, however, a petition was received on behalf of Alexander Croke,[2] Esq.,

---

[1] *House of Commons Journal*, February 17, 1815.

[2] Alexander Croke (1758-1842), knighted in 1816, was from 1801-1815 judge in the Vice-Admiralty Court, Nova Scotia. As a lawyer, he could defend his own interests.

who was now in Nova Scotia, which made further amendments necessary, and the Committee was empowered to send for persons, papers and records. Meanwhile the humbler individuals whose future was imperilled were also bestirring themselves. They applied to the Keeper of the Records in the Augmentation Office for a report on the history of Otmoor. This Report, which is published at length by Dunkin,[1] states that in spite of laborious research no mention of Otmoor could be found in any single record from the time of William the Conqueror to the present day. Even *Doomsday Book* contained no reference to it. Nowhere did it appear in what manor Otmoor was comprehended, nor was there any record that any of the lords of neighbouring manors had ever been made capable of enjoying any rights of common upon it. The custom of usage without stint, in fact, pointed to some grant before the memory of man, and made it unlikely that any lord of the manor had ever had absolute right of soil. Armed, no doubt, with this learned report, some ' Freeholders, Landholders, Cottagers and Persons ' residing in four parishes sent up a petition asking to be heard against the Bill. But they were too late : their petition was ordered to lie on the Table, and the Bill passed the Commons the same day (26th June) and received the Royal Assent on 12th July.

The Act directed that one-sixteenth of the whole (which was stated to be over 4000 acres) should be given to the Lord of the Manor of Beckley, Lord Abingdon, in compensation of his rights of soil, and one-eighth as composition for all tithes. Thus Lord Abingdon received, to start with, about 750 acres. The residue was to be allotted among the various parishes, townships and hamlets, each allotment to be held as a common pasture for the township. So far, beyond the fact that Lord Abingdon had taken off more than a sixth part of their common pasture, and that the pasture was now divided up into different parts, it did not seem that the ordinary inhabitants were much affected. The sting lay in the arrangements for the future of these divided common pastures. ' And if at any future time the major part in value of the several persons interested in such plot or parcels of land, should require a separate division of the said land, he (the commissioner) is directed to divide and allot the same among the several proprietors, in proportion to their individual rights and interests therein.' [2]

---

[1] Dunkin's *Oxfordshire*, vol. i. pp. 122-3.   [2] *Ibid.*, p. 123.

We have, fortunately, a very clear statement of the way in which the ' rights and interests ' of the poorer inhabitants of the Otmoor towns were regarded in the enclosure. These inhabitants, it must be remembered, had enjoyed rights of common without any stint from time immemorial, simply by virtue of living in the district. In a letter from ' An Otmoor Proprietor ' to the Oxford papers in 1830, the writer (Sir Alexander Croke himself ?), who was evidently a man of some local importance, explains that by the general rule of law a commoner is not entitled to turn on to the common more cattle than are sufficient to manure and stock the land to which the right of common is annexed. Accordingly, houses without land attached to them cannot, strictly speaking, claim a right of common. How then explain the state of affairs at Otmoor, where all the inhabitants, landed or landless, enjoyed the same rights ? By prescription, he answers, mere houses do in point of fact sometimes acquire a right of common, but this right, though it may be said to be without stint, is in reality always liable to be stinted by law. Hence, when a common like Otmoor is enclosed, the allotments are made as elsewhere in proportion to the amount of land possessed by each commoner, whilst a ' proportionable share ' is thrown in to those who own mere houses. But even this share, he points out, does not necessarily belong to the person who has been exercising the right of common, unless he happens to own his own house. It belongs to his landlord, who alone is entitled to compensation. A superficial observer might perhaps think this a hardship, but in point of fact it is quite just. The tenants, occupying the houses, must have been paying a higher rent in consideration of the right attached to the houses, and they have always been liable to be turned out by the landlord at will. ' They had no permanent interest, and it has been decided by the law that *no man can have any right in any common, as belonging to a house, wherein he has no interest but only habitation* : so that the poor, as such, had no right to the common whatever.' [1]

The results of the Act, framed and administered on these lines, were described by Dunkin,[2] writing in 1823, as follows : ' It now only remains to notice the effect of the operation of this act. On the division of the land allotted to the respective townships, a certain portion was assigned to each cottager in lieu of his accustomed commonage, but the

---

[1] Jackson's *Oxford Journal*, September 18, 1830.   [2] Vol. i. p. 124.

delivery of the allotment did not take place, unless the party to whom it was assigned paid his share of the expenses incurred in draining and dividing the waste : and he was also further directed to enclose the same with a fence. The poverty of the cottager in general prevented his compliance with these conditions, and he was necessitated to sell his share for any paltry sum that was offered. In the spring of 1819, several persons at Charlton and elsewhere made profitable speculations by purchasing these commons for £5 each, and afterwards prevailing on the commissioners to throw them into one lot, thus forming a valuable estate. In this way was Otmoor lost to the poor man, and awarded to the rich, under the specious idea of benefitting the public.' The expenses of the Act, it may be mentioned, came to something between £20,000 and £30,000, or more than the fee-simple of the soil. [1]

Enclosed Otmoor did not fulfil Arthur Young's hopes : '. . . instead of the expected improvement in the quality of the soil, it has been rendered almost totally worthless ; a great proportion being at this moment over-rated at 5s. an acre yearly rent, few crops yielding any more than barely sufficient to pay for labour and seed.' [2] This excess of expenses over profits was adduced by the ' Otmoor proprietor,' to whom we have already referred, as an illustration of the public-spirited self-sacrifice of the enclosers, who were paying out of their own pockets for a national benefit, and by making some, at any rate, of the land capable of cultivation, were enabling the poor to have ' an honest employment, instead of losing their time in idleness and waste.' [3] But fifteen years of this ' honest employment ' failed to reconcile the poor to their new position, and in 1830 they were able to express their feelings in a striking manner.[4]

In the course of his drainage operations, the commissioner had made a new channel for the river Ray, at a higher level, with the disastrous result that the Ray overflowed into a valuable tract of low land above Otmoor. For two years the farmers of this tract suffered severe losses (one farmer was said to have lost £400 in that time), then they took the law

[1] Jackson's *Oxford Journal*, September 11, 1830.

[2] *Ibid.*   [3] *Ibid.*, September 18.

[4] See Jackson's *Oxford Journal*, and *Oxford University and City Herald*, for September 11, 1830, and also *Annual Register*, 1830, Chron., p. 142, and Home Office Papers, for what follows.

into their own hands, and in June 1829 cut the embankments, so that the waters of the Ray again flowed over Otmoor and left their valuable land unharmed. Twenty-two farmers were indicted for felony for this act, but they were acquitted at the Assizes, under the direction of Mr. Justice Parke, on the grounds that the farmers had a right to abate the nuisance, and that the commissioner had exceeded his powers in making this new channel and embankment.

This judgment produced a profound impression on the Otmoor farmers and cottagers. They misread it to mean that all proceedings under the Enclosure Act were illegal and therefore null and void, and they determined to regain their lost privileges. Disturbances began at the end of August (28th August). For about a week, straggling parties of enthusiasts paraded the moor, cutting down fences here and there. A son of Sir Alexander Croke came out to one of these parties and ordered them to desist. He had a loaded pistol with him, and the moor-men, thinking, rightly or wrongly, that he was going to fire, wrested it from him and gave him a severe thrashing. Matters began to look serious : local sympathy with the rioters was so strong that special constables refused to be sworn in ; the High Sheriff accordingly summoned the Oxfordshire Militia, and Lord Churchill's troop of Yeomanry Cavalry was sent to Islip. But the inhabitants were not overawed. They determined to perambulate the bounds of Otmoor in full force, in accordance with the old custom. On Monday, 6th September, five hundred men, women and children assembled from the Otmoor towns, and they were joined by five hundred more from elsewhere. Armed with reap-hooks, hatchets, bill-hooks and duckets, they marched in order round the seven-mile-long boundary of Otmoor, destroying all the fences on their way. By noon their work of destruction was finished. ' A farmer in the neighbourhood who witnessed the scene gives a ludicrous description of the zeal and perseverance of the women and children as well as the men, and the ease and composure with which they waded through depths of mud and water and overcame every obstacle in their march. He adds that he did not hear any threatening expressions against any person or his property, and he does not believe any individuals present entertained any feeling or wish beyond the assertion of what they conceived (whether correctly or erroneously) to be their prescriptive and inalienable right, and of which they speak

precisely as the freemen of Oxford would describe their right
to Port Meadow.' [1]

By the time the destruction of fences was complete, Lord
Churchill's troop of yeomanry came up to the destroying
band : the Riot Act was read, but the moormen refused to
disperse.   Sixty or seventy of them were thereupon seized
and examined, with the result that forty-four were sent
off to Oxford Gaol in wagons, under an escort of yeomanry.
Now it happened to be the day of St. Giles' Fair, and the
street of St. Giles, along which the yeomanry brought their
prisoners, was crowded with countryfolk and townsfolk, most
of whom held strong views on the Otmoor question.   The
men in the wagons raised the cry ' Otmoor for ever,' the
crowd took it up, and attacked the yeomen with great
violence, hurling brickbats, stones and sticks at them from
every side.   The yeomen managed to get their prisoners as
far as the turning down Beaumont Street, but there they
were overpowered, and all forty-four prisoners escaped.
At Otmoor itself peace now reigned.   Through the broken
fences cattle were turned in to graze on all the enclosures,
and the villagers even appointed a herdsman to look after
them.   The inhabitants of the seven Otmoor towns formed
an association called ' the Otmoor Association,' which boldly
declared that ' the Right of Common on Otmoor was always
in the inhabitants, and that a non-resident proprietor had no
Right of Common thereon,' and determined to raise subscriptions for legal expenses in defence of their right, calling upon
' the pecuniary aid of a liberal and benevolent public . . .
to assist them in attempting to restore Otmoor once more to
its original state.' [2]

Meanwhile the authorities who had lost their prisoners once,
sent down a stronger force to take them next time, and although
at the Oxford City Sessions a bill of indictment against William
Price and others for riot in St. Giles and rescue of the prisoners
was thrown out, at the County Sessions the Grand Jury found
a true Bill against the same William Price and others for the
same offence, and also against Cooper and others for riot at
Otmoor.   The prisoners were tried at the Oxford Assizes next
month, before Mr. Justice Bosanquet and Sir John Patteson.
The jury returned a verdict which shows the strength of public
opinion.   ' We find the defendants guilty of having been present
at an unlawful assembly on the 6th September at Otmoor, but

[1] *Oxford University and City Herald*, September 11, 1830.   [2] *Ibid.*

it is the unanimous wish of the Jury to recommend all the parties to the merciful consideration of the Court.' The judges responded to this appeal and the longest sentence inflicted was four months' imprisonment.[1]

The original enclosure was now fifteen years old, but Otmoor was still in rebellion, and the Home Office Papers of the next two years contain frequent applications for troops from Lord Macclesfield, Lord-Lieutenant, Sir Alexander Croke and other magistrates. Whenever there was a full moon, the patriots of the moor turned out and pulled down the fences. How strong was the local resentment of the overriding of all the rights and traditions of the commoners may be seen not only from the language of one magistrate writing to Lord Melbourne in January 1832: ' all the towns in the neighbourhood of Otmoor are more or less infected with the feelings of the most violent, and cannot at all be depended on ' : but also from a resolution passed by the magistrates at Oxford in February of that year, declaring that no constabulary force that the magistrates could raise would be equal to suppressing the Otmoor outrages, and asking for soldiers. The appeal ended with this significant warning : 'Any force which Government may send down should not remain for a length of time together, but that to avoid the possibility of an undue connexion between the people and the Military, a succession of troops should be observed.' So long and so bitter was the civil war roused by an enclosure which Parliament had sanctioned in absolute disregard of the opinions or the traditions or the circumstances of the mass of the people it affected.

[1] Jackson's *Oxford Journal*, March 5, 1831.

CHAPTER V

THE VILLAGE AFTER ENCLOSURE

THE governing class continued its policy of extinguishing the old village life and all the relationships and interests attached to it, with unsparing and unhesitating hand; and as its policy progressed there were displayed all the consequences predicted by its critics. Agriculture was revolutionised: rents leapt up: England seemed to be triumphing over the difficulties of a war with half the world. But it had one great permanent result which the rulers of England ignored. The anchorage of the poor was gone.

For enclosure was fatal to three classes: the small farmer, the cottager, and the squatter. To all of these classes their common rights were worth more than anything they received in return. Their position was just the opposite of that of the lord of the manor. The lord of the manor was given a certain quantity of land (the conventional proportion was one-sixteenth[1]) in lieu of his surface rights, and that compact allotment was infinitely more valuable than the rights so compensated. Similarly the tithe-owner stood to gain with the increased rent. The large farmer's interests were also in enclosure, which gave him a wider field for his capital and enterprise. The other classes stood to lose.

For even if the small farmer received strict justice in the division of the common fields, his share in the legal costs and the additional expense of fencing his own allotments often overwhelmed him, and he was obliged to sell his property.[2]

[1] See the Evidence of Witnesses before the Committee on Commons Inclosure of 1844. (Baily, land-agent): 'General custom to give the Lord of Manor $\frac{1}{16}$th as compensation for his rights exclusive of the value of minerals and of his rights as a common right owner.' Another witness (Coulson, a solicitor) defined the surface rights as 'game and stockage,' and said that the proportion determined upon was the result of a bargain beforehand.

[2] 'Many small proprietors have been seriously injured by being obliged in pursuance of ill-framed private bills to enclose lands which never repaid the expense.' Marshall, *The Appropriation and Enclosure of Commonable and Intermixed Lands*, 1801, p. 52.

The expenses were always very heavy, and in some cases amounted to £5 an acre.[1] The lord of the manor and the tithe-owner could afford to bear their share, because they were enriched by enclosure : the classes that were impoverished by enclosure were ruined when they had to pay for the very proceeding that had made them the poorer. The promoter of the General Enclosure Bill of 1796, it will be remembered, had proposed to exempt the poor from the expense of fencing, but the Select Committee disapproved, and the only persons exempted in the cases we have examined were the lords of the manor or tithe-owners.

If these expenses still left the small farmer on his feet, he found himself deprived of the use of the fallow and stubble pasture, which had been almost as indispensable to him as the land he cultivated. ' Strip the small farms of the benefit of the commons,' said one observer, ' and they are all at one stroke levelled to the ground.' [2] It was a common clause in Enclosure Acts that no sheep were to be depastured on allotments for seven years.[3] The small farmer either emigrated

---

[1] COST OF ENCLOSURE.—The expenses of particular Acts varied very much. Billingsley in his *Report on Somerset* (p. 57) gives £3 an acre as the cost of enclosing a lowland parish, £2, 10s. for an upland parish.   The enclosure of the 12,000 acre King's Sedgmoor (*Ibid.*, p. 196) came (with the subdivisions) to no less than £59,624, 4s. 8d., or nearly £5 an acre.   Stanwell Enclosure, on the other hand, came to about 23s. an acre, and various instances given in the *Report for Bedfordshire* work out at about the same figure.   When the allotments to the tithe-owners and the lord of the manor were exempted, the sum per acre would of course fall more heavily on the other allottees, *e.g.* of Louth, where more than a third of the 1701 acres enclosed were exempt.   In many cases, of course, land was sold to cover expenses.   The cost of fencing allotments would also vary in different localities.   In Somerset, from 7s. 7d. to 8s. 7d. for 20 feet of quickset hedge was calculated, in Bedfordshire, 10s. 6d. per pole. See also for expense Hasbach, pp. 64, 65, and *General Report on Enclosures*, Appendix xvii.   Main Items :—

1. Country solicitor's fees for drawing up Bill and attending in town ;
2. Attendance of witnesses at House of Commons and House of Lords to prove that Standing Orders had been complied with ;
3. Expenses of persons to get signatures of consents and afterwards to attend at House of Commons to swear to them (it once cost from £70 to £80 to get consent of principal proprietor) ;
4. Expense of Parliamentary solicitor, 20 gs., but more if opposition ;
5. Expense of counsel if there was opposition ;
6. Parliamentary fees, see p. 76.

[2] *Inquiry into the Advantages and Disadvantages resulting from Bills of Enclosure*, 1780, p. 14.

[3] Cf. Ashelworth, Cheshunt, Knaresborough.

to America or to an industrial town, or became a day labourer. His fate in the last resort may perhaps be illustrated by the account given by the historian of *Oxfordshire* of the enclosure of Merton. ' About the middle of last century a very consider-able alteration was produced in the relative situation of different classes in the village. The Act of Parliament for the inclosure of the fields having annulled all leases, and the inclosure itself facilitated the plan of throwing several small farms into a few large bargains,[1] the holders of the farms who had hereto-fore lived in comparative plenty, became suddenly reduced to the situation of labourers, and in a few years were necessitated to throw themselves and their families upon the parish. The overgrown farmers who had fattened upon this alteration, feeling the pressure of the new burden, determined if possible to free themselves : they accordingly decided upon reducing the allowance of these poor to the lowest ratio,[2] and resolved to have no more servants so that their parishioners might experience no further increase from that source. In a few years the numbers of the poor rapidly declined : the more aged sank into their graves, and the youth, warned by their parents' sufferings, sought a settlement elsewhere. The farmers, rejoicing in the success of their scheme, procured the demolition of the cottages, and thus endeavoured to secure themselves and their successors from the future expenses of supporting an increased population, so that in 1821 the parish numbered only thirty houses inhabited by thirty-four families.' [3] Another writer gave an account of the results of a Norfolk enclosure. ' In passing through a village near Swaffham, in the County of Norfolk a few years ago, to my great morti-fication I beheld the houses tumbling into ruins, and the common fields all enclosed ; upon enquiring into the cause of this melancholy alteration, I was informed that a gentle-man of Lynn had bought that township and the next adjoin-ing to it : that he had thrown the one into three, and the other into four farms ; which before the enclosure were in about twenty farms : and upon my further enquiring what was becoming of the farmers who were turned out, the

---

[1] Previous to enclosure there were twenty-five farmers : the land is now divided among five or six persons only.

[2] It was then confidently said that several poor persons actually perished from want, and so great was the outcry that some of the farmers were hissed in the public market at Bicester.

[3] Dunkin's *Oxfordshire*, pp. 2 and 3.

answer was that some of them were dead and the rest were become labourers.' [1]

The effect on the cottager can best be described by saying that before enclosure the cottager was a labourer with land, after enclosure he was a labourer without land. The economic basis of his independence was destroyed. In the first place, he lost a great many rights for which he received no compensation. There were, for instance, the cases mentioned by Mr. Henry Homer (1719-1791), Rector of Birdingbury and Chaplain to Lord Leigh, in the pamphlet he published in 1769,[2] where the cottagers lost the privileges of cutting furze and turf on the common land, the proprietor contending that they had no right to these privileges, but only enjoyed them by his indulgence. In every other case, Mr. Homer urged, uninterrupted, immemorial usage gives a legal sanction even to encroachments. 'Why should the poor, as poor, be excluded from the benefit of this general Indulgence ; or why should any set of proprietors avail themselves of the inability of the poor to contend with them, to get possession of more than they enjoyed ? ' [3]

Another right that was often lost was the prescriptive right of keeping a cow. The *General Report on Enclosures* (p. 12) records the results of a careful inquiry made in a journey of 1600 miles, which showed that before enclosure cottagers often kept cows without a legal right, and that nothing was given them for the practice. Other cottagers kept cows by right of hiring their cottages and common rights, and on enclosure the land was thrown into a farm, and the cottager had to sell his cow. Two examples taken from the *Bedfordshire Report* illustrate the consequences of enclosure to the small man. One is from Maulden : [4] 'The common was very extensive. I conversed with a farmer, and several cottagers. One of them said, enclosing would ruin England ; it was worse than ten wars. Why, my friend, what have you lost by it ? *I kept four cows before the parish*

---

[1] F. Moore, *Considerations on the Exorbitant Price of Proprietors*, 1773, p. 22 ; quoted by Levy, p. 27.

[2] *Essay on the Nature and Method of ascertaining the specific Share of Proprietors upon the Inclosure of Common fields, with observations on the inconveniences of common fields, etc.*, p. 22.

[3] The Kirton, Sutterton and Wigtoft (Lincs) Acts prescribed a penalty for taking turf or sod after the passing of the Act, of £10, and in default of payment imprisonment in the House of Correction with hard labour for three months.

[4] P. 235.

*was enclosed, and now I don't keep so much as a goose ; and you
ask me what I lose by it !* ' [1]   The other is from Sandy : [2] ' This
parish was very peculiarly circumstanced ; it abounds with
gardeners, many cultivating their little freeholds, so that on
the enclosure, there were found to be sixty-three proprietors,
though nine-tenths, perhaps, of the whole belonged to Sir
P. Monoux and Mr. Pym.   These men kept cows on the
boggy common, and cut fern for litter on the warren, by which
means they were enabled to raise manure for their gardens,
besides fuel in plenty : the small allotment of an acre and a
half, however good the land, has been no compensation for
what they were deprived of.   They complain heavily, and
know not how they will now manage to raise manure.   This
was no reason to preserve the deserts in their old state, but
an ample one for giving a full compensation.'

Lord Winchilsea stated in his letter to the Board of Agriculture in 1796 : ' Whoever travels through the Midland
Counties and will take the trouble of inquiring, will generally
receive for answer that formerly there were a great many
cottagers who kept cows, but that the land is now thrown to
the farmers, and if he inquires still further, he will find that
in those parishes the Poor Rates have increased in an amazing
degree more than according to the average rise throughout
England.'

These cottagers often received nothing at all for the right
they had lost, the compensation going to the owner of the
cottage only.   But even those cottagers who owned their cottage
received in return for their common right something infinitely
less valuable.   For a tiny allotment was worth much less than
a common right, especially if the allotment was at a distance
from their cottage, and though the Haute Huntre Act binds
the commissioners to give Lord FitzWilliam an allotment near
his gardens, there was nothing in any Act that we have seen
to oblige the commissioners to give the cottager an allotment
at his door.   And the cottagers had to fence their allotments
or forfeit them.   Anybody who glances at an award will
understand what this meant.   It is easy, for example, to
imagine what happened under this provision to the following

[1] The only provision for the poor in the Maulden Act, (36 Geo. III. c. 65)
was a fuel allotment as a compensation for the ancient usage of cutting peat or
moor turf.   The trustees (rector, churchwarden and overseers) were to distribute
the turf to poor families, and were to pay any surplus from the rent of the
herbage to the poor rates.   [2] P. 240.

cottagers at Stanwell : Edmund Jordan (1½ acres) J. and F.
Ride (each 1¼ acres) T. L. Rogers (1¼ acres) Brooker Derby (1¼)
Mary Gulliver (1¼ acres) Anne Higgs (1¼) H. Isherwood (1¼)
William Kent (1¼) Elizabeth Carr (1 acre) Thomas Nash
(1 acre) R. Ride (just under 1 acre) William Robinson (just
under 1 acre) William Cox (¾ acre) John Carter (¾ acre)
William Porter (¾ acre) Thomas King (½ acre) John Hether-
ington (under ½ an acre) J. Trout (¼ acre and 4 perches)
and Charles Burkhead (12 perches).   It would be interesting
to know how many of these small parcels of land found their
way into the hands of Sir William Gibbons and Mr. Edmund
Hill.

The Louth award is still more interesting from this point
of view.   J. Trout and Charles Burkhead passing rich, the one
on ¼ acre and 4 perches, the other on 12 perches, had only to
pay their share of the expenses of the enclosure, and for their
own fencing.   Sir William Gibbons was too magnanimous
a man to ask them to fence his 500 acres as well.   But at
Louth the tithe-owners, who took more than a third of the
whole, were excused their share of the costs, and also had their
fencing done for them by the other proprietors.   The prebendary and the vicar charged the expenses of fencing their
600 acres on persons like Elizabeth Bryan who went off
with 39 perches, Ann Dunn (35 perches), Naomi Hodgson,
widow (35 perches), John Betts (34 perches), Elizabeth Atkins
(32 perches), Will Boswell (31 perches), Elizabeth Eycon
(28 perches), Ann Hubbard, widow (15 perches), and Ann
Metcalf, whose share of the spoil was 14 perches.   The award
shows that there were 67 persons who received an acre or
less.   Cottagers who received such allotments and had to
fence them had no alternative but to sell, and little to do
with the money but to drink it.   This is the testimony of the
General Report on Enclosures.[1]

The squatters, though they are often spoken of as cottagers,
must be distinguished from the cottager in regard to their
legal and historical position.   They were in a sense outside
the original village economy.   The cottager was, so to speak,
an aboriginal poor man : the squatter a poor alien.   He

---

[1] At St. Neots a gentleman complained to Arthur Young in 1791 that in the
enclosure which took place sixteen years before, 'the poor were ill-treated by
having about half a rood given them in lieu of a *cow keep*, the inclosure of which
land costing more than they could afford, they sold the lots at £5, the money
was drank out at the ale-house, and the men, spoiled by the habit, came, with
their families to the parish.'—*Annals of Agriculture*, vol. xvi. p. 482.

settled on a waste, built a cottage, and got together a few geese or sheep, perhaps even a horse or a cow, and proceeded to cultivate the ground.

The treatment of encroachments seems to have varied very greatly, as the cases analysed in the Appendix show, and there was no settled rule. Squatters of less than twenty years' standing seldom received any consideration beyond the privilege of buying their encroachment. Squatters of more than twenty or forty years' standing, as the case might be, were often allowed to keep their encroachments, and in some cases were treated like cottagers, with a claim to an allotment. But, of course, like the cottagers, they lost their common rights.

Lastly, enclosure swept away the bureaucracy of the old village : the viewers of fields and letters of the cattle, who had general supervision of the arrangements for pasturing sheep or cows in the common meadow, the common shepherd, the chimney peepers who saw that the chimneys were kept properly, the hayward, or pinder, who looked after the pound. Most of these little officials of the village court had been paid either in land or by fees. When it was proposed to abolish Parliamentary Enclosure, and to substitute a General Enclosure Bill, the Parliamentary officials, who made large sums out of fees from Enclosure Bills, were to receive compensation ; but there was no talk of compensation for the stolen livelihood of a pinder or a chimney peeper, as there had been for the lost pickings of the officials of Parliament, or as there was whenever an unhappy aristocrat was made to surrender one of his sinecures. George Selwyn, who had been Paymaster of the Works for twenty-seven years at the time that Burke's Act of 1782 deprived him of that profitable title, was not allowed to languish very long on the two sinecures that were left to him. In 1784 Pitt consoled him with the lucrative name of Surveyor-General of Crown Lands. The pinder and the viewer received a different kind of justice. For the rich there is compensation, as the weaver said in Disraeli's *Sybil,* but ' sympathy is the solace of the poor.' In this case, if the truth be told, even this solace was not administered with too liberal a hand.

All these classes and interests were scattered by enclosure, but it was not one generation alone that was struck down by the blow. For the commons were the patrimony of the poor. The commoner's child, however needy, was born with a spoon in his mouth. He came into a world in which he had a share and a place. The civilisation which was now submerged had spelt a sort of independence for the obscure lineage of the village. It had represented, too, the importance of the interest of the community in its soil, and in this aspect also the robbery of the present was less important than the robbery of the future. For one act of confiscation blotted out a principle of permanent value to the State.

The immediate consequences of this policy were only partially visible to the governing or the cultivated classes. The rulers of England took it for granted that the losses of individuals were the gains of the State, and that the distresses of the poor were the condition of permanent advance. Modern apologists have adopted the same view; and the popular resistance to enclosure is often compared to the wild and passionate fury that broke against the spinning and weaving machines, the symbols and engines of the Industrial Revolution. History has drawn a curtain over those days of exile and suffering, when cottages were pulled down as if by an invader's hand, and families that had lived for centuries in their dales or on their small farms and commons were driven before the torrent, losing

> 'Estate and house . . . and all their sheep,
> A pretty flock, and which for aught I know
> Had clothed the Ewbanks for a thousand years.'

Ancient possessions and ancient families disappeared. But the first consequence was not the worst consequence : so far from compensating for this misery, the ultimate result was still more disastrous. The governing class killed by this policy the spirit of a race. The petitions that are buried with their brief and unavailing pathos in the *Journals* of the House of Commons are the last voice of village independence, and the unnamed commoners who braved the dangers of resistance to send their doomed protests to the House of Commons that obeyed their lords, were the last of the English peasants. These were the men, it is not unreasonable to believe, whom Gray had in mind when he wrote :—

> 'Some village Hampden that with dauntless breast
> The little tyrant of his fields withstood.'

As we read the descriptions of the state of France before the Revolution, there is one fact that comforts the imagination and braces the heart. We read of the intolerable services of the peasant, of his forced labour, his confiscated harvests, his crushing burdens, his painful and humiliating tasks, including in some cases even the duty of protecting the sleep of the seigneur from the croaking of the neighbouring marshes. The mind of Arthur Young was filled with this impression of unsupportable servitude. But a more discerning eye might have perceived a truth that escaped the English traveller. It is contained in an entry that often greets us in the official reports on the state of the provinces : *ce seigneur litige avec ses vaissaux.* Those few words flash like a gleam of the dawn across this sombre and melancholy page. The peasant may be overwhelmed by the dîme, the taille, the corvée, the hundred and one services that knit his tenure to the caprice of a lord : he may be wretched, brutal, ignorant, ill-clothed, ill-fed, and ill-housed : but he has not lost his status : he is not a casual figure in a drifting proletariat : he belongs to a community that can withstand the seigneur, dispute his claims at law, resume its rights, recover its possessions, and establish, one day, its independence.

In England the aristocracy destroyed the promise of such a development when it broke the back of the peasant community. The enclosures created a new organisation of classes. The peasant with rights and a status, with a share in the fortunes and government of his village, standing in rags, but standing on his feet, makes way for the labourer with no corporate rights to defend, no corporate power to invoke, no property to cherish, no ambition to pursue, bent beneath the fear of his masters, and the weight of a future without hope. No class in the world has so beaten and crouching a history, and if the blazing ricks in 1830 once threatened his rulers with the anguish of his despair, in no chapter of that history could it have been written, ' This parish is at law with its squire.' For the parish was no longer the community that offered the labourer friendship and sheltered his freedom : it was merely the shadow of his poverty, his helplessness, and his shame. ' Go to an ale-house kitchen of an old enclosed country, and there you will see the origin of poverty and poor-rates. For whom are they to be sober ? For whom are they to save ? For the parish ? If I am diligent, shall I have leave to build a cottage ? If I am sober, shall I have land for a cow ? If I am frugal, shall I have half an acre of potatoes ? You offer no motives ; you have nothing but a parish officer and a workhouse !—Bring me another pot—.' [1]

[1] *Annals of Agriculture,* vol. xxxvi. p. 508.

CHAPTER VI

THE LABOURER IN 1795

In an unenclosed village, as we have seen, the normal labourer did not depend on his wages alone. His livelihood was made up from various sources. His firing he took from the waste, he had a cow or a pig wandering on the common pasture, perhaps he raised a little crop on a strip in the common fields. He was not merely a wage earner, receiving so much money a week or a day for his labour, and buying all the necessaries of life at a shop : he received wages as a labourer, but in part he maintained himself as a producer. Further, the actual money revenue of the family was not limited to the labourer's earnings, for the domestic industries that flourished in the village gave employment to his wife and children.

In an enclosed village at the end of the eighteenth century the position of the agricultural labourer was very different. All his auxiliary resources had been taken from him, and he was now a wage earner and nothing more. Enclosure had robbed him of the strip that he tilled, of the cow that he kept on the village pasture, of the fuel that he picked up in the woods, and of the turf that he tore from the common. And while a social revolution had swept away his possessions, an industrial revolution had swept away his family's earnings. To families living on the scale of the village poor, each of these losses was a crippling blow, and the total effect of the changes was to destroy their economic independence.

Some of these auxiliary resources were not valued very highly by the upper classes, and many champions of enclosure proved to their own satisfaction that the advantage, for example, of the right of cutting fuel was quite illusory. Such writers had a very superficial knowledge of the lot of the cottagers. They argued that it would be more economical for the labourer to spend on his ordinary employment the time he devoted to cutting fuel and turf, and to buy firing out of his wages : an argument from the theory of the division of labour that assumed that employment was constant. Fortunately we have, thanks to Davies, a very careful calculation that enables us to form rather a closer judgment. He estimates [1] that a man could cut nearly enough in a week to serve his family all the year, and as the farmers will give the carriage of it in return for the ashes, he puts the total cost at 10s. a year, or a little more than a week's wages.[2] If we compare this with his accounts of the cost of fuel elsewhere, we soon see how essential common fuel rights were to a labourer's economy. As Sidlesham in Surrey, for instance,[3] in the expenses of five families of labourers, the fuel varies from £1, 15s. 0d. up to £4, 3s. 0d., with an average of £2, 8s. 0d. per family. It must be remembered, too, that the sum of 10s. for fuel from the common is calculated on the assumption that the man would otherwise be working; whereas, in reality, he could cut his turf in slack times and in odd hours, when there was no money to be made by working for some one else.

There was another respect in which the resources of a labouring family were diminished towards the end of the century, and this too was a loss that the rich thought trifling. From time immemorial the labourer had sent his wife and children into the fields to glean or leaze after the harvest. The profits of gleaning, under the old, unimproved system of agriculture, were very considerable. Eden says of Rode in Northamptonshire, where agriculture was in a ' wretched state, from the land being in common-fields,' that ' several families will gather as much wheat as will serve them for bread the whole year, and as many beans as will keep a pig.' [4] From this point of view enclosure, with its improved methods of agriculture, meant a sensible loss to the poor of the parish, but even when there was less to be gleaned the privilege was by no means unimportant. A correspondent in the *Annals of Agriculture*,[5] writing evidently of land under improved cultivation in Shropshire, estimates that a wife can glean three or four bushels. The consumption of wheat, exclusive of other food, by a labourer's family he puts at half a bushel a week at least; the price of wheat at 13s. 6d. a bushel; the labourer's wages at 7s. or 8s. To such a family gleaning rights represented the equivalent of some six or seven weeks' wages.

With the introduction of large farming these customary

---

[1] Davies, *The Case of Labourers in Husbandry*, p. 15.
[2] In some instances it is reckoned as costing only 7s. *Ibid.*, see p. 185.
[3] Davies, p. 181.   [4] Eden, vol. ii. p. 547.   [5] Vol. xxv. p. 488.

rights were in danger. It was a nuisance for the farmer to have his fenced fields suddenly invaded by bands of women and children. The ears to be picked up were now few and far between, and there was a risk that the labourers, husbands and fathers of the gleaners, might wink at small thefts from the sheaves. Thus it was that customary rights, which had never been questioned before, and seemed to go back to the Bible itself, came to be the subject of dispute. On the whole question of gleaning there is an animated controversy in the *Annals of Agriculture* [1] between Capel Lofft,[2] a romantic Suffolk Liberal, who took the side of the gleaners, and Ruggles,[3] the historian, who argued against them. Capel Lofft was a humane and chivalrous magistrate who, unfortunately for the Suffolk poor, was struck off the Commission of the Peace a few years later, apparently at the instance of the Duke of Portland, for persuading the Deputy-Sheriff to postpone the execution of a girl sentenced to death for stealing, until he had presented a memorial to the Crown praying for clemency. The chief arguments on the side of the gleaners were (1) that immemorial custom gave legal right, according to the maxim, *consuetudo angliae lex est angliae communis*; (2) that Blackstone had recognised the right in his *Commentaries*, basing his opinion upon Hale and Gilbert, ' Also it hath been said, that by the common law and customs of England the poor are allowed to enter and glean on another's ground after harvest without being guilty of trespass, which humane provision seems borrowed from the Mosaic law ' (iii. 212, 1st edition); (3) that in Ireland the right was recognised by statutes of Henry VIII.'s reign, which modified it; (4) that it was a custom that helped to keep the poor free from degrading dependence on poor relief. It was argued, on the other hand, by those who denied the right to glean, that though the custom had existed from time immemorial, it did not rest on any basis of actual right, and that no legal sanction to it had ever been explicitly given, Blackstone and the authorities on whom he relied being too vague to be considered final.

---

[1] See *Annals of Agriculture*, vol. ix. pp. 13, 14, 165-167, 636-646, and vol. x. pp. 218-227.

[2] Capel Lofft (1751-1824) ; follower of Fox ; writer of poems and translations from Virgil and Petrarch ; patron of Robert Bloomfield, author of *Farmer's Boy*. Called by Boswell ' This little David of popular spirit.'

[3] Thomas Ruggles (1737-1813), author of *History of the Poor*, published in 1793, Deputy-Lieutenant of Essex and Suffolk.

Further, the custom was demoralising to the poor ; it led to idleness, ' how many days during the harvest are lost by the mother of a family and all her children, in wandering about from field to field, to glean what does not repay them the wear of their cloathes in seeking ' ; it led to pilfering from the temptation to take handfuls from the swarth or shock ; and it was deplorable that on a good-humoured permission should be grafted ' a legal claim, in its use and exercise so nearly approaching to licentiousness.'

Whilst this controversy was going on, the legal question was decided against the poor by a majority of judges in the Court of Common Pleas in 1788. One judge, Sir Henry Gould,[1] dissented in a learned judgment ; the majority based their decision partly on the mischievous consequences of the practice to the poor. The poor never lost a right without being congratulated by the rich on gaining something better. It did not, of course, follow from this decision that the practice necessarily ceased altogether, but from that time it was a privilege given by the farmer at his own discretion, and he could warn off obnoxious or ' saucy ' persons from his fields. Moreover, the dearer the corn, and the more important the privilege for the poor, the more the farmer was disinclined to largess the precious ears. Capel Lofft had pleaded that with improved agriculture the gleaners could pick up so little that that little should not be grudged, but the farmer found that under famine prices this little was worth more to him than the careless scatterings of earlier times.[2]

The loss of his cow and his produce and his common and traditional rights was rendered particularly serious to the labourer by the general growth of prices. For enclosure which had produced the agrarian proletariat, had raised the cost of

---

[1] Sir Henry Gould, 1710-1794.

[2] The *Annals of Agriculture* (vol. xvii. p. 293) contains a curious apology by a gleaner in 1791 to the owner of some fields, who had begun legal proceedings against her and her husband. 'Whereas I, Margaret Abree, wife of Thomas Abree, of the city of New Sarum, blacksmith, did, during the barley harvest, in the month of September last, many times wilfully and maliciously go into the fields of, and belonging to, Mr. Edward Perry, at Clarendon Park, and take with me my children, and did there leaze, collect, and carry away a quantity of barley. . . . Now we do hereby declare, that we are fully convinced of the illegality of such proceedings, and that no person has a right to leaze any sort of grain, or to come on any field whatsoever, without the consent of the owner ; and are also truly sensible of the obligation we are under to the said Edward Perry for his lenity towards us, inasmuch as the damages given, together with the heavy cost incurred, would have been much greater than we could possibly have discharged,

living for him.   The accepted opinion that under enclosure
England became immensely more productive tends to obscure
the truth that the agricultural labourer suffered in his character
of consumer, as well as in his character of producer, when the
small farms and the commons disappeared.   Not only had
he to buy the food that formerly he had produced himself,
but he had to buy it in a rising market.   Adam Smith admitted
that the rise of price of poultry and pork had been accelerated
by enclosure, and Nathaniel Kent laid stress on the diminution
in the supply of these and other small provisions.   Kent has
described the change in the position of the labourers in this
respect : ' Formerly they could buy milk, butter, and many
other small articles in every parish, in whatever quantity
they are wanted.   But since small farms have decreased in
number, no such articles are to be had ; for the great farmers
have no idea of retailing such small commodities, and those
who do retail them carry them all to town.   A farmer is even
unwilling to sell the labourer who works for him a bushel of
wheat, which he might get ground for three or four pence a
bushel.   For want of this advantage he is driven to the mealman or baker, who, in the ordinary course of their profit, get
at least ten per cent. of them, upon this principal article
of their consumption.' [1]   Davies, the author of *The Case o
Labourers in Husbandry*, thus describes the new method of
distribution : ' The great farmer deals in a wholesale way
with the miller : the miller with the mealman : the mealman
with the shopkeeper, of which last the poor man buys his
flour by the bushel.   For neither the miller nor the mealman
will sell the labourer a less quantity than a sack of flour, under
the retail price of shops, and the poor man's pocket will seldom
allow of his buying a whole sack at once.' [2]

and must have amounted to perpetual imprisonment, as even those who have
least disapproved of our conduct, would certainly not have contributed so large
a sum to deliver us from the legal consequences of it.   And we do hereby faithfully promise never to be guilty of the same, or any like offence in future.
Thomas Abree, Margaret Abree.   Her + Mark.'   It is interesting to compare
with this judge-made law of England the Mosaic precept : ' And when ye
reap the harvest of your land, thou shalt not make clean riddance of the
corners of thy field when thou reapest, neither shalt thou gather any gleaning
of thy harvest : thou shalt leave them unto the poor, and to the stranger '
(Leviticus xxiii. 22).

[1] Kent, *Hints*, p. 238 ; cf. John Wesley, *Works*, vol. iii. (3rd edition), p. 56.
[2] P. 34 ; cf. Marshall on the Southern Department, p. 9, ' Yorkshire bacon,
generally of the worst sort, is retailed to the poor from little chandlers' shops
at an advanced price, bread in the same way.'

It is clear from these facts that it would have needed a very large increase of wages to compensate the labourer for his losses under enclosure. But real wages, instead of rising, had fallen, and fallen far. The writer of the *Bedfordshire Report* (p. 67), comparing the period of 1730-50 with that of 1802-6 in respect of prices of wheat and labour, points out that to enable him to purchase equal quantities of bread in the second period and in the first, the pay of the day labourer in the second period should have been 2s. a day, whereas it was 1s. 6d. Nathaniel Kent, writing in 1796,[1] says that in the last forty or fifty years the price of provisions had gone up by 60 per cent., and wages by 25 per cent., ' but this is not all, for the sources of the market which used to feed him are in a great measure cut off since the system of large farms has been so much encouraged.' Professor Levy estimates that wages rose between 1760 and 1813 by 60 per cent., and the price of wheat by 130 per cent.[2] Thus the labourer who now lived on wages alone earned wages of a lower purchasing power than the wages which he had formerly supplemented by his own produce. Whereas his condition earlier in the century had been contrasted with that of Continental peasants greatly to his advantage in respect of quantity and variety of food, he was suddenly brought down to the barest necessities of life. Arthur Young had said a generation earlier that in France bread formed nineteen parts in twenty of the food of the people, but that in England all ranks consumed an immense quantity of meat, butter and cheese.[3] We know something of the manner of life of the poor in 1789 and 1795 from the family budgets collected by Eden and Davies from different parts of the country.[4] These budgets show that the labourers were rapidly sinking in this respect to the condition that Young had described as the condition of the poor in France. ' Bacon and other kinds of meat form a very small part of their diet, and cheese becomes a luxury.' But even on the meagre food that now became the ordinary fare of the cottage, the labourers could not make ends meet. All the budgets tell the same tale of impoverished diet accompanied by an overwhelming strain and an actual deficit. The normal labourer, even with constant employment, was no longer solvent.

---

[1] *Notes on the Agriculture of Norfolk*, p. 165.

[2] *Large and Small Holdings*, p. 11.

[3] Young's *Political Arithmetic*, quoted by Lecky, vol. vii. p. 263 note.

[4] See Appendix B for six of these budgets.

If we wish to understand fully the predicament of the labourer, we must remember that he was not free to roam over England, and try his luck in some strange village or town when his circumstances became desperate at home. He lived under the capricious tyranny of the old law of settlement, and enclosure had made that net a much more serious fact for the poor. The destruction of the commons had deprived him of any career within his own village ; the Settlement Laws barred his escape out of it. It is worth while to consider what the Settlement Laws were, and how they acted, and as the subject is not uncontroversial it will be necessary to discuss it in some detail.

Theoretically every person had one parish, and one only, in which he or she had a settlement and a right to parish relief. In practice it was often difficult to decide which parish had the duty of relief, and disputes gave rise to endless litigation. From this point of view eighteenth-century England was like a chessboard of parishes, on which the poor were moved about like pawns. The foundation of the various laws on the subject was an Act passed in Charles II.'s reign (13 and 14 Charles II. c. 12) in 1662. Before this Act each parish had, it is true, the duty of relieving its own impotent poor and of policing its own vagrants, and the infirm and aged were enjoined by law to betake themselves to their place of settlement, which might be their birthplace, or the place where they had lived for three years, but, as a rule, ' a poor family might, without the fear of being sent back by the parish officers, go where they choose, for better wages, or more certain employment.' [1]   This Act of 1662 abridged their liberty, and, in place of the old vagueness, established a new and elaborate system. The Act was declared to be necessary in the preamble, because ' by reason of some defects in the law, poor people are not restrained from going from one parish to another, and therefore do endeavour to settle themselves in those parishes where there is the best stock, the largest commons or wastes to build cottages, and the most woods for them to burn and destroy ; and when they have consumed it, then to another parish ; and at last become rogues and vagabonds ; to the great discouragement of parishes to provide stock, when it is liable to be devoured by strangers.' By the Act any new-comer, within forty days of arrival, could be ejected from a parish by an order from the magistrates, upon complaint from the parish officers, and removed to the

[1] Ruggles, *Annals of Agriculture*, vol. xiv. p. 205.

parish where he or she was last legally settled. If, however, the new-comer settled in a tenement of the yearly value of £10, or could give security for the discharge of the parish to the magistrates' satisfaction, he was exempt from this provision.

As this Act carried with it the consequence that forty days' residence without complaint from the parish officers gained the new-comer a settlement, it was an inevitable temptation to Parish A to smuggle its poor into Parish B, where forty days' residence without the knowledge of the parish officers would gain them a settlement. Fierce quarrels broke out between the parishes in consequence. To compose these it was enacted (1 James ii. c. 17) that the forty days' residence were to be reckoned only after a written notice had been given to a parish officer. Even this was not enough to protect Parish B, and by 3 William and Mary, c. 11 (1691) it was provided that this notice must be read in church, immediately after divine service, and then registered in the book kept for poor's accounts. Such a condition made it practically impossible for any poor man to gain a settlement by forty days' residence, unless his tenement were of the value of £10 a year, but the Act allowed an immigrant to obtain a settlement in any one of four ways ; (1) by paying the parish taxes ; (2) by executing a public annual office in the parish ; (3) by serving an apprenticeship in the parish ; (4) by being hired for a year's service in the parish. (This, however, only applied to the unmarried.) In 1697 (8 and 9 William iii. c. 30) a further important modification of the settlement laws was made. To prevent the arbitrary ejection of new-comers by parish officers, who feared that the fresh arrival or his children might somehow or other gain a settlement, it was enacted that if the new-comer brought with him to Parish B a certificate from the parish officers of Parish A taking responsibility for him, then he could not be removed till be became actually chargeable. It was further decided by this and subsequent Acts and by legal decisions, that the granting of a certificate was to be left to the discretion of the parish officers and magistrates, that the cost of removal fell on the certificating parish, and that a certificate holder could only gain a settlement in a new parish by renting a tenement of £10 annual value, or by executing a parish office, and that his apprentice or hired servant could not gain a settlement.

In addition to these methods of gaining a settlement there were four other ways, ' through which,' according to Eden,

' it is probable that by far the greater part of the labouring Poor . . . are actually settled.' [1]   (1) Bastards, with some exceptions, acquired a settlement by birth [2]; (2) legitimate children also acquired a settlement by birth if their father's, or failing that, their mother's legal settlement was not known ; (3) women gained a settlement by marriage ; (4) persons with an estate of their own were irremovable, if residing on it, however small it might be.

Very few important modifications had been made in the laws of Settlement during the century after 1697.   In 1722 (9 George I. c. 7) it was provided that no person was to obtain a settlement in any parish by the purchase of any estate or interest of less value than £30, to be ' bona fide paid,' a provision which suggests that parishes had connived at gifts of money for the purchase of estates in order to discard their paupers : by the same Act the payment of the scavenger or highway rate was declared not to confer a settlement.   In 1784 (24 George III. c. 6) soldiers, sailors and their families were allowed to exercise trades where they liked, and were not to be removable till they became actually chargeable ; and in 1793 (33 George III. c. 54) this latter concession was extended to members of Friendly Societies.   None of these concessions affected the normal labourer, and down to 1795 a labourer could only make his way to a new village if his own village would give him a certificate, or if the other village invited him.   His liberty was entirely controlled by the parish officers.

How far did the Settlement Acts operate?   How far did this body of law really affect the comfort and liberty of the poor ? The fiercest criticism comes from Adam Smith, whose fundamental instincts rebelled against so crude and brutal an interference with human freedom.   ' To remove a man who has committed no misdemeanour, from a parish where he chuses to reside, is an evident violation of natural liberty and justice. The common people of England, however, so jealous of their liberty, but, like the common people of most other countries, never rightly understanding wherein it consists, have now, for more than a century together, suffered themselves to be exposed to this oppression without a remedy.   Though men of reflex-

---

[1] Eden, vol. i. p. 180.

[2] The parish might have the satisfaction of punishing the mother by a year's hard labour (7 James I. c. 4, altered in 1810), but could not get rid of the child.

ion, too, have sometimes complained of the law of settlements as a public grievance ; yet it has never been the object of any general popular clamour, such as that against general warrants, an abusive practice undoubtedly, but such a one as was not likely to occasion any general oppression. There is scarce a poor man in England, of forty years of age, I will venture to say, who has not, in some part of his life, felt himself most cruelly oppressed by this ill-contrived law of settlements.' [1]

Adam Smith's view is supported by two contemporary writers on the Poor Law, Dr. Burn and Mr. Hay. Dr. Burn, who published a history of the Poor Law in 1764, gives this picture of the overseer : ' The office of an Overseer of the Poor seems to be understood to be this, to keep an extraordinary look-out to prevent persons coming to inhabit without certificates, and to fly to the Justices to remove them : and if a man brings a certificate, then to caution the inhabitants not to let him a farm of £10 a year, and to take care to keep him out of all parish offices.' [2] He further says that the parish officers will assist a poor man in taking a farm in a neighbouring parish, and give him £10 for the rent. Mr. Hay, M.P., protested in his remarks on the Poor Laws against the hardships inflicted on the poor by the Laws of Settlement. ' It leaves it in the breast of the parish officers whether they will grant a poor person a certificate or no.' [3] Eden, on the other hand, thought Adam Smith's picture overdrawn, and he contended that though there were no doubt cases of vexatious removal, the Laws of Settlement were not administered in this way everywhere. Howlett also considered the operation of the Laws of Settlement to be ' trifling,' and instanced the growth of Sheffield, Birmingham, and Manchester as proof that there was little interference with the mobility of labour.

A careful study of the evidence seems to lead to the conclusion that the Laws of Settlement were in practice, as they were on paper, a violation of natural liberty ; that they did not stop the flow of labour, but that they regulated it in the interest of the employing class. The answer to Howlett is given by Ruggles in the *Annals of Agriculture*.[4] He begins by saying that the Law of Settlement has made a poor family ' of necessity stationary ; and obliged them to rest satisfied with those wages they can obtain where their legal settle-

---

[1] *Wealth of Nations*, vol. i. p. 194.   [2] Quoted by Eden, vol. i. p. 347.
[3] See *Ibid.*, p. 296.   [4] Vol. xiv. pp. 205, 206.

ment happens to be; a restraint on them which ought to insure to them wages in the parish where they must remain, more adequate to their necessities, because it precludes them in a manner from bringing their labour, the only marketable produce they possess, to the best market; it is this restraint which has, in all manufacturing towns, been one cause of reducing the poor to such a state of miserable poverty; for, among the manufacturers, they have too frequently found masters who have taken, and continue to take every advantage, which strict law will give; of consequence, the prices of labour have been, in manufacturing towns, in an inverse ratio of the number of poor settled in the place; and the same cause has increased that number, by inviting foreigners, in times when large orders required many workmen; the masters themselves being the overseers, whose duty as parish officers has been opposed by their interest in supplying the demand.' In other words, when it suited an employer to let fresh workers in, he would, *qua* overseer, encourage them to come with or without certificates; but when they were once in and ' settled ' he would refuse them certificates to enable them to go and try their fortunes elsewhere, in parishes where a certificate was demanded with each poor new-comer.[1] Thus it is not surprising to find, from Eden's *Reports*, that certificates are never granted at Leeds and Skipton; seldom granted at Sheffield; not willingly granted at Nottingham, and that at Halifax certificates are not granted at present, and only three have been granted in the last eighteen years.

It has been argued that the figures about removals in different parishes given by Eden in his second and third volumes show that the Law of Settlement was ' not so black as it has been painted.' [2]   But in considering the small number of removals,

---

[1] An example of a parish where the interests of the employer and of the parish officers differed is given in the *House of Commons Journal* for February 4, 1788, when a petition was presented from Mr. John Wilkinson, a master iron-founder at Bradley, near Bilston, in the parish of Wolverhampton. The petitioner states ' that the present Demand for the Iron of his Manufacture and the Improvement of which it is capable, naturally encourage a very considerable Extension of his Works, but that the Experience he has had of the vexatious Effect, as well as of the constantly increasing Amount of Poor Rates to which he is subject, has filled him with Apprehensions of final Ruin to his Establishment; and that the Parish Officers . . . are constantly alarming his Workmen with Threats of Removal to the various Parishes from which the Necessity of employing skilful Manufacturers has obliged him to collect them.' He goes on to ask that his district shall be made extra-parochial to the poor rates.

[2] Hasbach, pp. 172-3.

we must also consider the large number of places where there is this entry, ' certificates are never granted.' It needed considerable courage to go to a new parish without a certificate and run the risk of an ignominious expulsion, and though all overseers were not so strict as the one described by Dr. Burn, yet the fame of one vexatious removal would have a far-reaching effect in checking migration. It is clear that the law must have operated in this way in districts where enclosures took away employment within the parish. Suppose Hodge to have lived at Kibworth-Beauchamp in Leicester-shire. About 1780, 3600 acres were enclosed and turned from arable to pasture; before enclosure the fields ' were solely applied to the production of corn,' and ' the Poor had then plenty of employment in weeding, reaping, threshing, etc., and could also collect a great deal of corn by gleaning.' [1] After the change, as Eden admits, a third or perhaps a fourth of the number of hands would be sufficient to do all the farm-ing work required. Let us say that Hodge was one of the superfluous two-thirds, and that the parish authorities refused him a certificate. What did he do? He applied to the overseer, who sent him out as a roundsman.[2] He would prefer to bear the ills he knew rather than face the unknown in the shape of a new parish officer, who might demand a certificate, and send him back with ignominy if he failed to produce one. If he took his wife and family with him there was even less chance of the demand for a certificate being waived.[3] So at Kibworth-Beauchamp Hodge and his com-panions remained, in a state of chronic discontent. ' The Poor complain of hard treatment from the overseers, and the overseers accuse the Poor of being saucy.' [4]

Now, at first sight, it seems obvious that it would be to the interest of a parish to give a poor man a certificate, if there were no market for his labour at home, in order to enable him to go elsewhere and make an independent living. This seems the reasonable view, but it is incorrect. In the same way, it would seem obvious that a parish would give slight relief to a person whose claim was in doubt rather than spend ten

---

[1] Eden, vol. ii. p. 384.   [2] See p. 148.

[3] The unborn were the special objects of parish officers' dread. At Derby the persons sent out under orders of removal are chiefly pregnant girls. (Eden, vol. ii. p. 126.) Bastards (see above) with some exceptions gained a settlement in their birthplace, and Hodge's legitimate children might gain one too if there was any doubt about the place of their parents' settlements.

[4] Eden, vol. ii. p. 383.

times the amount in contesting that claim at law. In point
of fact, in neither case do we find what seems the reasonable
course adopted. Parishes spent fortunes in lawsuits. And
to the parish authorities it would seem that they risked more
in giving Hodge a certificate than in obliging him to stay at
home, even if he could not make a living in his native place ;
for he might, with his certificate, wander a long way off, and
then fall into difficulties, and have to be fetched back at great
expense, and the cost of removing him would fall on the
certificating parish. There is a significant passage in the
Annals of Agriculture[1] about the wool trade in 1788. ' We
have lately had some hand-bills scattered about Bocking, I
am told, promising full employ to combers and weavers, that
would migrate to Nottingham. Even if they chose to try
this offer ; as probably a parish certificate for such a distance
would be refused ; it cannot be attempted.' Where parishes
saw an immediate prospect of getting rid of their superfluous
poor into a neighbouring parish with open fields or a
common, they were indeed not chary of granting certificates.
At Hothfield in Kent, for example, ' full half of the labouring poor are certificated persons from other parishes : the
above-mentioned common, which affords them the means of
keeping a cow, or poultry, is supposed to draw many Poor
into the parish ; certificated persons are allowed to dig
peat.'[2]

In the Rules for the government of the Poor in the hundreds
of Loes and Wilford in Suffolk[3] very explicit directions are
given about the granting of certificates. In the first place,
before any certificate is granted the applicant must produce an
examination taken before a Justice of the Peace, showing that
he belongs to one of the parishes within the hundred. Granted
that he has complied with this condition, then, (1) if he be
a labourer or husbandman no certificate will be granted him
out of the hundreds unless he belongs to the parish of Kenton,
and even in that case it is ' not to exceed the distance of three
miles ' ; (2) if he be a tradesman, artificer, or manufacturer
a certificate may be granted to him out of the hundreds, but
in no case is it to exceed the distance of twenty miles from

the parish to which he belongs. The extent of the hundreds was roughly fourteen miles by five and a half.

Eden, describing the neighbourhood of Coventry, says : 'In a country parish on one side the city, chiefly consisting of cottages inhabited by ribbon-weavers, the Rates are as high as in Coventry ; whilst, in another parish, on the opposite side, they do not exceed one-third of the City Rate : this is ascribed to the care that is taken to prevent manufacturers from settling in the parish.'[1] In the neighbourhood of Mollington (Warwickshire and Oxon) the poor rates varied from 2s. to 4s. in the pound. 'The difference in the several parishes, it is said, arises, in a great measure, from the facility or difficulty of obtaining settlements : in several parishes, a fine is imposed on a parishoner, who settles a newcomer by hiring, or otherwise, so that a servant is very seldom hired for a year. Those parishes which have for a long time been in the habit of using these precautions, are now very lightly burthened with Poor. This is often the case, where farms are large, and of course in few hands ; while other parishes, not politic enough to observe these rules, are generally burthened with an influx of poor neighbours.'[2] Another example of this is Deddington (Oxon) which like other parishes that possessed common fields suffered from an influx of small farmers who had been turned out elsewhere, whereas neighbouring parishes, possessed by a few individuals, were cautious in permitting newcomers to gain settlements.[3]

This practice of hiring servants for fifty-one weeks only was common : Eden thought it fraudulent and an evasion of the law that would not be upheld in a court of justice,[4] but he was wrong, for the 1817 Report on the Poor Law mentions among 'the measures, justifiable undoubtedly in point of law, which are adopted very generally in many parts of the kingdom, to defeat the obtaining a settlement, that of hiring labourers for a less period than a year ; from whence it naturally and necessarily follows, that a labourer may spend the season of

---

[1] Eden, vol. iii. p. 743.

[2] *Ibid.*   [3] *Ibid.*, vol. ii. p. 591.

[4] *Ibid.*, p. 654, *re* Litchfield. 'In two or three small parishes in this neighbourhood, which consist of large farms, there are very few poor : the farmers, in order to prevent the introduction of poor from other parishes, hire their servants for fifty-one weeks only. I conceive, however, that this practice would be considered, by a court of justice, as fraudulent, and a mere evasion in the master ; and that a servant thus hired, if he remained the fifty-second week with his master, on a fresh contract, would acquire a settlement in the parish.'

his health and industry in one parish, and be transferred in the decline of life to a distant part of the kingdom.'[1] We hear little about the feelings of the unhappy labourers who were brought home by the overseers when they fell into want in a parish which had taken them in with their certificate, but it is not difficult to imagine the scene. It is significant that the Act of 1795 (to which we shall refer later), contained a provision that orders of removal were to be suspended in cases where the pauper was dangerously ill.

From the Rules for the Government of the Poor in the Hundreds of Loes and Wilford, already alluded to, we learn some particulars of the allowance made for the removal of paupers. Twenty miles was to be considered a day's journey ; 2d. was to be allowed for one horse, and so on in proportion per mile : but if the distance were over twenty miles, or the overseer were obliged to be out all night, then 2s. was to be allowed for him, 1s. for his horse, and 6d. for each pauper.[2] It is improbable that such a scale of payment would induce the overseer to look kindly on the causes of his trouble : much less would a pauper be a *persona grata* if litigation over his settlement had already cost the parish large sums.

It has been necessary to give these particulars of the Law of Settlement for two reasons. In the first place, the probability of expulsion, ' exile by administrative order,' as it has been called, threw a shadow over the lives of the poor. In the second place, the old Law of Settlement became an immensely more important social impediment when enclosure and the great industrial inventions began to redistribute population. When the normal labourer had common rights and a strip and a cow, he would not wish to change his home on account of temporary distress : after enclosure he was reduced to a position in which his distress, if he stayed on in his own village, was likely to be permanent.

The want and suffering revealed in Davies' and Eden's budgets came to a crisis in 1795, the year of what may be called the revolt of the housewives. That year, when exceptional scarcity sharpened the edge of the misery caused by the changes we have summarised, was marked by a series of food riots all over England, in which a conspicuous part was taken by women. These disturbances are particularly interesting

[1] See *Annual Register*, 1817, p. 298.   [2] Eden, vol. ii. p. 689.

from the discipline and good order which characterise the conduct of the rioters. The rioters when they found themselves masters of the situation did not use their strength to plunder the shops : they organised distribution, selling the food they seized at what they considered fair rates, and handing over the proceeds to the owners. They did not rob : they fixed prices, and when the owner of provisions was making for a dearer market they stopped his carts and made him sell on the spot. At Aylesbury in March ' a numerous mob, consisting chiefly of women, seized on all the wheat that came to market, and compelled the farmers to whom it belonged to accept of such prices as they thought proper to name.' [1] In Devonshire the rioters scoured the country round Chudleigh, destroying two mills : ' from the great number of petticoats, it is generally supposed that several men were dressed in female attire.' [2] At Carlisle a band of women accompanied by boys paraded the streets, and in spite of the remonstrances of a magistrate, entered various houses and shops, seized all the grain, deposited it in the public hall, and then formed a committee to regulate the price at which it should be sold.[3] As Ipswich there was a riot over the price of butter, and at Fordingbridge, a certain Sarah Rogers, in company with other women started a cheap butter campaign. Sarah took some butter from Hannah Dawson ' with a determination of keeping it at a reduced price,' an escapade for which she was afterwards sentenced to three months' hard labour at the Winchester Assizes. ' Nothing but the age of the prisoner (being very young) prevented the Court from passing a more severe sentence.[4] At Bath the women actually boarded a vessel, laden with wheat and flour, which was lying in the river and refused to let her go. When the Riot Act was read they retorted that they were not rioting, but were resisting the sending of corn abroad, and sang God save the King. Although the owner took an oath that the corn was destined for Bristol, they were not satisfied, and ultimately soldiers were called in, and the corn was relanded and put into a warehouse.[5] In some places the soldiers helped the populace in their work of fixing prices : at Seaford, for example, they seized and sold meat and flour in the churchyard, and at Guildford they were the ringleaders in a movement to lower

[1] *Reading Mercury*, April 20, 1795 ; also *Ipswich Journal*, March 28.
[2] *Ipswich Journal*, April 18.   [3] *Ibid.*, August 8.
[4] *Ibid.*   *Ibid.*

the price of meat to 4d. a pound, and were sent out of the town by the magistrates in consequence.[1] These spontaneous leagues of consumers sprang up in many different parts, for in addition to the places already mentioned there were disturbances of sufficient importance to be chronicled in the newspapers, in Wiltshire, Suffolk, and Norfolk, whilst Eden states that at Deddington the populace seized on a boat laden with flour, but restored it on the miller's promising to sell it at a reduced price.[2]

These riots are interesting from many points of view. They are a rising of the poor against an increasing pressure of want, and the forces that were driving down their standard of life. They did not amount to a social rebellion, but they mark a stage in the history of the poor. To the rich they were a signal of danger. Davies declared that if the ruling classes learnt from his researches what was the condition of the poor, they would intervene to rescue the labourers from ' the abject state into which they are sunk.' Certainly the misery of which his budgets paint the plain surface could not be disregarded. If compassion was not a strong enough force to make the ruling classes attend to the danger that the poor might starve, fear would certainly have made them think of the danger that the poor might rebel. Some of them at any rate knew their Virgil well enough to remember that in the description of the threshold of Orcus, while ' senectus ' is ' tristis ' and ' egestas ' is ' turpis,' ' fames ' is linked with the more ominous epithet ' malesuada.' If a proletariat were left to starve despair might teach bad habits, and this impoverished race might begin to look with ravenous eyes on the lot of those who lived on the spoils and sinecures of the State. Thus fear and pity united to sharpen the wits of the rich, and to turn their minds to the distresses of the poor.

[1] *Reading Mercury*, April 27, 1795.
[2] Eden, vol. ii. p. 591. There was in fact hardly a county in which food riots did not break out. See Home Office Papers for 1795.

CHAPTER VII

THE REMEDIES OF 1795

THE collapse of the economic position of the labourer was the result of many causes, and in examining the various remedies that were proposed we shall see that they touch in turn on the several deficiencies that produced this failure. The governing fact of the situation was that the labourer's wages no longer sufficed to provide even a bare and comfortless existence. It was necessary then that his wages should be raised, or that the effects of the rise in prices should be counteracted by changes of diet and manner of life, or that the economic resources which formerly supplemented his earnings should in some way be restored, unless he was to be thrown headlong on to the Poor Law. We shall see what advice was given and what advice was taken in these momentous years.

DIET REFORM

A disparity between income and expenditure may be corrected by increasing income or by reducing expenditure. Many of the upper classes thought that the second method might be tried in this emergency, and that a judicious change of diet would enable the labourer to face the fall of wages with equanimity. The solution seemed to lie in the simple life. Enthusiasts soon began to feel about this proposal the sort of excitement that Robinson Crusoe enjoyed when discovering new resources on his island : an infinite vista of kitchen reform beckoned to their ingenious imaginations : and many of them began to persuade themselves that the miseries of the poor arose less from the scantiness of their incomes than from their own improvidence and unthriftiness.[1] The rich set an example in the worst days by cutting off pastry and restricting their servants to a quartern loaf a week each.[2] It was

---

[1] Eden, vol. i. p. 495.

[2] Resolution of Privy Council, July 6, 1795, and Debate and Resolution in House of Commons. *Parliamentary Register*, December 11, 1795, and Lord Sheffield in *Annals of Agriculture*, vol. xxv. p. 31.

surely not too much in these circumstances to ask the poor
to adapt their appetites to the changed conditions of their
lives, and to shake off what Pitt called ' groundless prejudices '
to mixed bread of barley, rye, and wheat.[1] Again oatmeal
was a common food in the north, why should it not be taken
in the south ?   If no horses except post horses and perhaps
cavalry horses were allowed oats, there would be plenty for
the poor.[2]   A Cumberland labourer with a wife and family
of five was shown by Eden [3] to have spent £7, 9s. 2d. a year
on oatmeal and barley, whereas a Berkshire labourer with
a wife and four children at home spent £36, 8s. a year on
wheaten bread alone.[4]   Clearly the starving south was to be
saved by the introduction of cheap cereals.

Other proposals of this time were to break against the opposition of the rich.   This broke against the opposition of the
poor.   All attempts to popularise substitutes failed, and the
poorer the labourer grew the more stubbornly did he insist
on wheaten bread.   ' Even household bread is scarcely ever
used : they buy the finest wheaten bread, and declare (what
I much doubt), that brown bread disorders their bowels.
Bakers do not now make, as they formerly did, bread of
unsifted flour : at some farmers' houses, however, it is still
made of flour, as it comes from the mill ; but this practice
is going much into disuse.   20 years ago scarcely any other
than brown bread was used.' [5]   At Ealing, when the charitable
rich raised a subscription to provide the distressed poor with
brown bread at a reduced price, many of the labourers thought
it so coarse and unpalatable that they returned the tickets
though wheaten bread was at 1s. 3d. the quartern loaf.[6]
Correspondent after correspondent to the *Annals of Agriculture* notes and generally deplores the fact that the poor,
as one of them phrases it, are too fine-mouthed to eat any but
the finest bread.[7]   Lord Sheffield, judging from his address
to Quarter Sessions at the end of 1795, would have had little
mercy on such grumblers.   After explaining that in his parish
relief was now given partly in potatoes, partly in wheaten
flour, and partly in oaten or barley flour, he declared : ' If
any wretches should be found so lost to all decency, and so

---

[1] See *Senator* for March 1, 1796, p. 1147.
[2] See Wilberforce's speech, *Parliamentary Register* and *Senator*, February
18, 1800.   [3] Eden, vol. ii. pp. 104-6.
    Ibid., p. 15.   [5] *Ibid.*, p. 280.   [6] *Ibid.*, p. 426.
[7] See *Annals of Agriculture*, vol. xxiv. pp. 63, 171, 177, 204, 285, 316, etc.

blind as to revolt against the dispensations of providence, and to refuse the food proposed for their relief, the parish officers will be justified in refusing other succour, and may be assured of support from the magistracy of the county.' [1]

To the rich, the reluctance of the labourer to change his food came as a painful surprise. They had thought of him as a roughly built and hardy animal, comparatively insensible to his surroundings, like the figure Lucretius drew of the primeval labourer :

> Et majoribus et solidis magis ossibus intus
> Fundatum, et validis aptum per viscera nervis ;
> Nec facile ex aestu, nec frigore quod caperetur,
> Nec novitate cibi, nec labi corporis ulla.

They did not know that a romantic and adventurous appetite is one of the blessings of an easy life, and that the more miserable a man's condition, and the fewer his comforts, the more does he shrink from experiments of diet. They were therefore surprised and displeased to find that labourers rejected soup, even soup served at a rich man's table, exclaiming, ' This is washy stuff, that affords no nourishment : we will not be fed on meal, and chopped potatoes like hogs.' [2] The dislike of change of food was remarked by the Poor Law Commissioners in 1834, who observed that the labourer had acquired or retained ' with the moral helplessness some of the other peculiarities of a child. He is often disgusted to a degree which other classes scarcely conceive possible, by slight differences in diet ; and is annoyed by anything that seems to him strange and new.' [3]

Apart from the constitutional conservatism of the poor there were good reasons for the obstinacy of the labourers.

---

[1] *Annals of Agriculture*, vol. xxv. p. 678.   [2] Eden, vol. i. p. 533.

[3] Perhaps the unpopularity of soup is partly explained by a letter published in the *Annals of Agriculture* in December 1795, vol. xxvi. p. 215. The writer says it is the custom for most families in the country ' to give their poor neighbours the pot liquor, that is, the liquor in which any meat has been boiled, and to which they sometimes add the broken bread from the parlour and kitchen tables : this,' he adds, ' makes but an indifferent mess.' The publications of the time contain numerous recipes for cheap soups : 'the power of giving an increased effect to Christian benevolence by these soups' (*Reports on Poor*, vol. i. p. 167) was eagerly welcomed. Cf. Mrs. Shore's account of stewed ox's head for the poor, according to which, at the cost of 2s. 6d. with the leavings of the family, a savoury mess for fifty-two persons could be prepared (*Ibid.*, p. 60).

Davies put one aspect of the case very well. ' If the working people of other countries are content with bread made of rye, barley, or oats, have they not milk, cheese, butter, fruits, or fish, to eat with that coarser bread ?   And was not this the case of our own people formerly, when these grains were the common productions of our land, and when scarcely wheat enough was grown for the use of the nobility and principal gentry ?   Flesh-meat, butter, and cheese, were then at such moderate prices, compared with the present prices, that poor people could afford to use them in common.   And with a competent quantity of these articles, a coarser kind of bread might very well satisfy the common people of any country.' [1]   He also states that where land had not been so highly improved as to produce much wheat, barley, oat-meal, or maslin bread were still in common use. Arthur Young himself realised that the labourer's attachment to wheaten bread was not a mere superstition of the palate. ' In the East of England I have been very generally assured, by the labourers who work the hardest, that they prefer the finest bread, not because most pleasant, but most contrary to a lax habit of body, which at once prevents all *strong* labour. The quality of the bread that is eaten by those who have meat, and perhaps porter and port, is of very little consequence indeed ; but to the hardworking man, who nearly lives on it, the case is abundantly different.' [2]   Fox put this point in a speech in the House of Commons in the debate on the high price of corn in November 1795. He urged gentlemen, who were talking of mixed bread for the people, ' not to judge from any experiment made with respect to themselves. I have myself tasted bread of different sorts, I have found it highly pleasant, and I have no doubt it is exceedingly wholesome. But it ought to be recollected how very small a part the article of bread forms of the provisions consumed by the more opulent classes of the community. To the poor it constitutes, the chief, if not the sole article of subsistence.' [3] The truth is that the labourer living on bread and tea had too delicate a digestion to assimilate the coarser cereals, and that there was, apart from climate and tradition, a very important difference between the labourer in the north and the labourer in the south, which the rich entirely overlooked. That differ-ence comes out in an analysis of the budgets of the Cumberland

[1] Davies, pp. 31-2.   [2] *Annals of Agriculture,* vol. xxv. p. 455.
[3] *Parliamentary Register,* November 2, 1795.

labourer and the Berkshire labourer. The Cumberland labourer who spent only £7, 9s. on his cereals, spent £2, 13s. 7d. a year on milk. The Berkshire labourer who spent £36, 8s. on wheaten bread spent 8s. 8d. a year on milk. The Cumberland family consumed about 1300 quarts in the year, the Berkshire family about two quarts a week. The same contrast appears in all budget comparisons between north and south. A weaver at Kendal (eight in the family) spends £12, 9s. on oatmeal and wheat, and £5, 4s. on milk.[1] An agricultural labourer at Wetherall in Cumberland (five in family) spends £7, 6s. 9d. on cereals and £2, 13s. 4d. on milk.[2] On the other side we have a labourer in Shropshire (four in family) spending £10, 8s. on bread (of wheat rye), and only 8s. 8d. on milk,[3] and a cooper at Frome, Somerset (seven in family) spending £45, 10s. on bread, and about 17s. on milk.[4] These figures are typical.[5]

Now oatmeal eaten with milk is a very different food from oatmeal taken alone, and it is clear from a study of the budgets that if oatmeal was to be acclimatised in the south, it was essential to increase the consumption of milk. But the great difference in consumption represented not a difference of demand, but a difference of supply. The southern labourer went without milk not from choice but from necessity. In the days when he kept cows he drank milk, for there was plenty of milk in the village. After enclosure, milk was not to be had. It may be that more cows were kept under the new system of farming, though this is unlikely, seeing that at this time every patch of arable was a gold-mine, but it is certainly true that milk became scarce in the villages. The new type of farmer did not trouble to sell milk at home. ' Farmers are averse to selling milk ; while poor persons who have only one cow generally dispose of all they can spare.'[6] The new farmer produced for a larger market : his produce was carried away, as Cobbett said, to be devoured by ' the idlers, the thieves, the prostitutes who are all taxeaters in the wens of Bath and London.' Davies argued, when pleading for the creation of small farms, ' The occupiers of these small farms, as well as the occupiers of Mr. *Kent's* larger cottages, would not think much of retailing to their poorer neighbours a little corn or a little milk, as they

[1] Eden, vol. iii. p. 769.   [2] *Ibid.*, vol. ii. p. 97.   [3] *Ibid.*, p. 621.
[4] *Ibid.*, p. 645.   [5] In many budgets no milk is included.
[6] *Reports on Poor*, vol. iv. p. 151.

might want, which the poor can now seldom have at all, and never but as a great favour from the rich farmers.'[1] Sir Thomas Bernard mentioned among the advantages of the Winchilsea system the ' no inconsiderable convenience to the inhabitants of that neighbourhood, that these cottagers are enabled to supply them, at a very moderate price, with milk, cream, butter, poultry, pig-meat, and veal : articles which, in general, are not worth the farmer's attention, and which, therefore, are supplied by speculators, who greatly enhance the price on the public.'[2] Eden[3] records that in Oxfordshire the labourers bitterly complain that the farmers, instead of selling their milk to the poor, give it to their pigs, and a writer in the Reports of the Society for Bettering the Condition of the Poor says that this was a practice not unusual in many parts of England.[4]

The scarcity of milk must be considered a contributory cause of the growth of tea-drinking, a habit that the philanthropists and Cobbett agreed in condemning. Cobbett declared in his *Advice to Young Men*[5] that ' if the slops were in fashion amongst ploughmen and carters, we must all be starved ; for the food could never be raised. The mechanics are half ruined by them.' In the Report on the Poor presented to the Hants Quarter Sessions in 1795,[6] the use of tea is described as ' a vain present attempt to supply to the spirits of the mind what is wanting to the strength of the body ; but in its lasting effects impairing the nerves, and therein equally injuring both the body and the mind.' Davies retorted on the rich who found fault with the extravagance of the poor in tea-drinking, by pointing out that it was their ' last resource.' ' The topic on which the declaimers against the extravagance of the poor display their eloquence with most success, is *tea-drinking*. Why should such people, it is asked, indulge in a luxury which is only proper for their betters ; and not rather content themselves with milk, which is in every form wholesome and nourishing ? Were it true that poor people could every where procure so excellent an article as milk, there would be then just reason to reproach them for giving the preference

---

[1] Davies, p. 104.   [2] *Reports on Poor*, vol. ii. p. 178.   [3] Vol. ii. p. 587.

[4] *Reports on Poor*, vol. i. p. 134 ; another reason for the dearth of milk was the growing consumption of veal in the towns. Davies says (p. 19), ' Suckling is here so profitable (to furnish veal for London) that the poor can seldom either buy or beg milk. '   [5] P. 27.

[6] See *Annals of Agriculture*, vol. xxv. pp. 367-8.

to the miserable infusion of which they are so fond. But it is not so. Wherever the poor can get milk, do they not gladly use it ? And where they cannot get it, would they not gladly exchange their tea for it ? [1] . . . Still you exclaim, *Tea is a luxury.* If you mean fine hyson tea, sweetened with refined sugar, and softened with cream, I readily admit it to be so. But *this* is not the tea of the poor. Spring water, just coloured with a few leaves of the lowest-priced tea, and sweetened with the brownest sugar, is the luxury for which you reproach them. To this they have recourse from mere necessity : and were they now to be deprived of this, they would immediately be reduced to bread and water. Tea-drinking is not the cause, but the consequence, of the distresses of the poor.' [2] We learn from the *Annals of Agriculture* that at Sedgefield in Durham [3] many of the poor declared that they had been driven to drinking tea from not being able to procure milk. [4]

No doubt the scarcity of milk helped to encourage a taste that was very quickly acquired by all classes in England, and not in England only, for, before the middle of the eighteenth century, the rapid growth of tea-drinking among the poor in the Lowlands of Scotland was affecting the revenue very seriously. [5] The English poor liked tea for the same reason that Dr. Johnson liked it, as a stimulant, and the fact that their food was monotonous and insipid made it particularly attractive. Eden shows that by the end of the eighteenth century it was in general use among poor families, taking the place both of beer and of milk, and excluding the substitutes that Eden wished to make popular. It seems perhaps less surprising to us than it did to him, that when the rich, who could eat or drink what they liked, enjoyed tea, the poor thought bread and tea a more interesting diet than bread and barley water.

A few isolated attempts were made to remedy the scarcity of milk, [6] which had been caused by enclosure and the con-

---

[1] Davies, p. 37.

[2] *Ibid.*, p. 39.   [3] *Annals of Agriculture*, vol. xxvi. p. 121.

[4] The dearness of malt was another fact which helped the introduction of tea. Cf. Davies, p. 38 : 'Time was when *small beer* was reckoned one of the necessaries of life, even in poor families.'

[5] Lecky, *History of England in Eighteenth Century*, vol. ii. p. 318.

[6] In connection with the dearth of milk it is important to notice the rise in the price of cheese. 'Poor people,' says Davies, (p. 19), 'reckon cheese the dearest article they can use' (cf. also p. 143), and in his comparison of prices in the middle of the eighteenth century with those of 1787-94 he gives the

solidation of farms.   Lord Winchilsea's projects have already
been described.   In the Reports of the Society for bettering
the Condition of the Poor, there are two accounts of plans
for supplying milk cheap, one in Staffordshire, where a respectable tradesman undertook to keep a certain number of cows
for the purpose in a parish where ' the principal number of
the poorer inhabitants were destitute of all means of procuring milk for their families,' [1] another at Stockton in Durham,
where the bishop made it a condition of the lease of a certain
farm, that the tenant should keep fifteen cows whose milk was
to be sold at $\frac{1}{2}$d. a pint to the poor.[2]   Mr. Curwen again, the
Whig M.P. for Carlisle, had a plan for feeding cows in the
winter with a view to providing the poor with milk.[3]

There was another way in which the enclosures had created
an insuperable obstacle to the popularising of ' cheap and
agreeable substitutes ' for expensive wheaten bread.   The
Cumberland housewife could bake her own barley bread in
her oven ' heated with heath, furze or brush-wood, the expence
of which is inconsiderable ' [4]; she had stretches of waste land at
her door where the children could be sent to fetch fuel.   ' There
is no comparison to the community,' wrote a contributor to
the *Annals of Agriculture*, [5] ' whether good wheat, rye, turnips,
etc., are not better than brakes, goss, furz, broom, and heath,'
but as acre after acre in the midlands and south was enclosed,
the fuel of the poor grew ever scantier.   When the common
where he had gleaned his firing was fenced off, the poor man
could only trust for his fuel to pilferings from the hedgerows.
To the spectator, furze from the common might seem ' gathered
with more loss of time than it appears to be worth ' [6]; to the
labourer whose scanty earnings left little margin over the

price of 112 lbs. of cheese at Reading Fair as from 17s. to 21s. in the first
period, and 40s. to 46s. in the second.   Retail cheese of an inferior sort had
risen from 2$\frac{1}{2}$d. or 3d. a lb. to 4$\frac{1}{2}$d. or 5d. (p. 65); cf. also correspondent in
Annals of Agriculture, vol. ii. p. 442.   'Every inhabitant of Bath must be
sensible that butter and cheese have risen in price one-third, or more, within
these twenty years.'   (Written in 1784).

[1] *Reports on Poor*, vol. i. p. 129.

[2] *Ibid.*, vol. iii. p. 78.

[3] *Annual Register*, 1806, p. 974; 'My local situation afforded me ample
means of knowing how greatly the lower orders suffered from being unable to
procure a supply of milk; and I am fully persuaded of the correctness of the
statement that the labouring poor lose a number of their children from the
want of a food so pre-eminently adapted to their support'; cf. also Curwen's
Hints.

[4] Eden, vol. i. p. 510.   [5] Vol. iii. p. 96.   [6] Eden, vol. iii. p. 694.

expense of bread alone, the loss of firing was not balanced by the economy of time.[1]

Insufficient firing added to the miseries caused by insufficient clothes and food. An ingenious writer in the *Annals of Agriculture*[2] suggested that the poor should resort to the stables for warmth, as was the practice in the duchy of Milan. Fewer would suffer death from want of fire in winter, he argued, and also it would be a cheap way of helping them, as it cost no fuel, for cattle were so obliging as to dispense warmth from their persons for nothing. But even this plan (which was not adopted) would not have solved the problem of cooking. The labourer might be blamed for his diet of fine wheaten bread and for having his meat (when he had any) roasted instead of made into soup, but how could cooking be done at home without fuel? ' No doubt, a labourer,' says Eden,[3] ' whose income was only £20 a year, would, in general, act wisely in substituting hasty-pudding, barley bread, boiled milk, and potatoes, for bread and beer ; but in most parts of this county, he is debarred not more by prejudice, than by local difficulties, from using a diet that requires cooking at home. The extreme dearness of fuel in Oxfordshire, compels him to purchase his dinner at the baker's ; and, from his unavoidable consumption of bread, he has little left for cloaths, in a country where warm cloathing is most essentially wanted.' In Davies' more racy and direct language, ' it is but little that in the present state of things the belly can spare for the back.'[4] Davies also pointed out the connection between dear fuel and the baker. ' Where fuel is scarce and dear, poor people find it cheaper to buy their bread of the baker than to bake for themselves. . . . But where fuel abounds, and costs only the trouble of cutting and carrying home, there they may save something by baking their own bread.'[5] Complaints of the pilfering of hedgerows were very common. ' Falstaff says " his soldiers found linen on every hedge " ; and I fear it is but too often the case, that labourers' children procure fuel from the same quarter.'[6] There were probably many families like the two described in Davies[7] who

---

[1] Cf. *Reports on Poor*, vol. i. p. 43 ; ' Where there are commons, the ideal advantage of cutting flags, peat, or whins, often causes a poor man to spend more time in procuring such fuel, than, if he reckoned his labour, would purchase for him double the quantity of good firing.'

[2] Vol. iv. p. 496.   [3] Vol. ii. p. 587.   [4] Davies, p. 28.

[5] *Ibid.*, p. 118.   [6] Eden, vol. iii. p. 805.   [7] P. 179.

spent nothing on fuel, which they procured 'by gathering cow-dung, and breaking their neighbours' hedges.'[1]

In some few cases, the benevolent rich did not content themselves with attempting to enforce the eighth commandment, but went to the root of the matter, helping to provide a substitute for their hedgerows. An interesting account of such an experiment is given in the *Reports on the Poor*,[2] by Scrope Bernard. 'There having been several prosecutions at the Aylesbury Quarter Sessions, for stealing fuel last winter, I was led to make particular inquiries, respecting the means which the poor at Lower Winchendon had of providing fuel. I found that there was no fuel then to be sold within several miles of the place; and that, amid the distress occasioned by the long frost, a party of cottagers had joined in hiring a person, to fetch a load of pit-coal from Oxford, for their supply. In order to encourage this disposition to acquire fuel in an honest manner,' a present was made to all this party of as much coal again as they had already purchased carriage free. Next year the vestry determined to help, and with the aid of private donations coal was distributed at 1s. 4d. the cwt. (its cost at the Oxford wharf), and kindling faggots at 1d. each. 'It had been said that the poor would not find money to purchase them, when they were brought: instead of which out of 35 poor families belonging to the parish, 29 came with ready money, husbanded out of their scanty means, to profit with eagerness of this attention to their wants; and among them a person who had been lately imprisoned by his master for stealing wood from his hedges.' Mr. Bernard concludes his account with some apt remarks on the difficulties of combining honesty with grinding poverty.[3]

[1] Cf. also Eden's description of a labourer's expenses, vol. iii. p. 797, where he says that whilst hedging and ditching, they are allowed to take home a faggot every evening, whilst the work lasts, 'but this is by no means sufficient for his consumption: his children, therefore, are sent into the fields, to collect wood where they can; and neither hedges nor trees are spared by the young marauders, who are thus, in some degree, educated in the art of thieving.'

[2] Vol. ii. p. 231.

[3] Cf. also for the difficulties of the poor in getting fuel, the account by the Rev. Dr. Glasse; *Reports on Poor*, vol. i. p. 58. 'Having long observed, that there is scarcely any article of life, in respect to which the poor are under greater difficulties, or for the supply of which they have stronger temptations to dishonest practices, than that of fuel,' he laid up in summer a store of coals in Greenford (Middlesex), and Wanstead, and sold them rather under original cost price, carriage free, in winter. 'The benefit arising from the relief afforded them in this article of coals, is obvious: they are habituated to pay for what they have;

MINIMUM WAGE

The attempts to reduce cottage expenditure were thus a failure. We must now describe the attempts to increase the cottage income. There were two ways in which the wages of the labourers might have been raised. One way, the way of combination, was forbidden by law. The other way was the fixing of a legal minimum wage in relation to the price of food. This was no new idea, for the regulation of wages by law was a venerable English institution, as old as the Statute of Edward III. The most recent laws on the subject were the famous Act of Elizabeth, an Act of James I., and an Act of George II. (1747). The Act of Elizabeth provided that the Justices of the Peace should meet annually and assess the wages of labourers in husbandry and of certain other workmen. Penalties were imposed on all who gave or took a wage in excess of this assessment. The Act of James I. was passed to remove certain ambiguities that were believed to have embarrassed the operation of the Act of Elizabeth, and among other provisions imposed a penalty on all who gave a wage below the wage fixed by the magistrates. The Act of 1747 [1] was passed because the existing laws were 'insufficient and defective,' and it provided that disputes between masters and men could be referred to the magistrates, 'although no rate or assessment of wages has been made that year by the Justices of the shire where such complaint shall be made.'

Two questions arise on the subject of this legislation, Was it operative? In whose interests was it administered, the interests of the employers or the interests of the employed? As to the first question there is a good deal of negative evidence to show that during the eighteenth century these laws were rarely applied. An example of an assessment (an assessment declaring a maximum) made by the Lancashire magistrates in 1725, was published in the *Annals of Agriculture* in 1795 [2] as an interesting curiosity, and the writer remarks: 'It appears from Mr. Ruggles' excellent *History of the Poor* that such orders must in general be searched for in earlier periods, and a

whereas at the shop they ran in debt. When their credit was at an end, they contrived to do without coals, by having recourse to wood-stealing; than which I know no practise which tends more effectually to introduce into young minds a habit of dishonesty; it is also very injurious to the farmer, and excites a degree of resentment in his breast, which, in many instances, renders him averse to affording relief to the poor, even when real necessity calls loudly for it.'

[1] 20 George II. c. 19. [2] *Annals of Agriculture*, vol. xxv. p. 305 ff.

friend of ours was much surprised to hear that any magistrates in the present century would venture on so bold a measure.' [1]

As to the second question, at the time we are discussing it was certainly taken for granted that this legislation was designed to keep wages down.   So implicitly was this believed that the Act of James I. which provided penalties in cases where wages were given below the fixed rate was generally ignored, and speakers and writers mentioned only the Act of Elizabeth, treating it as an Act for fixing a maximum.   Whitbread, for example, when introducing a Bill in 1795 to fix a minimum wage, with which we deal later, argued that the Elizabethan Act ought to be repealed because it fixed a maximum.   This view of the earlier legislation was taken by Fox, who supported Whitbread's Bill, and by Pitt who opposed it.   Fox said of the Act of Elizabeth that ' it secured the master from a risk which could but seldom occur, of being charged exorbitantly for the quantity of service ; but it did not authorise the magistrate to protect the poor from the injustice of a grinding and avaricious master, who might be disposed to take advantage of their necessities, and undervalue the rate of their services.' [2]   Pitt said that Whitbread ' imagined that he had on his side of the question the support of experience in this country, and appealed to certain laws upon the statute-book in confirmation of his proposition.   He did not find himself called upon to defend the principle of these statutes, but they were certainly introduced for purposes widely different from the object of the present bill.   They were enacted to guard the industry of the country from being checked by a general combination among labourers ; and the bill now under consideration was introduced solely for the purpose of remedying the inconveniences which labourers sustain from the disproportion existing between the price of labour and the price of living.' [3]   Only one speaker in the debates, Vansittart, afterwards Chancellor of the Exchequer, took the view that legislation was not needed because the Act of James I. gave the magistrates the powers with which Whitbread sought to arm them.

It was natural that many minds searching after a way of escape from the growing distress of the labourers, at a time when wages had not kept pace with prices, should have turned to the device of assessing wages by law in accordance

[1] *Annals of Agriculture*, vol. xxv. p. 298.
[2] *Parliamentary Register*, December 9, 1795.   [3] *Ibid.*, February 12, 1796.

with the price of provisions. If prices could not be assimilated to wages, could not wages be assimilated to prices? Nathaniel Kent, no wild visionary, had urged employers to raise wages in proportion to the increase of their profits, but his appeal had been without effect. But the policy of regulating wages according to the price of food was recommended in several quarters, and it provoked a great deal of discussion. Burke, whose days were closing in, was tempted to take part in it, and he put an advertisement into the papers announcing that he was about to publish a series of letters on the subject. The letters never appeared, but Arthur Young has described the visit he paid to Beaconsfield at this time and Burke's rambling thunder about ' the absurdity of regulating labour and the mischief of our poor laws,' and Burke's published works include a paper *Thoughts and Details on Scarcity*, presented to Pitt in November 1795. In this paper Burke argued that the farmer was the true guardian of the labourer's interest, in that it would never be profitable to him to underpay the labourer : an uncompromising application of the theory of the economic man, which was not less superficial than the Jacobins' application of the theory of the natural man.

In October 1795 Arthur Young sent out to the various correspondents of the Board of Agriculture a circular letter containing this question among others : ' It having been recommended by various quarter-sessions, that the price of labour should be regulated by that of bread corn, have the goodness to state what you conceive to be the advantages or disadvantages of such a system ? ' [1] Arthur Young was himself in favour of the proposal, and the Suffolk magistrates, at a meeting which he attended on the 12th of October, ordered : ' That the Members for this county be requested by the chairman to bring a bill into parliament, so to regulate the price of labour, that it may fluctuate with the average price of bread corn.' [2] Most of the replies were adverse, but the proposal found a warm friend in Mr. Howlett, the Vicar of Dunmow, who put into his answer some of the arguments which he afterwards developed in a pamphlet published in reply to Pitt's criticisms of Whitbread's Bill.[3] Howlett argued that Parliament had legislated with success to prevent combinations of workmen, and as an example he quoted the Acts of

---

[1] *Annals of Agriculture*, vol. xxv. p. 345.   [2] *Ibid.*, p. 316.

[3] *An Examination of Mr. Pitt's Speech in the House of Commons, February* 12, 1796.

8 George III., which had made the wages of tailors and silk-weavers subject to the regulations of the magistrates. It was just as necessary and just as practicable to prevent a combination of a different kind, that of masters. 'Not a combination indeed formally drawn up in writing and sanctioned under hand and seal, a combination, however, as certain (the result of contingencies or providential events) and as fatally efficacious as if in writing it had filled five hundred skins of parchment : a combination which has operated for many years with a force rapidly increasing, a combination which has kept back the hire of our labourers who have reaped down our fields, and has at length torn the clothes from their backs, snatched the food from their mouths, and ground the flesh from their bones.' Howlett, it will be seen, took the same view as Thelwall, that the position of the labourers was deteriorating absolutely and relatively. He estimated from a survey taken at Dunmow that the average family should be taken as five ; if wages had been regulated on this basis, and the labourer had been given per head no more than the cost of a pauper's keep in the workhouse sixty years ago, he would have been very much better off in 1795. He would himself take a higher standard. In reply to the argument that the policy of the minimum wage would deprive the labourers of all spur and incentive he pointed to the case of the London tailors ; they at any rate displayed plenty of life and ingenuity, and nobody could say that the London fashions did not change fast enough. Employers would no more raise wages without compulsion than they would make good roads without the aid of turnpikes or the prescription of statutes enforced by the magistrates. His most original contribution to the discussion was the argument that the legal regulation should not be left to the unassisted judgment of the magistrates : 'it should be the result of the clearest, fullest, and most accurate information, and at length be judiciously adapted to each county, hundred, or district in every quarter of the kingdom.' Howlett differed from some of the supporters of a minimum wage, in thinking that wages should be regulated by the prices of the necessaries of life, not merely by that of bread corn.

The same policy was advocated by Davies in *The Case of Labourers in Husbandry*.[1] Davies argued that if the minimum only were fixed, emulation would not be discouraged, for better workmen would both be more sure of employment

[1] P. 106 ff.

and also obtain higher wages. He suggested that the minimum wage should be fixed by calculating the sum necessary to maintain a family of five, or by settling the scale of day wages by the price of bread alone, treating the other expenses as tolerably steady. He did not propose to regulate the wages of any but day labourers, nor did he propose to deal with piecework, although piecework had been included in the Act of Elizabeth. He further suggested that the regulation should be in force only for half the year, from November to May, when the labourers' difficulties pressed hardest upon them. Unfortunately he coupled with his minimum wage policy a proposal to give help from the rates to families with more than five members, if the children were unable to earn.

But the most interesting of all the declarations in favour of a minimum wage was a declaration from labourers. A correspondent sent the following advertisement to the *Annals of Agriculture* :—

' The following is an advertisement which I cut out of a Norwich newspaper :—

" DAY LABOURERS

" At a numerous meeting of the day labourers of the little parishes of Heacham, Snettisham, and Sedgford, this day, 5th November, in the parish church of Heacham, in the county of Norfolk, in order to take into consideration the best and most peaceable mode of obtaining a redress of all the severe and peculiar hardships under which they have for many years so patiently suffered, the following resolutions were unanimously agreed to :—1st, That—*The labourer is worthy of his hire*, and that the mode of lessening his distresses, as hath been lately the fashion, by selling him flour under the market price, and thereby rendering him an object of a parish rate, is not only an indecent insult on his lowly and humble situation (in itself sufficiently mortifying from his degrading dependence on the caprice of his employer) but a fallacious mode of relief, and every way inadequate to a radical redress of the manifold distresses of his calamitous state. 2nd, That the price of labour should, at all times, be proportioned to the price of wheat, which should invariably be regulated by the average price of that necessary article of life ; and that the price of labour, as specified in the annexed plan, is not only well calculated to make the labourer happy without being injurious to the farmer, but it appears to us the only rational means of securing the permanent happiness of this valuable and useful class of men, and, if adopted in its full extent, will have an immediate and powerful effect in reducing, if it does not entirely annihilate, that disgraceful and enormous tax on the public—the POOR RATE.

" *Plan of the Price of Labour proportionate to the Price of Wheat*

		per last.				per day.
When wheat shall be		14 l.	the price of labour shall be			1s. 2d.
,,	,,	16	,,	,,	,,	1s. 4d.
,,	,,	18	,,	,,	,,	1s. 6d.
,,	,,	20	,,	,,	,,	1s. 8d.
,,	,,	22	,,	,,	,,	1s. 10d.
,,	,,	24	,,	,,	,,	2s. 0d.
,,	,,	26	,,	,,	,,	2s. 2d.
,,	,,	28	,,	,,	,,	2s. 4d.
,,	,,	30	,,	,,	,,	2s. 6d.
,,	,,	32	,,	,,	,,	2s. 8d.
,,	,,	34	,,	,,	,,	2s. 10d.
,,	,,	36	,,	,,	,,	3s. 0d.

And so on, according to this proportion.

" 3rd, That a petition to parliament to regulate the price of labour, conformable to the above plan, be immediately adopted ; and that the day labourers throughout the county be invited to associate and co-operate in this necessary application to parliament, as a peaceable, legal, and probable mode of obtaining relief ; and, in doing this, no time should be lost, as the petition must be presented before the 29th January 1796.

" 4th, That one shilling shall be paid into the hands of the treasurer by every labourer, in order to defray the expences of advertising, attending on meetings, and paying counsel to support their petition in parliament.

" 5th, That as soon as the sense of the day labourers of this county, or a majority of them, shall be made known to the clerk of the meeting, a general meeting shall be appointed, in some central town, in order to agree upon the best and easiest mode of getting the petition signed : when it will be requested that one labourer, properly instructed, may be deputed to represent two or three contiguous parishes, and to attend the above intended meeting with a list of all the labourers in the parishes he shall represent, and pay their respective subscriptions ; and that the labourer, so deputed, shall be allowed two shillings and six pence a day for his time, and two shillings and six pence a day for his expences.

" 6th, That Adam Moore, clerk of the meeting, be directed to have the above resolutions, with the names of the farmers and labourers who have subscribed to and approved them, advertised in one Norwich and one London paper ; when it is hoped that the above plan of a petition to parliament will not only be approved and immediately adopted by the day labourers of this county, but by the day labourers of every county in the kingdom.

" 7th, That all letters, *post paid*, addressed to Adam Moore, labourer, at Heacham, near Lynn, Norfolk, will be duly noticed." [1]

This is one of the most interesting and instructive documents of the time. It shows that the labourers, whose steady decline during the next thirty years we are about to trace, were animated by a sense of dignity and independence. Something of the old spirit of the commoners still survived. But there is no sequel to this incident. This great scheme of a labourers' organisation vanishes : it passes like a flash of summer lightning. What is the explanation ? The answer is to be found, we suspect, in the Treason and Sedition Acts that Pitt was carrying through Parliament in this very month. Under those Acts no language of criticism was safe, and fifty persons could not meet except in the presence of a magistrate, who had power to extinguish the meeting and arrest the speaker. Those measures inflicted even wider injury upon the nation than Fox and Sheridan and Erskine themselves believed.

The policy of a minimum wage was brought before Parliament in the winter of 1795, in a Bill introduced by Samuel Whitbread, one of the small band of brave Liberals who had stood by Fox through the revolutionary panic. Whitbread is a politician to whom history has done less than justice, and he is generally known only as an implacable opponent of the Peninsular War. That opposition he contrived to conduct, as we know from the *Creevey Papers*, in

---

[1] *Annals of Agriculture*, 1795, vol. xxv. p. 503.

such a way as to win and keep the respect of Wellington. Whitbread's disapproval of that war, of which Liberals like Holland and Lord John Russell, who took Fox's view of the difference of fighting revolutions by the aid of kings and fighting Napoleon by the aid of peoples, were strong supporters, sprang from his compassion for the miseries of the English poor. His most notable quality was his vivid and energetic sympathy ; he spent his life in hopeless battles, and he died by his own hand of public despair. The Bill he now introduced was the first of a series of proposals designed for the rescue of the agricultural labourers. It was backed by Sheridan and Grey,[1] and the members for Suffolk.

The object of the Bill [2] was to explain and amend the Act of Elizabeth, which empowered Justices of the Peace at or within six weeks of every General Quarter Sessions held at Easter to regulate the wages of labourers in husbandry. The provisions of the Bill were briefly as follows. At any Quarter Sessions the justices could agree, if they thought fit, to hold a General Sessions for carrying into execution the powers given them by the Act. If they thought good to hold such a General Sessions, the majority of them could ' rate and appoint the wages and fix and declare the hours of working of all labourers in husbandry, by the day, week, month or year, and with beer or cyder or without, respect being had to the value of money and the plenty or scarcity of the time.' This rate was to be printed and posted on the church doors, and was to hold good till superseded by another made in the same way. The rate was not to apply to any tradesman or artificer, nor to any labourer whose diet was wholly provided by his employer, nor to any labourer *bona fide* employed on piecework, nor to any labourer employed by the parish. The young, the old, and the infirm were also exempted from the provisions of the Act. It was to be lawful ' to contract with and pay to any male person, under the age of —— [3] years, or to any man who from age or infirmity or any other incapacity shall be unable to do the ordinary work of a labouring man, so much as he shall reasonably deserve for the work which he shall be able to do and shall do.' In case of complaint the decision as to the ability of the labourer rested with the justices.

With the above exceptions no labourer was to be hired under the appointed rates, and any contract for lower wages was

---

[1] *Parliamentary Debates.*   [2] Printed in *Parliamentary Papers* for 1795-6.
The age was not filled up.

void. If convicted of breaking the law, an employer was to be fined ; if he refused to pay the fine, his goods were to be distrained on, and if this failed to produce enough to pay the expenses, he could be committed to the common gaol or House of Correction. A labourer with whom an illegal contract was made was to be a competent witness.

The first discussions of the Bill were friendly in tone. On 25th November Whitbread asked for leave to bring it in. Sir William Young, Lechmere, Charles Dundas, and Sir John Rous all spoke with sympathy and approval. The first reading debate took place on 9th December, and though Whitbread had on that occasion the powerful support of Fox, who, while not concealing his misgivings about the Bill, thought the alternative of leaving the great body of the people to depend on the charity of the rich intolerable, an ominous note was struck by Pitt and Henry Dundas on the other side. The Bill came up for second reading on 12th February 1796.[1] Whitbread's opening speech showed that he was well aware that he would have to face a formidable opposition. Pitt rose at once after the motion had been formally seconded by one of the Suffolk members, and assailed the Bill in a speech that made an immediate and overwhelming impression. He challenged Whitbread's argument that wages had not kept pace with prices ; he admitted the hardships of the poor, but he thought the picture overdrawn, for their hardships had been relieved by ' a display of beneficence never surpassed at any period,' and he argued that it was a false remedy to use legislative interference, and to give the justices the power to regulate the price of labour, and to endeavour ' to establish by authority what would be much better accomplished by the unassisted operation of principles.' This led naturally to an attack on the restrictions on labour imposed by the Law of Settlement, and a discussion of the operation of the Poor Laws, and the speech ended, after a glance at the great possibilities of child employment, with the promise of measures which should restore the original purity of the Poor Laws, and make them a blessing instead of the curse they had become. The speech seems to have dazzled the House of Commons, and few stood up against the general opinion that Whitbread's proposal was dangerous, and that the whole question had better be left to Pitt. Lechmere, a Worcestershire member, was one of them, and he made an admirable little speech in which he

[1] For report of debate see *Parliamentary Register* for that date.

tried to destroy the general illusion that the poor could not be unhappy in a country where the rich were so kind. Whitbread himself defended his Bill with spirit and ability, showing that Pitt had not really found any substantial argument against it, and that Pitt's own remedies were all hypothetical and distant. Fox reaffirmed his dislike of compulsion, but restated at the same time his opinion that Whitbread's Bill, though not an ideal solution, was the best solution available of evils which pressed very hardly on the poor and demanded attention. General Smith pointed out that one of Pitt's remedies was the employment of children, and warned him that he had himself seen some of the consequences of the unregulated labour of children ' whose wan and pale complexions bespoke that their constitutions were already undermined, and afforded but little promise of a robust manhood, or of future usefulness to the community.' But the general sense of the House was reflected in the speeches of Buxton, Coxhead and Burdon, whose main argument was that the poor were not in so desperate a plight as Whitbread supposed, and that whatever their condition might be, Pitt was the most likely person to find such remedies as were practicable and effective. The motion for second reading was negatived without a division. The verdict of the House was a verdict of confidence in Pitt.

Four years later (11th February 1800) Whitbread repeated his attempt.[1] He asked for leave to bring in a Bill to explain and amend the Act of Elizabeth, and said that he had waited for Pitt to carry out his promises. He was aware of the danger of overpaying the poor, but artificers and labourers should be so paid as to be able to keep themselves and their families in comfort. He saw no way of securing this result in a time of distress except the way he had suggested. Pitt rose at once to reply. He had in the interval brought in and abandoned his scheme of Poor Law Reform. He had spent his only idea, and he was now confessedly without any policy at all. All that he could contribute was a general criticism of legislative interference, and another discourse on the importance of letting labour find its own level. He admitted the fact of scarcity, but he believed the labouring class seldom felt fewer privations. History scarcely provides a more striking spectacle of a statesman paying himself with soothing phrases in the midst of a social cyclone. The House was more than ever on his side. All the interests and instincts of class were disguised under

[1] See *Parliamentary Register*.

the gold dust of Adam Smith's philosophy. Sir William Young, Buxton, Wilberforce, Ellison, and Perceval attacked the Bill. Whitbread replied that charity as a substitute for adequate wages had mischievous effects, for it took away the independence of the poor, ' a consideration as valuable to the labourer as to the man of high rank,' and as for the argument that labour should be left to find its own level, the truth surely was that labour found its level by combinations, and that this had been found to be so great an evil that Acts of Parliament had been passed against it.

The date of the second reading of the Bill was hotly disputed : [1] the friends of the measure wanted it to be fixed for 28th April, so that Quarter Sessions might have time to deliberate on the proposals ; the opponents of the measure suggested 25th February, on the grounds that it was dangerous to keep the Bill in suspense so long : ' the eyes of all the labouring poor,' said Mr. Ellison, ' must in that interval be turned upon it.' The opponents won their point, and when the Bill came up for second reading its fate was a foregone conclusion. Whitbread made one last appeal, pleading the cause of the labourers bound to practical serfdom in parishes where the landowner was an absentee, employed at starvation wages by farmers, living in cottages let to them by farmers. But his appeal was unheeded : Lord Belgrave retorted with the argument that legislative interference with agriculture could not be needed, seeing that five hundred Enclosure Bills had passed the House during a period of war, and the Bill was rejected.

So died the policy of the minimum wage. Even later it had its adherents, for, in 1805, Sir Thomas Bernard criticised it [2] as the ' favourite idea of some very intelligent and benevolent men.' He mentioned as a *reductio ad absurdum* of the scheme, that had the rate of wages been fixed by the standard of 1780 when the quartern loaf was 6d. and the labourer's pay 9s. a week, the result in 1800 when the quartern loaf cost 1s. 9d. would have been a wage of £1, 11s. 6d.

When Whitbread introduced his large and comprehensive Poor Law Bill in 1807,[3] the proposal for a minimum wage was not included.

From an examination of the speeches of the time and of the answers to Arthur Young's circular printed in the *Annals of*

---

[1] See *Parliamentary Register*, February 14, 1800.
[2] *Reports on Poor*, vol. v. p. 23.   [3] See p. 179.

Agriculture, it is evident that there was a genuine fear among the opponents of the measure that if once wages were raised to meet the rise in prices it would not be easy to reduce them when the famine was over. This was put candidly by one of Arthur Young's correspondents : ' it is here judged more prudent to indulge the poor with bread corn at a reduced price than to raise the price of wages.' [1]

The policy of a minimum wage was revived later by a society called ' The General Association established for the Purpose of bettering the Condition of the Agricultural and Manufacturing Labourers.' Three representatives of this society gave evidence before the Select Committee on Emigration in 1827, and one of them pointed out as an illustration of the injustice with which the labourers were treated, that in 1825 the wages of agricultural labourers were generally 9s. a week, and the price of wheat 9s. a bushel, whereas in 1732 the wages of agricultural labour were fixed by the magistrates at 6s. a week, and the price of wheat was 2s. 9d. the bushel. In support of this comparison he produced a table from *The Gentleman's Magazine* of 1732 :—

Wheat in February 1732, 23s. to 25s. per quarter.
Wheat in March 1732, 20s. to 22s. per quarter.

Yearly wages appointed by the Justices to be taken by the servants in the county of Kent, not exceeding the following sums :

	£	s	d
Head ploughman waggoner or seedsman	£8	0	0
His mate .	4	0	0
Best woman	3	0	0
Second sort of woman	2	0	0
Second ploughman	6	0	0
His mate .	3	0	0
Labourers by day in summer		1	2
In winter		1	0

JUSTICES OF GLOUCESTER

	£	s	d
Head servant in husbandry	5	0	0
Second servant in husbandry	4	0	0
Driving boy under fourteen	1	0	0
Head maid servant or dairy servant	2	10	0
Mower in harvest without drink per day		1	2
With drink .		1	0

[1] *Annals of Agriculture,* vol. xxvi. p. 178.

Other day labourers with drink	1	0
From corn to hay harvest with drink . . .	0	8
Mowers and reapers in corn harvest with drink .	1	0
Labourers with diet	0	4
Without diet or drink	0	10
Carpenter wheelwright or mason without drink .	1	2
With drink	1	0

One of the witnesses pointed out that there were five millions of labourers making with their families eight millions, and that if the effect of raising their wages was to increase their expenditure by a penny a day, there would be an increase of consumption amounting to twelve millions a year. These arguments made little impression on the Committee, and the representations of the society were dismissed with contempt : ‘ It is from an entire ignorance of the universal operation of the principle of Supply and Demand regulating the rate of wages that all these extravagant propositions are advanced, and recommendations spread over the country which are so calculated to excite false hopes, and consequently discontent, in the minds of the labouring classes. Among the most extravagant are those brought forward by the Society established for the purpose of bettering the condition of the manufacturing and agricultural labourers.’

POOR LAW REFORM

Pitt, having secured the rejection of Whitbread’s Minimum Wage Bill in 1796, produced his own alternative : Poor Law Reform. It is necessary to state briefly what were the Poor Law arrangements at the time of his proposals.

The Poor Law system reposed on the great Act of Elizabeth (1601), by which the State had acknowledged and organised the duty to the poor which it had taken over from the Church. The parish was constituted the unit, and overseers, unsalaried and nominated by the J.P.’s, were appointed for administering relief, the necessary funds being obtained by a poor rate. Before 1722 a candidate for relief could apply either to the overseers or to the magistrate. By an Act passed in that year, designed to make the administration stricter, application was to be made first to the overseer. If the overseer rejected the application the claimant could submit his case to a magistrate, and the magistrate, after hearing the overseer’s objection, could order that relief should be given. There were, however, a number of parishes in which applications for relief were made to salaried guardians. These were the parishes that had adopted an Act known as Gilbert's Act, passed in 1782.[1] In these parishes,[2] joined in incorporations, the parish overseers were not abolished, for they still had the duty of collecting and accounting for the rates, but the distribution was in the hands of paid guardians, one for each parish, appointed by the justices out of a list of names submitted by the parishioners. In each set of incorporated parishes there was a ' Visitor ' appointed by the justices, who had practically absolute power over the guardians. If the guardians refused relief, the claimant could still appeal, as in the case of the overseers, to the justices.

Such was the parish machinery. The method of giving relief varied greatly, but the main distinction to be drawn is between (1) out relief, or a weekly pension of a shilling or two at home ; and (2) indoor relief, or relief in a workhouse, or poorhouse, or house of industry. Out relief was the earlier institution, and it held its own throughout the century, being the only form of relief in many parishes. Down to 1722 parishes that wished to build a workhouse had to get a special Act of Parliament. In that year a great impetus was given to the workhouse movement by an Act [3] which authorised overseers, with the consent of the vestry, to start workhouses, or to farm out the poor, and also authorised parishes to join together for this purpose. If applicants for relief refused to go into the workhouse, they forfeited their title to any relief at all. A great many workhouses were built in consequence of this Act : in 1732 there were stated to be sixty in the country, and about fifty in the metropolis.[4]

Even if the applicant for relief lived in a parish which had built or shared in a workhouse, it did not follow that he was forced into it. He lost his title to receive relief outside, but his fate would depend on the parish officers. In the parishes which had adopted Gilbert's Act the workhouse was reserved for the aged, for the infirm, and for young children. In most parishes there was out relief as well as indoor relief : in some parishes outdoor relief being allowed to applicants of a certain age or in special circumstances. In some parishes all outdoor

---

[1] 22 George III. c. 83.

[2] In 1834 there were 924 comprised in 67 incorporations (Nicholls, vol. ii. p. 91.   [3] 9 George I. c. 7.   [4] Eden, vol. i. p. 269.

relief had stopped by 1795.[1] There is no doubt that in most
parishes tho workhouse accommodation would have been quite
inadequate for the needs of the parish in times of distress. It
was quite common to put four persons into a single bed.

The workhouses were dreaded by the poor,[2] not only for the
dirt and disease and the devastating fevers that swept through
them,[3] but for reasons that are intelligible enough to any one
who has read Eden's descriptions. Those descriptions show
that Crabbe's picture is no exaggeration :—

> 'Theirs is yon House that holds the Parish-Poor,
> Whose walls of mud scarce bear the broken door ;
> There, where the putrid vapours, flagging, play,
> And the dull wheel hums doleful through the day ;—
> There Children dwell who know no Parents' care ;
> Parents, who know no Children's love, dwell there !
> Heart-broken Matrons on their joyless bed,
> Forsaken Wives and Mothers never wed ;
> Dejected Widows with unheeded tears,
> And crippled Age with more than childhood fears ;
> The Lame, the Blind, and, far the happiest they !
> The moping Idiot and the Madman gay.
> Here too the Sick their final doom receive,
> Here brought, amid the scenes of grief, to grieve,
> Where the loud groans from some sad chamber flow,
> Mixt with the clamours of the crowd below ;
> Here sorrowing, they each kindred sorrow scan,
> And the cold charities of man to man :
> Whose laws indeed for ruin'd Age provide,
> And strong compulsion plucks the scrap from pride ;
> But still that scrap is bought with many a sigh,
> And pride embitters what it can't deny.' [4]

A good example of this mixture of young and old, virtuous
and vicious, whole and sick, sane and mad, is given in Eden's
catalogue of the inmates of Epsom Workhouse in January
1796.[5] There were eleven men, sixteen women, and twenty-
three children. We read of J. H., aged forty-three, 'always . . .

---

[1] *E.g.* Oxford and Shrewsbury.

[2] There is a significant entry in the Abstracts of Returns to the 1775 Poor
Relief Committee in reference to the building of that death-trap, the Bulcamp
House of Industry. 'In the Expences for Building is included £500 for build-
ing a Part which was pulled down by a Mob.'

[3] At Heckingham in Norfolk a putrid fever, in 1774, killed 126 out of 220
inmates (Eden, vol. ii. p. 473, quoting Howlett) ; cf. also Ruggles, *History of
the Poor*, vol. ii. p. 266.

[4] 'The Village,' pp. 16 and 17.   [5] Eden, vol. iii. p. 694 ff.

somewhat of an idiot, he is now become quite a driveller ' ; of E. E., aged sixty-two, ' of a sluggish, stupid character ' ; of A. M., aged twenty-six, ' afflicted with a leprosy ' ; of R. M., aged seventy-seven, ' worn out and paralytic ' ; of J. R., aged seventeen, who has contracted so many disorderly habits that decent people will not employ him.   It is interesting to notice that it was not till 1790 that the Justices of the Peace were given any power of inspecting workhouses.

In 1796, before Pitt's scheme was brought in, the Act of 1722, which had been introduced to stiffen the administration of the Poor Laws, was relaxed.   An Act,[1] of which Sir William Young was the author, abolished the restriction of right to relief to persons willing to enter the workhouse, and provided that claimants could apply for relief directly to a magistrate. The Act declares that the restrictions had been found ' inconvenient and oppressive.'   It is evidence, of course, of the increasing pressure of poverty.

But to understand the arrangements in force at this time, and also the later developments, we must glance at another feature of the Poor Law system.   The Poor Laws were a system of employment as well as a system of relief.   The Acts before 1722 are all called Acts for the Relief of the Poor : the Act of 1722 speaks of ' the Settlement, Employment and Relief.'   That Act empowered parishes to farm out the poor to an employer.   Gilbert's Act of 1782 provided that in the parishes incorporated under that Act the guardians were not to send able-bodied poor to the poorhouse, but to find work for them or maintain them until work was found : the guardian was to take the wage and provide the labourer with a maintenance.   Thus there grew up a variety of systems of public employment : direct employment of paupers on parish work : the labour rate system, or the sharing out of the paupers among the ratepayers : the roundsman system by which pauper labour was sold to the farmers.[2]

---

[1] 36 George III. c. 23.

[2] The last of these systems had been included in a Bill introduced by Sir William Young in 1788. ' In order to relieve agricultural labourers, who are often, during the winter, out of employment, the vestry in every parish is empowered, by notice affixed to the church door, to settle a rate of wages to be paid to labourers out of employ, from the 30th Nov. to the 28th of Feb. ; and to distribute and send them round in rotation to the parishioners, proportionally as they pay to the Rates; to be paid by the person employing them two-thirds of the wages so settled, and one-third by the parish-officers out of the Rates.' —Eden, vol. i. p. 397.

This was the state of things that Pitt proposed to reform. His general ideas on the subject were put before the House of Commons in the debate on the second reading of Whitbread's Bill.[1] He thought that persons with large families should be treated as entitled to relief, that persons without a settlement, falling into want, should not be liable to removal at the caprice of the parish officer, that Friendly Societies should be encouraged, and that Schools of Industry should be established. 'If any one would take the trouble to compute the amount of all the earnings of the children who are already educated in this manner, he would be surprised, when he came to consider the weight which their support by their own labours took off the country, and the addition which, by the fruits of their toil, and the habits to which they were formed, was made to its internal opulence.' On 22nd December of that year, in a new Parliament, he asked for leave to bring in a Bill for the better Support and Maintenance of the Poor. He said the subject was too extensive to be discussed at that stage, that he only proposed that the Bill should be read a first and second time and sent to a committee where the blanks could be filled up, and the Bill printed before the holidays, 'in order that during the interval of Parliament it might be circulated in the country and undergo the most serious investigation.'[2] Sheridan hinted that it was unfortunate for the poor that Pitt had taken the question out of Whitbread's hands, to which Pitt replied that any delay in bringing forward his Bill was due to the time spent on taking advice. On 28th February of the next year (1797), while strangers were excluded from the Gallery, there occurred what the *Parliamentary Register* calls 'a conversation upon the farther consideration of the report of the Poor's Bill,' in which nobody but Pitt defended the Bill, and Sheridan and Joliffe attacked it. With this its Parliamentary history ends.

The main features of the Bill were these.[3] Schools of Industry were to be established in every parish or group of parishes. These schools were to serve two purposes. First, the young were to be trained there (this idea came, of course,

---

[1] *Parliamentary Register*, February 12, 1796.

[2] *Ibid.*, December 22, 1796.

[3] The Bill is printed in House of Commons Papers, 1796. The 'Heads of the Bill' as circulated appear in the *Annals of Agriculture*, vol. xxvi. pp. 260 ff. and 359 ff. Eden gives in the form of Appendices (1) the Heads of the Bill, (2) the Amendments introduced in Committee.

from Locke). Every poor man with more than two children who were not self-supporting, and every widow with more than one such child, was to be entitled to a weekly allowance in respect of each extra child. Every allowance child who was five years or over was to be sent to the School of Industry, unless his parent could instruct and employ him, and the proceeds of his work was to go towards the upkeep of the school. Secondly, grown-up people were to be employed there. The authorities were to provide ' a proper stock of hemp, flax, silk, cotton, wool, iron, leather or other materials, and also proper tools and implements for the employment of the poor,' and they were empowered to carry on all trades under this Act, ' any law or custom to the contrary notwithstanding.' Any person lawfully settled in a parish was entitled to be employed in the school ; any person residing in a parish, able and willing to be employed at the usual rates, was entitled to be employed there when out of work. Poor persons refusing to be employed there were not to be entitled to relief. The authorities might either pay wages at a rate fixed by the magistrates, or they might let the employed sell their products and merely repay the school for the material, or they might contract to feed them and take a proportion of their receipts. If the wages paid in the school were insufficient, they were to be supplemented out of the rates.

The proposals for outside relief were briefly and chiefly these. A person unable to earn the full rate of wages usually given might contract with his employer to work at an inferior rate, and have the balance between his earnings and an adequate maintenance made up by the parish. Money might be advanced under certain circumstances for the purchase of a cow or other animal, if it seemed likely that such a course would enable the recipient to maintain himself without the help of the parish. The possession of property up to thirty pounds was not to disqualify a person for relief. A parochial insurance fund was to be created, partly from private subscriptions and partly from the rates. No person was to be removed from a parish on account of relief for temporary disability or sickness.

The most celebrated and deadly criticism came from Bentham, who is often supposed to have killed the Bill. Some of his objections are captious and eristical, and he is a good deal less than just to the good elements of the scheme. Pitt deserves credit for one statesmanlike discovery, the discovery that it

is bad policy to refuse to help a man until he is ruined. His
cow-money proposal was also conceived in the right spirit if
its form was impracticable. But the scheme as a whole was
confused and incoherent, and it deserved the treatment it
received. It was in truth a huge patchwork, on which the
ideas of living and dead reformers were thrown together
without order or plan. As a consequence, its various parts
did not agree. It is surprising that the politician who had
attacked Whitbread's Bill as an interference with wages
could have included in his scheme the proposal to pay wages
in part out of rates. The whole scheme, though it would
have involved a great expenditure, would have produced
very much the same result as the Speenhamland system, by
virtue of this clause. Pitt showed no more judgment or foresight than the least enlightened of County Justices in introducing into a scheme for providing relief, and dealing with
unemployment, a proposal that could only have the effect
of reducing wages. The organisation of Schools of Industry
as a means of dealing with unemployment has sometimes been
represented as quite a new proposal, but it was probably
based on the suggestion made by Fielding in 1753 in his paper,
' A proposal for making an effectual provision for the poor,
for amending their morals, and for rendering them useful
members of society.' Fielding proposed the erection of a
county workhouse, which was to include a house of correction.
He drew up a sharp and drastic code which would have
authorised the committal to his County House, not only of
vagrants, but of persons of low degree found harbouring in
an ale-house after ten o'clock at night. But the workhouse
was not merely to be used as a penal settlement, it was to find
work for the unemployed. Any person who was unable to
find employment in his parish could apply to the minister or
churchwardens for a pass, and this pass was to give him the
right to claim admission to the County House where he was to
be employed. The County House was also to be provided
with instructors who could teach native and foreign manu-
factures to the inmates. Howlett, one of Pitt's critics,
was probably right in thinking that Pitt was reviving this
scheme.

The Bill excited general opposition. Bentham's analysis
is the most famous of the criticisms that have survived,
but in some senses his opposition was less serious than the
dismay of magistrates and ratepayers. Hostile petitions

poured into the House of Commons from London and from all parts of the country; among others there were petitions from Shrewsbury, Oswestry, Worcester, Bristol, Lincoln, Carmarthen, Bedford, Chester and Godalming.[1]   Howlett attacked the scheme on the ground of the danger of parish jobbery and corruption. Pitt apparently made no attempt to defend his plan, and he surrendered it without a murmur. We are thus left in the curious and disappointing position of having before us a Bill on the most important subject of the day, introduced and abandoned by the Prime Minister without a word or syllable in its defence. Whitbread observed[2] four years later that the Bill was brought in and printed, but never brought under the discussion of the House.   Pitt's excuse is significant: ' He was, as formerly, convinced of its propriety; but many objections had been started to it by those whose opinion he was bound to respect. Inexperienced himself in country affairs, and in the condition of the poor, he was diffident of his own opinion, and would not press the measure upon the attention of the House.'

Poor Law Reform was thus abandoned, but two attempts were made, at the instance of Pitt, one of them with success, to soften the brutalities of the Law of Settlement. Neither proposal made it any easier to gain a settlement, and Pitt very properly declared that they did not go nearly far enough. Pitt had all Adam Smith's just hatred of these restrictions, and in opposing Whitbread's Bill for a minimum wage he pointed to ' a radical amendment ' of the Law of Settlement as the true remedy. He was not the formal author of the Act of 1795, but it may safely be assumed that he was the chief power behind it. This Act[3] provided that nobody was to be removeable until he or she became actually chargeable to the parish. The preamble throws light on the working of the Settlement laws. It declares that ' Many industrious poor persons, chargeable to the parish, township, or   place where they live, merely from want of work there, would in any other place where sufficient employment is to be had, maintain themselves and families without being burthensome to any parish, township, or place ; and such poor persons are for the most part compelled to live in their own parishes, townships, or places, and are not permitted to inhabit else-where, under pretence that they are likely to become charge-

---

[1] *House of Commons Journal.*
[2] *Parliamentary Register*, February 11, 1800.   [3] 35 George III. c. 101.

able to the parish, township, or place into which they go for
the purpose of getting employment, although the labour of
such poor persons might, in many instances, be very beneficial
to such parish, township, or place.' The granting of certificates is thus admitted to have been ineffectual. The same
Act provided that orders of removal were to be suspended
in cases where the pauper was dangerously ill, a provision that
throws some light on the manner in which these orders had
been executed, and that no person should gain a settlement
by paying levies or taxes, in respect of any tenement of a
yearly value of less than ten pounds.[1]

From this time certificates were unnecessary, and if a
labourer moved from Parish A to Parish B he was no longer
liable to be sent back at the caprice of Parish B's officers until
he became actually chargeable, but, of course, if from any
cause he fell into temporary distress, for example, if he were
out of work for a few weeks, unless he could get private aid
from ' the opulent,' he had to return to his old parish. An
attempt was made to remedy this state of things by Mr. Baker
who, in March 1800, introduced a Bill [2] to enable overseers to
assist the deserving but unsettled poor in cases of temporary
distress. He explained that the provisions of the Bill would
apply only to men who could usually keep themselves, but
from the high cost of provisions had to depend on parochial
aid. He found a powerful supporter in Pitt, who argued
that if people had enriched a parish with their industry, it
was unfair that owing to temporary pressure they should
be removed to a place where they were not wanted, and that
it was better for a parish to suffer temporary inconvenience
than for numbers of industrious men to be rendered unhappy
and useless. But in spite of Pitt's unanswerable case, the
Bill, which was denounced by Mr. Buxton as ' oppressive to
the landed interest, by Lord Sheffield as ' subversive of the
whole economy of the country,' by Mr. Ellison as submerging
the middle ranks, and by Sir William Pulteney as being a

[1] For Whitbread's proposals to amend the Law of Settlement in 1807 see next
chapter. An attempt was made in 1819 (59 George III. c. 50) to define and
simplify the conditions under which the hiring of a tenement of £10 annual
value conferred the right to a settlement. The term of residence was extended
to a year, the nature of the tenement was defined, and it was laid down that the
rent must be £10, and paid for a whole year. But so unsuccessful was this piece
of legislation that it was found necessary to pass a second Act six years later
(1826, 6 George IV. c. 57), and a third Act in 1831 (1 William IV. c. 18).

[2] *Senator*, March 1800.

'premium for idleness and extravagance,' was rejected by thirty votes to twenty-three.[1]

ALLOTMENTS

Another policy that was pressed upon the governing class was the policy of restoring to the labourer some of the resources he had lost with enclosure, of putting him in such a position that he was not obliged to depend entirely on the purchasing power of his wages at the shop. This was the aim of the allotment movement. The propaganda failed, but it did not fail for the want of vigorous and authoritative support. We have seen in a previous chapter that Arthur Young awoke in 1801 to the social mischief of depriving the poor of their land and their cows, and that he wanted future Enclosure Acts to be juster and more humane. Cobbett suggested a large scheme of agrarian settlement to Windham in 1806. These proposals had been anticipated by Davies, whose knowledge of the actual life of the poor made him understand the important difference between a total and a partial dependence on wages. 'Hope is a cordial, of which the poor man has especially much need, to cheer his heart in the toilsome journey through life. And the fatal consequence of that policy, which deprives labouring people of the expectation of possessing any property in the soil, must be the extinction of every generous principle in their minds. . . . No gentleman should be permitted to pull down a cottage, until he had first erected another, upon one of Mr. Kent's plans, either on some convenient part of the waste, or on his own estate, with a certain quantity of land annexed.' He praised the Act of Elizabeth which forbade the erection of cottages with less than four acres of land around them, 'that poor people might secure for themselves a maintenance, and not be obliged on the loss of a few days labour to come to the parish,'[2] and urged that this prohibition, which had been repealed in 1775,[3] should be set up again.

---

[1] See Debates in *Senator*, March 31 and April 3, 1800, and *Parliamentary Register*. Cf. for removals for temporary distress, Sir Thomas Bernard's Charge to Overseers in the Hundred of Stoke. Bucks. *Reports on Poor*, vol. i. p. 260. 'With regard to the removal of labourers belonging to other parishes, consider thoroughly what you may lose, and what the individual may suffer, by the removal, before you apply to us on the subject. Where you have had, for a long time, the benefit of their labour, and where all they want is a little *temporary* relief, reflect whether, after so many years spent in your service, this is the *moment* and the *cause*, for removing them from the scene of their daily labour to a distant parish, etc.' (1798).

[2] Davies, pp. 102-4.   [3] 15 George III. c. 32.

The general policy of providing allotments was never tried, but we know something of individual experiments from the Reports of the Society for Bettering the Condition and Increasing the Comforts of the Poor. This society took up the cause of allotments very zealously, and most of the examples of private benevolence seem to have found their way into the pages of its reports.

These experiments were not very numerous. Indeed, the name of Lord Winchilsea recurs so inevitably in every allusion to the subject as to create a suspicion that the movement and his estates were coextensive. This is not the truth, but it is not very wide of the truth, for though Lord Winchilsea had imitators, those imitators were few. The fullest account of his estate in Rutlandshire is given by Sir Thomas Bernard.[1] The estate embraced four parishes—Hambledon, Egleton, Greetham, and Burley on the Hill. The tenants included eighty cottagers possessing one hundred and seventy-four cows. ' About a third part have all their land in severalty ; the rest of them have the use of a cow-pasture in common with others ; most of them possessing a small homestead, adjoining to their cottage ; every one of them having a good garden, and keeping one pig at least, if not more. . . . Of all the rents of the estate, none are more punctually paid than those for the cottagers' land.' In this happy district if a man seemed likely to become a burden on the parish his landlord and neighbours saved the man's self-respect and their own pockets as ratepayers, by setting him up with land and a cow instead. So far from neglecting their work as labourers, these proprietors of cows are described as ' most steady and trusty.' We have a picture of this little community leading a hard but energetic and independent life, the men going out to daily work, but busy in their spare hours with their cows, sheep, pigs, and gardens ; the women and children looking after the live stock, spinning, or working in the gardens : a very different picture from that of the landless and ill-fed labourers elsewhere.

Other landlords, who, acting on their own initiative, or at the instance of their agents, helped their cottagers by letting them land on which to keep cows were Lord Carrington and Lord Scarborough in Lincolnshire, and Lord Egremont on his Yorkshire estates (Kent was his agent). Some who were friendly to the allotments movement thought it a mistake to give allotments of arable land in districts where pasture land was not

[1] *Reports on Poor*, vol. ii. p. 171.

available. Mr. Thompson, who writes the account of Lord Carrington's cottagers with cows, thought that ' where cottagers occupy arable land, it is very rarely of advantage to them, and generally a prejudice to the estate.' [1]   He seems, however, to have been thinking more of small holdings than of allotments. ' The late Abel Smith, Esq., from motives of kindness to several cottagers on his estates in Nottinghamshire, let to each of them a small piece of arable land.   I have rode over that estate with Lord Carrington several times since it descended to him, and I have invariably observed that the tenants upon it, who occupy only eight or ten acres of arable land, are poor, and their land in bad condition. They would thrive more and enjoy greater comfort with the means of keeping two or three cows each than with three times their present quantity of arable land ; but it would be a greater mortification to them to be deprived of it than their landlord is disposed to inflict.' [2]   On the other hand, a striking instance of successful arable allotments is described by a Mr. Estcourt in the Reports of the Society for Bettering the Condition of the Poor.[3] The scene was the parish of Long Newnton in Wilts, which contained one hundred and forty poor persons, chiefly agricultural labourers, distributed in thirty-two families, and the year was 1800. The price of provisions was very high, and ' though all had a very liberal allowance from the poor rate ' the whole village was plunged in debt and misery. From this hopeless plight the parish was rescued by an allotment scheme that Mr. Estcourt established and described. Each cottager who applied was allowed to rent a small quantity of land at the rate of £1, 12s. an acre [4] on a fourteen years' lease : the quantity of land let to an applicant depended on the number in his family, with a maximum of one and a half acres : the tenant was to forfeit his holding if he received poor relief other than medical relief.   The offer was greedily accepted, two widows with large families and four very old and infirm persons being the only persons who did not apply for a lease. A loan of £44 was divided among the tenants to free them from their debts and give them a fresh start. They were allowed a third of their plot on Lady Day 1801, a second third on Lady Day 1802, and the remainder on Lady Day 1803. The results as recorded in 1805 were

---

[1] *Reports on Poor*, vol. ii. p. 136.   [2] *Ibid.*, p. 137.

[3] *Ibid.*, vol. v. p. 66.

[4] Mr. Estcourt mentions that the land ' would let to a farmer at about 20s. per acre now.'

astonishing.   None of the tenants had received any poor relief : all the conditions had been observed : the loan of £44 had long been repaid and the poor rate had fallen from £212, 16s. to £12, 6s.   'They are so much beforehand with the world that it is supposed that it must be some calamity still more severe than any they have ever been afflicted with that could put them under the necessity of ever applying for relief to the parish again. . . . The farmers of this parish allow that they never had their work better done, their servants more able, willing, civil, and sober, and that their property was never so free from depredation as at present.' [1]

Some philanthropists, full of the advantages to the poor of possessing live-stock, argued that it was a good thing for cottagers to keep cows even in arable districts.   Sir Henry Vavasour wrote an account in 1801 [2] of one of his cottagers who managed to keep two cows and two pigs and make a profit of £30 a year on three acres three perches of arable with a summer's gait for one of his cows.   The man, his wife, and his daughter of twelve worked on the land in their spare hours. The Board of Agriculture offered gold medals in 1801 for the best report of how to keep one or two cows on arable land, and Sir John Sinclair wrote an essay on the subject, reproduced in the account of ' Useful Projects ' in the *Annual Register*.[3] Sir John Sinclair urged that if the system was generally adopted it would remove the popular objections to enclosure.

Other advocates of the policy of giving the labourers land pleaded only for gardens in arable districts ; ' a garden,' wrote Lord Winchilsea, ' may be allotted to them in almost every situation, and will be found of infinite use to them.   In countries, where it has never been the custom for labourers to keep cows, it may be difficult to introduce it ; but where no gardens have been annexed to the cottages, it is sufficient to give the ground, and the labourer is sure to know what to do with it, and will reap an immediate benefit from it.   Of this I have had experience in several places, particularly in two parishes near Newport Pagnell, Bucks, where there never have been any gardens annexed to the labourers' houses, and where, upon land being allotted to them, they all, without a single exception, have cultivated their gardens extremely well, and profess receiving

[1] It is interesting to find that these allotments were still being let out success-fully in 1868. See p. 4145 of the Report on the Employment of Children, Young Persons, and Women in Agriculture, 1868.

[2] *Reports on Poor*, vol. iii. p. 329.   [3] 1803, p. 850.

the greatest benefits from them.' [1] ' A few roods of land, at a fair rent,' wrote a correspondent in the *Annals of Agriculture* in 1796,[2] ' would do a labourer as much good as wages almost doubled : there would not, then, be an idle hand in his family, and the man himself would often go to work in his root yard instead of going to the ale house.' [3] The interesting report on the ' Inquiry into the General State of the Poor ' presented at the Epiphany General Quarter Sessions for Hampshire and published in the *Annals of Agriculture*,[4] a document which does not display too much indulgence to the shortcomings of labourers, recommends the multiplication of cottages with small pieces of ground annexed, so that labourers might live nearer their work, and spend the time often wasted in going to and from their work, in cultivating their plot of ground at home. ' As it is chiefly this practice which renders even the state of slavery in the West Indies tolerable, what an advantage would it be to the state of free service here ! ' [5]

The experiments in the provision of allotments of any kind were few, and they are chiefly interesting for the light they reflect on the character of the labourer of the period. They show of what those men and women were capable whose degradation in the morass of the Speenhamland system is the last and blackest page in the history of the eighteenth century. Their rulers put a stone round their necks, and it was not their character but their circumstances that dragged them into the mire. In villages where allotments were tried the agricultural labourer is an upright and self-respecting figure. The immediate moral effects were visible enough at the time. Sir Thomas Bernard's account of the cottagers on Lord Winchilsea's estate contains the following reflections : ' I do not mean to assert that the English cottager, narrowed as he now is in the means and habits of life, may be immediately capable of taking that active and useful station in society, that is filled by those who are the subject of this paper. To produce so great an improvement in character and circumstances of life,

---

[1] *Reports on Poor*, vol. i. p. 100.   [2] Vol. xxvi. p. 4.

[3] The most distinguished advocate of this policy was William Marshall, the agricultural writer who published a strong appeal for the labourers in his book *On the Management of Landed Estates*, 1806, p. 155 ; cf. also Curwen's *Hints*, p. 239 : ' A farther attention to the cottager's comfort is attended with little cost ; I mean giving him a small garden, and planting that as well as the walls of his house with fruit trees.'   [4] Vol. xxv. p. 349.

[5] *Ibid.*, p. 358.

will require time and attention. The cottager, however, of this part of the county of Rutland, *is not of a different species from other English cottagers*; and if he had not been protected and encouraged by his landlord, he would have been the same hopeless and comfortless creature that we see in some other parts of England. The farmer (with the assistance of the steward) would have taken his land; the creditor, his cow and pig; and the workhouse, his family.'[1]

We have seen, in discussing enclosures, that the policy of securing allotments to the labourers in enclosure Acts was defeated by the class interests of the landlords. Why, it may be asked, were schemes such as those of Lord Winchilsea's adopted so rarely in villages already enclosed? These arrangements benefited all parties. There was no doubt about the demand; 'in the greatest part of this kingdom,' wrote one correspondent, 'the cottager would rejoice at being permitted to pay the utmost value given by the farmers, for as much land as would keep a cow, if he could obtain it at that price.'[2] The steadiness and industry of the labourers, stimulated by this incentive, were an advantage both to the landlords and to the farmers. Further, it was well known that in the villages where the labourers had land, poor rates were light.[3] Why was it that a policy with so many recommendations never took root? Perhaps the best answer is given in the following story. Cobbett proposed to the vestry of Bishops Walthams that they should ' ask the Bishop of Winchester to grant an acre of waste land to every married labourer. All, however, but the village schoolmaster voted against it, on the ground . . . that it would make the men " too saucy," that they would " breed more children " and " want higher wages." '[4]

The truth is that enclosures and the new system of farming had set up two classes in antagonism to allotments, the large farmer, who disliked saucy labourers, and the shopkeeper, who knew that the more food the labourer raised on his little estate the less would he buy at the village store. It had been to the interest of a small farmer in the old common-field village to have a number of semi-labourers, semi-owners who could help at the harvest: the large farmer wanted a permanent supply of labour which was absolutely at his command. Moreover, the roundsman system maintained his labourers for him when

---

[1] *Reports on Poor*, vol. ii. p. 184.   [2] *Ibid.*, p. 134.
[3] Cf. *Poor Law Report*, 1817, Appendix G, p. 4.
[4] Capes, *Rural Life in Hampshire*, p. 282.

he did not want them. The strength of the hostility of the
farmers to allotments is seen in the language of those few
landlords who were interested in this policy. Lord Winchilsea
and his friends were always urging philanthropists to proceed
with caution, and to try to reason the farmers out of their
prejudices. The Report of the Poor Law Commission in 1834
showed that these prejudices were as strong as ever. ' We can
do little or nothing to prevent pauperism ; the farmers will
have it : they prefer that the labourers should be slaves ;
they object to their having gardens, saying ' The more they
work for themselves, the less they work for us.' [1] This was
the view of Boys, the writer in agricultural subjects, who,
criticising Kent's declaration in favour of allotments, remarks :
' If farmers in general were to accommodate their labourers
with two acres of land, a cow and two or three pigs, they would
probably have more difficulty in getting their hard work done—
as the cow, land, etc., would enable them to live with less
earnings.' [2] Arthur Young and Nathaniel Kent made a great
appeal to landlords and to landlords' wives to interest themselves in their estates and the people who lived on them, but
landlords' bailiffs did not like the trouble of collecting a
number of small rents, and most landlords preferred to leave
their labourers to the mercy of the farmers. There was,
however, one form of allotment that the farmers themselves
liked : they would let strips of potato ground to labourers,
sometimes at four times the rent they paid themselves, getting
the land manured and dug into the bargain.[3]

The Select Vestry Act of 1819 [4] empowered parishes to buy
or lease twenty acres of land, and to set the indigent poor to
work on it, or to lease it out to any poor and industrious
inhabitant. A later Act of 1831 [5] raised the limit from twenty
to fifty acres, and empowered parishes to enclose fifty acres
of waste (with the consent of those who had rights on it) and
to lease it out for the same purposes. Little use was made of
these Acts, and perhaps the clearest light is thrown on the
extent of the allotment movement by a significant sentence
that occurs in the Report of the Select Committee on Allotments in 1843. ' It was not until 1830, when discontent

---

[1] *Poor Law Report*, 1834, p. 61 ; cf. *ibid.*, p. 185.

[2] Notes to Kent's *Norfolk*, p. 178.

[3] See *Poor Law Report*, 1834, p. 181, and *Allotments Committee*, 1843,
p. 108.   [4] 59 George III. c. 12.

[5] 1 and 2 William IV. c. 42.

had been so painfully exhibited amongst the peasantry of the
southern counties that this method of alleviating their situation
was much resorted to.' In other words, little was done till
labourers desperate with hunger had set the farmers' ricks
blazing.

THE REMEDY ADOPTED. SPEENHAMLAND

The history has now been given of the several proposals
made at this time that for one reason or another fell to the
ground. A minimum wage was not fixed, allotments were
only sprinkled with a sparing hand on an estate here and
there, there was no revolution in diet, the problems of local
supply and distribution were left untouched, the reconstruc-
tion of the Poor Law was abandoned. What means then did
the governing class take to tranquillise a population made
dangerous by hunger ? The answer is, of course, the Speenhamland Act. The Berkshire J.P.'s and some discreet persons
met at the Pelican Inn at Speenhamland [1] on 6th May 1795,
and there resolved on a momentous policy which was gradually adopted in almost every part of England.

There is a strange irony in the story of this meeting which
gave such a fatal impetus to the reduction of wages. It was
summoned in order to raise wages, and so make the labourer
independent of parish relief. At the General Quarter Sessions
for Berkshire held at Newbury on the 14th April, Charles
Dundas, M.P.,[2] in his charge to the Grand Jury [3] dwelt on the
miserable state of the labourers and the necessity of increasing
their wages to subsistence level, instead of leaving them to
resort to the parish officers for support for their families, as
was the case when they worked for a shilling a day. He
quoted the Acts of Elizabeth and James with reference to the
fixing of wages. The Court, impressed by his speech, decided
to convene a meeting for the rating of wages. The advertisement of the meeting shows that this was the only object in
view. 'At the General Quarter Sessions of the Peace for
this county held at Newbury, on Tuesday, the 14th instant,
the Court, having taken into consideration the great In-

---

[1] Speenhamland is now part of Newbury. The Pelican Inn has disappeared,
but the Pelican Posting House survives.

[2] Charles Dundas, afterwards Lord Amesbury, 1751-1832 ; Liberal M.P. for
Berkshire, 1794-1832, nominated by Sheridan for the Speakership in 1802 but
withdrew.

[3] *Reading Mercury*, April 20, 1795.

equality of Labourers' Wages, and the insufficiency of the same for the necessary support of an industrious man and his family ; and it being the opinion of the Gentlemen assembled on the Grand Jury, that many parishes have not advanced their labourers' weekly pay in proportion to the high price of corn and provisions, do (in pursuance of the Acts of Parliament, enabling and requiring them so to do, either at the Easter Sessions, yearly, or within six weeks next after) earnestly request the attendance of the Sheriff, and all the Magistrates of this County, at a Meeting intended to be held at the Pelican Inn in Speenhamland, on Wednesday, the sixth day of May next, at ten o'clock in the forenoon, for the purpose of consulting together with such discreet persons as they shall think meet, and they will then, having respect to the plenty and scarcity of the time, and other circumstances (if approved of) proceed to limit, direct, and appoint the wages of day labourers.' [1]

The meeting was duly held on 6th May.[2] Mr. Charles Dundas was in the chair, and there were seventeen other magistrates and discreet persons present, of whom seven were clergymen. It was resolved unanimously 'that the present state of the poor does require further assistance than has been generally given them.' Of the details of the discussion no records have come down to us, nor do we know by what majority the second and fatal resolution rejecting the rating of wages and substituting an allowance policy was adopted. According to Eden, the arguments in favour of adopting the rating of wages were ' that by enforcing a payment for labour, from the employers, in proportion to the price of bread, some encouragement would have been held out to the labourer, as what he would have received, would have been payment for labour. He would have considered it as his right, and not as charity.' [3] But these arguments were rejected, and a pious recommendation to employers to raise wages, coupled with detailed directions for supplementing those wages from parish funds, adopted instead.[4] The text of the second resolution runs thus : ' Resolved, that it is not expedient for the

---

[1] *Reading Mercury*, April 20, 1795.
[2] See *Ibid.*, May 11, 1795.   [3] Eden, vol. i. p. 578.
[4] On the same day a 'respectable meeting' at Basingstoke, with the Mayor in the chair, was advocating the fixing of labourers' wages in accordance with the price of wheat without any reference to parish relief,—*Reading Mercury*, May 11, 1795.

Magistrates to grant that assistance by regulating the wages of Day Labourers according to the directions of the Statutes of the 5th Elizabeth and 1st James : But the Magistrates very earnestly recommend to the Farmers and others throughout the county to increase the Pay of their Labourers in proportion to the present Price of Provisions ; and agreeable thereto the Magistrates now present have unanimously Resolved, That they will in their several divisions, make the following calculations and allowances for the relief of all poor and industrious men and their families, who, to the satisfaction of the Justices of their parish, shall endeavour (as far as they can), for their own support and maintenance, that is to say, when the gallon loaf of second flour, weighing 8 lbs. 11 oz. shall cost one shilling, then every poor and industrious man shall have for his own support 3s. weekly, either produced by his own or his family's labour or an allowance from the poor rates, and for the support of his wife and every other of his family 1s. 6d. When the gallon loaf shall cost 1s. 4d., then every poor and industrious man shall have 4s. weekly for his own, and 1s. 10d. for the support of every other of his family.

' And so in proportion as the price of bread rises or falls (that is to say), 3d. to the man and 1d. to every other of the family, on every penny which the loaf rises above a shilling.'

In other words, it was estimated that the man must have three gallon loaves a week, and his wife and each child one and a half.

It is interesting to notice that at this same famous Speenhamland meeting the justices ' wishing, as much as possible, to alleviate the Distresses of the Poor with as little burthen on the occupiers of the Land as possible ' recommended overseers to cultivate land for potatoes and to give the workers a quarter of the crop, selling the rest at one shilling a bushel ; overseers were also recommended to purchase fuel and to retail it at a loss.

The Speenhamland policy was not a full-blown invention of that unhappy May morning in the Pelican Inn. The principle had already been adopted elsewhere. At the Oxford Quarter Sessions on 13th January 1795, the justices had resolved that the following incomes were ' absolutely necessary for the support of the poor, industrious labourer, and that when the utmost industry of a family cannot produce the undermentioned sums, it must be made up by the overseer, exclusive of rent, viz. :—

' A single Man according to his labour.

' A Man and his Wife not less than 6s. a week.

' A Man and his Wife with one or two Small Children, not less than 7s. a week.

' And for every additional Child not less than 1s. a week.' This regulation was to be sent to all overseers within the county.[1]

But the Speenhamland magistrates had drawn up a table which became a convenient standard, and other magistrates found it the simplest course to accept the table as it stood. The tables passed rapidly from county to county. The allowance system spread like a fever, for while it is true to say that the northern counties took it much later and in a milder form, there were only two counties still free from it in 1834—Northumberland and Durham.

To complete our picture of the new system we must remember the results of Gilbert's Act. It had been the practice in those parishes that adopted the Act to reserve the workhouse for the infirm and to find work outside for the unemployed, the parish receiving the wages of such employment and providing maintenance. This outside employment had spread to other parishes, and the way in which it had been worked may be illustrated by cases mentioned by Eden, writing in the summer and autumn of 1795. At Kibworth-Beauchamp in Leicestershire, ' in the winter, and at other times, when a man is out of work, he applies to the overseer, who sends him from house to house to get employ : the housekeeper, who employs him, is obliged to give him victuals, and 6d. a day ; and the parish adds 4d.; (total 10d. a day;) for the support of his family: persons working in this manner are called rounds-men, from their going round the village or township for employ.' [2] At Yardley Goben, in Northamptonshire, every person who paid more than £20 rent was bound in his turn to employ a man for a day and to pay him a shilling.[3] At Maids Morton the roundsman got 6d. from the employer and 6d. or 9d. from the parish.[4] At Winslow in Bucks the system was more fully developed. ' There seems to be here a great want of employment : most labourers are (as it is termed,) *on the Rounds* ; that is, they go to work from one house to another *round* the parish. In winter, sometimes 40 persons are on the rounds. They are wholly paid by the parish, unless the householders choose to employ them ; and from these circumstances, labourers often become very lazy, and imperious. Children, about ten years old, are put

[1] See *Ipswich Journal*, February 7, 1795, and *Reading Mercury*, July 6, 1795.
[2] Eden, vol. ii. p. 384.   [3] *Ibid.*, p. 548.   [4] *Ibid.*, p. 27.

on the rounds, and receive from the parish from 1s. 6d. to 3s. a week.' [1] The Speenhamland systematised scale was easily grafted on to these arrangements. 'During the late dear season, the Poor of the parish went in a body to the Justices, to complain of their want of bread. The Magistrates sent orders to the parish officers to raise the earnings of labourers, to certain weekly sums, according to the number of their children ; a circumstance that should invariably be attended to in apportioning parochial relief. These sums were from 7s. to 19s. ; and were to be reduced, proportionably with the price of bread.' [2]

The Speenhamland system did not then spring Athene-like out of the heads of the justices and other discreet persons whose place of meeting has given the system its name. Neither was the unemployment policy thereafter adopted a sudden inspiration of the Parliament of 1796. The importance of these years is that though the governing classes did not then introduce a new principle, they applied to the normal case methods of relief and treatment that had hitherto been reserved for the exceptions. The Poor Law which had once been the hospital became now the prison of the poor. Designed to relieve his necessities, it was now his bondage. If a labourer was in private employment, the difference between the wage his master chose to give him and the recognised minimum was made up by the parish. Those labourers who could not find private employment were either shared out among the ratepayers, or else their labour was sold by the parish to employers, at a low rate, the parish contributing what was needed to bring the labourers' receipts up to scale. Crabbe has described the roundsman system :

' Alternate Masters now their Slave command,
  Urge the weak efforts of his feeble hand,
  And when his age attempts its task in vain,
  With ruthless taunts, of lazy poor complain.' [3]

The meshes of the Poor Law were spread over the entire labour system. The labourers, stripped of their ancient rights and their ancient possessions, refused a minimum wage and allotments, were given instead a universal system of pauperism. This was the basis on which the governing class rebuilt the English village. Many critics, Arthur Young and Malthus among them, assailed it, but it endured for forty years, and it was not disestablished until Parliament itself had passed through a revolution.

[1] Eden, vol. ii. p. 29.   [2] *Ibid.*, p. 32.   [3] 'The Village,' Book I.

CHAPTER VIII

AFTER SPEENHAMLAND

THE Speenhamland system is often spoken of as a piece of pardonable but disastrous sentimentalism on the part of the upper classes. This view overlooks the predicament in which these classes found themselves at the end of the eighteenth century. We will try to reconstruct the situation and to reproduce their state of mind. Agriculture, which had hitherto provided most people with a livelihood, but few people with vast fortunes, had become by the end of the century a great capitalist and specialised industry. During the French war its profits were fabulous, and they were due partly to enclosures, partly to the introduction of scientific methods, partly to the huge prices caused by the war. It was producing thus a vast surplus over and above the product necessary for mainten-ance and for wear and tear. Consequently, as students of Mr. Hobson's *Industrial System* will perceive, there arose an important social problem of distribution, and the Poor Law was closely involved with it.

This industry maintained, or helped to maintain, four principal interests : the landlords, the tithe-owners, the farmers, and the labourers. Of these interests the first two were repre-sented in the governing class, and in considering the mind of that class we may merge them into one. The sympathies of the farmers were rather with the landlords than with the labourers, but their interests were not identical. The labourers were unrepresented either in the Government or in the voting power of the nation. If the forces had been more equally matched, or if Parliament had represented all classes, the surplus income of agriculture would have gone to increase rents, tithes, profits, and wages. It might, besides turning the landlords into great magnates like the cotton lords of Lancashire, and throwing up a race of farmers with scarlet coats and jack boots, have raised permanently the standard and character of the labouring class, have given them a decent wage and decent cottages. The village population whose condition, as Whitbread said, was compared by supporters of the slave trade with that of the negroes in the West Indies, to its disadvantage, might have been rehoused on its share of this tremendous revenue. In fact, the revenue went solely to increase rent, tithes, and to some extent profits. The labourers alone had made no advance when the halcyon days of the industry clouded over and prices fell. The rent receiver received more rent than was needed to induce him to let his land, the farmer made larger profits than were necessary to induce him to apply his capital and ability to farming, but the labourer received less than was necessary to maintain him, the balance being made up out of the rates. Thus not only did the labourer receive no share of this surplus ; he did not even get his subsistence directly from the product of his labour. Now let us suppose that instead of having his wages made up out of the rates he had been paid a maintenance wage by the farmer. The extra cost would have come out of rent to the same extent as did the subsidy from the rates. The landlord therefore made no sacrifice in introducing the Speenhamland system, for though the farmers thought that they could obtain a reduction of rent more easily if they could plead high rates than if they pleaded the high price of labour,[1] it is obvious that the same conditions which produced a reduction of rents in the one case must ultimately have produced a reduction in the other. As it was, none of this surplus went to labour, and the proportion in which it was divided between landlord and farmer was not affected by the fact that the labourer was kept alive partly from the rates and not wholly from wages.[2]

Now the governing class which was confronted with the situation that we have described in a previous chapter consisted of two classes who had both contrived to slip off their obligations to the State. They were both essentially privileged classes. The landlords were not in the eye of history absolute owners ; they had held their land on several conditions, one of which was the liability to provide military services for the Crown, and this obligation they had commuted into a tax on the nation. Neither were the tithe-owners absolute owners in the eye of history. In early days all Church property was regarded as the patrimony of the poor, and the clergy were

[1] *Poor Law Report*, 1834, p. 60.
[2] The big landlord under this method shared the privilege of paying the labourer's wages with the smaller farmer.

bidden to use it *non quasi suis sed quasi commendatis.*
Dryden, in drawing the character of the Good Parson, had
described their obligations :

> ‘ True priests, he said, and preachers of the Word
> Were only stewards of their sovereign Lord :
> Nothing was theirs but all the public store,
> Intrusted riches to relieve the poor.’

It was recognised, as late as the reign of Henry iv., that
tithes were designed among other objects for the relief of the
poor.   An Act of that reign confirmed an earlier Act of
Richard ii. (15 Rich. ii. c. 6), which laid down that on the
appropriation of any parish church, money was to be paid
yearly of the fruits and profits of the said church to the
poor parishioners.   After this time the claims of the poor
fade from view.   Of course, great masses of tithe property had passed, by the time we are considering, into
secular hands.   The monasteries appropriated about a third
of the livings of England, and the tithes in these parishes
passed at the Reformation to the Crown, whence they passed
in grants to private persons.   No responsibility for the poor
troubled either the lay or spiritual owners of tithes, and though
they used the name of God freely in defending their claims,
they were stewards of God in much the same sense as George iv.
was the defender of the faith.   The landowners and tithe-
owners had their differences when it came to an Enclosure
Bill, but these classes had the same interests in the disposal
of the surplus profits of agriculture ; and both alike were in
a vulnerable position if the origin and history of their property
came under too fierce a discussion.

There was a special reason why the classes that had suddenly
become very much richer should dread too searching a discontent at this moment.   They had seen tithes, and all
seignorial dues abolished almost at a single stroke across the
Channel, and they were at this time associating constantly
with the emigrant nobility of France, whose prospect of re-
covering their estates seemed to fade into a more doubtful
distance with every battle that was fought between the
France who had given the poor peasant such a position as the
peasant enjoyed nowhere else, and her powerful neighbour
who had made her landlords the richest and proudest class
in Europe.   The French Convention had passed a decree
(November 1792), declaring that ‘ wherever French armies
shall come, all taxes, tithes, and privileges of rank are to be

abolished, all existing authorities cancelled, and provisional administrations elected by universal suffrage. The property of the fallen Government, of the privileged classes and their adherents to be placed under French protection.' This last sentence had an unpleasant ring about it; it sounded like a terse paraphrase of *non quasi suis sed quasi commendatis*. In point of fact there was not yet any violent criticism of the basis of the social position of the privileged classes in England. Even Paine, when he suggested a scheme of Old Age Pensions for all over fifty, and a dowry for every one on reaching the age of twenty-one, had proposed to finance it by death duties. Thelwall, who wrote with a not unnatural bitterness about the great growth of ostentatious wealth at a time when the poor were becoming steadily poorer, told a story which illustrated very well the significance of the philanthropy of the rich. ' I remember I was once talking to a friend of the charity and benevolence exhibited in this country, when stopping me with a sarcastic sneer, " Yes," says he, " we steal the goose, and we give back the giblets." " No," said a third person who was standing by, " giblets are much too dainty for the common herd, we give them only the pen feathers." ' [1] But the literature of Radicalism was not inflammatory, and the demands of the dispossessed were for something a good deal less than their strict due. The richer classes, however, were naturally anxious to soothe and pacify the poor before discontent spread any further, and the Speenhamland system turned out, from their point of view, a very admirable means to that end, for it provided a maintenance for the poor by a method which sapped their spirit and disarmed their independence. They were anxious that the labourers should not get into the way of expecting a larger share in the profits of agriculture, and at the same time they wanted to make them contented. Thelwall [2] stated that when he was in the Isle of Wight, the farmers came to a resolution to raise the price of labour, and that they were dissuaded by one of the greatest proprietors in the island, who called a meeting and warned the farmers that they would make the common people insolent and would never be able to reduce their wages again.

An account of the introduction of the system into Warwickshire and Worcestershire illustrates very well the state of mind in which this policy had its origin. ' In Warwickshire, the year 1797 was mentioned as the date of its commencement in that

[1] *Tribune*, vol. ii. p. 317.   [2] *Ibid.*, p. 339.

county, and the scales of relief giving it authority were published in each of these counties previously to the year 1800. It was apprehended by many at that time, that either the wages of labour would rise to a height from which it would be difficult to reduce them when the cause for it had ceased, or that during the high prices the labourers might have had to endure privations to which it would be unsafe to expose them. To meet the emergency of the time, various schemes are said to have been adopted, such as weekly distributions of flour, providing families with clothes, or maintaining entirely a portion of their families, until at length the practice became general, and a right distinctly admitted by the magistrates was claimed by the labourer to parish relief, on the ground of inadequate wages and number in family. I was informed that the consequences of the system were not wholly unforeseen at the time, as affording a probable inducement to early marriages and large families; but at this period there was but little apprehension on that ground. A prevalent opinion, supported by high authority, that population was in itself a source of wealth, precluded all alarm. The demands for the public service were thought to endure a sufficient draught for any surplus people; and it was deemed wise by many persons at this time to present the Poor Laws to the lower classes, as an institution for their advantage, peculiar to this country; and to encourage an opinion among them, that by this means their own share in the property of the kingdom was recognised.' [1] To the landlords the Speenhamland system was a safety-valve in two ways. The farmers got cheap labour, and the labourers got a maintenance, and it was hoped thus to reconcile both classes to high rents and the great social splendour of their rulers. There was no encroachment on the surplus profits of agriculture, and landlords and tithe-owners basked in the sunshine of prosperity. It would be a mistake to represent the landlords as deliberately treating the farmers and the labourers on the principle which Cæsar boasted that he had applied with such success, when he borrowed money from his officers to give it to his soldiers, and thus contrived to attach both classes to his interest; but that was in effect the result and the significance of the Speenhamland system.

This wrong application of those surplus profits was one element in the violent oscillations of trade during the generation after the war. A long war adding enormously to the

[1] Poor Law Commission Report of 1834, p. 126.

expenditure of Government must disorganise industry seriously in any case, and in this case the demoralisation was increased by a bad currency system. The governing class, which was continually meditating on the subject of agricultural distress, holding inquiries, and appointing committees, never conceived the problem as one of distribution. The Select Committee of 1833 on Agriculture, for example, expressly disclaims any interest in the question of rents and wages, treating these as determined by a law of Nature, and assuming that the only question for a Government was the question of steadying prices by protection. What they did not realise was that a bad distribution of profits was itself a cause of disturbance. The most instructive speech on the course of agriculture during the French war was that in which Brougham showed in the House of Commons, on 9th April 1816, how the country had suffered from over-production during the wild elation of high prices, and how a tremendous system of speculative farming had been built up, entangling a variety of interests in this gamble. If those days had been employed to raise the standard of life among the labourers and to increase their powers of consumption, the subsequent fall would have been broken. The economists of the time looked on the millions of labourers as an item of cost, to be regarded like the price of raw material, whereas it is clear that they ought to have been regarded also as affording the best and most stable of markets. The landlord or the banker who put his surplus profits into the improvement and cultivation of land, only productive under conditions that could not last and could not return, was increasing unemployment in the future, whereas if the same profits had been distributed in wages among the labourers, they would have permanently increased consumption and steadied the vicissitudes of trade. Further, employment would have been more regular in another respect, for the landowner spent his surplus on luxuries, and the labourer spent his wages on necessaries.

Now labour might have received its share of these profits either in an increase of wages, or in the expenditure of part of the revenue in a way that was specially beneficial to it. Wages did not rise, and it was a felony to use any pressure to raise them. What was the case of the poor in regard to taxation and expenditure? Taxation was overwhelming. A Herefordshire farmer stated that in 1815 the rates and taxes on a farm of three hundred acres in that county were :—

	£	s.	d.
Property tax, landlord and tenant . . .	95	16	10
Great tithes	64	17	6
Lesser tithes	29	15	0
Land tax	14	0	0
Window lights	24	1	6
Poor rates, landlord	10	0	0
Poor rates, tenant	40	0	0
Cart-horse duty, landlord, 3 horses . . .	2	11	0
Two saddle horses, landlord	9	0	0
Gig	6	6	0
Cart-horse duty, tenant	7	2	0
One saddle horse, tenant	2	13	6
Landlord's malt duty on 60 bushels of barley .	21	0	0
Tenant's duty for making 120 bushels of barley into malt	42	0	0
New rate for building shire hall, paid by landlord	9	0	0
New rate for building shire hall, paid by tenant .	3	0	0
Surcharge	2	8	0
	£383	11	4[1]

The *Agricultural and Industrial Magazine*, a periodical published by a philanthropical society in 1833, gave the following analysis of the taxation of a labourer earning £22, 10s. a year :—

		£	s.	d.
1.	Malt	4	11	3
2.	Sugar	0	17	4
3.	Tea and Coffee	1	4	0
4.	Soap	0	13	0
5.	Housing	0	12	0
6.	Food	3	0	0
7.	Clothes	0	10	0
		£11	7	7

But in the expenditure from this taxation was there a single item in which the poor had a special interest ?   The great mass of the expenditure was war expenditure, and that was not expenditure in which the poor were more interested than the

[1] See Curtler's *Short History of Agriculture*, p. 249.

rest. Indeed, much of it was expenditure which could not be associated directly or indirectly with their interests, such as the huge subsidies to the courts of Europe. Nearly fifty millions went in these subventions, and if some of them were strategical others were purely political. Did the English labourer receive any profit from the two and a half millions that Pitt threw to the King of Prussia, a subsidy that was employed for crushing Kosciusko and Poland, or from the millions that he gave to Austria, in return for which Austria ceded Venice to Napoleon? Did he receive any benefit from the million spent every year on the German legion, which helped to keep him in order in his own country? Did he receive any benefit from the million and a half which, on the confession of the Finance Committee of the House of Commons in 1810, went every year in absolute sinecures? Did he receive any benefit from the interest on the loans to the great bankers and contractors, who made huge profits out of the war and were patriotic enough to lend money to the Government to keep it going? Did he receive any benefit from the expenditure on crimping boys or pressing seamen, or transporting and imprisoning poachers and throwing their families by thousands on the rates? Pitt's brilliant idea of buying up a cheap debt out of money raised by a dear one cost the nation twenty millions, and though Pitt considered the Sinking Fund his best title to honour, nobody will pretend that the poor of England gained anything from this display of his originality.[1] In these years Government was raising by taxation or loans over a hundred millions, but not a single penny went to the education of the labourer's children, or to any purpose that made the perils and difficulties of his life more easy to be borne. If the sinecures had been reduced by a half, or if the great money-lenders had been treated as if their claims to the last penny were not sacrosanct, and had been made to take their share of the losses of the time, it would have been possible to set up the English cottager with allotments on the modest plan proposed by Young or Cobbett, side by side with the great estates with which that expenditure endowed the bankers and the dealers in scrip.

Now, so long as prices kept up, the condition of the labourer was masked by the general prosperity of the times. The governing class had found a method which checked the demand for

[1] Smart, *Economic Annals*, p. 36.

higher wages and the danger that the labourer might claim a share in the bounding wealth of the time. The wolf was at the door, it is true, but he was chained, and the chain was the Speenhamland system. Consequently, though we hear complaints from the labourers, who contended that they were receiving in a patronising and degrading form what they were entitled to have as their direct wages, the note of rebellion was smothered for the moment. At this time it was a profitable proceeding to grow corn on almost any soil, and it is still possible to trace on the unharvested downs of Dartmoor the print of the plough that turned even that wild moorland into gold, in the days when Napoleon was massing his armies for invasion. During these years parishes did not mind giving aid from the rates on the Speenhamland scale, and, though under this mischievous system population was advancing wildly, there was such a demand for labour that this abundance did not seem, as it seemed later, a plague of locusts, but a source of strength and wealth. The opinion of the day was all in favour of a heavy birth rate, and it was generally agreed, as we have seen, that Pitt's escapades in the West Indies and elsewhere would draw off the surplus population fast enough to remove all difficulties. But although the large farmers prayed incessantly to heaven to preserve Pitt and to keep up religion and prices, the day came when it did not pay to plough the downs or the sands, and tumbling prices brought ruin to the farmers whose rents and whole manner of living were fixed on the assumption that there was no serious danger of peace, and that England was to live in a perpetual heyday of famine prices.

With the fall in prices, the facts of the labourer's condition were disclosed. Doctors tell us that in some cases of heart disease there is a state described as compensation, which may postpone failure for many years. With the fall in 1814 compensation ceased, and the disease which it obscured declared itself. For it was now no longer possible to absorb the redundant population in the wasteful roundsman system, and the maintenance standard tended to fall with the growing pressure on the resources from which the labourer was kept. By this time all labour had been swamped in the system. The ordinary village did not contain a mass of decently paid labourers and a surplus of labourers, from time to time redundant, for whom the parish had to provide as best it could. It contained a mass of labourers, all of them underpaid, whom the parish had to keep alive in the way most convenient to the farmers. Bishop

Berkeley once said that it was doubtful whether the prosperity that preceded, or the calamities that succeeded, the South Sea Bubble had been the more disastrous to Great Britain : that saying would very well apply to the position of the agricultural labourer in regard to the rise and the fall of prices. With the rise of prices the last patch of common agriculture had been seized by the landlords, and the labourer had been robbed even of his garden ; [1] with the fall, the great mass of labourers were thrown into destitution and misery. We may add that if that prosperity had been briefer, the superstition that an artificial encouragement of population was needed—the superstition of the rich for which the poor paid the penalty— would have had a shorter life. As it was, at the end of the great prosperity the landlords were enormously rich ; rents had in some cases increased five-fold between 1790 and 1812 : [2] the large farmers had in many cases climbed into a style of life which meant a crash as soon as prices fell ; the financiers had made great and sudden fortunes ; the only class for whom a rise in the standard of existence was essential to the nation, had merely become more dependent on the pleasure of other classes and the accidents of the markets. The purchasing power of the labourer's wages had gone down.

The first sign of the strain is the rioting of 1816. In that year the spirit which the governing class had tried to send to sleep by the Speenhamland system, burst out in the first of two peasants' revolts. Let us remember what their position was. They were not the only people overwhelmed by the fall in prices. Some landlords, who had been so reckless and extravagant as to live up to the enormous revenue they were receiving, had to surrender their estates to the new class of bankers and money-lenders that had been made powerful by the war. Many farmers, who had taken to keeping liveried servants and to copying the pomp of their landlords, and who had staked everything on the permanence of prices, were now submerged. Small farmers too, as the answers sent to the questions issued this year by the Board of Agriculture show, became paupers. The labourer was not the only sufferer. But he differed

---

[1] 'It was during the war that the cottagers of England were chiefly deprived of the little pieces of land and garden, and made solely dependent for subsistence on the wages of their daily labour, or the poor rates. Land, and the produce of it, had become so valuable, that the labourer was envied the occupation of the smallest piece of ground which he possessed : and even "the bare-worn common" was denied.'—*Kentish Chronicle*, December 14, 1830.   [2] Curtler, p. 243.

from the other victims of distress in that he had not benefited, but, as we have seen, had lost, by the prosperity of the
days when the plough turned a golden furrow. His housing
had not been improved; his dependence had not been made
less abject or less absolute; his wages had not risen; and in
many cases his garden had disappeared. When the storm
broke over agriculture his condition became desperate. In
February 1816 the Board of Agriculture sent out a series of
questions, one of which asked for an account of the state of
the poor, and out of 273 replies 237 reported want of employment and distress, and 25 reported that there was not
unemployment or distress.[1] One of the correspondents
explained that in his district the overseer called a meeting
every Saturday, when he put up each labourer by name to
auction, and they were let generally at from 1s. 6d. to 2s. per
week and their provisions, their families being supported by
the parish.[2]

In 1816 the labourers were suffering both from unemployment and from high prices. In 1815, as the *Annual Register* [3]
puts it, ' much distress was undergone in the latter part of the
year by the trading portion of the community. This source of
private calamity was unfortunately coincident with an extraordinary decline in agricultural prosperity, immediately
proceeding from the greatly reduced price of corn and other
products, which bore no adequate proportion to the exorbitant
rents and other heavy burdens pressing upon the farmer.' At
the beginning of 1816 there were gloomy anticipations of a fall
in prices, and Western [4] moved a series of resolutions designed
to prevent the importation of corn. But as the year advanced
it became evident that the danger that threatened England
was not the danger of abundance but the danger of scarcity.
A bitterly cold summer was followed by so meagre a harvest
that the price of corn rose rapidly beyond the point at which
the ports were open for importation. But high prices which
brought bidders at once for farms that had been unlet made
bread and meat dear to the agricultural labourer, without
bringing him more employment or an advance of wages, and
the riots of 1816 were the result of the misery due to this
combination of misfortunes.

---

[1] *Agricultural State of the Kingdom*, Board of Agriculture, 1816, p. 7.
[2] *Ibid.*, pp. 250-1.   [3] P. 144.
[4] C. C. Western (1767-1844); whig M.P., 1790-1832; chief representative of
agricultural interests; made peer in 1833.

The riots broke out in May of that year, and the counties affected were Norfolk, Suffolk, Huntingdon and Cambridgeshire. Nightly assemblies were held, threatening letters were sent, and houses, barns and ricks were set on fire. These fires were a prelude to a more determined agitation, which had such an effect on the authorities that the Sheriff of Suffolk and Mr. Willet, a banker of Brandon near Bury, hastened to London to inform the Home Secretary and to ask for the help of the Government in restoring tranquillity. Mr. Willet's special interest in the proceedings is explained in a naïve sentence in the *Annual Register*: ' A reduction in the price of bread and meat was the avowed object of the rioters. They had fixed a maximum for the price of both. They insisted that the lowest price of wheat must be half a crown a bushel, and that of prime joints of beef fourpence per pound. Mr. Willet, a butcher at Brandon, was a marked object of their ill-will, in which Mr. Willet, the banker, was, from the similarity of his name, in danger of sharing. This circumstance, and a laudable anxiety to preserve the public peace, induced him to take an active part and exert all his influence for that purpose.' [1] The rioters numbered some fifteen hundred, and they broke up into separate parties, scattering into different towns and villages. In the course of their depredations the house of the right Mr. Willet was levelled to the ground, after which the wrong Mr. Willet, it is to be hoped, was less restless.[2] ' They were armed with long, heavy sticks, the ends of which, to the extent of several inches, were studded with short iron spikes, sharp at the sides and point. Their flag was inscribed " *Bread or Blood!* " and they threatened to march to London.' [3]

During the next few days there were encounters between insurgent mobs in Norwich and Bury and the yeomanry, the dragoons, and the West Norfolk Militia. No lives seem to have been lost, but a good deal of property was destroyed, and a number of rioters were taken into custody. The *Times* of 25th May says, in an article on these riots, that wages had been reduced to a rate lower than the magistrates thought

---

[1] *Annual Register*, 1816, Chron., p. 67.

[2] The disturbances at Brandon ceased immediately on the concession of the demands of the rioters; flour was reduced to 2s. 6d. a stone, and wages were raised for two weeks to 2s. a head. The rioters were contented, and peace was restored.—*Times*, May 23, 1816.

[3] *Annual Register*, 1816, Chron., p. 67.

reasonable, for the magistrates, after suppressing a riot near Downham, acquiesced in the propriety of raising wages, and released the offenders who had been arrested with a suitable remonstrance. There was a much more serious battle at Littleport in the Isle of Ely, when the old fighting spirit of the fens seems to have inspired the rioters. They began by driving from his house a clergyman magistrate of the name of Vachel, after which they attacked several houses and extorted money. They then made for Ely, where they carried out the same programme. This state of anarchy, after two or three days, ended in a battle in Littleport in which two rioters were killed, and seventy-five taken prisoners. The prisoners were tried next month by a Special Commission : twenty-four were capitally convicted; of these five were hung, five were transported for life, one was transported for fourteen years, three for seven years, and ten were imprisoned for twelve months in Ely gaol.[1] The spirit in which one of the judges, Mr. Christian, the Chief Justice of the Isle of Ely, conducted the proceedings may be gathered from his closing speech, in which he said that the rioters were receiving ' great wages ' and that ' any change in the price of provisions could only lessen that superfluity, which, I fear, they too frequently wasted in drunkenness.' [2]

The pressure of the changed conditions of the nation on this system of maintenance out of the rates is seen, not only in the behaviour of the labourers, but also in the growing anxiety of the upper classes to control the system, and in the tenacity with which the parishes contested settlement claims. This is the great period of Poor Law litigation. Parish authorities kept a stricter watch than ever on immigrants. In 1816, for example, the Board of Agriculture reported that according to a correspondent ' a late legal decision, determining that keeping a cow gained a settlement, has deprived many cottagers of that comfort, as it is properly called.' [3] This decision was remedied by the 1819 Act [4] to amend the Settlement Laws

[1] *Cambridge Chronicle*, June 28, 1816.

[2] *Times*, June 26. A curious irony has placed side by side with the account in the *Annual Register* of the execution of the five men who were hung for their share in this spasm of starvation and despair, the report of a meeting, with the inevitable Wilberforce in the chair, for raising a subscription for rebuilding the Protestant Church at Copenhagen, which had been destroyed by the British Fleet at the bombardment of Copenhagen in 1807.

[3] *Agricultural State of the Kingdom*, p. 13.   [4] 59 George III. c. 50,

as regards renting tenements, and the Report on the Poor Law in 1819 states that in consequence there 'will no longer be an obstacle to the accommodation which may be afforded in some instances to a poor family, by renting the pasturage of a cow, or some other temporary profit from the occupation of land.'[1] Lawsuits between parishes were incessant, and in 1815 the money spent on litigation and the removal of paupers reached the gigantic figure of £287,000.

In Parliament, too, the question of Poor Law Reform was seen to be urgent, but the problem assumed a particular and very limited shape. The significance of this development can be illustrated by comparing the character and the fate of a measure Whitbread had introduced in 1807 with the character and the fate of the legislation after Waterloo.

Whitbread's scheme had aimed at (1) improving and humanising the Law of Settlement ; (2) reforming the administration of the Poor Law as such in such a way as to give greater encouragement to economy and a fairer distribution of burdens ; (3) stimulating thrift and penalising idleness in the labourers ; (4) reforming unemployment policy.

The proposals under the first head provided that settlement might be gained by five years' residence as a householder, if the householder had not become chargeable or been convicted of crime, or been absent for more than six weeks in a year. Two Justices of the Peace were to have power on complaint of the parish authorities to adjudicate on the settlement of any person likely to become chargeable, subject to an appeal to Quarter Sessions.

The proposals under the second head aimed partly at vestry reform and partly at rating reform. In those parishes where there was an open vestry, all ratepayers were still equal as voters, but Whitbread proposed to give extra voting power at vestry meetings in proportion to assessment.[2] He wished to reform rating, by making stock in trade and personal property (except farming stock), which produced profit liable to assessment, by authorising the vestry to exempt such occupiers of cottages as they should think fit, and by giving power to the Justices of the Peace to strike out of the rate any person

---

[1] See *Annual Register*, 1819, p. 320.

[2] Those assessed at £100 were to have two votes, those at £150 three votes, and those at £400 four votes. Whitbread did not propose to copy the provision of Gilbert's Act, which withdrew all voting power in vestries in parishes that adopted that Act from persons assessed at less than £5.

occupying a cottage not exceeding five pounds in yearly value, who should make application to them, such exemptions not to be considered parochial relief. He also proposed that the county rate should be charged in every parish in proportion to the assessed property in the parish, and that any parish whose poor rate was for three years more than double the average of the parish rate in the county, should have power to apply to Quarter Sessions for relief out of county stock.

Whitbread's proposals for stimulating thrift and penalising idleness were a strange medley of enlightenment and childishness. He proposed to give the parish officers power to build cottages which were to be let at the best rents that were to be obtained : but the parish officers might with the consent of the vestry allow persons who could not pay rent to occupy them rent free, or at a reduced rent. He proposed also to create a National Bank, something of the nature of a Post Office Savings Bank, to be employed both as a savings bank and an insurance system for the poor. With these two excellent schemes he combined a ridiculous system of prizes and punishments for the thrifty and the irresponsible. Magistrates were to be empowered to give rewards (up to a maximum of £20) with a badge of good conduct, to labourers who had brought up large families without parish help, and to punish any man who appeared to have become chargeable from idleness or misconduct, and to brand him with the words, ' criminal Poor.'

In his unemployment policy Whitbread committed the fatal mistake, common to almost all the proposals of the time, of mixing up poor relief with wages in a way to depress and demoralise the labour market. The able-bodied unemployed, men, youths, or single women, were to be hired out by parish officers at the best price to be obtained. The wages were to be paid to the worker. If the worker was a single man or woman, or a widower with no children dependent on him, his or her earnings were to be made up by the parish to a sum necessary to his or her subsistence. If he or she had children, they were to be made up to three-quarters, or four-fifths, or the full average rate, according to the number of children. No single man or woman was to be hired out for more than a year, and no man or woman with dependent children for more than a month.

The proposals were attacked vigorously by two critics who were not often found in company, Cobbett and Malthus. Cobbett criticised the introduction of plural voting at vestry

meetings in an excellent passage in the *Political Register*.[1]
' Many of those who pay rates are but a step or two from
pauperism themselves ; and they are the most likely persons
to consider duly the important duty of doing, in case of relief,
what they would be done unto. " But," Mr. Whitbread will
say, " is it right for these persons to *give away the money of
others*." It is *not* the money of others, any more than the
amount of tithes is the farmer's money. The maintenance
of the poor is a charge upon the land, a charge duly considered
in every purchase and in every lease. Besides, as the law
now stands, though every parishioner has a vote in vestry,
must it not be evident, to every man who reflects, that a man
of large property and superior understanding will have weight
in proportion ? That he will, in fact, have *many votes* ? If
he play the tyrant, even little men will rise against him, and
it is right they should have the power of so doing ; but, while
he conducts himself with moderation and humanity, while
he behaves as he ought to do to those who are beneath him
in point of property, there is no fear but he will have a
sufficiency of weight at every vestry. The votes of the inferior
persons in the parish are, in reality, dormant, unless in cases
where some innovation, or some act of tyranny, is attempted.
They are, like the sting of the bee, weapons merely of defence.'

Malthus' criticisms were of a very different nature.[2] He
objected particularly to the public building of cottages, and
the assessment of personal property to the rates. He argued
that the scarcity of houses was the chief reason ' why the
Poor Laws had not been so extensive and prejudicial in their
effects as might have been expected.' If a stimulus was
given to the building of cottages there would be no check on
the increase of population. A similar tendency he ascribed
to the rating of personal property. The employers of labour
had an interest in the increase of population, and therefore
in the building of cottages. This instinct was at present held
in check by consideration of the burden of the rates. If,
however, they could distribute that burden more widely,
this consideration would have much less weight. Population would increase and wages would consequently go down.
' It has been observed by Dr. Adam Smith that no efforts of
the legislature had been able to raise the salary of curates

---

[1] *Political Register*, August 29, 1807, p. 329.
[2] Letter to Samuel Whitbread, M.P., on his proposed Bill for the Amendment of the Poor Laws, 1807.

to that price which seemed necessary for their decent maintenance : and the reason which he justly assigns is that the bounties held out to the profession by the scholarships and fellowships of the universities always occasioned a redundant supply. In the same manner, if a more than usual supply of labour were encouraged by the premiums of small tenements, nothing could prevent a great and general fall in its price.'

The Bill was introduced in 1807, before the fall of the Whig Ministry, and it went to a Committee. But the Tory Parliament elected that year to support Portland and his anti-Catholic Government was unfriendly, and the county magistrates to whom the draft of the Bill was sent for criticisms were also hostile. Whitbread accordingly proceeded no further. At this time the Speenhamland system seemed to be working without serious inconvenience, and there was therefore no driving power behind such proposals. But after 1815 the conditions had changed, and the apathy of 1807 had melted away. The ruling class was no longer passive and indifferent about the growth of the Speenhamland system : both Houses of Parliament set inquiries on foot, schemes of emigration were invited and discussed, and measures of Vestry Reform were carried. But the problem was no longer the problem that Whitbread had set out to solve. Whitbread had proposed to increase the share of property in the control of the poor rates, but he had also brought forward a constructive scheme of social improvement. The Vestry Reformers of this period were merely interested in reducing the rates : the rest of Whitbread's programme was forgotten.

In 1818 an Act [1] was passed which established plural voting in vestries, every ratepayer whose rateable value was £50 and over being allowed a vote for every £25 of rateable property. In the following year an Act [2] was passed which allowed parishes to set up a select vestry, and ordained that in these parishes the overseers should give such relief as was ordered by the Select Vestry, and further allowed the appointment of salaried assistant overseers. These changes affected the administration of the Speenhamland system very considerably : and the salaried overseers made themselves hated in many parishes by the Draconian régime which they introduced. The parish cart, or the cart to which in some parishes men and women who asked for relief were harnessed, was one of the innovations of this period. The administrative methods

[1] 58 George III. c. 69.   [2] 59 George III. c. 12.

that were adopted in these parishes are illustrated by a fact
mentioned by a clerk to the magistrates in Kent, in October
1830.[1] The writer says that there was a severe overseer at
Ash, who had among other applicants for relief an unemployed
shepherd, with a wife and five children living at Margate,
thirteen miles away. The shepherd was given 9s. a week,
but the overseer made him walk to Ash every day except
Sunday for his eighteenpence. The shepherd walked his
twenty-six miles a day on such food as he could obtain out of
his sh...re of the 9s. for nine weeks, and then his strength could
hold out no longer. The writer remarked that the shepherd
was an industrious and honest man, out of work through no
fault of his own. It was by such methods that the salaried
overseers tried to break the poor of the habit of asking for
relief, and it is not surprising that such methods rankled in
the memories of the labourers. In this neighbourhood the
writer attributed the fires of 1830 more to this cause than to
any other.

These attempts to relieve the ratepayer did nothing to
relieve the labourer from the incubus of the system. His
plight grew steadily worse. A Committee on Agricultural
Wages, of which Lord John Russell was chairman, reported
in 1824 that whereas in certain northern counties, where the
Speenhamland system had not yet taken root, wages were 12s.
to 15s., in the south they varied from 8s. or 9s. a week to 3s.
for a single man and 4s. 6d. for a married man.[2] In one part
of Kent the lowest wages in one parish were 6d. a day, and
in the majority of parishes 1s. a day. The wages of an
unmarried man in Buckinghamshire in 1828, according to a
clergyman who gave evidence before the Committee of that
year on the Poor Laws, were 3s. a week, and the wages of a
married man were 6s. a week. In one parish in his neighbourhood the farmers had lately reduced the wages of able-
bodied married men to 4s. a week. Thus the Speenhamland
system had been effective enough in keeping wages low, but
as a means of preserving a minimum livelihood it was breaking down by this time on all sides. We have seen from the
history of Merton in Oxfordshire[3] what happened in one
parish long before the adversities of agriculture had become
acute. It is easy from this case to imagine what happened

---

[1] H. O. Papers, Municipal and Provincial.
[2] Of course the system was only one of the causes of this difference in wages.
[3] P. 99.

when the decline in employment and agriculture threw a steadily increasing burden on the system of maintenance from the rates. In some places, as the Commissioners of 1834 reported, the labourers were able by intimidation to keep the system in force, but though parishes did not as a rule dare to abandon or reform the system, they steadily reduced their scale.

The most direct and graphic demonstration of this fact, which has not apparently ever been noticed in any of the voluminous discussions of the old Poor Law system, is to be seen in the comparison of the standards of life adopted at the time the system was introduced with the standards that were adopted later. In 1795, as we have seen, the magistrates at Speenhamland recommended an allowance of three gallon loaves for each labourer, and a gallon loaf and a half for his wife and for each additional member of his family. This scale, it must be remembered, was not peculiar to Berkshire. It was the authoritative standard in many counties. We are able to compare this with some later scales, and the comparison yields some startling results. In Northamptonshire in 1816 the magistrates fixed a single man's allowance at 5s., and the allowance for a man and his wife at 6s., the price of wheat the quartern loaf being 11½d.[1] On this scale a man is supposed to need a little over two and a half gallon loaves, and a man and his wife a little more than three gallon loaves, or barely more than a single man was supposed to need in 1795. This is a grave reduction, but the maintenance standard fell very much lower before 1832. For though we have scales for Cambridgeshire and Essex for 1821 published in the Report of the Poor Law Commission of 1834,[2] which agree roughly with the Northamptonshire scale (two gallon loaves for a man, and one and a half for a woman), in Wiltshire, according to the complicated scale adopted at Hindon in 1817, a man was allowed one and three-fifths gallon loaves, and a woman one and one-tenth.[3] A Hampshire scale, drawn up in 1822 by eight magistrates, of whom five were parsons, allowed only one gallon loaf a head, with 4d. a week per head in addition to a family of four persons, the extra allowance being reduced by a penny in cases where there were six in the family, and by

---

[1] See *Agricultural State of the Kingdom*, Board of Agriculture, p. 231, and Cobbett, *Political Register*, October 5, 1816.   [2] Pp. 21 and 23.

[3] The table is given in the Report of the Committee on the Poor Laws, 1828.

twopence in cases where there were more than six.[1] The Dorsetshire magistrates in 1826 allowed a man the equivalent of one and a half gallon loaves and a penny over, and a woman or child over fourteen one and one-sixth.[2] We have a general statement as to the scales in force towards the end of our period in a passage in M'Culloch's *Political Economy* quoted in the *Edinburgh Review* for January 1831 (p. 353): ' The allowance scales now issued from time to time by the magistrates are usually framed on the principle that every labourer should have a gallon loaf of standard wheaten bread weekly for every member of his family and one over : that is four loaves for three persons, five for four, six for five, and so on.' That is, a family of four persons would have had seven and a half gallon loaves in 1795, and only five gallon loaves in 1831.

Now the Speenhamland scale did not represent some easy and luxurious standard of living ; it represented the minimum on which it was supposed that a man employed in agriculture could support life. In thirty-five years the standard had dropped, according to M'Culloch's statement, as much as a third, and this not because of war or famine, for in 1826 England had had eleven years of peace, but in the ordinary course of the life of the nation. Is such a decline in the standard of life recorded anywhere else in history ?

How did the labourers live at all under these conditions ? Their life was, of course, wretched and squalid in the extreme. Cobbett describes a group of women labourers whom he met by the roadside in Hampshire as ' such an assemblage of rags as I never saw before even amongst the hoppers at Farnham.' Of the labourers near Cricklade he said : ' Their dwellings are little better than pig-beds, and their looks indicate that their food is not nearly equal to that of a pig. These wretched hovels are stuck upon little beds of ground on the *roadside* where the space has been wider than the road demanded. In many places they have not two rods to a hovel. It seems as if they had been swept off the fields by a hurricane, and had dropped and found shelter under the banks on the roadside. Yesterday morning was a sharp frost, and this had set the poor creatures to digging up their little plots of potatoes. In my

[1] Cobbett, *Political Register*, September 21, 1822. Cobbett wrote one of his liveliest articles on this scale, setting out the number of livings held by the five parsons, and various circumstances connected with their families.

[2] *Ibid.*, September 9, 1826.

whole life I never saw human wretchedness equal to this; no, not even amongst the free negroes in America who, on an average, do not work one day out of four.' [1] The labourers' cottages in Leicestershire he found were 'hovels made of mud and straw, bits of glass or of old cast-off windows, without frames or hinges frequently, and merely stuck in the mud wall. Enter them and look at the bits of chairs or stools, the wretched boards tacked together to serve for a table, the floor of pebble broken or of the bare ground; look at the thing called a bed, and survey the rags on the backs of the inhabitants.' [2] A Dorsetshire clergyman, a witness before the Committee on Wages in 1824, said that the labourers lived almost entirely on tea and potatoes; a Bedfordshire labourer said that he and his family lived mainly on bread and cheese and water, and that sometimes for a month together he never tasted meat; a Suffolk magistrate described how a labourer out of work, convicted of stealing wood, begged to be sent at once to a House of Correction, where he hoped to find food and employment. If Davies had written an account of the labouring classes in 1820 or 1830, the picture he drew in 1795 would have seemed bright in comparison. But even this kind of life could not be supported on such provision as was made by the parish. How, then, did the labourers maintain any kind of existence when society ceased to piece together a minimum livelihood out of rates and wages?

For the answer to this question we must turn to the history of crime and punishment; to the Reports of the Parliamentary Committees on Labourers' Wages (1824), on the Game Laws (1823 and 1828), on Emigration (1826 and 1827), on Criminal Commitments and Convictions and Secondary Punishments (1827, 1828, 1831, and 1832), and the evidence of those who were in touch with this side of village life. From these sources we learn that, rate aid not being sufficient to bring wages to the maintenance level, poaching, smuggling, and ultimately thieving were called in to rehabilitate the labourer's economic position. [3] He was driven to the wages of crime. The history of the agricultural labourer in this generation is written in the code of the Game Laws, the growing brutality of the

---

[1] *Rural Rides*, p. 17.　　　[2] *Ibid.*, p. 609.

[3] The farmers were usually sympathetic to poaching as a habit, but it was not so much from a perception of its economic tendencies, as from a general resentment against the Game Laws.

Criminal Law, and the preoccupation of the rich with the efficacy of punishment.

We know from Fielding with what sort of justice the magistrates treated persons accused of poaching in the reign of George III.'s grandfather, but when he wrote his account of Squire Western, and when Blackstone wrote that the Game Laws had raised up a little Nimrod in every manor, the blood of men and boys had not yet been spilt for the pleasures of the rich. It is only after Fielding and Blackstone were both in their graves that this page of history became crimson, and that the gentlemen of England took to guarding their special amusements by methods of which a Member of Parliament declared that the nobles of France had not ventured on their like in the days of their most splendid arrogance. The little Nimrods who made and applied their code were a small and select class. They were the persons qualified under the law of Charles II. to shoot game, *i.e.* persons who possessed a freehold estate of at least £100 a year, or a leasehold estate of at least £150 a year, or the son or heir-apparent of an esquire or person of higher degree. The legislation that occupies so much of English history during a period of misery and famine is devoted to the protection of the monopoly of this class, comprising less than one in ten thousand of the people of England. A Member of Parliament named Warburton said in the House of Commons that the only parallel to this monopoly was to be found in Mariner's account of the Tonga Islands, where rats were preserved as game. Anybody might eat rats there, but nobody was allowed to kill them except persons descended from gods or kings.

With the general growth of upper-class riches and luxury there came over shooting a change corresponding with the change that turned hunting into a magnificent and extravagant spectacle. The habit set in of preserving game in great masses, of organising the battue, of maintaining armies of keepers. In many parts of the country, pheasants were now introduced for the first time. Whereas game had hitherto kept something of the wildness, and vagrancy, and careless freedom of Nature, the woods were now packed with tame and docile birds, whose gay feathers sparkled among the trees, before the eyes of the half-starved labourers breaking stones on the road at half a crown a week. The change is described by witnesses such as Sir James Graham and Sir Thomas Baring, magistrates respectively in Cumberland and Hampshire, before the Select

Committee on Criminal Commitments and Convictions in 1827. England was, in fact, passing through a process precisely opposite to that which had taken place in France : the sport of the rich was becoming more and more of an elaborate system, and more of a vested interest.   This development was marked by the growth of an offensive combination among game preservers ; in some parts of the country game associations were formed, for the express purpose of paying the costs of prosecutions, so that the poacher had against him not merely a bench of game preservers, but a ring of squires, a sort of Holy Alliance for the punishment of social rebels, which drew its meshes not round a parish but round a county.   Simultaneously, as we have seen, a general change was coming over the circumstances and position of the poor.   The mass of the people were losing their rights and independence ; they were being forced into an absolute dependence on wages, and were living on the brink of famine.   These two developments must be kept in mind in watching the building up of the game code in the last phase of the ancient régime.

The Acts for protecting game passed after the accession of George III. are in a crescendo of fierceness.   The first important Act was passed in 1770.   Under this Act any one who killed game of any kind between sunsetting and sunrising, or used any gun, or dog, snare, net, or other engine for destroying game at night, was, on conviction by one witness before one Justice of the Peace, to be punished with imprisonment for not less than three months or more than six.   For a subsequent offence he was to be imprisoned for not more than twelve months or less than six, and to be whipped publicly between the hours of twelve and one o'clock.   This was light punishment compared with the measures that were to follow.   In the year 1800, the year of Marengo, when all England was braced up for its great duel with the common enemy of freedom and order, and the labourers were told every day that they would be the first to suffer if Napoleon landed in England, the English Parliament found time to pass another Act to punish poachers, and to teach justice to mend her slow pace.   By this Act when two or more persons were found in any forest, chase, park, wood, plantation, paddock, field, meadow, or other open or enclosed ground, having any gun, net, engine, or other instrument, with the intent to destroy, take, or kill game, they were to be seized by keepers or servants, and on conviction before a J.P., they were to be treated as rogues and vagabonds

under the Act of 1744, *i.e.* they were to be punished by imprisonment with hard labour ; an incorrigible rogue, *i.e.* a
second offender, was to be imprisoned for two years with
whipping.   Further, if the offender was over twelve years
of age, the magistrates might sentence him to serve in the
army or navy.   If an incorrigible rogue escaped from the
House of Correction he was to be liable to transportation for
seven years.

Two consequences followed from this Act. Now that punishment was made so severe, the poacher had a strong reason for
violence : surrender meant service in a condemned regiment,
and he therefore took the risks of resistance.   The second
consequence was the practice of poaching in large groups.
The organisation of poaching gangs was not a natural development of the industry ; it was adopted in self-defence.[1]   This
Act led inevitably to those battles between gamekeepers and
labourers that became so conspicuous a feature of English life
at this time, and in 1803 Lord Ellenborough passed an Act
which provided that any persons who presented a gun or tried
to stab or cut ' with intent to obstruct, resist, or prevent the
lawful apprehension or detainer of the person or persons so
stabbing or cutting, or the lawful apprehension or detainer of
any of his, her, or their accomplices for any offences for which
he, she, or they may respectively be liable by law to be apprehended, imprisoned, or detained,' should suffer death as a
felon.   In 1816, when peace and the fall of prices were bringing
new problems in their train, there went through Parliament,
without a syllable of debate, a Bill of which Romilly said
that no parallel to it could be found in the laws of any country
in the world.   By that Act a person who was found at night
unarmed, but with a net for poaching, in any forest, chase, or
park was to be punished by transportation for seven years.
This Act Romilly induced Parliament to repeal in the following
year, but the Act that took its place only softened the law to
the extent of withdrawing this punishment from persons found
with nets, but without guns or bludgeons : it enacted that any
person so found, armed with gun, crossbow, firearms, bludgeon,
or any other offensive weapon, was to be tried at Quarter
Sessions, and if convicted, to be sentenced to transportation for
seven years : if such offender were to return to Great Britain

[1] See Cobbett ; *Letters to Peel* ; *Political Register* ; and Dr. Hunt's evidence
before the Select Committee on Criminal Commitments and Convictions,
1827.

before his time was over, he was to be transported for the rest of his life.[1]

This savage Act, though by no means a dead letter, as Parliamentary Returns show, seems to have defeated its own end, for in 1828 it was repealed, because, as Lord Wharn-cliffe told the House of Lords, there was a certain reluctance on the part of juries to convict a prisoner, when they knew that conviction would be followed by transportation. The new Act of 1828, which allowed a person to be convicted before two magistrates, reserved transportation for the third offence, punishing the first offence by three months', and the second by six months' imprisonment. But the convicted person had to find sureties after his release, or else go back to hard labour for another six months if it was a first offence, or another twelve months if it was his second. Further, if three men were found in a wood and one of them carried a gun or bludgeon, all three were liable to be transported for fourteen years.[2] Althorp's Bill of 1831 which abolished the qualifications of the Act of Charles II., gave the right to shoot to every landowner who took out a certificate, and made the sale of game legal, proposed in its original form to alter these punishments, making that for the first and second offences rather more severe (four and eight months), and that for the third, two years' imprisonment. In Committee in the House of Commons the two years were reduced to one year on the proposal of Orator Hunt. The House of Lords, however, restored the punishments of the Act of 1828.

These were the main Acts for punishing poachers that were passed during the last phase of the ancient régime. How large a part they played in English life may be imagined from

---

[1] A manifesto was published in a Bath paper in reply to this Act; it is quoted by Sydney Smith, *Essays*, p. 263: 'TAKE NOTICE.—We have lately heard and seen that there is an act passed, and whatever poacher is caught destroying the game is to be transported for seven years.—*This is English Liberty!*

'Now we do swear to each other that the first of our company that this law is inflicted on, that there shall not be one gentleman's seat in our country escape the rage of fire. The first that impeaches shall be shot. We have sworn not to impeach. You may think it a threat, but they will find it a reality. The Game Laws were too severe before. The Lord of all men sent these animals for the peasants as well as for the prince. God will not let his people be oppressed. He will assist us in our undertaking, and we will execute it with caution.'

[2] The Archbishop of Canterbury prosecuted a man under this Act in January 1831, for rescuing a poacher from a gamekeeper without violence, on the ground that he thought it his duty to enforce the provisions of the Act.

a fact mentioned by the Duke of Richmond in 1831.[1] In the three years between 1827 and 1830 one in seven of all the criminal convictions in the country were convictions under the Game Code. The number of persons so convicted was 8502, many of them being under eighteen. Some of them had been transported for life, and some for seven or fourteen years. In some years the proportion was still higher.[2] We must remember, too, what kind of judges had tried many of these men and boys. 'There is not a worse-constituted tribunal on the face of the earth,' said Brougham in 1828, ' not even that of the Turkish Cadi, than that at which summary convictions on the Game Laws constantly take place ; I mean a bench or a brace of sporting justices. I am far from saying that, on such subjects, they are actuated by corrupt motives ; but they are undoubtedly instigated by their abhorrence of that *caput lupinum*, that *hostis humani generis*, as an Honourable Friend of mine once called him in his place, that *fera naturæ*—a poacher. From their decisions on those points, where their passions are the most likely to mislead them, no appeal in reality lies to a more calm and unprejudiced tribunal ; for, unless they set out any matter illegal on the face of the conviction, you remove the record in vain.' [3]

The close relation of this great increase of crime to the general distress was universally recognised. Cobbett tells us that a gentleman in Surrey asked a young man, who was cracking stones on the roadside, how he could live upon half a crown a week. 'I don't live upon it,' said he. 'How do you live then ? ' 'Why,' said he, ' I *poach* : it is better to be hanged than to be starved to death.' [4] This story receives illustration after illustration in the evidence taken by Parliamentary Committees. The visiting Justices of the Prisons in Bedfordshire reported in 1827 that the great increase in commitments, and particularly the number of commitments for offences against the Game Laws, called for an inquiry. More than a third of the commitments during the last quarter had been for such offences. The Report continues :—

' In many parishes in this county the wages given to young

---

[1] House of Lords, September 19, 1831.

[2] A magistrate wrote to Sir R. Peel in 1827 to say that many magistrates sent in very imperfect returns of convictions, and that the true number far exceeded the records.—Webb, *Parish and County*, p. 598 note.

[3] *Brougham Speeches*, vol. ii. p. 373.

[4] *Political Register*, March 29, 1823, vol, xxiv. p. 796,

unmarried agricultural labourers, in the full strength and vigour of life, seldom exceed 3s. or 3s. 6d. a week, paid to them, generally, under the description of roundsmen, by the overseers out of the poor rates ; and often in the immediate vicinity of the dwellings of such half-starved labourers there are abundantly-stocked preserves of game, in which, during a single night, these dissatisfied young men can obtain a rich booty by snaring hares and taking or killing pheasants . . . offences which they cannot be brought to acknowledge to be any violation of private property. Detection generally leads to their imprisonment, and imprisonment introduces these youths to familiarity with criminals of other descriptions, and thus they become rapidly abandoned to unlawful pursuits and a life of crime.' [1] Mr. Orridge, Governor of the Gaol of Bury St. Edmunds, gave to the Committee on Commitments and Convictions [2] the following figures of prisoners committed to the House of Correction for certain years :—

1805, 221	1815, 387	1824, 457
1806, 192	1816, 476	1825, 439
1807, 173	1817, 430	1826, 573.

He stated that the great increase in the number of commitments began in the year 1815 with the depression of agriculture and the great dearth of employment : that men were employed on the roads at very low rates : that the commitments under the Game Laws which in 1810 were five, in 1811 four, and in 1812 two, were seventy-five in 1822, a year of great agricultural distress, sixty in 1823, sixty-one in 1824, and seventy-one in 1825. Some men were poachers from the love of sport, but the majority from distress. Mr. Pym, a magistrate in Cambridgeshire, and Sir Thomas Baring, a magistrate for Hampshire, gave similar evidence as to the cause of the increase of crime, and particularly of poaching, in these counties. Mr. Bishop, a Bow Street officer, whose business it was to mix with the poachers in public-houses and learn their secrets, told the Committee on the Game Laws in 1823 that there had not been employment for the labouring poor in most of the places he had visited. Perhaps the most graphic picture of the relation of distress to crime is given in a pamphlet, *Thoughts and Suggestions on the Present Condition of the Country*, published in 1830 by Mr. Potter Macqueen, late M.P. for Bedford.

'In January 1829, there were ninety-six prisoners for trial

[1] Select Committee on Criminal Commitments and Convictions, 1827, p. 30.
Ibid., p. 39.

in Bedford Gaol, of whom seventy-six were able-bodied men, in the prime of life, and, chiefly, of general good character, who were driven to crime by sheer want, and who would have been valuable subjects had they been placed in a situation, where, by the exercise of their health and strength, they could have earned a subsistence. There were in this number eighteen poachers, awaiting trial for the capital offence of using arms in self-defence when attacked by game-keepers; of these eighteen men, one only was not a parish pauper, and he was the agent of the London poulterers, who, passing under the apparent vocation of a rat-catcher, paid these poor creatures more in one night than they could obtain from the overseer for a week's labour. I conversed with each of these men singly, and made minutes of their mode of life. The two first I will mention are the two brothers, the Lilleys, in custody under a charge of firing on and wounding a keeper, who endeavoured to apprehend them whilst poaching. They were two remarkably fine young men, and very respectably connected. The elder, twenty-eight years of age, married, with two small children. When I inquired how he could lend himself to such a wretched course of life, the poor fellow replied : ' Sir, I had a pregnant wife, with one infant at her knee, and another at her breast ; I was anxious to obtain work, I offered myself in all directions, but without success ; if I went to a distance, I was told to go back to my parish, and when I did so, I was allowed . . . What ? Why, for myself, my babes, and my wife, in a condition requiring more than common support, and unable to labour, I was allowed 7s. a week for all ; for which I was expected to work on the roads from light to dark, and to pay three guineas a year for the hovel which sheltered us.' The other brother, aged twenty-two, unmarried, received 6d. a day. These men were hanged at the spring assizes. Of the others, ten were single men, their ages varying from seventeen to twenty-seven. Many had never been in gaol before, and were considered of good character. Six of them were on the roads at 6d. per day. Two could not obtain even this pittance. One had been refused relief on the ground that he had shortly previous obtained a profitable piece of job-work, and one had existed on 1s. 6d. during the fortnight before he joined the gang in question. Of five married men, two with wife and two children received 7s., two with wife and one child 6s., and one with wife and four small children 11s.' [1]

[1] Quoted in *Times*, December 18, 1830.

If we wish to obtain a complete picture of the social life of the time, it is not enough to study the construction of this vindictive code.   We must remember that a sort of civil war was going on between the labourers and the gamekeepers. The woods in which Tom Jones fought his great fight with Thwackum and Blifil to cover the flight of Molly Seagrim now echoed on a still and moonless night with the din of a different sort of battle : the noise of gunshots and blows from bludgeons, and broken curses from men who knew that, if they were taken, they would never see the English dawn rise over their homes again : a battle which ended perhaps in the death or wounding of a keeper or poacher, and the hanging or transportation of some of the favourite Don Quixotes of the village.   A witness before the Committee on the Game Laws said that the poachers preferred a quiet night.   Crabbe, in the poacher poem (Book XXI. of *Tales of the Hall*) which he wrote at the suggestion of Romilly, takes what would seem to be the more probable view that poachers liked a noisy night :

' It was a night such bold desires to move
Strong winds and wintry torrents filled the grove ;
The crackling boughs that in the forest fell,
The cawing rooks, the cur's affrighted yell ;
The scenes above the wood, the floods below,
Were mix'd, and none the single sound could know ;
" Loud blow the blasts," they cried, " and call us as they blow." '

Such an encounter is put into cold arithmetic in an official return like this [1] :—

' An account of the nineteen persons committed to Warwick Gaol for trial at the Lent Assizes 1829 for shooting and wounding John Slinn at Combe Fields in the County of Warwick whilst endeavouring to apprehend them for destroying game in the night with the result thereof :—

| Above 14 and under 20 years of age. | Above 20 years of age. | Capitally convicted and reprieved with— | | | Admitted to Evidence. |
		Transportation for life.	Transportation for 14 years.	Imprisonment with hard labour in House of Correction for 2 years.	
11	8	7	9	1	2

[1] Return of Convictions under the Game Laws from 1827 to 1830.   Ordered by the House of Commons to be printed, February 14, 1831, p. 4.

Seven peasants exiled for life, nine exiled for fourteen years, and two condemned to the worst exile of all. In that village at any rate there were many homes that had reason to remember the day when the pleasures of the rich became the most sacred thing in England.

But the warfare was not conducted only by these methods. For the gentlemen of England, as for the genius who fought Michael and Gabriel in the great battle in the sixth book of *Paradise Lost*, science did not spread her light in vain. There was a certain joy of adventure in a night skirmish, and a man who saw his wife and children slowly starving, to whom one of those golden birds that was sleeping on its perch the other side of the hedge, night after night, till the day when it should please the squire to send a shot through its purple head, meant comfort and even riches for a week, was not very much afraid of trusting his life and his freedom to his quick ear, his light foot, or at the worst his powerful arm. So the game preservers invented a cold and terrible demon : they strewed their woods with spring guns, that dealt death without warning, death without the excitement of battle, death that could catch the nimblest as he slipped and scrambled through the hiding bracken. The man who fell in an affray fell fighting, his comrades by his side ; it was a grim and uncomforted fate to go out slowly and alone, lying desolate in the stained bushes, beneath the unheeding sky. It is not clear when these diabolical engines, as Lord Holland called them, were first introduced, but they were evidently common by 1817, when Curwen made a passionate protest in the House of Commons, and declared, ' Better the whole race of game was extinct than that it should owe its preservation to such cruel expedients.' [1] Fortunately for England the spring guns, though they scattered murder and wounds freely enough (Peel spoke in 1827 of ' daily accidents and misfortunes '), did not choose their victims with so nice an eye as a Justice of the Peace, and it was often a gamekeeper or a farm servant who was suddenly tripped up by this lurking death. By 1827 this state of things had become such a scandal that Parliament intervened and passed an Act, introduced in the Lords by Lord Suffield, who had made a previous attempt in 1825, to make the setting of spring guns a misdemeanour.[2]

[1] *Hansard*, June 9, 1817.

[2] Scotland was exempted from the operation of this statute, for whilst the Bill was going through Parliament, a case raised in a Scottish Court ended in a

The Bill did not pass without considerable opposition. Tennyson, who introduced it in the Commons, declared that the feudal nobility in ancient France had never possessed a privilege comparable with this right of killing and maiming, and he said that the fact that Coke of Norfolk [1] and Lord Suffield, both large game preservers, refused to employ them showed that they were not necessary. Members of both Houses of Parliament complained bitterly of the 'morbid sensibility' that inspired the proposal, and some of them defended spring guns as a labour-saving machine, speaking of them with the enthusiasm that a manufacturer might bestow on the invention of an Arkwright or a Crompton. One member of the House of Commons, a Colonel French, opposed the Bill with the argument that the honest English country gentleman formed ' the very subject and essence of the English character,' while Lord Ellenborough opposed it in the other House on the ground that it was contrary to the principles of the English law, which gave a man protection for his property in proportion to the difficulty with which it could be defended by ordinary means.

The crime for which men were maimed or killed by these engines or torn from their homes by summary and heartless justice was, it must be remembered, no crime at all in the eyes of the great majority of their countrymen. At this time the sale of game was prohibited under stern penalties, and yet every rich man in London, from the Lord Mayor downwards, entertained his guests with game that he had bought from a poulterer. How had the poulterer bought it ? There was no secret about the business. It was explained to two Select Committees, the first of the House of Commons in 1823, and the second of the House of Lords in 1828, by poulterers who lived by these transactions, and by police officers who did nothing to interfere with them. Daniel Bishop, for example, one of the chief Bow Street officers, described the arrangements to the Committee in 1823.[2]

' Can you state to the Committee, how the Game is brought from the poachers up to London, or other market ? . . . The poachers generally meet the coachman or guards of the mails or vans, and deliver it to them after they are out of a town,

unanimous decision by the six Judges of the High Court of Justiciary that killing by a spring gun was murder. Hence the milder provisions of this Act were not required. See *Annual Register*, 1827, p. 185, and Chron., p. 116.

[1] That Coke of Norfolk did not err on the side of mercy towards poachers is clear from his record. His biographer (Mrs. Stirling) states that one of his first efforts in Parliament was to introduce a Bill to punish night poaching.   [2] P. 29 ff.

they do not deliver it in a town; then it is brought up to London, sometimes to their agents; but the coachmen and guards mostly have their friends in London where they know how to dispose of it, and they have their contracts made at so much a brace. . . . There is no intermediate person between the poacher and the coachman or guard that conveys it to town? . . . Very seldom; generally the head of the gang pays the rest of the men, and he sends off the Game. . . . When the game arrives in London, how is it disposed of? . . . They have their agents, the bookkeepers at most of the inns, the porters who go out with the carts; any persons they know may go and get what quantity they like, by sending an order a day or two before; there are great quantities come up to Leadenhall and Newgate markets.'

Nobody in London thought the worse of a poulterer for buying poached game; and nobody in the country thought any the worse of the poacher who supplied it. A witness before the Committee in 1823 said that in one village the whole of the village were poachers, ' the constable of the village, the shoe-maker and other inhabitants of the village.' Another witness before the Lords in 1828 said that occupiers and unqualified proprietors agreed with the labourers in thinking that poaching was an innocent practice.

Those who wished to reform the Game Laws argued that if the sale of game were legalised, and if the anomalous qualifications were abolished, the poacher's prize would become much less valuable, and the temptation would be correspondingly diminished. This view was corroborated by the evidence given to the Select Committees. But all such proposals were bitterly attacked by the great majority of game preservers. Lord Londonderry urged against this reform in 1827 ' that it would deprive the sportsman of his highest gratification . . . the pleasure of furnishing his friends with presents of game: nobody would care for a present which everybody could give '![1] Other game preservers argued that it was sport that made the English gentlemen such good officers, on which the *Edinburgh Review* remarked: ' The hunting which Xenophon and Cicero praise as the best discipline for forming great generals from its being war in miniature must have been very unlike pheasant shooting.'[2] Lord Deerhurst declared, when the proposal was made fourteen years earlier, that this was not the time to dis-gust resident gentlemen. The English aristocracy, like the

[1] *Annual Register*, 1827, p. 184. [2] *Edinburgh Review*, December 1831.

French, would only consent to live in the country on their own terms.   When the squires threatened to turn *émigrés* if anybody else was allowed to kill a rabbit, or if a poacher was not put to risk of life and limb, Sydney Smith gave an answer that would have scandalised the House of Commons, ' If gentlemen cannot breathe fresh air without injustice, let them putrefy in Cranbourne Court.'

But what about the justice of the laws against poachers ? To most members of Parliament there would have been an element of paradox in such a question.   From the discussions on the subject of the Game Laws a modern reader might suppose that poachers were not men of flesh and blood, but some kind of vermin.   There were a few exceptions.   In 1782, when Coke of Norfolk, acting at the instance of the magistrates of that county, proposed to make the Game Laws more stringent, Turner, the member for York, made a spirited reply ; he ' exclaimed against those laws as cruel and oppressive on the poor : he said it was a shame that the House should always be enacting laws for the safety of gentlemen ; he wished they would make a few for the good of the poor. . . . For his own part, he was convinced, that if he had been a common man, he would have been a poacher, in spite of all the laws ; and he was equally sure that the too great severity of the laws was the cause that the number of poachers had increased so much.' [1] Fox (29th April 1796) protested with vigour against the morality that condemned poachers without mercy, and condoned all the vices of the rich, but he, with Sheridan, Curwen, Romilly, and a few others were an infinitesimal minority.

The aristocracy had set up a code, under which a man or boy who had offended against the laws, but had done nothing for which any of his fellows imputed discredit to him, was snatched from his home, thrown into gaol with thieves and criminals, and perhaps flung to the other side of the world, leaving his family either to go upon the rates or to pick up a living by such dishonesties as they could contrive.   This last penalty probably meant final separation.   Mr. T. G. B. Estcourt, M.P., stated in evidence before the Select Committee on Secondary Punishments in 1831 [2] that as men who had been transported were not brought back at the public expense, they scarcely ever returned,[3] that agricultural labourers

---

[1] *Parliamentary Register*, February 25, 1782.   [2] P. 42.

[3] ' Speaking now of country and agricultural parishes, I do not know above one instance in all my experience.'

specially dreaded transportation, because it meant ‘entire separation’ from ‘former associates, relations, and friends,’ and that since he and his brother magistrates in Wiltshire had taken to transporting more freely, committals had decreased. The special misery that transportation inflicted on men of this class is illustrated in Marcus Clarke's famous novel, *For the Term of His Natural Life*. In the passage describing the barracoon on the transport ship, Clarke throws on the screen all the different types of character—forgers, housebreakers, cracksmen, footpads—penned up in that poisonous prison. ‘The poacher grimly thinking of his sick wife and children would start as the night-house ruffian clapped him on the shoulder and bade him with a curse to take good heart and be a man.’ Readers of Mr. Hudson's character sketches of the modern Wiltshire labourer can imagine the scene. To the lad who had never been outside his own village such a society must have been unspeakably alien and terrible : a ring of callous and mocking faces, hardened, by crime and wrong and base punishment, to make bitter ridicule of all the memories of home and boyhood and innocence that were surging and breaking round his simple heart.

The growing brutality of the Game Laws, if it is the chief, is not the only illustration of the extent to which the pressure of poverty was driving the labourers to press upon law and order, and the kind of measures that the ruling class took to protect its property. Another illustration is the Malicious Trespass Act.

In 1820 Parliament passed an Act which provided that any person convicted before a single J.P. within four months of the act of doing any malicious injury to any building, hedge, fence, tree, wood, or underwood was to pay damage not exceeding £5, and if he was unable to pay these damages he was to be sent to hard labour in a common gaol or House of Correction for three months. The law before the passing of this Act was as it is to-day, *i.e.* the remedy lay in an action at law against the trespasser, and the trespasser under the Act of William and Mary had to pay damages. The Act of 1820 was passed without any debate that is reported in *Hansard*, but it is not unreasonable to assume that it was demanded for the protection of enclosures and game preserves.[1] This Act

[1] Some Enclosure Acts prescribed special penalties for the breaking of fences. See cases of Haute Huntre and Croydon in Appendix.

exempted one set of persons entirely, ' persons engaged in hunting, and qualified persons in pursuit of game.' These privileged gentlemen could do as much injury as they pleased.

One clause provided that every male offender under sixteen who did not pay damages, and all costs and charges and expenses forthwith, might be sent by the magistrate to hard labour in the House of Correction for six weeks. Thus a child who broke a bough from a tree by the roadside might be sent by the magistrate, who would in many cases be the owner of the tree, to the House of Correction, there to learn the ways of criminals at an age when the magistrate's own children were about half-way through their luxurious education. This was no *brutum fulmen*. Children were sent to prison in great numbers.[1] Brougham said in 1828 : ' There was a Bill introduced by the Rt. Hon. Gentleman opposite for extending the payment of expenses of witnesses and prosecutors out of the county rates. It is not to be doubted that it has greatly increased the number of Commitments, and has been the cause of many persons being brought to trial, who ought to have been discharged by the Magistrates. The habit of committing, from this and other causes, has grievously increased everywhere of late, and especially of boys. Eighteen hundred and odd, many of them mere children, have been committed in the Warwick district during the last seven years.' [2]   The Governor of the House of Correction in Coldbath Fields, giving evidence before the Committee on Secondary Punishments in 1831, said that he had under his charge a boy of ten years old who had been in prison eight times. Capper, the Superintendent of the Convict Establishment, told the same Committee that some of the boy convicts were so young that they could scarcely put on their clothes, and that they had to be dressed. Richard Potter's diary for 1813 contains this entry : ' Oct. 13.—I was attending to give evidence against a man. Afterwards, two boys, John and Thomas Clough, aged 12 and 10 years, were tried and found guilty of stealing some Irish linen out of Joseph Thorley's warehouse during the dinner hour. The Chairman sentenced them to seven years' transportation. On its being pronounced, the Mother of those unfortunate boys came to the Bar to her children, and with them was in great agony, imploring mercy of the Bench. With difficulty the children were removed.

[1] See Mr. Estcourt's evidence before Select Committee on Secondary Punishments, 1831, p. 41.

[2] *Present State of the Law*, p. 41.

The scene was so horrifying I could remain no longer in court.' [1]
Parliament put these tremendous weapons into the hands of
men who believed in using them, who administered the law
on the principle by which Sir William Dyott regulated his
conduct as a magistrate, that ' nothing but the terror of human
suffering can avail to prevent crime.'

The class that had, in Goldsmith's words, hung round ' our
paltriest possessions with gibbetts' never doubted its power
to do full justice to the helpless creatures who tumbled into
the net of the law.   Until 1836 a man accused of a felony was
not allowed to employ counsel to make his defence in the Court.
His counsel (if he could afford to have one) could examine and
cross-examine witnesses, and that was all ; the prisoner,
whatever his condition of mind, or his condition of body, had
to answer the speech of the prosecuting counsel himself.   In
nine cases out of ten he was quite an unlearned man ; he was
swept into the glare of the Court blinking from long months of
imprisonment in dark cells ; the case against him was woven
into a complete and perfect story by the skilled fingers of a
lawyer, and it was left to this rude and illiterate man, by the
aid of his own memory and his own imagination, his life on the
razor's edge, his mind bewildered by his strange and terrible
surroundings, to pick that story to pieces, to expose what was
mere and doubtful inference, to put a different complexion on
a long and tangled set of events, to show how a turn here or
a turn there in the narrative would change black into white
and apparent guilt into manifest innocence.   Sydney Smith,
whose opinions on the importance of giving the poor a fair trial
were as enlightened as his opinions on their proper treatment
in prison were backward, has described the scene.

' It is a most affecting moment in a Court of Justice, when the
evidence has all been heard, and the Judge asks the prisoner
what he has to say in his defence.   The prisoner who has (by
great exertions, perhaps of his friends) saved up money enough
to procure Counsel, says to the Judge " that he leaves his defence
to his Counsel."   We have often blushed for English humanity
to hear the reply.   " Your Counsel cannot speak for you, you
must speak for yourself " ; and this is the reply given to a poor
girl of eighteen—to a foreigner—to a deaf man—to a stammerer
—to the sick—to the feeble—to the old—to the most abject and
ignorant of human beings ! . . . How often have we seen a poor

[1] *From Ploughshare to Parliament*, p. 186 ; the *Annual Register* for 1791
records the execution of two boys at Newport for stealing, one aged fourteen and
the other fifteen.

wretch, struggling against the agonies of his spirit, and the rude-
ness of his conceptions, and his awe of better-dressed men and
better-taught men, and the shame which the accusation has
brought upon his head, and the sight of his parents and children
gazing at him in the Court, for the last time perhaps, and after
a long absence ! ' [1]

Brougham said in the House of Commons that there was
no man who visited the Criminal Courts who did not see the
fearful odds against the prisoner. This anomaly was peculiar
to England, and in England it was peculiar to cases of felony.
Men tried for misdemeanours, or for treason, or before the
House of Lords could answer by the mouth of counsel. It was
only in those cases where the prisoners were almost always poor
and uneducated men and women, as Lord Althorp pointed out
in an admirable speech in the House of Commons, that the
accused was left to shift for himself. Twice, in 1824 and in
1826, the House of Commons refused leave to bring in a Bill
to redress this flagrant injustice, encouraged in that refusal not
only by Canning, but, what is much more surprising, by Peel.

The favourite argument against this reform, taking precedence
of the arguments that to allow persons the aid of counsel in
putting their statement of fact would make justice slower, more
expensive, and more theatrical, was the contention that the
judge did, in point of fact, represent the interest of the prisoner :
a confused plea which it did not require any very highly developed gift of penetration to dissect. But how far, in point
of fact, were the judges able to enter into the poor prisoner's
mind ? They had the power of sentencing to death for
hundreds of trivial offences. It was the custom to pass the
brutal sentence which the law allowed to be inflicted for
felonies, and then to commute it in all except a few cases. By
what considerations did judges decide when to be severe ?
Lord Ellenborough told Lauderdale that he had left a man to
be hanged at the Worcester Assizes because he lolled out his
tongue and pretended to be an idiot, on which Lauderdale asked
the Chief Justice what law there was to punish that particular
offence with death. We learn from Romilly's *Memoirs* [2]
that one judge left three men to be hanged for thefts at the
Maidstone Assizes because none of them could bring a witness
to his character.

The same disposition to trust to the discretion of the judge,
which Camden described as the law of tyrants, explains the

---

[1] Sydney Smith, *Essays*, p. 487.   [2] Vol. ii. p. 153.

vitality of the system of prescribing death as the punishment for hundreds of paltry offences. During the last fifty years the energy of Parliament in passing Enclosure Acts had been only rivalled by its energy in creating capital offences. The result was a penal code which had been condemned by almost every Englishman of repute of the most various opinions, from Blackstone, Johnson, and Goldsmith to Burke and Bentham. This system made the poor man the prey of his rich neighbours. The most furious punishments were held *in terrorem* over the heads of prisoners, and the wretched man who was caught in the net was exposed to all the animosities that he might have provoked in his ordinary life. Dr. Parr put this point writing to Romilly in 1811.

' There is, indeed, one consideration in the case of bad men which ought to have a greater weight than it usually has in the minds of the Judges. Dislike from party, quarrels with servants or neighbours, offence justly or unjustly taken in a quarrel, jealousy about game, and twenty other matters of the same sort, frequently induce men to wish to get rid of a convicted person : and well does it behove every Judge to be sure that the person who recommends the execution of the sentence is a man of veracity, of sense, of impartiality and kindness of nature in the habitual character of his mind. I remember hearing from Sergeant Whitaker that, while he was trying a man for a capital offence at Norwich, a person brought him a message from the late Lord Suffield, " that the prisoner was a good-for-nothing fellow, and he hoped the Judge would look to him " ; and the Sergeant kindled with indignation, and exclaimed in the hearing of the Court, " Zounds ! would Sir Harbord Harbord have me condemn the man before I have tried him ? " What Sir Harbord did during the trial, many squires and justices of the peace, upon other occasions, do after it ; and were I a Judge, I should listen with great caution to all unfavourable representations. The rich, the proud, the irascible, and the vindictive are very unfit to estimate the value of life to their inferiors.' [1]

We can see how the squires and the justices would close in round a man of whom they wanted, with the best intentions in the world, to rid their parish, woods, and warrens, when the punishment he was to receive turned on his reputation as it was estimated by the gentlemen of his neighbourhood.

---

[1] Romilly, *Memoirs*, vol. ii. p. 181.

Was Sir Harbord Harbord very far removed from the state of mind described in the Sixth Satire of Juvenal ?

> ' " Pone crucem servo." " Meruit quo crimine servus
> Supplicium ? quis testis adest ? quis detulit ? Audi :
> Nulla unquam de morte hominis cunctatio longa est."
> " O demens, ita servus homo est ? nil fecerit, esto :
> Hoc volo, sic jubeo, sit pro ratione voluntas." '

And Sir Harbord Harbord had in hundreds of cases what he had not in this case, the power to wreak his anger on ' a good-for-nothing fellow.'

When Romilly entered on his noble crusade and tried very cautiously to persuade Parliament to repeal the death penalty in cases in which it was rarely carried out, he found the chief obstacle in his way was the fear that became common among the governing class at this time, the fear that existing methods of punishment were ceasing to be deterrent. In 1810 he carried his Bill, for abolishing this penalty for the crime of stealing privately to the amount of five shillings in a shop, through the House of Commons, and the Bill was introduced in the House of Lords by Lord Holland. There it was rejected by twenty-one to eleven, the majority including the Archbishop of Canterbury and six other bishops.[1] The chief speeches against the Bill were made by Eldon and Ellenborough. Ellenborough argued that transportation was regarded, and justly regarded, by those who violated the law as ' a summer airing by an easy migration to a milder climate.'

The nightmare that punishment was growing gentle and attractive to the poor came to haunt the mind of the governing class. It was founded on the belief that as human wretchedness was increasing, there was a sort of law of Malthus, by which human endurance tended to outgrow the resources of repression. The agricultural labourers were sinking into such a deplorable plight that some of them found it a relief to be committed to the House of Correction, where, at least, they obtained food and employment, and the magistrates began to fear in consequence that ordinary punishments could no longer be regarded as deterrent, and to reason that some condition had yet to be discovered which would be more miserable than the general existence of the poor. The justices who punished Wiltshire poachers found such an El Dorado of unhappiness in transportation. But disturbing rumours

---

[1] It was again rejected in 1813 by twenty to fifteen, the majority including five bishops.

came to the ears of the authorities that transportation was not thought a very terrible punishment after all, and the Government sent out to Sir George Arthur, the Governor of Van Diemen's Land, certain complaints of this kind. The answer which the Governor returned is published with the Report of the Committee on Secondary Punishments, and the complete correspondence forms a very remarkable set of Parliamentary Papers. The Governor pointed out that these complaints, which made such an impression on Lord Melbourne, came from employers in Australia, who wanted to have greater control over their servants. Arthur was no sentimentalist; his sympathies had been drilled in two hard schools, the army and the government of prisoners; his account of his own methods shows that in describing the life of a convict he was in no danger of falling into the exaggerations or the rhetoric of pity. In these letters he made it very clear that nobody who knew what transportation meant could ever make the mistake of thinking it a light punishment. The ordinary convict was assigned to a settler. ' Deprived of liberty, exposed to all the caprice of the family to whose service he may happen to be assigned, and subject to the most summary laws, the condition of a convict in no respect differs from that of a slave, except that his master cannot apply corporal punishment by his own hands or those of his overseer, and has a property in him for a limited period only.' Further, ' idleness and insolence of expression, or even of looks, anything betraying the insurgent spirit, subjects him to the chain-gang, or the triangle, or to hard labour on the roads.' [1] We can imagine what the life of an ordinary convict might become. In earlier days every convict who went out began as an assigned servant, and it was only for misconduct in the colony or on the way thither that he was sent to a Penal Settlement, but the growing alarm of the ruling class on the subject of punishment led to a demand for more drastic sentences, and shortly after the close of our period Lord Melbourne introduced a new system, under which convicts might be sentenced from home to the Penal Settlement, and any judge who thought badly of a prisoner might add this hideous punishment to transportation.

The life of these Settlements has been described in one of the most vivid and terrible books ever written. Nobody can read Marcus Clarke's great novel without feeling that the methods of barbarism had done their worst and most

---

[1] *Correspondence on the Subject of Secondary Punishments*, 1834, p. 22.

devilish in Macquarie Harbour and Port Arthur. The lot of the prisoners in *Resurrection* is by comparison a paradise. Not a single feature that can revolt and stupefy the imagination is wanting to the picture. Children of ten committing suicide, men murdering each other by compact as an escape from a hell they could no longer bear, prisoners receiving a death sentence with ecstasies of delight, punishments inflicted that are indistinguishable from torture, men stealing into the parched bush in groups, in the horrible hope that one or two of them might make their way to freedom by devouring their comrades—an atmosphere in which the last faint glimmer of self-respect and human feeling was extinguished by incessant and degrading cruelty. Few books have been written in any language more terrible to read. Yet not a single incident or feature is imaginary : the whole picture is drawn from the cold facts of the official reports.[1] And this system was not the invention of some Nero or Caligula ; it was the system imposed by men of gentle and refined manners, who talked to each other in Virgil and Lucan of liberty and justice, who would have died without a murmur to save a French princess from an hour's pain or shame, who put down the abominations of the Slave Trade, and allowed Clive and Warren Hastings to be indicted at the bar of public opinion as monsters of inhumanity ; and it was imposed by them from the belief that as the poor were becoming poorer, only a system of punishment that was becoming more brutal could deter them from crime.

If we want to understand how completely all their natural feelings were lost in this absorbing fear, we must turn to the picture given by an observer who was outside their world ; an observer who could enter into the misery of the punished, and could describe what transportation meant to boys of nine and ten, exposed to the most brutal appetites of savage men ; to chained convicts, packed for the night in boxes so narrow that they could only lie on one side; to crushed and broken men, whose only prayer it was to die. From him we learn how these scenes and surroundings impressed a mind that could look upon a convict settlement as a society of living men and boys, and not merely as the Cloaca Maxima of property and order.[2]

---

[1] See Select Committee on Secondary Punishments, 1831, and Select Committee on Transportation, 1838.

[2] See evidence of Dr. Ullathorne, Roman Catholic Vicar-General of New Holland and Van Diemen's Land, before the 1838 Committee on Transportation.

CHAPTER IX

THE ISOLATION OF THE POOR

THE upper classes, to whom the fact that the labourers were more wretched in 1830 than they had been in 1795 was a reason for making punishment more severe, were not deliberately callous and cruel in their neglect of all this growing misery and hunger. Most of those who thought seriously about it had learnt a reasoned insensibility from the stern Sibyl of the political economy in fashion, that strange and partial interpretation of Adam Smith, Malthus and Ricardo which was then in full power. This political economy had robbed poverty of its sting for the rich by representing it as Nature's medicine, bitter indeed, but less bitter than any medicine that man could prescribe. If poverty was sharper at one time than another, this only meant that society was more than ever in need of this medicine. But the governing class as a whole did not think out any such scheme or order of society, or master the new science of misery and vice. They thought of the poor not in relation to the mysterious forces of Nature, but in relation to the privileges of their own class in which they saw no mystery at all. Their state of mind is presented in a passage in Bolingbroke's *Idea of a Patriot King.* ' As men are apt to make themselves the measure of all being, so they make themselves the final cause of all creation. Thus the reputed orthodox philosophers in all ages have taught that the world was made for man, the earth for him to inhabit, and all the luminous bodies in the immense expanse around us for him to gaze at. Kings do no more, nay not so much, when they imagine themselves the final cause for which societies were formed and governments instituted.' If we read ' the aristocracy ' for ' kings ' we shall have a complete analysis of the social philosophy of the ruling class. It was from this centre that they looked out upon the world. When the misery of the poor reacted on their own comfort, as in the case of poaching or crime or the pressure on the rates, they were aware of it and took measures to protect their property, but of any social problem outside these relations they were entirely unconscious. Their philosophy and their religion taught them that it was the duty of the rich to be benevolent, and of the poor to be patient and industrious. The rich were ready to do their part, and all they asked of the poor was that they should learn to bear their lot with resignation. Burke had laid down the true and full philosophy of social life once and for all. ' Good order is the foundation of all good things. To be enabled to acquire, the people, without being servile, must be tractable and obedient. The magistrate must have his reverence, the laws their authority. The body of the people must not find the principles of natural subordination by art rooted out of their minds. They must respect that property of which they cannot partake. They must labour to obtain what by labour can be obtained; and when they find, as they commonly do, the success disproportioned to the endeavour, they must be taught their consolation in the final proportions of eternal justice.' [1]

The upper classes, looking upon the world in this way, considered that it was the duty of the poor man to adapt himself, his tastes, his habits, and his ambitions, to the arrangements of a society which it had pleased Providence to organise on this interesting plan. We have in the pages of Eden the portrait of the ideal poor woman, whose life showed what could be done if poverty were faced in the proper spirit. ' Anne Hurst was born at Witley in Surrey : there she lived the whole period of a long life, and there she died. As soon as she was thought able to work, she went to service : there, before she was twenty, she married James Strudwick, who, like her own father, was a day labourer. With this husband she lived, a prolific, hardworking, contented wife, somewhat more than fifty years. He worked more than threescore years on one farm, and his wages, summer and winter, were regularly a shilling a day. He never asked more nor was never offered less. They had between them seven children : and lived to see six daughters married and three the mothers of sixteen children : all of whom were brought up, or are bringing up, to be day labourers. Strudwick continued to work till within seven weeks of the day of his death, and at the age of four score, in 1787, he closed, in peace, a not inglorious life ; for, to the day of his death, he never received a farthing in the way of parochial aid. His wife survived him about seven years, and though bent with age

[1] *Reflections on the Revolution in France* (fourth edition), p. 359.

and infirmities, and little able to work, excepting as a weeder in a gentleman's garden, she also was too proud to ask or receive any relief from the parish. For six or seven of the last years of her life, she received twenty shillings a year from the person who favoured me with this account, which he drew up from her own mouth. With all her virtue, and all her merit, she yet was not much liked in her neighbourhood ; people in affluence thought her haughty, and the Paupers of the parish, seeing, as they could not help seeing, that her life was a reproach to theirs, aggravated all her little failings. Yet, the worst thing they had to say of her was, that she was proud ; which, they said, was manifested by the way in which she buried her husband. Resolute, as she owned she was, to have the funeral, and everything that related to it, what she called decent, nothing could dissuade her from having handles to his coffin and a plate on it, mentioning his age. She was also charged with having behaved herself crossly and peevishly towards one of her sons-in-law, who was a mason and went regularly every Saturday evening to the ale house as he said just to drink a pot of beer. James Strudwick in all his life, as she often told this ungracious son-in-law, never spent five shillings in any idleness : luckily (as she was sure to add) he had it not to spend. A more serious charge against her was that, living to a great age, and but little able to work, she grew to be seriously afraid, that, at last, she might become chargeable to the parish (the heaviest, in her estimation, of all human calamities), and that thus alarmed she did suffer herself more than once, during the exacerbations of a fit of distempered despondency, peevishly (and perhaps petulantly) to exclaim that God Almighty, by suffering her to remain so long upon earth, seemed actually to have forgotten her.' 'Such,' concludes Eden, 'are the simple annals of Dame Strudwick : and her historian, partial to his subject, closes it with lamenting that such village memoirs have not oftener been sought for and recorded.'[1] This was the ideal character for the cottage. How Eden or anybody else would have hated this poor woman in whom every kindly feeling had been starved to death if she had been in his own class ! We know from Creevey what his friends thought of ' the stingy kip ' Lambton when they found themselves under his roof, where ' a round of beef at a side table was run at with as much keenness as a banker's shop before a stoppage.' A little peevishness or even petulance with God Almighty would

[1] Eden, vol. i. p. 579.

not have seemed the most serious charge that could be brought against such a neighbour. But if every villager had had Dame Strudwick's hard and narrow virtues, and had crushed all other tastes and interests in the passion for living on a shilling a day in a cold and bitter independence, the problem of preserving the monopolies of the few without disorder or trouble would have been greatly simplified. There would have been little danger, as Burke would have said, that the fruits of successful industry and the accumulations of fortune would be exposed to ' the plunder of the negligent, the disappointed, and the unprosperous.'

The way in which the ruling class regarded the poor is illustrated in the tone of the discussions when the problem of poverty had become acute at the end of the eighteenth century. When Pitt, who had been pestered by Eden to read his book, handed a volume to Canning, then his secretary, that brilliant young politician spent his time writing a parody on the grotesque names to be found in the Appendix, and it will be recollected that Pitt excused himself for abandoning his scheme for reforming the Poor Law, on the ground that he was inexperienced in the condition of the poor. It was no shame to a politician to be ignorant of such subjects. The poor were happy or unhappy in the view of the ruling class according to the sympathy the rich bestowed on them. If there were occasional misgivings they were easily dispelled. Thus one philosopher pointed out that though the position of the poor man might seem wanting in dignity or independence, it should be remembered by way of consolation that he could play the tyrant over his wife and children as much as he liked.[1] Another train of soothing reflections was started by such papers as that published in the *Annals of Agriculture* in 1797, under the title ' On the Comforts enjoyed by the Cottagers compared to those of the ancient Barons.' In such a society a sentiment like that expressed by Fox when supporting Whitbread's Bill in 1795, that ' it was not fitting in a free country that the great body of the people should depend on the charity of the rich,' seemed a challenging paradox. Eden thought this an extraordinary way of looking at the problem, and retorted that it was gratifying to see how ready the rich were to bestow their benevolent attentions. This was the point of view of Pitt and of almost all the speakers in the debate that followed Fox's outburst, Buxton going so far as to say that owing to those

[1] *Reports on Poor*, vol. ii. p. 325.

attentions the condition of the poor had never been ' so eligible.' Just as the boisterous captain in *Evelina* thought it was an honour to a wretched Frenchwoman to be rolled in British mud, so the English House of Commons thought that poverty was turned into a positive blessing by the kindness of the rich.

Writing towards the end of the ancient régime, Cobbett maintained that in his own lifetime the tone and language of society about the poor had changed very greatly for the worse, that the old name of ' the commons of England ' had given way to such names as ' the lower orders,' ' the peasantry,' and ' the population,' and that when the poor met together to demand their rights they were invariably spoken of by such contumelious terms as ' the populace ' or ' the mob.' ' In short, by degrees beginning about fifty years ago the industrious part of the community, particularly those who create every useful thing by their labour, have been spoken of by everyone possessing the power to oppress them in any degree in just the same manner in which we speak of the animals which compose the stock upon a farm. This is not the manner in which the forefathers of us, the common people, were treated.' [1] Such language, Cobbett said, was to be heard not only from ' taxdevourers, bankers, brewers, monopolists of every sort, but also from their clerks, from the very shopkeepers and waiters, and from the fribbles stuck up behind the counter to do the business that ought to be done by a girl.' This is perhaps only another way of saying that the isolation of the poor was becoming a more and more conspicuous feature of English society.

Many causes combined to destroy the companionship of classes, and most of all the break-up of the old village which followed on the enclosures and the consolidation of farms. In the old village, labourers and cottagers and small farmers were neighbours. They knew each other and lived much the same kind of life. The small farmer was a farmer one day of the week and a labourer another; he married, according to Cobbett, the domestic servant of the gentry, a fact that explains the remark of Sophia Western's maid to the landlady of the inn, ' and let me have the bacon cut very nice and thin, for I can't endure anything that 's gross. Prythee try if you can't do a little tolerably for once ; and don't think you have a farmer's wife or some of those creatures in the house.' The new

---

[1] *Political Register*, vol. lxxviii. p. 710.

farmer lived in a different latitude. He married a young lady from the boarding school. He often occupied the old manor house.[1] He was divided from the labourer by his tastes, his interests, his ambitions, his display and whole manner of life. The change that came over the English village in consequence was apparent to all observers with social insight. When Goldsmith wanted to describe a happy village he was careful to choose a village of the old kind, with the farmers ' strangers alike to opulence and to poverty,' and Crabbe, to whose sincere and realist pen we owe much of our knowledge of the social life of the time, gives a particularly poignant impression of the cold and friendless atmosphere that surrounded the poor :

> ' Where Plenty smiles, alas ! she smiles for few,
> And those who taste not, yet behold her store,
> Are as the slaves that dig the golden ore,
> The wealth around them makes them doubly poor.' [2]

Perhaps the most vivid account of the change is given in a letter from Cobbett in the *Political Register* for 17th March 1821,[3] addressed to Mr. Gooch :—

' I hold a return to *small farms* to be *absolutely necessary* to a restoration to anything like an English community ; and I am quite sure, that the ruin of the present race of farmers, generally, is a necessary preliminary to this. . . . The life of the husbandman cannot be that of *a gentleman* without injury to society at large. When farmers become *gentlemen* their labourers become *slaves.* A *Virginian* farmer, as he is called, very much resembles a *great farmer* in England ; but then, the Virginian's work is done by slaves. It is in those States of America, where the farmer is only the *first labourer* that all the domestic virtues are to be found, and all that public-spirit and that valour, which are the safeguards of American independence, freedom, and happiness. You, Sir, with others, complain of the increase of the *poor-rates.* But, you seem to forget, that, in the destruction of the small farms, as separate farms, small-farmers have become mere hired labourers. . . . Take England throughout *three farms have been turned into one within fifty years,* and the far greater part of the change has taken place within the last *thirty years* ; that is to say, since the commencement of the deadly system of PITT. Instead of families of small farmers with all their exertions, all their decency of dress and of manners, and all their scrupulousness as to character, we have *families of paupers,* with all the improvidence and wrecklessness belonging to an irrevocable sentence of poverty

---

[1] Hasbach, p. 131.   [2] 'Village,' Book I.   [3] Vol. xxxviii. p. 750 ff.

for life. Mr. CURWEN in his *Hints on Agriculture*, observes that he saw some where in Norfolk, I believe it was, *two hundred* farmers worth from *five to ten thousand pounds each*; and exclaims "What a *glorious* sight!" In commenting on this passage in the Register, in the year 1810, I observed "Mr. CURWEN only saw the *outside* of the sepulchre; if he had seen the *two or three thousand* half-starved labourers of these two hundred farmers, and the *five or six thousand* ragged wives and children of those labourers; if the farmers had brought those with them, the sight would not have been so *glorious.*"'

A practice referred to in the same letter of Cobbett's that tended to widen the gulf between the farmer and the labourer was the introduction of bailiffs : ' Along with enormous prices for corn came in the employment of *Bailiffs* by farmers, a natural consequence of large farms ; and to what a degree of insolent folly the system was leading, may be guessed from an observation of Mr. ARTHUR YOUNG, who recommended, that the Bailiff should have a good horse to ride, and a *bottle of port wine every day at his dinner* : while in the same work, Mr. YOUNG gives great numbers of rules for saving labour upon a farm. A pretty sort of farm where the bailiff was to have a bottle of port wine at his dinner ! The custom was, too, to bring bailiffs from some *distant part*, in order to prevent them from having any feeling of compassion for the labourers. *Scotch* bailiffs above all, were preferred, as being thought harder than any others that could be obtained ; and thus (with shame I write the words !) the farms of *England*, like those of *Jamaica*, were supplied with drivers from Scotland ! . . . Never was a truer saying, than that of the common people, that a Scotchman makes a " good *sole*, but a d——d bad *upper leather.*" '[1] Bamford, speaking of 1745, says : ' Gentlemen then lived as they ought to live : as real gentlemen will ever be found living : in kindliness with their neighbours ; in openhanded charity towards the poor, and in hospitality towards all friendly comers. There were no grinding bailiffs and land stewards in those days to stand betwixt the gentleman and his labourer or his tenant : to screw up rents and screw down livings, and to invent and transact all little meannesses for so much per annum.'[2] Cobbett's prejudice against Scotsmen, the race of ' feelosofers,' blinded him to virtues which were notoriously theirs, as in his round declaration that all the hard work of agriculture was done by Englishmen and

[1] Cobbett's *Political Register*, March 17, 1821, p. 779.
[2] Bamford, *Passages in the Life of a Radical*, p. 38.

Irishmen, and that the Scotsmen chose such tasks as 'peeping into melon frames.' But that his remarks upon the subject of the introduction of Scottish bailiffs reflected a general feeling may be seen from a passage in Miss Austen's *Emma*, ' Mr. Graham intends to have a Scotch bailiff for his new estate. Will it answer ? Will not the old prejudice be too strong ? '

The change in the status of the farmer came at a time of a general growth of luxury. All classes above the poor adopted a more extravagant and ostentatious style and scale of living. This was true, for example, of sporting England. Fox-hunting dates from this century. Before the eighteenth century the amusement of the aristocracy was hunting the stag, and that of the country squire was hunting the hare. It was because Walpole kept beagles at Richmond and used to hunt once a week that the House of Commons has always made Saturday a holiday. In the Peninsular War, Wellington kept a pack of hounds at headquarters, but they were fox-hounds. In its early days fox-hunting had continued the simpler traditions of hare-hunting, and each small squire kept a few couple of hounds and brought them to the meet. Gray has described his uncle's establishment at Burnham, where every chair in the house was taken up by a dog. But as the century advanced the sport was organised on a grander scale : the old buck-hounds and slow horses were superseded by more expensive breeds, and far greater distances were covered. Fox-hunting became the amusement both of the aristocracy and of the squires, and it resembled rather the pomp and state of stag-hunting than the modest pleasures of Walpole and his friends. In all other directions there was a general increase of magnificence in life. The eighteenth century was the century of great mansions, and some of the most splendid palaces of the aristocracy were built during the distress and famine of the French war. The ambitions of the aristocracy became the ambitions of the classes that admired them, as we know from Smollett, and Sir William Scott in 1802, speaking in favour of the non-residence of the clergy, 'expressly said that they and their families ought to appear at watering-places, and that this was amongst the means of making them respected by their flocks!'[1]

The rich and the poor were thus growing further and further apart, and there was nobody in the English village to inter-

[1] *Rural Rides*, p. 460.

pret these two worlds to each other. M. Babeau has pointed out that in France, under the ancient régime, the lawyers represented and defended in some degree the rights of the peasants. This was one consequence of the constant litigation between peasants and seigneurs over communal property. The lawyers who took the side of the peasants lived at their expense it is true, but they rendered public services, they presented the peasants' case before public opinion, and they understood their ideas and difficulties. This explains a striking feature of the French Revolution, the large number of local lawyers who became prominent as champions of revolutionary ideas. One of Burke's chief complaints of the Constituent Assembly was that it contained so many country attorneys and notaries, 'the fomenters and conductors of the petty war of village vexation.'[1] In England the lawyers never occupied this position, and it is impossible to imagine such a development taking place there. The lawyers who interested themselves in the poor were enlisted not in the defence of the rights of the commoners but in the defence of the purses of the parishes. For them the all-important question was not what rights the peasant had against his lord, but on which parish he had a claim for maintenance.

The causes of litigation were endless : if a man rented a tenement of the annual value of £10 he acquired a settlement. But his rental might not have represented the annual value, and so the further question would come up, Was the annual value actually £10 ? ' If it may be really not far from that sum, and the family of the pauper be numerous, the interests of the contending parishes, supported by the conflicting opinions of their respective surveyors, leads to the utmost expense and extremity of litigation.'[2] If the annual value were not in dispute there might be nice and intricate questions about the kind of tenement and the nature of the tenure : if the settlement was claimed in virtue of a contract of hiring, was the contract ' general, special, customary, retrospective, conditional, personal ' or what not ?[3] If the settlement was claimed in virtue of apprenticeship,[4] what was the nature of the indentures and so on. If claimed for an estate of £30, was the estate really worth £30, and how was it acquired ? These are a few of the questions in dispute, and to add to the confusion ' on

[1] *Reflections*, p. 61. [2] *Poor Law Report*, 1817.
[3] Cf. *Ibid.*, 1834, p. 161.
[4] Cf. case of apprentice, *Annual Register*, 1819, p. 195.

no branch of the law have the judgments of the superior court been so contradictory.' [1]

Thus the principal occupation of those lawyers whose business brought them into the world of the poor was of a nature to draw their sympathies and interests to the side of the possessing classes, and whereas peasants' ideas were acclimatised outside their own class in France as a consequence of the character of rural litigation and of rural lawyers, the English villager came before the lawyer, not as a client, but as a danger; not as a person whose rights and interests had to be explored and studied, but as a person whose claims on the parish had to be parried or evaded.   It is not surprising, therefore, to find that both Fielding and Smollett lay great stress on the reputation of lawyers for harshness and extortion in their treatment of the poor, regarding them, like Carlyle, as 'attorneys and law beagles who hunt ravenous on the earth.'   Readers of the adventures of Sir Launcelot Greaves will remember Tom Clarke ' whose goodness of heart even the exercise of his profession had not been able to corrupt.   Before strangers he never owned himself an attorney without blushing, though he had no reason to blush for his own practice, for he constantly refused to engage in the cause of any client whose character was equivocal, and was never known to act with such industry as when concerned for the widow and orphan or any other object that sued *in forma pauperis.'*   Fielding speaks in a foot-note to *Tom Jones* of the oppression of the poor by attorneys, as a scandal to the law, the nation, Christianity, and even human nature itself.

There was another class that might, under different circumstances, have helped to soothe and soften the isolation of the poor, but the position and the sympathies of the English Church made this impossible.   This was seen very clearly by Adam Smith, who was troubled by the fear that ' enthusiasm,' the religious force so dreaded by the men of science and reason, would spread among the poor, because the clergy who should have controlled and counteracted it were so little in touch with the mass of the people.   Under the government of the Anglican Church, as set up by the Reformation, he pointed out,

---

[1] *Poor Law Report,* 1817 ; in some cases there were amicable arrangements to keep down legal expenses ; *e.g.* at Halifax (Eden), the overseer formed a society of the officers of adjoining parishes.   Cases were referred to them, and the decision of the majority was accepted.

' the clergy naturally endeavour to recommend themselves to the sovereign, to the court, and to the nobility and gentry of the country, by whose influence they chiefly expect to obtain preferment.' [1]   He added that such a clergy are very apt to neglect altogether the means of maintaining their influence and authority with the lower ranks of life.   The association of the Anglican Church with the governing class has never been more intimate and binding than it was during the eighteenth century. This was true alike of bishops and of clergy.   The English bishop was not a gay Voltairean like the French, but he was just as zealous a member of the privileged orders, and the system over which he presided and which he defended was a faint copy of the gloriously coloured scandals of the French Church.   The prelates who lived upon those scandals were described by Robespierre, with a humour that he did not often indulge, as treating the deity in the same way as the mayor of the palace used to treat the French kings.   ' Ils l'ont traité comme jadis les maires du palais traitèrent les descendants de Clovis pour régner sous son nom et se mettre à sa place.   Ils l'ont relégué dans le ciel comme dans un palais, et ne l'ont appelé sur la terre que pour demander a leur profit des dîmes, des richesses, des honneurs, des plaisirs et de la puissance.' When Archbishop Dillon declared against the civil constitution he said that he and his colleagues acted as gentlemen and not as theologians.   The Archbishop of Aix spoke of tithes as a voluntary offering from the piety of the faithful.   ' As to that,' said the Duke de la Rochefoucault, ' there are now forty thousand cases in the Courts.'   Both these archbishops would have found themselves quite at home among the spiritual peers in the House of Lords, where the same decorous hypocrisies mingled with the same class atmosphere.   For the English bishops, though they were not libertines like the French, never learnt so to be Christians as to forget to be aristocrats, and their religious duties were never allowed to interfere with the demands of scholarship or of pleasure.   Perhaps the most distinguished product of this régime was Bishop Watson of Llandaff, who invented an improved gunpowder and defended Christianity against Paine and Gibbon.   These were his diversions ; his main business was carried on at his magnificent country seat on the banks of Windermere.   He was bishop for thirty-four years, and during the whole of that time he never lived within his diocese, preferring to play the part of the grand

---

[1] *Wealth of Nations*, vol. iii. p. 234.

seigneur planting trees in Westmorland. He has left a sympathetic and charming account of what he modestly calls his retirement from public life, an event not to be confused with abdication of his see, and of how he built the palace where he spent the emoluments of Llandaff and the long autumn of his life.

It was natural to men who lived in this atmosphere to see politics through the spectacles of the aristocracy. To understand how strongly the view that the Church existed to serve the aristocracy, and the rest of the State through the aristocracy, was fixed in the minds of the higher clergy, we have only to look at the case of a reformer like Bishop Horsley. The bishop is chiefly known as a preacher, a controversialist, and the author of the celebrated dictum that the poor had nothing to do with the laws except to obey them. His battle with Priestley has been compared to the encounter of Bentley and Collins, a comparison that may not give Horsley more, but certainly gives Priestley less than his due. When he preached before the House of Lords on the death of Louis xvi. his audience rose and stood in silent reverence during his peroration. The cynical may feel that it was not difficult to inspire emotion and awe in such a congregation on such a subject at such a time, but we know from De Quincey that Horsley's reputation as a preacher stood remarkably high. He was one of the leaders of the Church in politics; for our purposes it is more important to note that he was one of the reforming bishops. Among other scandals he attacked the scandal of non-residence, and he may be taken as setting in this regard the strictest standard of his time; yet he did not scruple to go and live in Oxford for some years as tutor to Lord Guernsey, during the time that he was Rector of Newington, as plain a confession as we could want that in the estimation of the most public-spirited of the clergy the nobility had the first claims on the Church. These social sympathies were confirmed by common political interests. The privileges of the aristocracy and of the bishops were in fact bound up together, and both bishops and aristocracy had good reason to shrink from breaking a thread anywhere. Perhaps the malicious would find the most complete and piquant illustration of the relations of the Church and the governing class in the letter written by Dr. Goodenough to Addington, who had just made him Dean of Rochester, when the clerkship of the Pells, worth £3000 a year, was about to become vacant. ' I understand that Colonel Barré is in a very precarious state. I hope you will have the fortitude to nominate Harry to be his successor.' Harry, Addington's son, was a boy at Winchester. The father's fortitude rose to the emergency : the dean blossomed a little later into a bishop.

But if the French and the English bishops both belonged to the aristocracy in feelings and in habits, a great difference distinguishes the rank and file of the clergy in the two countries. The French priest belonged by circumstances and by sympathy to the peasant class. The bishop regarded the country curé as *un vilain sentant le fumier*, and treated him with about as much consideration as the seigneur showed to his dependants. The priest's quarrel with the bishop was like the peasant's quarrel with the seigneur : for both priest and peasant smarted under the arrogant airs of their respective superiors, and the bishop swallowed up the tithes as the seigneur swallowed up the feudal dues. Sometimes the curé put himself at the head of a local rebellion. In the reign of Louis xv. the priests round Saint-Germain led out their flocks to destroy the game which devoured their crops, the campaign being announced and sanctified from the pulpit. In the Revolution the common clergy were largely on the side of the peasants. Such a development was inconceivable in England. As the curé's windows looked to the village, the parson's windows looked to the hall. When the parson's circumstances enabled him to live like the squire, he rode to hounds, for though, as Blackstone tells us, Roman Canon Law, under the influence of the tradition that St. Jerome had once observed that the saints had eschewed such diversions, had interdicted *venationes et sylvaticas vagationes cum canibus et accipitribus* to all clergymen, this early severity of life had vanished long before the eighteenth century. He treated the calls of his profession as trifling accidents interrupting his normal life of vigorous pleasure. On becoming Bishop of Chester, Dr. Blomfield astonished the diocese by refusing to license a curate until he had promised to abstain from hunting, and by the pain and surprise with which he saw one of his clergy carried away drunk from a visitation dinner. One rector, whom he rebuked for drunkenness, replied with an injured manner that he was never drunk on duty.

There were, it is true, clergymen of great public spirit and devoted lives, and such men figure in these pages, but the Church, as a whole, was an easy-going society, careful of its pleasures and comforts, living with the moral ideas and as far as possible in the manner of the rich. The rivalry of the Methodist movement had given a certain stimulus to zeal, and the Vicar of Corsley in Wilts,[1] for example, added a second service to the duties of the Sunday, though guarding himself expressly against the admission of any obligation to make it permanent. But it was found impossible to eradicate from the system certain of the vices that belong to a society which is primarily a class. Some of the bishops set themselves to reduce the practice of non-residence. Porteus, Bishop of London, devoted a great part of his charge to his clergy in 1790 to this subject, and though he pleaded passionately for reform he cannot be said to have shut his eyes to the difficulties of the clergy. ' There are, indeed, two impediments to constant residence which cannot easily be surmounted ; the first is (what unfortunately prevails in some parts of this diocese) unwholesomeness of situation ; the other is the possession of a second benefice. Yet even these will not justify *a total and perpetual* absence from your cures. The unhealthiness of many places is of late years by various improvements greatly abated, and there are now few so circumstanced as not to admit of residence there in *some* part of the year without any danger to the constitution.' Thus even Bishop Porteus, who in this very charge reminded the clergy that they were called by the titles of stewards, watchmen, shepherds, and labourers, never went the length of thinking that the Church was to be expected to minister to the poor in all weathers and in all climates.

The exertions of the reforming bishops did not achieve a conspicuous success, for the second of the difficulties touched on by Porteus was insurmountable. In his *Legacy to Parsons*, Cobbett, quoting from the *Clerical Guide*, showed that 332 parsons shared the revenues of 1496 parishes, and 500 more shared those of 1524. Among the pluralists were Lord Walsingham, who besides enjoying a pension of £700 a year, was Archdeacon of Surrey, Prebendary of Winchester, Rector of Calbourne, Rector of Fawley, perpetual Curate of Exbury, and Rector of Merton ; the Earl of Guildford, Rector of Old Alresford, Rector of New Alresford, perpetual Curate of Medsted, Rector of St. Mary, Southampton, including the great parish of South Stoneham, Master of St. Cross Hospital, with the revenue of the parish of St. Faith along with it. There were three Pretymans dividing fifteen benefices, and

[1] *Life in an English Village*, by Maude F. Davies, p. 58.

Wellington's brother was Prebendary of Durham, Rector of Bishopwearmouth, Rector of Chelsea, and Rector of Therfield. This method of treating the parson's profession as a comfortable career was so closely entangled in the system of aristocracy, that no Government which represented those interests would ever dream of touching it. Parliament intervened indeed, but intervened to protect those who lived on these abuses. For before 1801 there were Acts of Parliament on the Statute Book (21 Henry VIII. c. 13, and 13 Elizabeth c. 20), which provided certain penalties for non-residence. In 1799 a certain Mr. Williams laid informations against hundreds of the clergy for offences against these Acts. Parliament replied by passing a series of Acts to stay proceedings, and finally in 1803 Sir William Scott, member for the University of Oxford, passed an Act which allowed the bishops to authorise parsons to reside out of their parishes. It is not surprising to find that in 1812, out of ten thousand incumbents, nearly six thousand were non-resident.

In the parishes where the incumbent was non-resident, if there was a clergyman at all in the place, it was generally a curate on a miserable pittance. Bishop Porteus, in the charge already mentioned, gives some interesting information about the salaries of curates : ' It is also highly to the honour of this Diocese that in general the stipends allowed to the curates are more liberal than in many other parts of the kingdom. In several instances I find that the stipend for one church only is £50 a year ; for two £60 and the use of a parsonage ; and in the unwholesome parts of the Diocese £70 and even £80 (that is £40 for each church), with the same indulgence of a house to reside in.' Many of the parishes did not see much of the curate assigned to them. ' A man must have travelled very little in the kingdom,' said Arthur Young in 1798, ' who does not know that country towns abound with curates who never see the parishes they serve, but when they are absolutely forced to it by duty.' [1] But the ill-paid curate, even when he was resident and conscientious, as he often was, moved like the pluralist rector in the orbit of the rich. He was in that world though not of it. All his hopes hung on the squire. To have taken the side of the poor against him would have meant ruin, and the English Church was not a nursery of this kind of heroism. It is significant that almost every eighteenth-century novelist puts

[1] *Inquiry into the State of the Public Mind among the Lower Classes*, p. 27.

at least one sycophantic parson in his or her gallery of portraits.[1]

In addition to the social ties that drew the clergy to the aristocracy, there was a powerful economic hindrance to their friendship with the poor. De Tocqueville thought that the tithe system brought the French priest into interesting and touching relations with the peasant : a view that has seemed fanciful to later historians, who are more impressed by the quarrels that resulted. But De Tocqueville himself could scarcely argue that the tithe system helped to warm the heart of the labourer to the Church of England in cases such as those recorded in the Parliamentary Paper issued in 1833, in which parson magistrates sent working men to prison for refusing to pay tithes to their rector. Day labouring men had originally been exempted from liability to pay tithes, but just as the French Church brought more and more of the property and industry of the State within her confiscating grasp, so the English Parliament, from the reign of William III., had been drawing the parson's net more closely round the labourer. Moreover, as we shall see in a later chapter, the question of tithes was in the very centre of the social agitations that ended in the rising of 1830 and its terrible punishment. In this particular quarrel the farmers and labourers were on the same side, and the parsons as a body stood out for their own property with as much determination as the landlords.

In one respect the Church took an active part in oppressing the village poor, for Wilberforce and his friends started, just before the French Revolution, a Society for the Reformation of Manners, which aimed at enforcing the observance of Sunday, forbidding any kind of social dissipation, and repressing freedom of speech and of thought whenever they refused to conform to the superstitions of the morose religion that was then in fashion. This campaign was directed against the license of the poor alone. There were no stocks for the Sabbath-breakers of Brooks's : a Gibbon might take what liberties he pleased with religion : the wildest Methodist never tried to shackle the loose tongues or the loose lives of the gay rich. The attitude of the Church to the excesses of this class is well depicted in Fielding's account of Parson Supple, who never remonstrated with Squire Western for swearing, but preached so vigorously

[1] The parsons under Squire Allworthy's roof, the parson to whom Pamela appealed in vain, and, most striking of all, Mr. Collins in *Pride and Prejudice*.

in the pulpit against the habit that the authorities put the laws very severely in execution against others, ' and the magistrate was the only person in the parish who could swear with impunity.' This description might seem to border on burlesque, but there is an entry in Wilberforce's diary that reveals a state of mind which even Fielding would have found it impossible to caricature. Wilberforce was staying at Brighton, and this is his description of an evening he spent at the Pavilion with the first gentleman of Europe : ' The Prince and Duke of Clarence too very civil. Prince showed he had read Cobbett. Spoke strongly of the blasphemy of his late papers and most justly.' [1] We can only hope that Sheridan was there to enjoy the scene, and that the Prince was able for once to do justice to his strong feelings in language that would not shock Wilberforce's ears.

Men like Wilberforce and the magistrates whom he inspired did not punish the rich for their dissolute behaviour ; they only found in that behaviour another argument for coercing the poor. As they watched the dishevelled lives of men like George Selwyn, their one idea of action was to punish a village labourer for neglecting church on Sunday morning. We have seen how the cottagers paid in Enclosure Bills for their lords' adventures at play. They paid also for their lords' dissipations in the loss of innocent pleasures that might have brought some colour into their grey lives. The more boisterous the fun at Almack's, the deeper the gloom thrown over the village. The Select Committee on Allotments that reported in 1843 found one of the chief causes of crime in the lack of recreations. Sheridan at one time and Cobbett at another tried to revive village sports, but social circumstances were too strong for them. In this respect the French peasant had the advantage. Babeau's picture of his gay and sociable Sunday may be overdrawn, but a comparison of Crabbe's description of the English Sunday with contemporary descriptions of Sunday as it was spent in a French village, shows that the spirit of common gaiety, killed in England by Puritanism and by the destruction of the natural and easy-going relations of the village community, survived in France through all the tribulations of poverty and famine. The eighteenth-century French village still bore a resemblance in fact to the mediæval English village, and Goldsmith has recorded in *The Traveller* his impressions of ' mirth and social ease.' Babeau gives an

[1] *Life*, vol. iv. p. 277.

account of a great variety of village games, from the violent
contests in Brittany for the ' choule,' in one of which fourteen
players were drowned, to the gentler dances and the children's
romps that were general in other parts of France, and Arthur
Young was very much struck by the agility and the grace that
the heavy peasants displayed in dancing on the village green.
Windham, speaking in a bad cause, the defence of bull-baiting
in 1800, laid stress on the contrast : ' In the south of France
and in Spain, at the end of the day's labour, and in the cool of
the evening's shade, the poor dance in mirthful festivity on
the green, to the sound of the guitar.   But in this country no
such source of amusement presents itself.   If they dance, it
must be often in a marsh, or in the rain, for the pleasure of
catching cold.   But there is a substitute in this country well
known by the name of *Hops*.   We all know the alarm which the
very word inspires, and the sound of the fiddle calls forth the
magistrate to dissolve the meeting.   Men bred in ignorance
of the world, and having no opportunity of mixing in its scenes
or observing its manners, may be much worse employed than
in learning something of its customs from theatrical representations ; but if a company of strolling players make their appearance in a village, they are hunted immediately from it as a
nuisance, except, perhaps, there be a few people of greater
wealth in the neighbourhood, whose wives and daughters
patronize them.' [1]   Thus all the influences of the time conspired
to isolate the poor, and the changes, destructive of their freedom
and happiness, that were taking place in their social and
economic surroundings, were aggravated by a revival of Puritanism which helped to rob village life of all its natural melody
and colour.

[1] *Parliamentary Register*, April 18, 1800.

CHAPTER X

THE VILLAGE IN 1830

WE have described the growing misery of the labourer, the increasing rigours of the criminal law, and the insensibility of the upper classes, due to the isolation of the poor. What kind of a community was created by the Speenhamland system after it had been in force for a generation? We have, fortunately, a very full picture given in a Parliamentary Report that is generally regarded as one of the landmarks of English history. We cannot do better than set out the main features of the Report of the Poor Law Commissioners of 1834, and the several effects they traced to this system.

The first effect is one that everybody could have anticipated : the destruction of all motives for effort and ambition. Under this system ' the most worthless were sure of *something*, while the prudent, the industrious, and the sober, with all their care and pains, obtained *only something*; and even that scanty pittance was doled out to them by the overseer.'[1] All labourers were condemned to live on the brink of starvation, for no effort of will or character could improve their position. The effect on the imagination was well summed up in a rhetorical question from a labourer who gave evidence to a Commissioner. ' When a man has his spirit broken what is he good for?'[2] The Poor Law Commissioners looked at it from a different point of view : ' The labourer feels that the existing system, though it generally gives him low wages, always gives him work. It gives him also, strange as it may appear, what he values more, a sort of independence. He need not bestir himself to seek work ; he need not study to please his master ; he need not put any restraint upon his temper ; he need not ask relief as a favour. He has all a slave's security for subsistence, without his liability to punishment. . . . All the other classes of society are exposed to the vicissitudes of hope and fear ; he alone has nothing to lose or to gain.'[3]

[1] Report of the Poor Law Commission, 1834, p. 243.   [2] *Ibid.*, p. 84.
[3] *Ibid.*, pp. 56-7.

But it is understating the result of the system on individual enterprise to say that it destroyed incentives to ambition ; for in some parishes it actually proscribed independence and punished the labourer who owned some small property. Wages under these conditions were so low that a man with a little property or a few savings could not keep himself alive without help from the parish, but if a man was convicted of possessing anything he was refused parish help. It was dangerous even to look tidy or neat, ' ragged clothes are kept by the poor, for the express purpose of coming to the vestry in them.' [1] The Report of the Commissioners on this subject recalls Rousseau's description of the French peasant with whom he stayed in the course of his travels, who, when his suspicions had been soothed, and his hospitable instincts had been warmed by friendly conversation, produced stores of food from the secret place where they had been hidden to escape the eye of the tax-collector. A man who had saved anything was ruined. A Mr. Hickson, a Northampton manufacturer and landowner in Kent, gave an illustration of this.

' The case of a man who has worked for me will show the effect of the parish system in preventing frugal habits. This is a hard-working, industrious man, named William Williams. He is married, and had saved some money, to the amount of about £70, and had two cows ; he had also a sow and ten pigs. He had got a cottage well furnished ; he was a member of a benefit club at Meopham, from which he received 8s. a week when he was ill. He was beginning to learn to read and write, and sent his children to the Sunday School. He had a legacy of about £46, but he got his other money together by saving from his fair wages as a waggoner. Some circumstances occurred which obliged me to part with him. The consequence of this labouring man having been frugal and saved money, and got the cows, was that no one would employ him, although his superior character as a workman was well known in the parish. He told me at the time I was obliged to part with him : " Whilst I have these things I shall get no work ; I must part with them all ; I must be reduced to a state of beggary before any one will employ me." I was compelled to part with him at Michaelmas ; he has not yet got work, and he has no chance of getting any until he has become a pauper ; for until then the paupers will be preferred to him. He cannot get work in his own parish, and he will not be

[1] Report of the Poor Law Commission, 1834, p. 244.

allowed to get any in other parishes.   Another instance of the same kind occurred amongst my workmen.   Thomas Hardy, the brother-in-law of the same man, was an excellent work-man, discharged under similar circumstances ; he has a very industrious wife.   They have got two cows, a well-furnished cottage, and a pig and fowls.   Now he cannot get work, because he has property.   The pauper will be preferred to him, and he can qualify himself for it only by becoming a pauper. If he attempts to get work elsewhere, he is told that they do not want to fix him on the parish.   Both these are fine young men, and as excellent labourers as I could wish to have.   The latter labouring man mentioned another instance of a labouring man in another parish (Henstead), who had once had more property than he, but was obliged to consume it all, and is now working on the roads.' [1]   This effect of the Speenhamland arrangements was dwelt on in the evidence before the Com-mittee on Agricultural Labourers' Wages in 1824.   Labourers had to give up their cottages in a Dorsetshire village because they could not become pensioners if they possessed a cottage, and farmers would only give employment to village pensioners. Thus these cottagers who had not been evicted by enclosure were evicted by the Speenhamland system.

It is not surprising that in the case of another man of independent nature in Cambridgeshire, who had saved money and so could get no work, we are told that the young men pointed at him, and called him a fool for not spending his money at the public-house, ' adding that then he would get work.' [2] The statesmen who condemned the labourer to this fate had rejected the proposal for a minimum wage, on the ground that it would destroy emulation.

There was one slight alleviation of this vicious system, which the Poor Law Commissioners considered in the very different light of an aggravation.   If society was to be re-organised on such a basis as this, it was at any rate better that the men who were made to live on public money should not be grateful to the ratepayers.   The Commissioners were pained by the insolence of the paupers.   ' The parish money,' said a Sussex labourer, ' is now chucked to us like as to a dog,' [3] but the labourers did not lick the hand that threw it.   All through the Report we read complaints of the ' insolent, dis-contented, surly pauper,' who talks of ' right ' and ' income,'

[1] Report of the Poor Law Commission, 1834, pp. 78-9.   [2] *Ibid.*, p. 80.
[3] *Ibid.*, p. 291.

and who will soon fight for these supposed rights and income
'unless some step is taken to arrest his progress to open
violence.' The poor emphasised this view by the terms they
applied to their rate subsidies, which they sometimes called
'their reglars,' sometimes 'the county allowance,' and sometimes 'The Act of Parliament allowance.' Old dusty rent-
books of receipts and old dirty indentures of apprenticeship
were handed down from father to son with as much care as
if they had been deeds of freehold property, as documentary
evidence to their right to a share in the rates of a particular
parish.[1] Of course there was not a uniform administration,
and the Commissioners reported that whilst in some districts
men were disqualified for relief if they had any wages, in others
there was no inquiry into circumstances, and non-necessitous
persons dipped like the rest into the till. In many cases only
the wages received during the last week or fortnight were taken
into account, and thus the allowance would be paid to some
persons who at particular periods received wages in excess of
the scale. This accounts for the fact stated by Thorold
Rogers from his own experience that there were labourers
who actually saved considerable sums out of the system.

The most obvious and immediate effect was the effect
which had been foreseen without misgiving in Warwickshire
and Worcestershire. The married man was employed in
preference to the bachelor, and his income rose with the birth
of each child. But there was one thing better than to marry
and have a family, and that was to marry a mother of
bastards, for bastards were more profitable than legitimate
children, since the parish guaranteed the contribution for
which the putative father was legally liable. It was easier to
manage with a family than with a single child. As one young
woman of twenty-four with four bastard children put it, 'If
she had one more she should be very comfortable.'[2] Women
with bastard children were thus very eligible wives. The effect
of the whole system on village morals was striking and widespread, and a witness from a parish which was overwhelmed
with this sudden deluge of population said to the Commission,
'the eighteen-penny children will eat up this parish in ten
years more, unless some relief be afforded us.'[3] Before this
period, if we are to believe Cobbett, it had been rare for a
woman to be with child at the time of her marriage; in

[1] Report of the Poor Law Commission, 1834, p. 94.   [2] *Ibid.*, p. 172.
[3] *Ibid.*, p. 66.

these days of demoralisation and distress it became the habit.

The effects produced by this system on the recipients of relief were all of them such as might have been anticipated, and in this respect the Report of the Commissioners contained no surprises. It merely illustrated the generalisations that had been made by all Poor Law Reformers during the last fifteen years. But the discovery of the extent of the corruption which the system had bred in local government and administration was probably a revelation to most people. It demoralised not only those who received but those who gave. A network of tangled interests spread over local life, and employers and tradesmen were faced with innumerable temptations and opportunities for fraud. To take the case of the overseer first. Suppose him to be a tradesman : he was liable to suffer in his custom if he refused to relieve the friends, or it might be the workmen of his customers. It would require a man of almost superhuman rigidity of principle to be willing not only to lose time and money in serving a troublesome and unprofitable office, but to lose custom as well.[1] From the resolve not to lose custom he might gradually slip down to the determination to reimburse himself for ' the vexatious demands ' on his time, till a state of affairs like that in Slaugham came about.

' Population, 740. Expenditure, £1706. The above large sum of money is expended principally in orders on the village shops for flour, clothes, butter, cheese, etc. : the tradesmen serve the office of overseer by turns ; the two last could neither read nor write.' [2]

If the overseer were a farmer there were temptations to pay part of the wages of his own and his friends' labourers out of parish money, or to supply the workhouse with his own produce. The same temptations beset the members of vestries, whether they were open or select. ' Each vestryman, so far as he is an immediate employer of labour, is interested in keeping down the rate of wages, and in throwing part of their payment on others, and, above all, on the principal object of parochial fraud, the tithe-owner : if he is the owner of cottages, he endeavours to get their rent paid by the parish ; if he keeps a shop, he struggles to get allowance for his customers or debtors ; if he deals in articles used in the workhouse, he tries to increase the workhouse consumption ; if

[1] Report of the Poor Law Commission, 1834, pp. 98-104.   [2] *Ibid.*, p. 100.

he is in humble circumstances, his own relations or friends may be among the applicants.'[1] Mr. Drummond, a magistrate for Hants and Surrey, said to the Committee on Labourers' Wages in 1824, that part of the poor-rate expenditure was returned to farmers and landowners in exorbitant cottage rents, and that the farmers always opposed a poor man who wished to build himself a cottage on the waste.

In the case of what was known as the ' labour rate ' system, the members of one class combined together to impose the burden of maintaining the poor on the shoulders of the other classes. By this system, instead of the labourer's wages being made up to a fixed amount by the parish, each rate-payer was bound to employ, and to pay at a certain rate, a certain number of labourers, whether he wanted them or not. The number depended sometimes on his assessment to the poor rate, sometimes on the amount of acres he occupied (of the use to which the land was put no notice was taken, a sheep-walk counting for as much as arable fields) : when the occupiers of land had employed a fixed number of labourers, the surplus labourers were divided amongst all the rate-payers according to their rental. This plan was superficially fair, but as a matter of fact it worked out to the advantage of the big farmers with much arable land, and pressed hard on the small ones who cultivated their holdings by their own and their children's labour, and, in cases where they were liable to the rate, on the tradesmen who had no employment at which to set an agricultural labourer. After 1832 (2 and 3 William IV. c. 96) the agreement of three-fourths of the rate-payers to such a system was binding on all, and the large farmers often banded together to impose it on their fellow ratepayers by intimidation or other equally unscrupulous means : thus at Kelvedon in Essex we read : ' There was no occasion in this parish, nor would it have been done but for a junto of powerful landholders, putting down opposition by exempting a sufficient number, to give themselves the means of a majority.'[2]

Landlords in some cases resorted to Machiavellian tactics in order to escape their burdens.

' Several instances have been mentioned to us, of parishes nearly depopulated, in which almost all the labour is performed by persons settled in the neighbouring villages or towns ; drawing from them, as allowance, the greater part of their

[1] Report of the Poor Law Commission, 1834, p. 108. [2] *Ibid.*, p. 210.

subsistence.'[1] This method is described more at length in the following passage :—

'When a parish is in the hands of only one proprietor, or of proprietors so few in number as to be able to act, and to compel their tenants to act, in unison, and adjoins to parishes in which property is much divided, they may pull down every cottage as it becomes vacant, and prevent the building of new ones. By a small immediate outlay they may enable and induce a considerable portion of those who have settlements in their parish to obtain settlements in the adjoining parishes : by hiring their labourers for periods less than a year, they may prevent the acquisition of new settlements in their own. They may thus depopulate their own estates, and cultivate them by means of the surplus population of the surrounding district.'[2] A clergyman in Reading[3] said that he had between ten and twenty families living in his parish and working for the farmers in their original parish, whose cottages had been pulled down over their heads. Occasionally a big proprietor of parish A, in order to lessen the poor rates, would, with unscrupulous ingenuity, take a farm in parish B, and there hire for the year a batch of labourers from A : these at the end of their term he would turn off on to the mercies of parish B which was now responsible for them, whilst he sent for a fresh consignment from parish A.[4]

The Report of the Commission is a remarkable and searching picture of the general demoralisation produced by the Speenhamland system, and from that point of view it is most graphic and instructive. But nobody who has followed the history of the agricultural labourer can fail to be struck by its capital omission. The Commissioners, in their simple analysis of that system, could not take their eyes off the Speenhamland goblin, and instead of dealing with that system as a wrong and disastrous answer to certain difficult questions, they treated the system itself as the one and original source of all evils. They sighed for the days when ' the paupers were a small disreputable minority, whose resentment was not to be feared, and whose favour was of no value,' and ' all other classes were anxious to diminish the number of applicants, and to reduce the expenses of their maintenance.'[5] They did not realise that the governing class had not created a Frankenstein monster for the mere pleasure of its creation ; that they had not set out

---

[1] Report of the Poor Law Commission, 1834, p. 73. [2] *Ibid.*, p. 157.
[3] *Ibid.*, p. 158. [4] *Ibid.*, p. 161. [5] *Ibid.*, p. 130.

to draw up an ideal constitution, as Rousseau had done for the Poles. In 1795 there was a fear of revolution, and the upper classes threw the Speenhamland system over the villages as a wet blanket over sparks. The Commissioners merely isolated the consequences of Speenhamland and treated them as if they were the entire problem, and consequently, though their report served to extinguish that system, it did nothing to rehabilitate the position of the labourer, or to restore the rights and status he had lost. The new Poor Law was the only gift of the Reformed Parliament to the agricultural labourer ; it was an improvement on the old, but only in the sense that the east wind is better than the sirocco.

What would have happened if either of the other two remedies had been adopted for the problem to which the Speenhamland system was applied, it is impossible to say. But it is easy to see that the position of the agricultural labourer, which could not have been worse, might have been very much better, and that the nation, as apart from the landlords and money-lords, would have come out of this whirlpool much stronger and much richer. This was clear to one correspondent of the Poor Law Commission, whose memorandum, printed in an Appendix,[1] is more interesting and profound than any contribution to the subject made by the Commissioners themselves. M. Chateauvieux set out an alternative policy to Speenhamland, which, if the governing class of 1795 or the governing class of 1834 had been enlightened enough to follow it, would have set up a very different labouring class in the villages from the helpless proletariat that was created by the enclosures.

‘ Mais si au lieu d’opérer le partage des biens communaux, l’administration de la commune s’était bornée à louer pour quelques années des parcelles des terres qu’elle possède en vaine pâture, et cela à très bas prix, aux journaliers domiciliés sur son territoire, il en serait résulté :

‘ (1) Que le capital de ces terres n’aurait point été aliéné et absorbé dans la propriété particulière.

‘ (2) Que ce capital aurait été néanmoins utilisé pour la reproduction.

‘ (3) Qu’il aurait servi à l’amélioration du sort des pauvres qui l’auraient défriché, de toute la différence entre le prix du

---

[1] Appendix F, No. 3, to 1st Report of Commissioners.

loyer qu'ils en auraient payé, et le montant du revenu qu'ils auraient obtenu de sa recolte.

'(4) Que la commune aurait encaissé le montant de ses loyers, et aurait augmenté d'autant les moyens dont elle dispose pour le soulagement de ces pauvres.'

M. Chateauvieux understood better than any of the Commissioners, dominated as they were by the extreme individualist economy of the time, the meaning of Bolingbroke's maxim that a wise minister considers his administration as a single day in the great year of Government; but as a day that is affected by those which went before and must affect those which are to come after. A Government of enclosing landowners was perhaps not to be expected to understand all that the State was in danger of losing in the reckless alienation of common property.

What of the prospects of the other remedy that was proposed? At first sight it seems natural to argue that had Whitbread's Minimum Wage Bill become an Act of Parliament it would have remained a dead letter. The administration depended on the magistrates and the magistrates represented the rent-receiving and employing classes. A closer scrutiny warrants a different conclusion. At the time that the Speenhamland plan was adopted there were many magistrates in favour of setting a minimum scale. The Suffolk magistrates, for example, put pressure on the county members to vote for Whitbread's Bill, and those members, together with Grey and Sheridan, were its backers. The Parliamentary support for the Bill was enough to show that it was not only in Suffolk that it would have been adopted; there were men like Lechmere and Whitbread scattered about the country, and though they were men of far more enlightened views than the average J.P., they were not without influence in their own neighbourhoods. It is pretty certain, therefore, that if the Bill had been carried, it would have been administered in some parts of the country. The public opinion in support of the Act would have been powerfully reinforced by the pressure of the labourers, and this would have meant a more considerable stimulus than might at first be supposed, for the Report of the Poor Law Commissioners shows that the pressure of the labourers was a very important factor in the retention of the allowance system in parishes where the overseers wished to abandon it, and if the labourers could coerce the local authorities into continuing the Speenhamland system, they could have coerced the magistrates into making an assessment of wages.   The labourers were able by a show of violence to raise wages and to reduce prices temporarily, as is clear from the history of 1816 and 1830.   It is not too much to suppose that they could have exercised enough influence in 1795 to induce magistrates in many places to carry out a law that was on the Statute Book.   Further, it is not unreasonable to suppose that agricultural labourers' unions to enforce the execution of the law would have escaped the monstrous Combination Law of 1799 and 1800, for even in 1808 the Glasgow and Lancashire cotton-weavers were permitted openly to combine for the purpose of seeking a legal fixing of wages.[1]

If assessment had once become the practice, the real struggle would have arisen when the great prosperity of agriculture began to decline; at the time, that is, when the Speenhamland system began to show those symptoms of strain that we have described.   Would the customary wage, established under the more favourable conditions of 1795, have stood against that pressure ?   Would the labourers have been able to keep up wages, as critics of the Whitbread Bill had feared that they would ?   In considering the answers to that question, we have to reckon with a force that the debaters of 1795 could not have foreseen.   In 1795 Cobbett was engaged in the politics and polemics of America, and if any member of the House of Commons knew his name, he knew it as the name of a fierce champion of English institutions, and a fierce enemy of revolutionary ideas ; a hero of the *Anti-Jacobin* itself.   In 1810 Cobbett was rapidly making himself the most powerful tribune that the English poor have ever known.   Cobbett's faults are plain enough, for they are all on the surface.   His egotism sometimes seduced his judgment ; he had a strongly perverse element in his nature ; his opinion of any proposals not his own was apt to be petulant and peevish, and it might perhaps be said of him that he generally had a wasp in his bonnet. These qualities earned for him his title of the Contentious Man.   They would have been seriously disabling in a Cabinet Minister, but they did not affect his power of collecting and mobilising and leading the spasmodic forces of the poor.

Let us recall his career in order to understand what his influence would have been if the labourers had won their customary wage in 1795, and had been fighting to maintain it fifteen or twenty years later.   His adventures began early.

[1] See Webb's *History of Trade Unionism*, p. 59.

When he was thirteen his imagination was fired by stories the gardener at Farnham told him of the glories of Kew. He ran away from home, and made so good an impression on the Kew gardener that he was given work there. His last coppers on that journey were spent in buying Swift's *Tale of a Tub*. He returned home, but his restless dreams drove him again into the world. He tried to become a sailor, and ultimately became a soldier. He left the army, where he had made his mark and received rapid promotion, in order to expose a financial scandal in his regiment, but on discovering that the interests involved in the countenance of military abuses were far more powerful than he had supposed, he abandoned his attempt and fled to France. A few months later he crossed to America, and settled down to earn a living by teaching English to French refugees. This peaceful occupation he relinquished for the congenial excitements of polemical journalism, and he was soon the fiercest pamphleteer on the side of the Federals, who took the part of England, in their controversies with the Democrats, who took the part of the Revolution. So far as the warfare of pamphlets went, Cobbett turned the scale. The Democrats could not match his wit, his sarcasm, his graphic and pointed invectives, his power of clever and sparkling analysis and ridicule. This warfare occupied him for nearly ten years, and he returned to England in time to have his windows broken for refusing to illuminate his house in celebration of the Peace of Amiens. In 1802 he started the *Political Register*. At that time he was still a Tory, but a closer study of English life changed his opinions, and four years later he threw himself into the Radical movement. The effect of his descent on English politics can only be compared to the shock that was given to the mind of Italy by the French methods of warfare, when Charles VIII. led his armies into her plains to fight pitched battles without any of the etiquette or polite conventions that had graced the combats of the condottieri. He gave to the Reform agitation an uncompromising reality and daring, and a movement which had become the dying echo of a smothered struggle broke into storm and thunder. Hazlitt scarcely exaggerated his dæmonic powers when he said of him that he formed a fourth estate of himself.

Now Cobbett may be said to have spent twenty years of his life in the effort to save the labourers from degradation and ruin. He was the only man of his generation who regarded politics from this standpoint. This motive is the key to his career. He saw in 1816 that the nation had to choose between its sinecures, its extravagant army, its rulers' mad scheme of borrowing at a higher rate to extinguish debt, for which it was paying interest at a low rate, its huge Civil List and privileged establishments, the interests of the fund-holders and contractors on the one hand, and its labourers on the other. In that conflict of forces the labourer could not hold his own. Later, Cobbett saw that there were other interests, the interests of landowners and of tithe-holders, which the State would have to subordinate to national claims if the labourer was to be saved. In that conflict, too, the labourer was beaten. He was unrepresented in Parliament, whereas the opposing interests were massed there. Cobbett wanted Parliamentary Reform, not like the traditional Radicals as a philosophy of rights, but as an avalanche of social power. Parliamentary Reform was never an end to him, nor the means to anything short of the emancipation of the labourer. In this, his main mission, Cobbett failed. The upper classes winced under his ruthless manners, and they trembled before his Berserker rage, but it is the sad truth of English history that they beat him. Now if, instead of throwing himself against this world of privilege and vested interests in the hopes of wringing a pittance of justice for a sinking class, it had been his task to maintain a position already held, he would have fought under very different conditions. If, when prices began to fall, there had been a customary wage in most English villages, the question would not have been whether the ruling class was to maintain its privileges and surplus profits by letting the labourer sink deeper into the morass, but whether it was to maintain these privileges and profits by taking something openly from him. It is easier to prevent a dog from stealing a bone than to take the bone out of his mouth. Cobbett was not strong enough to break the power of the governing class, but he might have been strong enough to defend the customary rights of the labouring class. As it was, the governing class was on the defensive at every point. The rent receivers, the tithe owners, the mortgagers, the lenders to the Government and the contractors all clung to their gains, and the food allowance of the labourer slowly and steadily declined.

There was this great difference between the Speenhamland system and a fixed standard of wages. The Speenhamland system after 1812 was not applied so as to maintain an equilibrium between the income and expenditure of the labourer : it was applied to maintain an equilibrium between social forces. The scale fell not with the fall of prices to the labourer, but with the fall of profits to the possessing classes. The minimum was not the minimum on which the labourer could live, but the minimum below which rebellion was certain. This was the way in which wages found their own level. They gravitated lower and lower with the growing weakness of the wage-earner. If Cobbett had been at the head of a movement for preserving to the labourer a right bestowed on him by Act of Parliament, either he would have succeeded, or the disease would have come to a crisis in 1816, instead of taking the form of a lingering and wasting illness. Either, that is, other classes would have had to make the economies necessary to keep the labourers' wages at the customary point, or the labourers would have made their last throw before they had been desolated and weakened by another fifteen years of famine.

There is another respect in which the minimum wage policy would have profoundly altered the character of village society. It would have given the village labourers a bond of union before they had lost the memories and the habits of their more independent life ; it would have made them an organised force, something like the organised forces that have built up a standard of life for industrial workmen. An important passage in Fielding's *Tom Jones* shows that there was material for such combination in the commoners of the old village. Fielding is talking of his borrowings from the classics and he defends himself with this analogy : ' The ancients may be considered as a rich common, where every person who hath the smallest tenement in Parnassus hath a free right to batten his muse : or, to place it in a clearer light, we moderns are to the ancients what the poor are to the rich. By the poor here I mean that large and venerable body which in English we call the mob. Now whoever hath had the honour to be admitted to any degree of intimacy with this mob must well know, that it is one of their established maxims to plunder and pillage their rich neighbours without any reluctance : and that this is held to be neither sin nor crime among them. And so constantly do they abide and act by this maxim, that in every parish almost in the kingdom there is a kind of confederacy ever carrying on against a certain person of opulence called the squire whose property is considered as free booty by all his poor neighbours ; who, as they conclude that there is no manner of guilt in such depredations, look upon it as a point of honour and moral obligation to conceal and to preserve each other from punishment on all such occasions.   In like manner are the ancients such as Homer, Virgil, Horace, Cicero and the rest to be esteemed among us writers as so many wealthy squires from whom we, the poor of Parnassus, claim an immemorial custom of taking whatever we can come at.' [1]

It would not have been possible to create a great labourers' union before the Combination Laws were repealed in 1824, but if the labourers had been organised to defend their standard wage, they would have established a tradition of permanent association in each village.   The want of this was their fatal weakness.   All the circumstances make the spirit of combination falter in the country.   In towns men are face to face with the brutal realities of their lives, unsoftened by any of the assuaging influences of brook and glade and valley. Men and women who work in the fields breathe something of the resignation and peace of Nature ; they bear trouble and wrong with a dangerous patience.   Discontent moves, but it moves slowly, and whereas storms blow up in the towns, they beat up in the country.   That is one reason why the history of the anguish of the English agricultural labourer so rarely breaks into violence.   Castlereagh's Select Committee in 1817 rejoiced in the discovery that ' notwithstanding the alarming progress which has been made in extending disaffection, its success has been confined to the principal manufacturing districts, and that scarcely any of the agricultural population have lent themselves to these violent projects.'   There is a Russian saying that the peasant must ' be boiled in the factory pot ' before a revolution can succeed.   And if it is difficult in the nature of things to make rural labourers as formidable to their masters as industrial workers, there is another reason why the English labourer rebelled so reluctantly and so tardily against what Sir Spencer Walpole called, in the true spirit of a classical politician, ' his inevitable and hereditary lot.'   Village society was constantly losing its best and bravest blood. Bamford's description of the poacher who nearly killed a gamekeeper's understrapper in a quarrel in a public-house, and then hearing from Dr. Healey that his man was only stunned, promised the doctor that if there was but one single hare on Lord Suffield's estates, that hare should be in the

[1] *Tom Jones*, Bk. XII. chap. i.

doctor's stew-pot next Sunday, reminds us of the loss a village suffered when its poachers were snapped up by a game-preserving bench, and tossed to the other side of the world. During the years between Waterloo and the Reform Bill the governing class was decimating the village populations on the principle of the Greek tyrant who flicked off the heads of the tallest blades in his field ; the Game Laws, summary jurisdiction, special commissions, drove men of spirit and enterprise, the natural leaders of their fellows, from the villages where they might have troubled the peace of their masters. The village Hampdens of that generation sleep by the shores of Botany Bay. Those who blame the supine character of the English labourer forget that his race, before it had quite lost the memories and the habits of the days of its independence and its share in the commons, was passed through this sieve. The scenes we shall describe in the next chapter show that the labourers were capable of great mutual fidelity when once they were driven into rebellion. If they had had a right to defend and a comradeship to foster from the first, Cobbett, who spent his superb strength in a magnificent onslaught on the governing class, might have made of the race whose wrongs he pitied as his own, an army no less resolute and disciplined than the army O'Connell made of the broken peasants of the West.

CHAPTER XI

THE LAST LABOURERS' REVOLT

Where not otherwise stated the authorities for the two following chapters are the Home Office Papers for the time (Municipal and Provincial, Criminal, Disturbances, Domestic, etc.), the *Times* and local papers.

I

A TRAVELLER who wished to compare the condition of the English and the French rural populations in 1830 would have had little else to do than to invert all that had been written on the subject by travellers a century earlier. At the beginning of the eighteenth century England had the prosperous and France the miserable peasantry. But by the beginning of the nineteenth century the French peasant had been set free from the impoverishing and degrading services which had made his lot so intolerable in the eyes of foreign observers ; he cultivated his own land, and lived a life, spare, arduous, and exacting but independent. The work of the Revolution had been done so thoroughly in this respect that the Bourbons, when Wellington and the allies lifted them back on to their throne, could not undo it. It is true that the future of the French peasants was a subject of some anxiety to English observers, and that M'Culloch committed himself to the prediction that in half a century, owing to her mass of small owners, France would be the greatest pauper-warren in Europe. If any French peasant was disturbed by this nightmare of the political economy of the time, he had the grim satisfaction of knowing that his position could hardly become worse than the position that the English labourer already occupied. He would have based his conclusion, not on the wild language of revolutionaries, but on the considered statement of those who were so far from meditating revolution that they shrank even from a moderate reform of Parliament. Lord Carnarvon said in one House of Parliament that the English labourer had been reduced to a plight more abject than that of any race in Europe ; English landlords reproduced in the other that very parallel between the English labourer and the West Indian negro which had figured so conspicuously in Thelwall's lectures. Thelwall, as Canning reminded him in a savage parody on the Benedicite, got pelted for his pains. Since the days of those lectures all Europe had been overrun by war, and England alone had escaped what Pitt had called the liquid fire of Jacobinism. There had followed for England fifteen years of healing peace. Yet at the end of all this time the conquerors of Napoleon found themselves in a position which they would have done well to exchange with the position of his victims. The German peasant had been rescued from serfdom ; Spain and Italy had at least known a brief spell of less unequal government. The English labourer alone was the poorer ; poorer in money, poorer in happiness, poorer in sympathy, and infinitely poorer in horizon and in hope. The riches that he had been promised by the champions of enclosure had faded into something less than a maintenance. The wages he received without land had a lower purchasing power than the wages he had received in the days when his wages were supplemented by common rights. The standard of living which was prescribed for him by the governing class was now much lower than it had been in 1795.

This was not part of a general decline. Other classes for whom the rulers of England prescribed the standard had advanced during the years in which the labourers had lost ground. The King's Civil List had been revised when provisions rose. The salaries of the judges had been raised by three several Acts of Parliament (1799, 1809, and 1825), a similar course had been taken in the case of officials. Those who have a taste for the finished and unconscious cynicism of this age will note— recollecting that the upper classes refused to raise wages in 1795 to meet the extra cost of living, on the ground that it would be difficult afterwards to reduce them—that all the upper-class officials, whose salaries were increased because living was more expensive, were left to the permanent enjoyment of that increase. The lives of the judges, the landlords, the parsons, and the rest of the governing class were not become more meagre but more spacious in the last fifty years. During that period many of the great palaces of the English nobility had been built, noble libraries had been collected, and famous galleries had grown up, wing upon wing. The agricultural labourers whose fathers had eaten meat, bacon, cheese, and vegetables were living on bread and potatoes. They had lost their gardens, they had ceased to brew their beer in their cottages. In their work they had no sense of ownership or interest. They no longer ' sauntered after cattle ' on the open common, and at twilight they no longer ' played down the setting sun'; the games had almost disappeared from the English village, their wives and children were starving before their eyes, their homes were more squalid, and the philosophy of the hour taught the upper classes that to mend a window or to put in a brick to shield the cottage from damp or wind was to increase the ultimate miseries of the poor. The sense of sympathy and comradeship, which had been mixed with rude and unskilful government, in the old village had been destroyed in the bitter days of want and distress. Degrading and repulsive work was invented for those whom the farmer would not or could not employ. De Quincey, wishing to illustrate the manners of eighteenth-century France, used to quote M. Simond's story of how he had seen, not very long before the Revolution, a peasant ploughing with a team consisting of a donkey and a woman. The English poor could have told him that half a century later there were English villages in which it was the practice of the overseer to harness men and women to the parish cart, and that the sight of an idiot woman between the shafts was not unknown within a hundred miles of London.[1] Men and women were living on roots and sorrel ; in the summer of the year 1830 four harvest labourers were found under a hedge dead of starvation, and Lord Winchilsea, who mentioned the fact in the House of Lords, said that this was not an exceptional case. The labourer was worse fed and worse housed than the prisoner, and he would not have been able to keep body and soul together if he had not found in poaching or in thieving or in smuggling the means of eking out his doles and wages.

The feelings of this sinking class, the anger, dismay, and despair with which it watched the going out of all the warm comfort and light of life, scarcely stir the surface of history. The upper classes have told us what the poor ought to have thought of these vicissitudes ; religion, philosophy, and political economy were ready with alleviations and explanations which seemed singularly helpful and convincing to the rich. The voice of the poor themselves does not come to our ears. This great population seems to resemble nature, and to bear all the storms that beat upon it with a strange silence and resignation.

[1] See Fawley, p. 279.

But just as nature has her power of protest in some sudden upheaval, so this world of men and women—an underground world as we trace the distance that its voices have to travel to reach us—has a volcanic character of its own, and it is only by some volcanic surprise that it can speak the language of remonstrance or menace or prayer, or place on record its consciousness of wrong. This world has no member of Parliament, no press, it does not make literature or write history; no diary or memoirs have kept alive for us the thoughts and cares of the passing day. It is for this reason that the events of the winter of 1830 have so profound an interest, for in the scenes now to be described we have the mind of this class hidden from us through all this period of pain, bursting the silence by the only power at its command. The demands presented to the farmer, the parson, and the squire this winter tell us as much about the South of England labourer in 1830 as the cahiers tell us of the French peasants in 1789.

We have seen that in 1795 and in 1816 there had been serious disturbances in different parts of England. These had been suppressed with a firm hand, but during hard winters sporadic violence and blazing hay-stacks showed from time to time that the fire was still alive under the ashes. The rising of 1830 was far more general and more serious ; several counties in the south of England were in state bordering on insurrection ; London was in a panic, and to some at least of those who had tried to forget the price that had been paid for the splendour of the rich, the message of red skies and broken mills and mob diplomacy and villages in arms sounded like the summons that came to Hernani. The terror of the landowners during those weeks is reflected in such language as that of the Duke of Buckingham, who talked of the country being in the hands of the rebels, or of one of the Barings, who said in the House of Commons that if the disorders went on for three or four days longer they would be beyond the reach of almost any power to control them. This chapter of social history has been overshadowed by the riots that followed the rejection of the Reform Bill. Every one knows about the destruction of the Mansion House at Bristol, and the burning of Nottingham Castle ; few know of the destruction of the hated workhouses at Selborne and Headley. The riots at Nottingham and Bristol were a prelude to victory ; they were the wild shout of power. If the rising of 1830 had succeeded, and won back for the labourer his lost livelihood, the day when the Headley work-house was thrown down would be remembered by the poor as the day of the taking of the Bastille. But this rebellion failed, and the men who led that last struggle for the labourer passed into the forgetfulness of death and exile.

Kent was the scene of the first disturbances. There had been some alarming fires in the west of the county during the summer, at Orpington and near Sevenoaks. In one case the victim had made himself unpopular by pulling down a cottage built on a common adjoining his property, and turning out the occupants. How far these fires were connected with later events it is impossible to say : the authors were never dis-covered. The first riot occurred at Hardres on Sunday the 29th of August, when four hundred labourers destroyed some threshing machines.[1] Next day two magistrates with a hundred special constables and some soldiers went to Hardres Court, and no more was heard of the rioters. The *Spectator* early next year announced that it had found as a result of inquiries that the riots began with a dispute between farmers over a threshing machine, in the course of which a magistrate had expressed strong views against the introduction of these machines. The labourers proceeded to destroy the machine, whereupon, to their surprise, the magistrate turned on them and punished them ; in revenge they fired his ricks. ' A farmer in another village, talking of the distress of the labourers, said, " Ah, I should be well pleased if a plague were to break out among them, and then I should have their carcases as manure, and right good stuff it would make for my hops." This speech, which was perhaps only intended as a brutal jest, was reported ; it excited rage instead of mirth, and the stacks of the jester were soon in a blaze. This act of incendiarism was open and deliberate. The incendiary is known, and not only has he not been tried, he has not even been charged.' [2] Cobbett, on the other hand, maintained that the occasion of the first riots was the importation of Irish labourers, a practice now some years old, that might well inflame resentment, at a time when the governing class was continually contending that the sole cause of distress was excessive population, and that the true solution was the removal of surplus labourers to the colonies.

Whatever the actual origin of the first outbreak may have been, the destruction of machinery was to be a prominent feature of this social war. This was not merely an instinct

[1] *Kent Herald*, September 2, 1830.   [2] *Times*, January 3, 1831.

of violence, there was method and reason in it. Threshing
was one of the few kinds of work left that provided the labourer
with a means of existence above starvation level. A landowner
and occupier near Canterbury wrote to the *Kent Herald*,[1] that
in his parish, where no machines had been introduced, there
were twenty-three barns. He calculated that in these barns
fifteen men at least would find employment threshing corn up
till May. If we suppose that each man had a wife and three
children, this employment would affect seventy-five persons.
'An industrious man who has a barn never requires poor
relief; he can earn from 15s. to 20s. per week; he considers it
almost as his little freehold, and that in effect it certainly is.'
It is easy to imagine what the sight of one of these hated
engines meant to such a parish; the fifteen men, their wives
and families would have found cold comfort, when they had
become submerged in the morass of parish relief, in the reflection
that the new machine extracted for their master's and the
public benefit ten per cent. more corn than they could hammer
out by their free arms. The destruction of threshing machines
by bands of men in the district round Canterbury continued
through September practically unchecked. By the end of the
month three of the most active rioters were in custody, and
the magistrates were under the pleasant illusion that there
would be voluntary surrenders. In this they were disappointed, and the disturbances spread over a wider area,
which embraced the Dover district. Early in October there
was a riot at Lyminge, at which Sir Edward Knatchbull and
the Rev. Mr. Price succeeded in arresting the ringleaders, and
bound over about fifty other persons. Sir Edward Knatchbull,
in writing to the Home Office, stated that the labourers said
'they would rather do anything than encounter such a winter
as the last.' Mr. Price had to pay the penalty for his active
part in this affair, and his ricks were fired.
   Large rewards were promised from the first to informers,
these rewards including a wise offer of establishment elsewhere,
but the prize was refused, and rick-burning spread steadily
through a second month. Threatening letters signed 'Swing,'
a mysterious name that for the next few weeks spread
terror over England, were received by many farmers and
landowners. The machine-breakers were reported not to
take money or plunder, and to refuse it if offered. Their
programme was extensive and formidable. When the High

[1] September 30, 1830.

Sheriff attended one of their meetings to remonstrate with them, they listened to his homily with attention, but before dispersing one of them said, ' We will destroy the corn-stacks and threshing machines this year, next year we will have a turn with the parsons, and the third we will make war upon the statesmen.' [1]

On 24th October seven prisoners were tried at the East Kent Quarter Sessions, for machine-breaking. They pleaded guilty, and were let off with a lenient sentence of three days' imprisonment and an harangue from Sir Edward Knatchbull. Hitherto all attempts to discover the incendiaries had been baffled, but on 21st October a zealous magistrate wrote to the Home Office to say that he had found a clue. He had apprehended a man called Charles Blow, and since the evidence was not sufficient to warrant committal for arson, he had sent him to Lewes Jail as a vagrant for three months. ' In com-pany with Blow was a girl of about ten years of age (of the name of Mary Ann Johnson), but of intelligence and cunning far beyond her age. It having been stated to me that she had let fall some expressions which went to show that she could if she pleased communicate important information, I committed her also for the same period as Blow.' Now the fires in question had taken place in Kent, and the vagrants were apprehended in Sussex, consequently the officials of both counties meddled with the matter and between them spoilt the whole plan, for Mary Ann and her companion were ques-tioned by so many different persons that they were put on their guard, and failed to give the information that was ex-pected. Thus at any rate, Lord Camden, the Lord-Lieutenant, explained their silence, but he did not despair, ' if the Parties cannot even be convicted I am apt to think their Committal now will do good, though they may be to be liberated after-wards, but nothing is so likely to produce alarm and produce evidence as a Committal for a Capital Crime.' However, as no more is heard of Mary Ann, it may be assumed that when she had served her three months she left Lewes Jail a sadder and a wiser child.

Towards the end of October, after something of a lull in the middle of the month, the situation became more serious. Dis-satisfaction, or, as some called it, ' frightful anarchy,' spread to the Maidstone and Sittingbourne districts. Sir Robert Peel was anxious to take strong measures. ' I beg to repeat to you

[1] *Brighton Chronicle*, October 6, quoted in *Times*, October 14.

that I will adopt any measure—will incur any expense at the public charge—that can promote the suppression of the outrages in Kent and the detection of the offenders.' A troop of cavalry was sent to Sittingbourne. In the last days of October, mobs scoured the country round Maidstone, demanding half a crown a day wages and constant employment, forcing all labourers to join them, and levying money, beer, and provisions. At Stockbury, between Maidstone and Sittingbourne, one of these mobs paraded a tricolour and a black flag. On 30th October the Maidstone magistrates went out with a body of thirty-four soldiers to meet a mob of four hundred people, about four miles from Maidstone, and laid hold of the three ringleaders. The arrests were made without difficulty or resistance, from which it looks as if these bands of men were not very formidable, but the officer in command of the soldiers laid stress in his confidential report on the dangers of the situation and the necessity for fieldpieces, and Peel promptly ordered two pieces of artillery to be dispatched.

At the beginning of November disturbances broke out in Sussex, and the movement developed into an organised demand for a living wage. By the middle of the month the labourers were masters over almost all the triangle on the map, of which Maidstone is the apex and Hythe and Brighton are the bases. The movement, which was more systematic, thorough, and successful in this part of the country than anywhere else, is thus described by the special correspondent of the *Times*, 17th November : ' Divested of its objectionable character, as a dangerous precedent, the conduct of the peasantry has been admirable. There is no ground for concluding that there has been any extensive concert amongst them. Each parish, generally speaking, has risen *per se* ; in many places their proceedings have been managed with astonishing coolness and regularity ; there has been little of the ordinary effervescence displayed on similar occasions. The farmers have notice to meet the men : a deputation of two or more of the latter produce a written statement, well drawn up, which the farmers are required to sign ; the spokesman, sometimes a Dissenting or Methodist teacher, fulfils his office with great propriety and temper. Where disorder has occurred, it has arisen from dislike to some obnoxious clergyman, or tithe man, or assistant overseer, who has been trundled out of the parish in a wheelbarrow, or drawn in triumph in a load of ballast by a dozen old women. The farmers universally agreed to the demands they made: that is, they were not mad enough to refuse requests which they could not demonstrate to be unreasonable in themselves, and which were urged by three hundred or four hundred men after a barn or two had been fired, and each farmer had an incendiary letter addressed to him in his pocket.'

There was another development of the movement which is not noted in this account by the correspondent of the *Times*. It often happened that the farmers would agree to pay the wages demanded by the labourers, but would add that they could not continue to pay those wages unless rents and tithes were reduced. The labourers generally took the hint and turned their attention to tithes and rents, particularly to tithes. Their usual procedure was to go in a body to the rector, often accompanied by the farmers, and demand an abatement of tithes, or else to attend the tithe audit and put some not unwelcome pressure upon the farmers to prevent them from paying.

It must not be supposed that the agitation for a living wage was confined to the triangular district named above, though there it took a more systematic shape. Among the Home Office Papers is a very interesting letter from Mr. D. Bishop, a London police officer, written from Deal on 11th November, describing the state of things in that neighbourhood: 'I have gone to the different Pot Houses in the Villages, disguised among the Labourers, of an evening and all their talk is about the wages, some give 1s. 8d. per day some 2s. some 2s. 3d. . . . all they say they want is 2s. 6d. per day and then they say they shall be comfortable. I have every reason to believe the Farmers will give the 2s. 6d. per day after a bit . . . they are going to have a meeting and I think it will stop all outrages.'

The disturbances in Sussex began with a fire on 3rd November at an overseer's in Battle. The explanation suggested by the authorities was that the paupers had been 'excited by a lecture lately given here publicly by a person named Cobbett.' Next night there was another fire at Battle; but it was at Brede, a village near Rye, that open hostilities began. As the rising at Brede set the fashion for the district, it is perhaps worth while to describe it in some detail.[1]

For a long time the poor of Brede had smarted under the

---

[1] For Brede see H. O. Papers, Extracts from Poor Law Commissioners' Report, published 1833, and newspapers.

insults of Mr. Abel, the assistant overseer, who, among other innovations, had introduced one of the hated parish carts, and the labourers were determined to have a reckoning with him. After some preliminary discussions on the previous day, the labourers held a meeting on 5th November, and deputed four men to negotiate with the farmers. At the conference which resulted, the following resolutions, drawn up by the labourers, were signed by both parties [1] :—

' Nov. 5, 1830. At a meeting held this day at the Red Lion, of the farmers, to meet the poor labourers who delegated David Noakes Senior, Thomas Henley, Joseph Bryant and Th. Noakes, to meet the gentlemen this day to discuss the present distress of the poor. . . . Resolution 1. The gentlemen agree to give to every able-bodied labourer with wife and two children 2s. 3d. per day, from this day to the 1st of March next, and from the 1st of March to the 1st of Oct. 2s. 6d. per day, and to have 1s. 6d. per week with three children, and so on according to their family. Resolution 2. The poor are determined to take the present overseer, Mr. Abell, out of the parish to any adjoining parish and to use him with civility.'

The meeting over, the labourers went to Mr. Abel's house with their wives and children and some of the farmers, and placed the parish cart at his door. After some hammering at the gates, Mr. Abel was persuaded to come out and get into the cart. He was then solemnly drawn along by women and children, accompanied by a crowd of five hundred, to the place of his choice, Vine Hall, near Robertsbridge, on the turnpike road, where he was deposited with all due solemnity. Mr. Abel made his way to the nearest magistrate to lodge his complaint, while the people of the parish returned home and were regaled with beer by the farmers : ' and Mr. Coleman . . . he gave every one of us half a pint of Beer, women and men, and Mr. Reed of Brede High gave us a Barrel because we had done such a great thing in the Parish as to carry that man away, and Mr. Coleman said he never was better pleased in his life than with the day's work which had been done.' [2]

The parish rid of Mr. Abel, the next reform in the new era was to be the reduction of tithes, and here the farmers needed the help of the labourers. What happened is best told in the

---

[1] They were signed by G. S. Hele, minister, by eight farmers and the four labourer delegates.   [2] Affidavit in H. O. Papers.

words of one of the chief actors.   He describes how, a little
before the tithe audit, his employer came to him when he was
working in the fields and suggested that the labourers should
see if they could ' get a little of the tithe off ' ; they were only
to show themselves and not to take any violent action.   Other
farmers made the same suggestions to their labourers.   ' We
went to the tithe audit and Mr. Hele came out and spoke to
us a good while and I and David Noakes and Thomas Noakes
and Thomas Henley answered him begging as well as we could
for him to throw something off for us and our poor Children
and to set up a School for them and Mr. Hele said he would see
what he could do.

' Mr. Coleman afterwards came out and said Mr. Hele had
satisfied them all well and then Mr. Hele came out and we
made our obedience to him and he to us, and we gave him
three cheers and went and set the Bells ringing and were all
as pleased as could be at what we had done.'

The success of the Brede rising had an immediate effect on
the neighbourhood, and every parish round prepared to deport
its obnoxious overseer and start a new life on better wages.
Burwash, Ticehurst, Mayfield, Heathfield, Warbleton and
Ninfield were among the parishes that adopted the Brede
programme.   Sometimes the assistant overseer thought it
wise to decamp before the cart was at his door.   Sometimes
the mob was aggressive in its manners.   ' A very considerable
Mob,' wrote Sir Godfrey Webster from Battle Abbey on 9th
November, ' to the amount of nearly 500, having their Parish
Officer in custody drawn in a Dung Cart, attempted to enter
this town at eleven o'clock this Morning.'   The attempt was
unsuccessful, and twenty of the rioters were arrested.   The
writer of this letter took an active part throughout the disturbances.   In this emergency he seems to have displayed
great zeal and energy.   A second letter of his on 12th
November gives a good description of the state of affairs round
Mayfield.   ' The Collector of Lord Carrington's Tithes had
been driven out of the Parish and the same Proceeding was
intended to be adopted towards the Parish Officer who fled
the place, it had been intended by the Rioters to have taken
by Force this Morning as many Waggons as possible (forcibly)
carried off the Tithe Corn and distributed it amongst themselves
in case of interruption they were resolved to burn it.   One of
the most violent and dangerous papers I have yet seen (a copy
of which I enclose) was carried round the 3 adjoining Parishes

and unfortunately was assented to by too many Occupiers of Land. I arrived in Time to prevent its circulation at Mayfield a small Town tho' populous parish 3000. By apprehending the Bearer of the Paper who acted as Chief of the Party and instantly in presence of a large Mob committing him for Trial I succeeded in repressing the tumultuous action then going on, and by subsequently calling together the Occupiers of Land, and afterwards the Mob (composed wholly of Agricultural Labourers) I had the satisfaction of mediating an arrangement between them perfectly to the content of each party, and on my leaving Mayfield this afternoon tranquillity was perfectly restored at that Place.' The violent and dangerous paper enclosed ran thus : ' Now gentlemen this is wat we intend to have for a maried man to have 2s. and 3d. per Day and all over two children 1s. 6d. per head a week and if a Man has got any boys or girls over age for to have employ that they may live by there Labour and likewise all single men to have 1s. 9d. a day per head and we intend to have the rents lowered likewise and this is what we intend to have before we leave the place and if ther is no alteration we shall proceed further about it. For we are all at one and we will keep to each other.'

At Ringmer in Sussex the proceedings were marked by moderation and order. Lord Gage, the principal landowner of the neighbourhood, knowing that disturbances were imminent, met the labourers by appointment on the village green. There were about one hundred and fifty persons present. By this time magistrates in many places had taken to arresting arbitrarily the ringleaders of the men, and hence when Lord Gage, who probably had no such intention, asked for the leader or captain nobody came forward, but a letter was thrown into the ring with a general shout. The letter which Lord Gage picked up and took to the Vestry for consideration read as follows : ' We the labourers of Ringmer and surrounding villages, having for a long period suffered the greatest privations and endured the most debasing treatment with the greatest resignation and forbearance, in the hope that time and circumstances would bring about an amelioration of our condition, till, worn out by hope deferred and disappointed in our fond expectations, we have taken this method of assembling ourselves in one general body, for the purpose of making known our grievances, and in a peaceable, quiet, and orderly manner, to ask redress ; and we would rather appeal to the good sense of the magistracy, instead of inflaming the passions of our fellow labourers, and ask those gentlemen who have done us the favour of meeting us this day whether 7d. a day is sufficient for a working man, hale and hearty, to keep up the strength necessary to the execution of the labour he has to do ?   We ask also, is 9s. a week sufficient for a married man with a family, to provide the common necessaries of life ? Have we no reason to complain that we have been obliged for so long a period to go to our daily toil with only potatoes in our satchels, and the only beverage to assuage our thirst the cold spring ; and on retiring to our cottages to be welcomed by the meagre and half-famished offspring of our toilworn bodies ?   All we ask, then, is that our wages may be advanced to such a degree as will enable us to provide for ourselves and families without being driven to the overseer, who, by the bye, is a stranger amongst us, and as in most instances where permanent overseers are appointed, are men callous to the ties of nature, lost to every feeling of humanity, and deaf to the voice of reason.   We say we want wages sufficient to support us, without being driven to the overseer to experience his petty tyranny and dictation.   We therefore ask for married men 2s. 3d. per day to the first of March, and from that period to the first of October 2s. 6d. a day : for single men 1s. 9d. a day to the first of March, and 2s. from that time to the first of October.   We also request that the permanent overseers of the neighbouring parishes may be directly discharged, particularly Finch, the governor of Ringmer poorhouse and overseer of the parish, that in case we are obliged, through misfortune or affliction, to seek parochial relief, we may apply to one of our neighbouring farmers or tradesmen, who would naturally feel some sympathy for our situation, and who would be much better acquainted with our characters and claims.   This is what we ask at your hands—this is what we expect, and we sincerely trust this is what we shall not be under the painful necessity of demanding.'

While the Vestry deliberated the labourers remained quietly in the yard of the poorhouse.   One of them, a veteran from the Peninsular War who had lost a limb, contrasted his situation on 9d. a day with that of the Duke of Wellington whose ' skin was whole ' and whose pension was £60,000 a year.   After they had waited some time, they were informed that their demands were granted, and they dispersed to their homes with huzzas and tears of joy, and as a sign of the new and auspicious era they broke up the parish grindstone, a memory of the evil past.[1]

An important feature of the proceedings in Kent and Sussex was the sympathy of other classes with the demands of the labourers. The success of the movement in Kent and Sussex, and especially of the rising that began at Brede, was due partly, no doubt, to the fact that smuggling was still a common practice in those counties, and that the agricultural labourers thus found their natural leaders among men who had learnt audacity, resourcefulness, and a habit of common action in that school of danger. But the movement could not have made such headway without any serious attempt to suppress it if the other classes had been hostile. There was a general sense that the risings were due to the neglect of the Government. Mr. Hodges, one of the Members for Kent, declared in the House of Commons on 10th December that if the Duke of Wellington had attended to a petition received from the entire Grand Jury of Kent there would have been no disturbances.[2]

The same spirit is displayed in a letter written by a magistrate at Battle, named Collingwood. ' I have seen three or four of our parochial insurrections, and been with the People for hours alone and discussing their matters with them which they do with a temper and respectful behaviour and an intelligence which must interest everyone in their favor. The poor in the Parishes in the South of England, and in Sussex and Kent greatly, have been ground to the dust in many instances by the Poor Laws. Instead of happy peasants they are made miserable and sour tempered paupers. Every Parish has its own peculiar system, directed more strictly, and executed with more or less severity or harshness. A principal tradesman in Salehurst (Sussex) in one part of which, Robertsbridge, we had our row the other night, said to me these words " You attended our meeting the other day and voted with me against the two principal Rate payers in this parish, two Millers, paying the people in two gallons of bad flour instead of money. You heard how saucy they were to their betters, can you wonder if

---

[1] *Times*, November 25.

[2] The petition was as follows : ' We feel that in justice we ought not to suffer a moment to pass away without communicating to your Grace the great and unprecedented distress which we are enabled from our own personal experience to state prevails among all the peasantry to a degree not only dreadful to individuals, but also to an extent which, if not checked, must be attended with serious consequences to the national prosperity.' Mr. Hodges does not mention the date, merely stating that it was sent to Wellington when Prime Minister.

they are more violent to their inferiors ? They never call a
man Tom, Dick etc. but you d——d rascal etc., at every
word, and force them to take their flour. Should you wonder
that they are dissatisfied ? " These words he used to me a
week before our Robertsbridge Row. Each of these Parochial
Rows differs in character as the man whom they select as leader
differs in impudence or courage or audacity or whatever you
may call it. If they are opposed at the moment, their resistance
shows itself in more or less violent outrages ; personally I
witnessed but one, that of Robertsbridge putting Mr. Johnson
into the cart, and that was half an accident. I was a stranger
to them, went among them and was told by hundreds after
that most unjustifiable assault that I was safe among them as
in my bed, and I never thought otherwise. One or two desperate
characters, and such there are, may at any moment make the
contest of Parish A differ from that of Parish B, but their
spirit, as far as regards loyalty and love for the King and Laws,
is, I believe, on my conscience, sound. I feel convinced that
all the cavalry in the world, if sent into Sussex, and all the
spirited acts of Sir Godfrey Webster, who, however, is invaluable
here will (not ?) stop this spirit from running through Hampshire, Wiltshire, Somersetshire, where Mr. Hobhouse, your
predecessor, told me the other day that they have got the
wages for single men down to 6s. per week (on which they
cannot live) through many other counties. In a week you
will have demands for cavalry from Hampshire under the same
feeling of alarm as I and all here entertained : the next week
from Wiltshire, Dorsetshire, and all the counties in which the
poor Rates have been raised for the payment of the poor up
to Essex and the very neighbourhood of London, where Mr.
Geo. Palmer, a magistrate, told me lately that the poor single
man is got down to 6s. I shall be over to-morrow probably at
Benenden where they are resolved not to let either Mr. Hodges's
taxes, the tithes or the King's taxes be paid. So I hear, and
so I dare say two or three carter boys may have said. I shall
go to-morrow and if I see occasion will arrest some man, and
break his head with my staff. But do you suppose that that
(though a show of vigor is not without avail) will prevent
Somersetshire men from crying out, when the train has got to
them, we will not *live* on 6s. per week, for living it is not, but
a long starving, and we will have tithes and taxes, and I know
not what else done away with. The only way to stop them is
to run before the evil. Let the Hampshire Magistrates and

Vestries raise the wages before the Row gets to their County, and you will stop the thing from spreading, otherwise you will not, I am satisfied. In saying all this, I know that I differ with many able and excellent Magistrates, and my opinion may be wrong, but I state it to you.'

It is not surprising that magistrates holding these opinions acted rather less vigorously than the central Government wished, and that Lord Camden's appeals to them not to let their political feelings and ' fanciful Crotchets ' [1] interfere with their activity were unsuccessful. But even had all the magistrates been united and eager to crush the risings they could not act without support from classes that were reluctant to give it. The first thought of the big landed proprietors was to re-establish the yeomanry, but they found an unexpected obstacle in the temper of the farmers. The High Sheriff, after consultation with the Home Secretary, convened a meeting for this purpose at Canterbury on 1st November, but proceedings took an unexpected turn, the farmers recommending as a preferable alternative that public salaries should be reduced, and the meeting adjourned without result. There were similar surprises at other meetings summoned with this object, and landlords who expected to find the farmers rallying to their support were met with awkward resolutions calling for reductions in rent and tithes. The *Kent Herald* went so far as to say that only the dependents of great landowners will join the yeomanry, ' this most unpopular corps.' The magistrates found it equally difficult to enlist special constables, the farmers and tradesmen definitely refusing to act in this capacity at Maidstone, at Cranbrook, at Tonbridge, and at Tonbridge Wells,[2] as well as in the smaller villages. The chairman of the Battle magistrates wrote to the Home Office to say that he intended to reduce his rents in the hope that the farmers would then consent to serve.

Even the Coast Blockade Service was not considered trustworthy. ' It is the last force,' wrote one magistrate, ' I should resort to, on account of the feeling which exists between them and the people hereabouts.' [3] In the absence of local help, the magistrates had to rely on military aid to quell a mob, or to execute a warrant. Demands for troops from different quarters were incessant, and sometimes querulous. ' If you cannot send a military force,' wrote one indignant country gentleman from Heathfield on 14th November, ' for God's sake, say so, without delay, in order that we may remove our families to a

[1] H, O, Papers,   [2] *Ibid,*   [3] *Ibid,*

place of safety from a district which want of support renders us totally unable longer to defend.' [1] Troops were despatched to Cranbrook, but when the Battle magistrates sent thither for help they were told to their great annoyance that no soldiers could be spared. The Government indeed found it impossible to supply enough troops. ' My dear Lord Liverpool,' wrote Sir Robert Peel on 15th November, ' since I last saw you I have made arrangements for sending every disposable cavalry soldier into Kent and the east part of Sussex. General Dalbiac will take the command. He will be at Battel to-day to confer with the Magistracy and to attempt to establish some effectual plan of operations against the rioters.'

The 7th Dragoon Guards at Canterbury were to provide for East Kent ; the 2nd Dragoon Guards at Maidstone were to provide for Mid-Kent ; and the 5th Dragoon Guards at Tunbridge Wells for the whole of East Sussex. Sir Robert Peel meanwhile thought that the magistrates should themselves play a more active part, and he continually expressed the hope that they would ' meet and concert some effectual mode of resisting the illegal demands.' [2] He deprecated strongly the action of certain magistrates in yielding to the mobs. Mr. Collingwood, who has been mentioned already, received a severe reproof for his behaviour at Goudhurst, where he had adopted a conciliatory policy and let off the rioters on their own recognisances. ' We did not think the case a very strong one,' he wrote on 18th November, ' or see any very urgent necessity for the apprehension of Eaves, nor after Captain King's statement that he had not felt a blow, could we consider the assault of a magistrate proved. The whole parish unanimously begged them off, and said that their being discharged on their own recognisances would probably contribute to the peace of the parish.'

The same weakness, or sympathy, was displayed by magistrates in the western part of Sussex, where the rising spread after the middle of November. In the Arundel district the magistrates anticipated disturbances by holding a meeting of the inhabitants to fix the scale of wages. The wages agreed on were ' 2s. a day wet and dry and 1s. 6d. a week for every child (above 2) under 4,' during the winter : from Lady Day to Michaelmas 14s. a week, wet and dry, with the same allowance for children. A scale was also drawn up for lads and young men. The mobs were demanding 14s. a week all

[1] H. O. Papers.   [2] *Ibid.*

the year round, but they seem to have acquiesced in the Arundel scale, and to have given no further trouble. At Horsham, the labourers adopted more violent measures and met with almost universal sympathy. There was a strong Radical party in that town, and one magistrate described it later as ' a hot Bed of Sedition.' Attempts were made, without success, to show that the Radicals were at the bottom of the disturbances. The district round Horsham was in an agitated state. Among others who received threatening letters was Sir Timothy Shelley of Field Place. The letter was couched in the general spirit of Shelley's song to the men of England :—

> ' Men of England, wherefore plough,
> For the lords who lay ye low,'

which his father may, or may not, have read. The writer urged him, ' if you wish to escape the impending danger in this world and in that which is to come,' to go round to the miserable beings from whom he exacted tithes, ' and enquire and hear from there own lips what disstres there in.' Like many of these letters, it contained at the end a rough picture of a knife, with ' Beware of the fatel daggar ' inscribed on it.

In Horsham itself the mob, composed of from seven hundred to a thousand persons, summoned a vestry meeting in the church. Mr. Sanctuary, the High Sheriff for Sussex, described the episode in a letter to the Home Office on the same day (18th November). The labourers, he said, demanded 2s. 6d. a day, and the lowering of rents and tithes: ' all these complaints were attended to——thought reasonable and complied with,' and the meeting dispersed quietly. Anticipating, it may be, some censure, he added, ' I should have found it quite impossible to have prevailed upon any person to serve as special constable——most of the tradespeople and many of the farmers considering the demands of the people but just (and) equitable——indeed many of them advocated (them)——a doctor spoke about the taxes——but no one backed him——that was not the object of the meeting.' A lady living at Horsham wrote a more vivid account of the day's work. She described how the mob made everybody come to the church. Mr. Simpson, the vicar, went without more ado, but Mr. Hurst, senior, owner of the great tithes, held out till the mob seized a chariot from the King's Arms and dragged it to his door. Whilst the chariot was being brought he slipped out, and entered the church with his two sons. All the gentlemen stood up at the altar, while the farmers encouraged the labourers in the body of the church. ' Mr. Hurst held out so long that it was feared blood would be shed, the Doors were shut till the Demands were granted, no lights were allowed, the Iron railing that surrounds the Monuments torn up, and the sacred boundary between the chancel and Altar overleapt before he would yield.' Mr. Hurst himself wrote to the Home Office to say that it was only the promise to reduce rents and tithes that had prevented serious riots, but he met with little sympathy at headquarters. ' I cannot concur,' wrote Sir Robert Peel, ' in the opinion of Mr. Hurst that it was expedient or necessary for the Vestry to yield to the demands of the Mob. In every case that I have seen, in which the mob has been firmly and temperately resisted, they have given way without resorting to personal violence.' A neighbouring magistrate, who shared Sir Robert Peel's opinion about the affair, went to Horsham a day or two later to swear in special constables. He found that out of sixty-three ' respectable householders ' four only would take the oath. Meanwhile the difficulties of providing troops increased with the area of disturbances. ' I have requested that every effort may be made to reinforce the troops in the western part of Sussex,' wrote Sir Robert Peel to a Horsham magistrate on 18th November, ' and you may judge of the difficulty of doing so, when I mention to you that the most expeditious mode of effecting this is to bring from Dorchester *the only* cavalry force that is in the West of England. This, however, shall be done, and 100 men (infantry) shall be brought from the Garrison of Portsmouth.'

Until the middle of November the rising was confined to Kent, Sussex and parts of Surrey, with occasional fires and threatening letters in neighbouring counties. After that time the disturbances became more serious, spreading not only to the West of Sussex, but to Berkshire, Hampshire, and Wiltshire. On 22nd November the Duke of Buckingham wrote from Avington in Hampshire to the Duke of Wellington : ' Nothing can be worse than the state of this neighbourhood. I may say that this part of the country is wholly in the hands of the rebels . . . 1500 rioters are to assemble to-morrow morning, and will attack any farmhouses where there are threshing machines. They go about levying contributions on every gentleman's house. There are very few magistrates ; and what there are are completely cowed.   In short, something decisive must instantly be done.'

The risings in these counties differed in some respects from the rising in Kent and Sussex.   The disturbances were not so much like the firing of a train of discontent, they were rather a sudden and spontaneous explosion.   They lasted only about a week, and were well described in a report of Colonel Brotherton, one of the two military experts sent by Lord Melbourne to Wiltshire to advise the magistrates.   He wrote on 28th November : ' The insurrectionary movement seems to be directed by no plan or system, but merely actuated by the spontaneous feeling of the peasantry and quite at random.' The labourers went about in larger numbers, combining with the destruction of threshing machines and the demand for higher wages a claim for ' satisfaction ' as they called it in the form of ready money.   It was their practice to charge £2 for breaking a threshing machine, but in some cases the mobs were satisfied with a few coppers.   The demand for ready money was not a new feature, for many correspondents of the Home Office note in their letters that the mobs levied money in Kent and Sussex, but hitherto this ' sturdy begging,' as Cobbett called it, had been regarded by the magistrates as unimportant.   The wages demanded in these counties were 2s. a day, whereas the demands in Kent and usually in Sussex had been for 2s. 6d. or 2s. 3d.   Wages had fallen to a lower level in Hampshire, Berkshire and Wiltshire.   The current rate in Wiltshire was 7s., and Colonel Mair, the second officer sent down by the Home Office, reported that wages were sometimes as low as 6s.   It is therefore not surprising to learn that in two parishes the labourers instead of asking for 2s. a day, asked only for 8s. or 9s. a week.   In Berkshire wages varied from 7s. to 9s., and in Hampshire the usual rate seems to have been 8s.

The rising in Hampshire was marked by a considerable destruction of property.   At Fordingbridge, the mob under the leadership of a man called Cooper, broke up the machinery both at a sacking manufactory and at a manufactory of threshing machines.   Cooper was soon clothed in innumerable legends : he was a gipsy, a mysterious gentleman, possibly the renowned ' Swing ' himself.   At the Fordingbridge riots he rode on horseback and assumed the title of Captain Hunt. His followers addressed him bareheaded.   In point of fact he was an agricultural labourer of good character, a native of

East Grimstead in Wilts, who had served in the artillery in
the French War. Some two months before the riots his wife
had robbed him, and then eloped with a paramour. This
unhinged his self-control; he gave himself up to drink and
despair, and tried to forget his misery in reckless rioting.
Near Andover again a foundry was destroyed by a mob, after
the ringleader, Gilmore, had entered the justices' room at
Andover, where the justices were sitting, and treated with
them on behalf of the mob. Gilmore also was a labourer;
he was twenty-five years old and had been a soldier.

The most interesting event in the Hampshire rising was the
destruction of the workhouses at Selborne and Headley.
Little is reported of the demolition of the poorhouse at
Selborne. The indictment of the persons accused of taking
part in it fell through on technical grounds, and as the
defendants were also the persons charged with destroying the
Headley workhouse, the prosecution in the Selborne case
was abandoned. The mob first went to Mr. Cobbold, Vicar
of Selborne, and demanded that he should reduce his tithes,
telling him with some bluntness ' we must have a touch of
your tithes : we think £300 a year quite enough for you . . . £4
a week is quite enough.' Mr. Cobbold was thoroughly alarmed,
and consented to sign a paper promising to reduce his tithes,
which amounted to something over £600, by half that sum.
The mob were accompanied by a good many farmers who had
agreed to raise wages if the labourers would undertake to
obtain a reduction of tithes, and these farmers signed the
paper also. After Mr. Cobbold's surrender the mob went on
to the workhouse at Headley, which served the parishes of
Bramshott, Headley and Kingsley. Their leader was a certain
Robert Holdaway, a wheelwright, who had been for a short
time a publican. He was a widower, with eight small children,
described by the witnesses at his trial as a man of excellent
character, quiet, industrious, and inoffensive. The master
of the workhouse greeted Holdaway with ' What, Holdy, are
you here ? ' ' Yes, but I mean you no harm nor your wife
nor your goods : so get them out as soon as you can, for the
house must come down.' The master warned him that there
were old people and sick children in the house. Holdaway
promised that they should be protected, asked where they
were, and said the window would be marked. What followed
is described in the evidence given by the master of the workhouse : ' There was not a room left entire, except that in which

the sick children were.   These were removed into the yard on
two beds, and covered over, and kept from harm all the time.
This was done by the mob.   They were left there because
there was no room for them in the sick ward.   The sick ward
was full of infirm old paupers.   It was not touched, but of all
the rest of the place not a room was left entire.'   The farmers
looked on whilst the destruction proceeded, and one at least
of the labourers in the mob declared afterwards that his master
had forced him to join.

In Wiltshire also the destruction of property was not confined to threshing machines.   At Wilton, the mob, under the
leadership of a certain John Jennings, aged eighteen,[1] who
declared that he ' was going to break the machinery to make
more work for the poor people,' did £500 worth of damage in a
woollen mill.   Another cloth factory at Quidhampton was also
injured ; in this affair an active part was taken by a boy even
younger than Jennings, John Ford, who was only seventeen
years old.[2]

The riot which attracted most attention of all the disturbances in Wiltshire took place at Pyt House, the seat of Mr. John
Benett, M.P. for the county.   Mr. Benett was a well-known
local figure, and had given evidence before several Committees
on Poor Laws.   The depth of his sympathy with the labourers
may be gauged by the threat that he uttered before the Committee of 1817 to pull down his cottages if Parliament should
make length of residence a legal method of gaining a settlement.   Some member of the Committee suggested that if there
were no cottages there would be no labourers, but Mr. Benett
replied cheerfully enough that it did not matter to a labourer
how far he walked to his work: ' I have many labourers
coming three miles to my farm every morning during the
winter ' (the hours were six to six) ' and they are the most
punctual persons we have.'   At the time he gave this evidence,
he stated that about three-quarters of the labouring population
in his parish of Tisbury received relief from the poor rates in aid
of wages, and he declared that it was useless to let them small
parcels of land.   The condition of the poor had not improved
in Mr. Benett's parish between 1817 and 1830, and Lord
Arundel, who lived in it, described it as ' a Parish in which the
Poor have been more oppressed and are in greater misery as a

---

[1] Transported for life to New South Wales.

[2] Ford was capitally convicted and sentenced to transportation for life, but
his sentence was commuted to imprisonment.

whole than any Parish in the Kingdom.' [1]   It is not surprising that when the news of what had been achieved in Kent and Sussex spread west to Wiltshire, the labourers of Tisbury rose to demand 2s. a day, and to destroy the threshing machines. A mob of five hundred persons collected, and their first act was to destroy a threshing machine, with the sanction of the owner, Mr. Turner, who sat by on horseback, watching them.   They afterwards proceeded to the Pyt House estate.   Mr. Benett met them, parleyed and rode with them for some way ; they behaved politely but firmly, telling him their intentions. One incident throws a light on the minds of the actors in these scenes.   ' I then,' said Mr. Benett afterwards, ' pointed out to them that they could not trust each other, for any man, I said, by informing against ten of you will obtain at once £500.' It was an adroit speech, but as it happened the Wiltshire labourers, half starved, degraded and brutalised, as they might be, had a different standard of honour from that imagined by this magistrate and member of Parliament, and the devilish temptation he set before them was rejected.   The mob destroyed various threshing machines on Mr. Benett's farms, and refused to disperse ; at last, after a good deal of sharp language from Mr. Benett, they threw stones at him.   At the same time a troop of yeomanry from Hindon came up and received orders to fire blank cartridges above the heads of the mob.   This only produced laughter ; the yeomanry then began to charge ; the mob took shelter in the plantations round Pyt House and stoned the yeomanry, who replied by a fierce onslaught, shooting one man dead on the spot,[2] wounding six by cutting off fingers and opening skulls, and taking a great number of prisoners.   At the inquest at Tisbury on the man John Harding, who was killed, the jury returned a verdict of justifiable homicide, and the coroner refused to grant a warrant for burial, saying that the man's action was equivalent to *felo de se*.   Hunt stated in the House of Commons that the foreman of the jury was the father of one of the yeomen.

We have seen that in these counties the magistrates took a very grave view of the crime of levying money from house-holders.   This was often done by casual bands of men and boys, who had little connection with the organised rising. An examination of the cases described before the Special

---

[1] H. O. Papers.

[2] According to local tradition he was killed not by the yeomanry but by a farmer, before the troop came up.   See Hudson, *A Shepherd's Life*, p. 248.

Commissions gives the impression that in point of fact there was very little danger to person or property. A farmer's wife at Aston Tirrold in Berkshire described her own experience to the Abingdon Special Commission. A mob came to her house and demanded beer. Her husband was out and she went to the door. 'Bennett was spokesman. He said " Now a little of your beer if you please." I answered " Not a drop." He asked " Why ? " and I said " I cannot give beer to encourage riot." Bennett said " Why you don't call this rioting do you ? " I said " I don't know what you call it, but it is a number of people assembled together to alarm others : but don't think I 'm afraid or daunted at it." Bennett said " Suppose your premises should be set on fire ? " I said " Then I certainly should be alarmed but I don't suppose either of you intends doing that." Bennett said " No, we do not intend any such thing, I don't wish to alarm you and we are not come with the intention of mischief." ' The result of the dialogue was that Bennett and his party went home without beer and without giving trouble.

It was natural that when mob-begging of this kind became fashionable, unpopular individuals should be singled out for rough and threatening visits. Sometimes the assistant over-seers were the objects of special hatred, sometimes the parson. It is worth while to give the facts of a case at St. Mary Bourne in Hampshire, because stress was laid upon it in the subsequent prosecutions as an instance of extraordinary violence. The clergyman, Mr. Easton, was not a favourite in his parish, and he preached what the poor regarded as a harsh and a hostile sermon. When the parish rose, a mob of two hundred forced their way into the vicarage and demanded money, some of them repeating, ' Money or blood.' Mrs. Easton, who was rather an invalid, Miss Lucy Easton, and Master Easton were downstairs, and Mrs. Easton was so much alarmed that she sent Lucy upstairs to fetch 10s. Meanwhile Mr. Easton had come down, and was listening to some extremely unsympathetic criticisms of his performances in the pulpit. ' Damn you,' said Daniel Simms,[1] ' where will your text be next Sunday ? ' William Simms was equally blunt and uncompromising. Meanwhile Lucy had brought down the half-sovereign, and Mrs. Easton gave it to William Simms,[2] who thereupon cried ' All out,' and the mob left the Eastons at peace.

[1] Transported for life to New South Wales.
[2] Transported for life to New South Wales.

One representative of the Church was distinguished from most of the country gentlemen and clergymen of the time by his treatment of one of these wandering mobs. Cobbett's letter to the Hampshire parsons, published in the *Political Register*, 15th January 1831, contains an account of the conduct of Bishop Sumner, the Bishop of Winchester. ' I have, at last, found a Bishop of the *Law* Church to *praise*. The facts are these : the Bishop, in coming from Winchester to his palace at Farnham, was met about a mile before he got to the latter place, by a band of sturdy beggars, whom some call robbers. They stopped his carriage, and asked for some money, which he gave them. But he did not *prosecute* them : he had not a man of them called to account for his conduct, but, the next day, set *twenty-four labourers to constant work*, opened his Castle to the distressed of all ages, and supplied all with food and other necessaries who stood in need of them. This was becoming a Christian teacher.' Perhaps the bishop remembered the lines from Dryden's *Tales from Chaucer*, describing the spirit in which the good parson regarded the poor :

> ' Who, should they steal for want of his relief,
> He judged himself accomplice with the thief.'

There was an exhibition of free speaking at Hungerford, where the magistrates sat in the Town Hall to receive deputations from various mobs, in connection with the demand for higher wages. The magistrates had made their peace with the Hungerford mob, when a deputation from the Kintbury mob arrived, led by William Oakley, a young carpenter of twenty-five. Oakley addressed the magistrates in language which they had never heard before in their lives and were never likely to hear again. ' You have not such d——d flats to deal with now, as you had before ; we will have 2s. a day till Lady Day, and 2s. 6d. afterwards for labourers and 3s. 6d. for tradesmen. And as we are here we will have £5 before we leave the place or we will smash it. . . . You gentlemen have been living long enough on the good things, now is our time and we will have them. You gentlemen would not speak to us now, only you are afraid and intimidated.' The magistrates acceded to the demands of the Kintbury mob and also gave them the £5, after which they gave the Hungerford mob £5, because they had behaved well, and it would be unjust to treat them worse than their Kintbury neighbours. Mr. Page, Deputy-Lieutenant for Berks, sent Lord Melbourne some tales about this same

Kintbury mob, which was described by Mr. Pearse, M.P., as a set of 'desperate savages.' 'I beg to add some anecdotes of the mob yesterday to illustrate the nature of its component parts. They took £2 from Mr. Cherry a magistrate and broke his Machine. Afterwards another party came and demanded One Pound——when the two parties had again formed into one, they passed by Mr. Cherry's door and said they had taken one pound too much, which they offered to return to him which it is said he refused—they had before understood that Mrs. Cherry was unwell and therefore came only in small parties. A poor woman passed them selling rabbitts, some few of the mob took some by force, the ringleader ordered them to be restored. At a farmer's where they had been regaled with bread cheese and beer one of them stole an umbrella : the ringleader hearing of it, as they were passing the canal threw him into it and gave him a good ducking.' [1]

In the early days of the rising in Hampshire, Wiltshire and Berkshire, there was a good deal of sympathy with the labourers. The farmers in many cases made no objection to the destruction of their threshing machines. One gentleman of Market Lavington went so far as to say that ' nearly all the Wiltshire Farmers were willing to destroy or set aside their machines.' ' My Lord,' wrote Mr. Williams, J.P., from Marlborough, ' you will perhaps be surprised to hear that the greatest number of the threshing machines destroyed have been put out for the Purpose by the Owners themselves.' The Duke of Buckingham complained that in the district round Avington ' the farmers have not the Spirit and in some instances not the Wish to put down ' disturbances.[2] At a meeting in Winchester, convened by the Mayor to preserve the peace (reported in the *Hampshire Chronicle* of 22nd November), Dr. Newbolt, a clergyman and magistrate, described his own dealings with one of the mobs. The mob said they wanted 12s. a week wages : this he said was a reasonable demand. He acted as mediator between the labourers and farmers, and as a result of his efforts the farmers agreed to these terms, and the labourers returned to work, abandoning their project of a descent on Winchester. The Mayor of Winchester also declared that the wages demanded were not unreasonable, and he laid stress on the fact that the object of the meeting was not to appoint special constables to come into conflict with the people, but merely to preserve the peace.

[1] H. O. Papers.   [2] *Ibid.*

Next week Dr. Newbolt put an advertisement into the *Hampshire Chronicle*, acknowledging the vote of thanks that had been passed to him, and reaffirming his belief that conciliation was the right policy.[1] At Overton, in Hampshire, Henry Hunt acted as mediator between the farmers and a hungry and menacing mob. Such was the fear of the farmers that they gave him unlimited power to make promises on their behalf : he promised the labourers that their wages should be raised from 9s. to 12s., with house rent in addition, and they dispersed in delight.

Fortune had so far smiled upon the rising, and there was some hope of success. If the spirit that animated the farmers, and in Kent many of the landowners, had lasted, the winter of 1830 might have ended in an improvement of wages and a reduction of rents and tithes throughout the south of England. In places where the decline of the labourer had been watched for years without pity or dismay, magistrates were now calling meetings to consider his circumstances, and the Home Office Papers show that some, at any rate, of the country gentlemen were aware of the desperate condition of the poor. Unhappily the day of conciliatory measures was a brief one. Two facts frightened the upper classes into brutality : one was the spread of the rising, the other the scarcity of troops.[2] As the movement spread, the alarm of the authorities inspired a different policy, and even those landowners who recognised that the labourers were miserable, thought that they were in the presence of a rising that would sweep them away unless they could suppress it at once by drastic means. They pictured the labourers as Huns and the mysterious Swing as a second Attila, and this panic they contrived to communicate to the other classes of society.

Conciliatory methods consequently ceased; the upper classes substituted action for diplomacy, and the movement rapidly collapsed. Little resistance was offered, and the terrible hosts of armed and desperate men melted down into groups of weak

---

[1] Ten days later, after Lord Melbourne's circular of December 8, Dr. Newbolt changed his tone. Writing to the Home Office he deprecated the censure implied in that circular, and stated that his conduct was due to personal infirmities and threats of violence : indeed he had subsequently heard from a certain Mr. Wickham that 'I left his place just in time to save my own life, as some of the Mob had it in contemplation to drag me out of the carriage, and to destroy me upon the spot, and it was entirely owing to the interference of some of the better disposed of the Peasantry that my life was preserved.'

[2] See p. 258.

and ill-fed labourers, armed with sticks and stones. On 26th November the *Times* could report that seventy persons had been apprehended near Newbury, and that ' about 60 of the most forward half-starved fellows' had been taken into custody some two miles from Southampton. Already the housing of the Berkshire prisoners was becoming a problem, the gaols at Reading and Abingdon being overcrowded : by the end of the month the Newbury Mansion House and Workhouse had been converted into prisons. This energy had been stimulated by a circular letter issued on 24th November, in which Lord Melbourne urged the lord-lieutenants and the magistrates to use firmness and vigour in quelling disturbances, and virtually promised them immunity for illegal acts done in discharge of their duty. A village here and there continued to give the magistrates some uneasiness, for example, Broughton in Hants, ' an open village in an open country . . . where there is no Gentleman to overawe them,' [1] but these were exceptions. The day of risings was over, and from this time forward, arson was the only weapon of discontent. At Charlton in Wilts, where ' the magistrates had talked of 12s. and the farmers had given 10s.,' a certain Mr. Polhill, who had lowered the wages one Saturday to 9s., found his premises in flame. ' The poor,' remarked a neighbouring magistrate, ' naturally consider that they will be beaten down again to 7s.' [2] By 4th December the *Times* correspondent in Wiltshire and Hampshire could report that quiet was restored, that the peasantry were cowed, and that men who had been prominent in the mobs were being picked out and arrested every day. He gave an amusing account of the trials of a special correspondent, and of the difficulties of obtaining information. 'The circular of Lord Melbourne which encourages the magistrates to seize suspected persons, and promises them impunity if the motives are good (such is the construction of the circular in these parts), and which the magistrates are determined to act upon, renders inquiries unsafe, and I have received a few good natured hints on this head. Gentlemen in gigs and post chaises are peculiar objects of jealousy. A cigar, which is no slight comfort in this humid atmosphere, is regarded on the road as a species of pyrotechnical tube ; and even an eye glass is in danger of being metamorphosed into a newly invented air gun, with which these *gentlemen* ignite stacks and barns as they pass. An innocent enquiry of whose house or farm

[1] H. O. Papers.   [2] *Ibid.*

is that? is, under existing circumstances, an overt act of incendiarism.'

In such a state of feeling, it was not surprising that labourers were bundled into prison for sour looks or discontented conversation. A zealous magistrate wrote to the Home Office on 13th December after a fire near Maidenhead, to say that he had committed a certain Greenaway to prison on the following evidence: 'Dr. Vansittart, Rector of Shottesbrook, gave a sermon a short time before the fire took place, recommending a quiet conduct to his Parishioners. Greenaway said openly in the churchyard, we have been quiet too long. His temper is bad, always discontented and churlish, frequently changing his Master from finding great difficulty in maintaining a large family from the Wages of labour.'

Meanwhile the rising had spread westward to Dorset and Gloucestershire, and northward to Bucks. In Dorsetshire and Gloucestershire, the disturbances were much like those in Wiltshire. In Bucks, in addition to the usual agricultural rising, with the breaking of threshing machines and the demand for higher wages, there were riots in High Wycombe, and considerable destruction of paper-making machinery by the unemployed. Where special grievances existed in a village, the labourers took advantage of the rising to seek redress for them. Thus at Walden in Bucks, in addition to demanding 2s. a day wages with 6d. for each child and a reduction of tithes, they made a special point of the improper distribution of parish gifts. 'Another person said that buns used to be thrown from the church steeple and beer given away in the churchyard, and a sermon preached on the bun day. Witness (the parson) told them that the custom had ceased before he came to the parish, but that he always preached a sermon on St. George's day, and two on Sundays, one of which was a volunteer. He told them that he had consulted the Archdeacon on the claim set up for the distribution of buns, and that the Archdeacon was of opinion that no such claim could be maintained.'

At Benson or Bensington, in Oxfordshire, the labourers, after destroying some threshing machines, made a demonstration against a proposal for enclosure. Mr. Newton, a large proprietor, had just made one of many unsuccessful attempts to obtain an Enclosure Act for the parish. Some thousand persons assembled in the churchyard expecting that Mr. Newton would try to fix the notice on the church door, but as he did not venture to appear, they proceeded to his house, and made him promise never again to attempt to obtain an Enclosure Act.[1]

The movement for obtaining higher wages by this rude collective bargaining was extinguished in the counties already mentioned by the beginning of December, but disturbances now developed over a larger area. A 'daring riot' took place at Stotfold in Bedfordshire. The labourers met together to demand exemption from taxes, dismissal of the assistant overseer, and the raising of wages to 2s. a day. The last demand was refused, on which the labourers set some straw alight in a field to alarm the farmers. Mr. Whitbread, J.P., brought a hundred special constables, and arrested ten ringleaders, after which the riot ceased. There were disturbances in Norfolk, Suffolk, and Essex; and in many other counties the propertied classes were terrified from time to time by the news of fires. In Cambridgeshire there were meetings of labourers to demand higher wages, in some places with immediate success, and one magistrate was alarmed by rumours of a design to march upon Cambridge itself on market day. In Devonshire Lord Ebrington reported an agitation for higher wages with encouragement from the farmers. He was himself impressed by the low wages in force, and had raised them in places still quiet ; a mistake for which he apologised. Even Hereford, 'this hitherto submissive and peaceful county,' was not unaffected. In Northamptonshire there were several fires, and also risings round Peterborough, Oundle and Wellingborough, and a general outbreak in the Midlands was thought to be imminent. Hayricks began to blaze as far north as Carlisle. Swing letters were delivered in Yorkshire, and in Lincolnshire the labourer was said to be awakening to his own importance. There were in fact few counties quite free from infection, and a leading article appeared in the *Times* on 6th December, in which it was stated that never had such a dangerous state of things existed to such an extent in England, in the period of well-authenticated records. 'Let the rich be taught that Providence will not suffer them to oppress their fellow creatures with impunity. Here are tens of thousands of Englishmen, industrious, kind-hearted, but broken-hearted beings, exasperated into madness by insufficient food and clothing, by utter want of necessaries for themselves and their unfortunate families.'

[1] See *Oxford University and City Herald*, November 20 and 27, 1830.

Unfortunately Providence, to whom the *Times* attributed these revolutionary sentiments, was not so close to the scene as Lord Melbourne, whose sentiments on the subject were very different. On 8th December he issued a circular, which gave a death-blow to the hope that the magistrates would act as mediators on behalf of the labourers. After blaming those magistrates who, under intimidation, had advised the establishment of a uniform rate of wages, the Home Secretary went on, ' Reason and experience concur in proving that a compliance with demands so unreasonable in themselves, and urged in such a manner, can only lead, and probably within a very short period of time, to the most disastrous results.' He added that the justices had ' no general legal authority to settle the amount of the wages of labour.' The circular contained a promise on the part of the Government that they would adopt ' every practicable and reasonable measure ' for the alleviation of the labourers' privations.

From this time the magistrates were everywhere on the alert for the first signs of life and movement among the labourers, and they forbade meetings of any kind. In Suffolk and Essex the labourers who took up the cry for higher wages were promptly thrown into prison, and arbitrary arrests became the custom. The movement was crushed, and the time for retribution had come. The gaols were full to overflowing, and the Government appointed Special Commissions to try the rioters in Hampshire, Wiltshire, Dorset, Berks, and Bucks. Brougham, who was now enjoying the office in whose pompous manner he must have lisped in his cradle, told the House of Lords on 2nd December, ' Within a few days from the time I am addressing your Lordships, the sword of justice shall be unsheathed to smite, if it be necessary, with a firm and vigorous hand, the rebel against the law.'

The disturbances were over, but the panic had been such that the upper classes could not persuade themselves that England was yet tranquil. As late as Christmas Eve the Privy Council gave orders to the archbishop to prepare ' a form of prayer to Almighty God, on account of the troubled state of certain parts of the United Kingdom.' The archbishop's composition, which was published after scores of men and boys had been sentenced to transportation for life, must have been recited with genuine feeling by those clergymen who had either broken, or were about to break, their agreement to surrender part of their tithes. One passage ran as follows :

' Restore, O Lord, to Thy people the quiet enjoyment of the many and great blessings which we have received from Thy bounty : defeat and frustrate the malice of wicked and turbulent men, and turn their hearts : have pity, O Lord, on the simple and ignorant, who have been led astray, and recall them to a sense of their duty ; and to persons of all ranks and conditions in this country vouchsafe such a measure of Thy grace, that our hearts being filled with true faith and devotion, and cleansed from all evil affections, we may serve Thee with one accord, in duty and loyalty to the King, in obedience to the laws of the land, and in brotherly love towards each other. . . .'

We shall see in the next chapter what happened to ' the simple and ignorant ' who had fallen into the hands of the English judges.

CHAPTER XII

THE LAST LABOURERS' REVOLT

II

The bands of men and boys who had given their rulers one moment of excitement and lively interest in the condition of the poor had made themselves liable to ferocious penalties. For the privileged classes had set up a code under which no labourer could take a single step for the improvement of the lot of his class without putting his life and liberties in a noose. It is true that the savage laws which had been passed against combination in 1799 and 1800 had been repealed in 1824, and that even under the less liberal Act of the following year, which rescinded the Act of 1824, it was no longer a penal offence to form a Trades Union. But it is easy to see that the labourers who tried to raise their wages were in fact on a shelving and most perilous slope. If they used threats or intimidation or molested or obstructed, either to get a labourer to join with them or to get an employer to make concessions, they were guilty of a misdemeanour punishable with three months' imprisonment. They were lucky if they ran no graver risk than this. Few of the prosecutions at the Special Commissions were under the Act of 1825. A body of men holding a meeting in a village where famine and unemployment were chronic, and where hardly any one had been taught to read or write, might very soon find themselves becoming what the Act of 1714 called a riotous assembly, and if a magistrate took alarm and read the Riot Act, and they did not disperse within one hour, every one of them might be punished as a felon. The hour's interval did not mean an hour's grace, for, as Mr. Justice Alderson told the court at Dorchester, within that hour 'all persons, even private individuals, may do anything, using force even to the last extremity to prevent the commission of a felony.'

There were at least three ways in which labourers meeting together to demonstrate for higher wages ran a risk of losing their lives, if any of their fellows got out of hand from temper, or from drink, or from hunger and despair. Most of the prosecutions before the Special Commissions were prosecutions under three Acts of 1827 and 1828, consolidating the law on the subject of offences against property and offences against the person. Under the eighth section of one Act (7 and 8 George IV. c. 30), any persons riotously or tumultuously assembled together who destroyed any house, stable, coach-house, outhouse, barn, granary, or any building or erection or machinery used in carrying on any trade or manufacture were to suffer death as felons. In this Act there is no definition of riot, and therefore ' the common law definition of a riot is resorted to, and in such a case if any one of His Majesty's subjects was terrified there was a sufficient terror and alarm to substantiate that part of the charge.' [1] Under the sixth section of another Act, any person who robbed any other person of any chattel, money, or valuable security was to suffer death as a felon. Now if a mob presented itself before a householder with a demand for money, and the householder in fear gave even a few coppers, any person who was in that mob, whether he had anything to do with this particular transaction or not, whether he was aware or ignorant of it, was guilty of robbery, and liable to the capital penalty. Under section 12 of the Act of the following year, generally known as Lansdowne's Act, which amended Ellenborough's Act of 1803, it was a capital offence to attempt to shoot at a person, or to stab, cut, or wound him, with intent to murder, rob, or maim. Under this Act, as it was interpreted, if an altercation arose and any violence was offered by a single individual in the mob, the lives of the whole band were forfeit. This was put very clearly by Baron Vaughan : ' There seems to be some impression that unless the attack on an individual is made with some deadly weapons, those concerned are not liable to capital punishment ; but it should be made known to all persons that if the same injury were inflicted by a blow of a stone, all and every person forming part of a riotous assembly is equally guilty as he whose hand may have thrown it, and all alike are liable to death.' Under section 4 of one Act of 1827 the penalty for destroying a threshing machine was transportation for seven years, and under section 17 the penalty for firing a rick was death. These were the terrors hanging over the village labourers of whom several hundreds were now awaiting their trial.

[1] Russell, *On Crimes and Misdemeanours*, p. 371.

The temper of the judges was revealed in their charges to the Grand Juries.   In opening the Maidstone Assizes on 14th December, Mr. Justice Bosanquet [1] declared that though there might be some distress it was much exaggerated, and that he was sure that those whom he had the honour to address would find it not only their duty but their pleasure to lend an ear to the wants of the poor.[2]   Mr. Justice Taunton [3] was even more reassuring on this subject at the Lewes Assizes : the distress was less than it had been twelve months before.   ' I regret to say,' he went on, ' there are persons who exaggerate the distress and raise up barriers between different classes— who use the most inflammatory language—who represent the rich as oppressors of the poor.   It would be impertinent in me to say anything to you as to your treatment of labourers or servants.   That man must know little of the gentry of England, whether connected with the town or country, who represents them as tyrants to the poor, as not sympathising in their distress, and as not anxious to relieve their burdens and to promote their welfare and happiness.' [4]   In opening the Special Commission at Winchester Baron Vaughan [5] alluded to the theory that the tumults had arisen from distress and admitted that it might be partly true, but, he continued, ' every man possessed of the feelings common to our nature must deeply lament 'it, and endeavour to alleviate it (as you gentlemen no doubt have done and will continue to do), by every means which Providence has put within his power.' If individuals were aggrieved by privations and injuries, they must apply to the Legislature, which alone could afford them relief, ' but it can never be tolerated in any country which professes to acknowledge the obligations of municipal law, that any man or body of men should be permitted to sit in judgment upon their own wrongs, or to arrogate to themselves the power of redressing them.   To suffer it would be to relapse into the barbarism of savage life and to dissolve the very elements by which society is held together.' [6]   The opinions of the Bench on the sections of the Act (7 and 8 George IV. c. 30) under which men could be hung for assembling riotously and breaking machinery were clearly expressed by Mr. Justice

---

[1] Sir J. B. Bosanquet (1773-1847).

[2] *Times*, December 15, 1830.   [3] Sir W. E. Taunton (1773-1835).

[4] The *Times* on December 25 quoted part of this charge in a leading article with some sharp strictures.

[5] Sir John Vaughan (1769-1839).   [6] *Times*, December 21, 1830.

Parke [1] (afterwards Lord Wensleydale) at Salisbury : ' If that law ceases to be administered with due firmness, and men look to it in vain for the security of their rights, our wealth and power will soon be at an end, and our capital and industry would be transferred to some more peaceful country, whose laws are more respected or better enforced.' [2]   By another section of that Act seven years was fixed as the maximum penalty for breaking a threshing machine. Mr. Justice Alderson [3] chafed under this restriction, and he told two men, Case and Morgan, who were found guilty at the Salisbury Special Commission of going into a neighbouring parish and breaking a threshing machine, that had the Legislature foreseen such crimes as theirs, it would have enabled the court to give them a severer sentence. [4]

Mr. Justice Park [5] was equally stern and uncompromising in defending the property of the followers of the carpenter of Nazareth against the unreasoning misery of the hour. Summing up in a case at Aylesbury, in which one of the charges was that of attempting to procure a reduction of tithes, he remarked with warmth : ' It was highly insolent in such men to require of gentlemen, who had by an expensive education qualified themselves to discharge the sacred duties of a Minister of the Gospel, to descend from that station and reduce themselves to the situation of common labourers.' [6]

Few judges could resist the temptation to introduce into their charges a homily on the economic benefits of machinery. Mr. Justice Park was an exception, for he observed at Aylesbury that the question of the advantages of machinery was outside the province of the judges, ' and much mischief often resulted from persons stepping out of their line of duty.' [7] Mr. Justice Alderson took a different view, and the very next day he was expounding the truths of political economy at Dorchester, starting with what he termed the ' beautiful and simple illustration ' of the printing press. [8] The illustration must have

---

[1] Sir James Parke (1782-1868).

[2] *Times*, January 3, 1831.   [3] Sir E. H. Alderson (1787-1857).

[4] *Times*, January 6, 1831. Cf. letter of Mr. R. Pollen, J.P., afterwards one of Winchester Commissioners, to Home Office, November 26 : ' It may be worth considering the law, which exempts all *Threshing Machines* from capital punishment, should such scenes as these occur again amongst the agricultural classes. I confess I view with great regret that they have found the mode of combining, which I had hoped was confined to the manufacturing classes.'

[5] Sir J. A. Park (1763-1838).   [6] *Times*, January 15, 1831.

[7] *Ibid.*, January 12, 1831.   [8] *Ibid.*

seemed singularly intimate and convincing to the labourers in
the dock who had never been taught their letters.

Such was the temper of the judges. Who and what were the
prisoners before them ? After the suppression of the riots,
the magistrates could pick out culprits at their leisure, and
when a riot had involved the whole of the village the temptation to get rid by this method of persons who for one reason
or another were obnoxious to the authorities was irresistible.
Hunt, speaking in the House of Commons,[1] quoted the case of
Hindon ; seven men had been apprehended for rioting and
they were all poachers. Many of the prisoners had already
spent a month in an overcrowded prison ; almost all of them
were poor men ; the majority could not read or write.[2] Few
could afford counsel, and it must be remembered that counsel
could not address the court on behalf of prisoners who were
being tried for breaking machines, or for belonging to a mob
that asked for money or destroyed property. By the rules of
the gaol, the prisoners at Salisbury were not allowed to see
their attorney except in the presence of the gaoler or his
servant. The labourers' ignorance of the law was complete and
inevitable. Many of them thought that the King or the
Government or the magistrates had given orders that machines
were to be broken. Most of them supposed that if a person
from whom they demanded money threw it down or gave it
without the application of physical force, there was no question
of robbery. We have an illustration of this illusion in a trial
at Winchester when Isaac Hill, junior, who was charged with
breaking a threshing machine near Micheldever, for which
the maximum penalty was seven years, pleaded in his defence
that he had not broken the machine and that all that he did
' was to ask the prosecutor civilly for the money, which the
mob took from him, and the prosecutor gave it to him, and
that he thanked him very kindly for it,' [3] an admission which
made him liable to a death penalty. A prisoner at Salisbury,
when he was asked what he had to say in his defence to the
jury, replied : ' Now, my Lord, I 'se got nothing to say to 'em,
I doant knaow any on 'em.' [4] The prisoners were at this

---

[1] February 8, 1831.

[2] There are no statistics for Wilts, Hants, Bucks, and Dorsetshire prisoners.
At Reading out of 138 prisoners 37 could read, and 25 of the 37 could also write.
At Abingdon, out of 47, 17 could read, and 6 of them could also write. In
Wilts and Hants the proportion was probably smaller, as the people were more
neglected.   [3] *Times*, December 24, 1830.   [4] *Ibid.*, January 8, 1831.

further disadvantage that all the witnesses whom they could call as to their share in the conduct of a mob had themselves been in the mob, and were thus liable to prosecution. Thus when James Lush (who was afterwards selected for execution) and James Toomer appealed to a man named Lane, who had just been acquitted on a previous charge, to give evidence that they had not struck Mr. Pinniger in a scuffle, Mr. Justice Alderson cautioned Lane that if he acknowledged that he had been in the mob he would be committed. Lane chose the safer part of silence.[1] In another case a witness had the courage to incriminate himself. When the brothers Simms were being tried for extorting money from Parson Easton's wife, a case which we have already described, Henry Bunce, called as a witness for the defence, voluntarily declared, in spite of a caution from the judge (Alderson), that he had been present himself and that William Simms did not use the expression ' blood or money.' He was at once ordered into custody. ' The prisoner immediately sprung over the bar into the dock with his former comrades, seemingly unaffected by the decision of the learned judge.' [2]

Perhaps the darkest side of the business was the temptation held out to prisoners awaiting trial to betray their comrades. Immunity or a lighter sentence was freely offered to those who would give evidence. Stokes, who was found guilty at Dorchester of breaking a threshing machine, was sentenced by Mr. Justice Alderson to a year's imprisonment, with the explanation that he was not transported because ' after you were taken into custody, you gave very valuable information which tended greatly to further the ends of justice.' [3] These transactions were not often dragged into the daylight, but some negotiations of this character were made public in the trial of Mr. Deacle next year. Mr. Deacle, a well-to-do gentleman farmer, was tried at the Lent Assizes at Winchester for being concerned in the riots. One of the witnesses against him, named Collins, admitted in cross-examination that he believed he should have been prosecuted himself, if he had not promised to give evidence against Mr. Deacle ; another witness, named Barnes, a carpenter, stated in cross-examination that during the trials at the Special Commission, ' he being in the dock, and about to be put on his trial, the gaoler Beckett called him out, and took

---

[1] *Times*, January 7, 1831.
[2] *Ibid.*, December 24, 1830. Henry Bunce was transported for life to New South Wales.   [3] *Ibid.*, January 14.

him into a room where there were Walter Long, a magistrate, and another person, whom he believed to be Bingham Baring, who told him that he should not be put upon his trial if he would come and swear against Deacle.' When the next witness was about to be cross-examined, the counsel for the prosecution abruptly abandoned the case.[1]

The first Special Commission was opened at Winchester with suitable pomp on 18th December. Not only the prison but the whole town was crowded, and the inhabitants of Winchester determined to make the best of the windfall. The jurymen and the *Times* special correspondent complained bitterly of the abnormal cost of living, the latter mentioning that in addition to extraordinary charges for beds, 5s. a day was exacted for firing and tallow candles, bedroom fire not included. The three judges sent down as commissioners were Baron Vaughan, Mr. Justice Parke, and Mr. Justice Alderson. With them were associated two other commissioners, Mr. Sturges Bourne, of assistant overseer fame, and Mr. Richard Pollen. The Duke of Wellington, as Lord-Lieutenant, sat on the Bench. The Attorney-General, Mr. Sergeant Wild, and others appeared to prosecute for the Crown. The County took up every charge, the Government only the more serious ones.

There were three hundred prisoners, most of them charged with extorting money by threats or with breaking machinery. What chance had they of a fair trial ? They started with the disabilities already described. They were thrown by batches into the dock ; the pitiless law was explained to the jury ; extenuating circumstances were ruled out as irrelevant. ' We do not come here,' said Mr. Justice Alderson, ' to inquire into grievances. We come here to decide law.' But though evidence about wages or distress was not admitted, the judges did not scruple to give their own views of the social conditions which had produced these disturbances. Perhaps the most flagrant example was provided by a trial which happily was for a misdemeanour only. Seven men were indicted for conspiring together and riotously assembling for the purpose of raising wages and for compelling others to join them. The labourers of the parish of Fawley had combined together for two objects, the first to raise their wages, which stood at 9s. a week, the second to get rid of the assistant overseer, who had introduced a parish cart, to which he had

---

[1] Cobbett, *Political Register*, vol. lxxiii. p. 535, and local papers.

harnessed women and boys, amongst others an idiot woman, named Jane Stevens. The labourers determined to break up the cart, but they desisted on the promise of a farmer that a horse should be bought for it. Lord Cavan was the large landowner of the parish. He paid his men as a rule 9s. a week, but two of them received 10s. The mob came up to his house to demand an increase of wages : Lord Cavan was out, quelling rioters elsewhere. Lady Cavan came down to see them. ' Seeing you are my neighbours and armed,' said she, ' yet, as I am an unprotected woman, I am sure you will do no harm.' The labourers protested that they meant no harm, and they did no harm. ' I asked them,' said Lady Cavan afterwards, in evidence, ' why they rose then, there was no apparent distress round Eaglehurst, and the wages were the same as they had been for several years. I have been in several of their cottages and never saw any appearance of distress. They said they had been oppressed long and would bear it no longer.' One man told her that he had 9s. a week wages and 3s. from the parish, he had heard that the 3s. was to be discontinued. With the common-sense characteristic of her class Lady Cavan assured him that he was not improving his position by idling. The labourers impressed the Cavan men, and went on their peaceful way round the parish. The farmers who gave evidence for the prosecution were allowed to assert that there was no distress, but when it came to evidence for the defence a stricter standard of relevancy was exacted. One witness for the prisoners said of the labourers : ' The men were in very great distress ; many of the men had only a few potatoes in their bag when they came to work.' ' The learned judges objected to this course of examination being continued : it might happen that through drinking a man might suffer distress.' The Attorney-General, in his closing speech, asserted again that the prisoners did not seem to have been in distress. Baron Vaughan, in summing up, said that men were not to assemble and conspire together for the purpose of determining what their wages should be. ' That which at first might be in itself a lawful act, might in the event become illegal. . . . A respectful statement or representation of their grievances was legal, and to which no one would object, but the evidence, if they believed it, showed that the conduct of this assembly was far from being respectful. No one could feel more for the distresses of the people than he did, but he would never endure that persons should by physical strength compel wages to be raised. There was no country where charity fell in a purer stream than in this. Let the man make his appeal in a proper and respectful manner, and he might be assured that appeal would never be heard in vain. . . . His Lordship spoke very highly of the conduct of Lady Cavan. She had visited the cottages of all those who lived in the neighbourhood, she knew they were not distressed, and she also felt confident from her kindness to them that they would not offer her any violence.' All seven were found guilty ; four were sentenced to six months hard labour, and three to three months.

Very few, however, of the cases at Winchester were simple misdemeanours, for in most instances, in addition to asking for higher wages, the labourers had made themselves liable to a prosecution for felony, either by breaking a threshing machine or by asking for money. Those prisoners who had taken part in the Fordingbridge riots, or in the destruction of machinery near Andover, or in the demolition of the Headley Workhouse, were sentenced to death or to transportation for life. Case after case was tried in which prisoners from different villages were indicted for assault and robbery. The features varied little, and the spectators began to find the proceedings monotonous. Most of the agricultural population of Hampshire had made itself liable to the death penalty, if the authorities cared to draw the noose. The three hundred who actually appeared in Court were like the men on whom the tower of Siloam fell.

A case to which the prosecution attached special importance arose out of an affair at the house of Mr. Eyre Coote. A mob of forty persons, some of whom had iron bars, presented themselves before Mr. Coote's door at two o'clock in the morning. Two bands of men had already visited Mr. Coote that evening, and he had given them beer : this third band was a party of stragglers. Mr. Coote stationed his ten servants in the portico, and when the mob arrived he asked them, ' What do you want, my lads ? ' ' Money,' was the answer. ' Money,' said Mr. Coote, ' you shan't have.' One of the band seemed to Mr. Coote about to strike him. Mr. Coote seized him, nine of the mob were knocked down and taken, and the rest fled. Six of the men were prosecuted for feloniously demanding money. Baron Vaughan remarked that outrages like this made one wonder whether one was in a civilised country, and he proceeded to raise its moral tone by sentencing all the prisoners to transportation for life, except one, Henry Eldridge, who was reserved for execution. He had been already capitally convicted of complicity in the Fordingbridge riots, and this attempt to ' enter the sanctuary of Mr. Eyre Coote's home ' following upon that crime, rendered him a suitable ' sacrifice to be made on the altar of the offended justice ' of his country.

In many of the so-called robberies punished by the Special Commissions the sums taken were trifling. George Steel, aged eighteen, was sentenced to transportation for life for obtaining a shilling, when he was in liquor, from Jane Neale : William Sutton, another boy of eighteen, was found guilty of taking 4d. in a drunken frolic : Sutton, who was a carter boy receiving 1s. 6d. a week and his food, was given an excellent character by his master, who declared that he had never had a better servant. The jury recommended him to mercy, and the judges responded by sentencing him to death and banishing him for life. George Clerk, aged twenty, and E. C. Nutbean, aged eighteen, paid the same price for 3d. down and the promise of beer at the Greyhound. Such cases were not exceptional, as any one who turns to the reports of the trials will see.

The evidence on which prisoners were convicted was often of the most shadowy kind. Eight young agricultural labourers, of ages varying from eighteen to twenty-five, were found guilty of riotously assembling in the parish of St. Lawrence Wootten and feloniously stealing £2 from William Lutely Sclater of Tangier Park. ' We want to get a little satisfaction from you ' was the phrase they used. Two days later another man, named William Farmer, was charged with the same offence. Mr. Sclater thought that Farmer was like the man in the mob who blew a trumpet or horn, but could not swear to his identity. Other witnesses swore that he was with the mob elsewhere, and said, ' Money wa want and money wa will hae.' On this evidence he was found guilty, and though Mr. Justice Alderson announced that he felt warranted in recommending that he should not lose his life, ' yet, it was his duty,' he continued, ' to state that he should for this violent and disgraceful outrage be sent out of the country, and separated for life from those friends and connections which were dear to him here : that he should have to employ the rest of his days in labour, at the will and for the profit of another, to show the people of the class to which the prisoner belonged that they cannot with impunity lend their aid to such outrages against the peace and security of person and property.'

We have seen that at the time of the riots it was freely stated that the farmers incited the labourers to make disturbances. Hunt went so far as to say in the House of Commons that in nineteen cases out of twenty the farmers encouraged the labourers to break the threshing machines. The county authorities evidently thought it unwise to prosecute the farmers, although it was proved in evidence that there were several farmers present at the destruction of the Headley Workhouse, and at the demonstration at Mr. Cobbold's house. Occasionally a farmer, in testifying to a prisoner's character, would admit that he had been in a mob himself. In such cases the judge administered rebukes, but the prosecution took no action. There was, however, one exception. A small farmer, John Boys, of the parish of Owslebury, had thrown himself heartily into the labourers' cause. A number of small farmers met and decided that the labourers' wages ought to be raised. Boys agreed to take a paper round for signature. The paper ran as follows : ' We the undersigned are willing to give 2s. per day for able-bodied married men, and 9s. per week for single men, on consideration of our rents and tithes being abated in proportion.' In similar cases, as a rule, the farmers left it to the labourers to collect signatures, and Boys, by undertaking the work himself, made himself a marked man. He had been in a mob which extorted money from Lord Northesk's steward at Owslebury, and for this he was indicted for felony. But the jury, to the chagrin of the prosecution, acquitted him. What followed is best described in the report of Sergeant Wilde's speech in the House of Commons (21st July 1831). ' Boyce was tried and acquitted : but he (Mr. Wilde) being unable to account for the acquittal, considering the evidence to have been clear against him, and feeling that although the jury were most respectable men, they might possibly entertain some sympathy for him in consequence of his situation in life, thought it his duty to send a communication to the Attorney-General, stating that Boyce was deeply responsible for the acts which had taken place : that he thought he should not be allowed to escape, and recommending that he be tried before a different jury in the other Court. The Attorney-General sent to him (Mr. Wilde) to come into the other Court, and the result was that Boyce was then tried and convicted.' In the other more complaisant

Court, Farmer Boys and James Fussell, described as a genteel young man of about twenty, living with his mother, were found guilty of heading a riotous mob for reducing rents and tithes and sentenced to seven years' transportation.[1]

This was not the only case in which the sympathies of the jury created a difficulty. The Home Office Papers contain a letter from Dr. Quarrier, a Hampshire magistrate, who had been particularly vigorous in suppressing riots, stating that Sir James Parke discharged a jury at the Special Commission ' under the impression that they were reluctant to convict the Prisoners which was more strongly impressed upon the mind of the Judge, by its being reported to his Lordship that " some of the Gosport Jurors had said, while travelling in the stage coach to Winchester, that they would not convict in cases where the Labourers had been driven to excess by Poverty and low Wages ! " It was ascertained that some of those empannelled upon the acquitting Jury were from Gosport, which confirmed the learned Judge in the determination to discharge them.' [2]

An interesting feature of the trials at Winchester was the number of men just above the condition of agricultural labourers who threw in their lot with the poor : the village mechanics, the wheelwrights, carpenters, joiners, smiths, and the bricklayers, shoemakers, shepherds and small holders were often prominent in the disturbances. To the judges this fact was a riddle. The threshing machines had done these men no injury ; they had not known the sting of hunger ; till the time of the riots their characters had been as a rule irreproachable. *Nemo repente turpissimus fuit*, and yet apparently these persons had suddenly, without warning, turned into the ' wicked and turbulent men ' of the archbishop's prayer. Such culprits deserved, in the opinions of the bench, severer punishment than the labourers, whom their example should have kept in the paths of obedience and peace.[3] Where the law permitted, they were sentenced to

---

[1] Fussell's sentence was commuted to imprisonment. Boys was sent to Van Diemen's Land.

[2] H. O. Papers, Municipal and Provincial. Hants, 1831, March 24.

[3] As early as November 26, Mr. Richard Pollen, Chairman of Quarter Sessions and afterwards a commissioner at Winchester, had written to the Home Office, ' I have directed the Magistrates' attention very much to the class of People found in the Mobs many miles from their own homes, Taylors, Shoemakers etc., who have been found always very eloquent, they are universally politicians : they should be, I think, selected.'—H. O. Papers.

transportation for life. One heinous offender of this type, Gregory, a carpenter, was actually earning 18s. a week in the service of Lord Winchester. But the most interesting instances were two brothers, Joseph and Robert Mason, who lived at Bullington. They rented three or four acres, kept a cow, and worked for the neighbouring farmers as well. Joseph, who was thirty-two, had a wife and one child ; Robert, who was twenty-four, was unmarried. Between them they supported a widowed mother. Their characters were exemplary, and the most eager malice could detect no blot upon their past. But their opinions were dangerous : they regularly took in Cobbett's *Register* and read it aloud to twenty or thirty of the villagers. Further, Joseph had carried on foot a petition for reform to the king at Brighton from a hundred and seventy-seven ' persons, belonging to the working and labouring classes ' of Wonston, Barton Stacey and Bullington, and was reported to have given some trouble to the king's porter by an importunate demand for an audience. The recital of these facts gave rise to much merriment at his trial, and was not considered irrelevant by judges who ruled out all allusions to distress.[1] An interesting light is thrown on the history of this petition by a fragment of a letter, written by Robert Mason to a friend, which somehow fell into the hands of a Captain Thompson of Longparish, and was forwarded by him to the Home Office as a valuable piece of evidence.

' *P.S.*—Since I wrote the above I have saw and talked with two persons who say " Bullington Barton and Sutton has sent a petition and why not Longparish Hursborne and Wherwell send another." I think as much, to be sure if we had all signed one, one journey and expense would have served but what is expence ? Why I would engage to carry a Petition and deliver it at St. James for 30 shillings, and to a place like Longparish what is that ? If you do send one pray do not let Church property escape your notice. There is the Church which cost Longparish I should think nearly £1500 yearly : yes and there is an old established Chaple which I will be bound does not cost £25 annually. For God sake . . .' (illegible).

The first charge brought against the Masons was that of robbing Sir Thomas Baring's steward of £10 at East Stratton.

---

[1] For a full account of the incident, including the text of the petition and list of signatures, see Cobbett's *Two-penny Trash*, July 1, 1832.

The money had been taken by one of the mobs; the Masons were acquitted. They were next put on their trial together with William Winkworth, a cobbler and a fellow reader of Cobbett, and ten others, for a similar offence. This time they were accused of demanding £2 or £5 from Mr. W. Dowden of Micheldever. The Attorney-General, in opening the case, drew attention to the circumstances of the Masons and Winkworth, saying that the offence with which they were charged was of a deeper dye, because they were men of superior education and intelligence. A humane clergyman, Mr. Cockerton, curate of Stoke Charity, gave evidence to the effect that if the men had been met in a conciliatory temper in the morning they would have dispersed. Joseph Mason and William Winkworth were found guilty, and sentenced, in the words of the judge, to 'be cut off from all communion with society' for the rest of their lives. Robert Mason was still unconvicted, but he was not allowed to escape. The next charge against him was that of going with a mob which extorted five shillings from the Rev. J. Joliffe at Barton Stacey. He admitted that he had accompanied the mob, partly because the labourers had urged him to do so, partly because he hoped that Mr. Joliffe, being accustomed to public speaking, would be able to persuade the labourers to disperse before any harm was done. There was no evidence to show that he had anything to do with the demand for money. He was found guilty and sentenced to transportation for life. When asked what he had to say for himself, he replied, 'If the learned Counsel, who has so painted my conduct to you, was present at that place and wore a smock frock instead of a gown, and a straw hat instead of a wig, he would now be standing in this dock instead of being seated where he is.'

Six men were reserved for execution, and told that they must expect no mercy on this side of the grave: Cooper, the leader in the Fordingbridge riots; Holdaway, who had headed the attack on Headley Workhouse; Gilmore, who had entered the justices' room in Andover 'in rather a violent manner' and parleyed with the justices, and afterwards, in spite of their remonstrances, been a ringleader in the destruction of a foundry in the parish of Upper Clatford; Eldridge, who had taken part in the Fordingbridge riot and also 'invaded the sanctuary' of Mr. Eyre Coote's home; James Aunalls, a lad of nineteen, who had extorted money at night with threats of a fire, from a person whom he bade look over the hills, where a fire was subsequently seen, and Henry Cook. Cook was a ploughboy of nineteen, who could neither read nor write. For most of his life, since the age of ten, he had been a farm hand. For six months before the riots he had been employed at sawing, at 10s. a week, but at the time of the rising he was out of work. After the riots he got work as a ploughboy at about 5s. a week till his arrest. Like the other lads of the neighbourhood he had gone round with a mob, and he was found guilty, with Joseph Mason, of extorting money from William Dowden. For this he might have got off with transportation for life, but another charge was preferred against him. Mr. William Bingham Baring, J.P., tried, with the help of some of his servants, to quell a riot at Northingdon Down Farm. Silcock, who seemed the leader of the rioters, declared that they would break every machine. Bingham Baring made Silcock repeat these words several times and then seized him. Cook then aimed a blow at Bingham Baring with a sledge-hammer and struck his hat. So far there was no dispute as to what had happened. One servant of the Barings gave evidence to the effect that he had saved his master's life by preventing Cook from striking again ; another afterwards put in a sworn deposition to the effect that Cook never attempted to strike a second blow. All witnesses agreed that Bingham Baring's hat had suffered severely : some of them said that he himself had been felled to the ground. Whatever his injuries may have been, he was seen out a few hours later, apparently in perfect health ; next day he was walking the streets of Winchester ; two days later he was presented at Court, and within a week he was strong enough to administer a sharp blow himself with his stick to a handcuffed and unconvicted prisoner, a display of zeal for which he had to pay £50. Cook did not put up any defence. He was sentenced to death.

Perhaps it was felt that this victim to justice was in some respects ill chosen, for reasons for severity were soon invented. He was a heavy, stolid, unattractive boy, and his appearance was taken to indicate a brutal and vicious disposition. Stories of his cruelties to animals were spread abroad. ' The fate of Henry Cook,' said the *Times* correspondent (3rd January 1831), ' excites no commiseration. From everything I have heard of him, justice has seldom met with a more appropriate sacrifice. He shed some tears shortly after hearing his doom, but has since relapsed into a brutal insensibility to his fate.' His age was raised to thirty, his wages to 30s. a week. Denman described him in the House of Commons, after his execution, as a carpenter earning 30s. a week, who had struck down one of the family of his benefactor, and had only been prevented from killing his victim by the interposition of a more faithful individual. This is the epitaph written on this obscure ploughboy of nineteen by the upper classes. His own fellows, who probably knew him at least as well as a Denman or a Baring, regarded his punishment as murder. Cobbett tells us that the labourers of Micheldever subscribed their pennies to get Denman's misstatements about Cook taken out of the newspapers. When his body was brought home after execution, the whole parish went out to meet it, and he was buried in Micheldever churchyard in solemn silence.[1]

Bingham Baring himself, as has been mentioned, happened to offend against the law by an act of violence at this time. He was not like Cook, a starving boy, but the son of a man who was reputed to have made seven millions of money, and was called by Erskine the first merchant in Europe. He did not strike his victim in a riot, but in cold blood. His victim could not defend himself, for he was handcuffed. The man struck was a Mr. Deacle, a small farmer who had had his own threshing machine broken, and was afterwards arrested with his wife, by Bingham Baring and a posse of magistrates, on suspicion of encouraging the rioters. Deacle's story was that Baring and the other magistrates concerned in the arrest treated his wife with great insolence in the cart in which they drove the Deacles to prison, and that Bingham Baring further struck him with a stick. For this Deacle got £50 damages in an action he brought against Baring. ' This verdict,' said the *Morning Herald*, ' seemed to excite the greatest astonishment ; for most of the Bar and almost every one in Court said, if on the jury, they would have given at least £5000 for so gross and wanton an insult and unfeeling conduct towards those who had not offered the least resistance ; the defendants not addressing the slightest evidence in palliation or attempting to justify it.' The judge, in summing up, ' could not help remarking that the handcuffing was, to say the least of it, a very harsh proceeding towards a lady and gentleman who had been perfectly civil and quiet.' Meanwhile the case of the magistrates against the Deacles had collapsed in the most inglorious manner. Though they had handcuffed these two

[1] It is said in Micheldever to-day that the snow never lies on his grave.

unresisting people, they had thought it wiser not to proceed against them. Deacle, however, insisted on being tried, and by threatening the magistrates with an action, he obliged them to prosecute. He was tried at the Assizes, and, as we have seen, the trial came to an abrupt conclusion under circumstances that threw the gravest suspicion on the methods of the authorities.[1] Meanwhile the treatment these two persons had received (and we can imagine from their story how innocent poor people, without friends or position, were handled) had excited great indignation, and the newspapers were full of it. There were petitions sent up to Parliament for a Committee of Inquiry. Now the class to which Cook was unlucky enough to belong had never sent a single member to Parliament, but the Baring family had five Members in the House of Commons at this very moment, one of whom had taken part with Bingham Baring in the violent arrest of the Deacles. The five, moreover, were very happily distributed, one of them being Junior Lord of the Treasury in Grey's Government and husband of Grey's niece, and another an important member of the Opposition and afterwards Chancellor of the Exchequer under Peel. The Barings therefore were in less danger of misrepresentation or misunderstanding ; the motion for a Committee was rejected by a great majority on the advice of Althorp and Peel ; the leader of the House of Commons came forward to testify that the Barings were friends of his, and the discussion ended in a chorus of praise for the family that had been judged so harshly outside the walls of Parliament.

When the Special Commission had finished its labours at Winchester, 101 prisoners had been capitally convicted ; of these 6 were left for execution. The remaining 95 were, with few exceptions, transported for life. Of the other prisoners tried, 36 were sentenced to transportation for various periods, 65 were imprisoned with hard labour, and 67 were acquitted. Not a single life had been taken by the rioters, not a single person wounded. Yet the riots in this county alone were punished by more than a hundred capital convictions, or almost double the number that followed the devilish doings of Lord George Gordon's mob. The spirit in which Denman regarded the proceedings is illustrated by his speech in the House of Commons on the amnesty debate : ' No fewer than a hundred persons were capitally convicted at Winchester, of offences for every one of which their lives might have been

[1] See p. 277.

justly taken, and ought to have been taken, if examples to such
an extent had been necessary.' [1]

These sentences came like a thunderclap on the people of
Winchester, and all classes, except the magistrates, joined in
petitions to the Government for mercy. The *Times* correspondent wrote as follows :—

'WINCHESTER, Friday Morning, 7*th Jan.*
'The scenes of distress in and about the jail are most terrible.
The number of men who are to be torn from their homes and
connexions is so great that there is scarcely a hamlet in the
county into which anguish and tribulation have not entered.
Wives, sisters, mothers, children, beset the gates daily, and the
governor of the jail informs me that the scenes he is obliged to
witness at the time of locking up the prison are truly heart-
breaking.

'You will have heard before this of the petitions which have
been presented to the Home Office from Gosport, Portsmouth,
Romsey, Whitchurch, and Basingstoke, praying for an extension
of mercy to all the men who now lie under sentence of death.
A similar petition has been got up in this city. It is signed by
the clergy of the Low Church, some of the bankers, and every
tradesman in the town without exception. Application was made
to the clergy of the Cathedral for their signatures, but they
refused to give them, except conditionally, upon reasons which
I cannot comprehend. They told the petitioners, as I am
informed, that they would not sign any such petition unless the
grand jury and the magistracy of the county previously affixed
their names to it. Now such an answer, as it appears to me, is an
admission on their part that no mischief would ensue from not
carrying into effect the dreadful sentence of the law ; for I cannot conceive that if they were of opinion that mischief would
ensue from it, they would sign the petition, even though it were
recommended by all the talent and respectability of the Court of
Quarter Sessions. I can understand the principles on which
that man acts, who asserts and laments the necessity of vindicat-
ing the majesty of the law by the sacrifice of human life ; but
I cannot understand the reasons of those who, admitting that
there is no necessity for the sword of justice to strike the
offender, decline to call upon the executive government to stay
its arm, and make their application for its mercy dependent on
the judgment, or it may be the caprice, of an influential aristocracy. Surely, of all classes of society, the clergy is that which
ought not to be backward in the remission of offences. They are
daily preaching mercy to their flocks, and it wears but an ill grace
when they are seen refusing their consent to a practical applica-

[1] February 8, 1831.

tion of their own doctrines. Whatever my own opinion may be, as a faithful recorder of the opinions of those around me, I am bound to inform you, that, except among the magistracy of the county, there is a general, I had almost said a universal, opinion among all ranks of society, that no good will be effected by sacrificing human life.' [1]

This outburst of public opinion saved the lives of four of the six men who had been left for execution. The two who were hung were Cooper and Cook. But the Government and the judges were determined that the lessons of civilisation should not be wanting in impressiveness or in dignity. They compelled all the prisoners who had been condemned by the Commission to witness the last agonies of the two men whom public opinion had been unable to rescue. The account given in the *Times* of 17th January shows that this piece of refined and spectacular discipline was not thrown away, and that the wretched comrades of the men who were hanged suffered as acutely as Denman or Alderson themselves could have desired. ' At this moment I cast my eyes down into the felons' yard, and saw many of the convicts weeping bitterly, some burying their faces in their smock frocks, others wringing their hands convulsively, and others leaning for support against the wall of the yard and unable to cast their eyes upwards.' This was the last vision of English justice that each labourer carried to his distant and dreaded servitude, a scene that would never fade from his mind. There was much that England had not taught him. She had not taught him that the rich owed a duty to the poor, that society owed any shelter to the freedom or the property of the weak, that the mere labourer had a share in the State, or a right to be considered in its laws, or that it mattered to his rulers in what wretchedness he lived or in what wretchedness he died. But one lesson she had taught him with such savage power that his simple memory would not forget it, and if ever in an exile's gilding dreams he thought with longing of his boyhood's famine-shadowed home, that inexorable dawn would break again before his shrinking eyes and he would thank God for the wide wastes of the illimitable sea.

The Special Commission for Wiltshire opened at Salisbury

[1] *Times*, January 8, 1831. The *Times* of the same day contains an interesting petition from the Birmingham Political Union on behalf of all the prisoners tried before the Special Commissions.

on 2nd January 1831. The judges were the same as those at Winchester; the other commissioners were Lord Radnor, the friend of Cobbett, and Mr. T. G. B. Estcourt. Lord Lansdowne, the Lord-Lieutenant, sat on the bench. The foreman of the Grand Jury was Mr. John Benett, who has already figured in these pages as the proprietor whose property was destroyed and the magistrate who committed the culprits. There were three hundred prisoners awaiting trial.

The method in which the prosecutions were conducted in Wiltshire, though it did not differ from the procedure followed in Hampshire and elsewhere, provoked some criticism from the lawyers. The prosecutions were all managed by the county authorities. The clerks of the committing magistrates in the different districts first took the depositions, and then got up all the prosecutions in their capacity of solicitors to the same magistrates prosecuting as county authorities, to the exclusion of the solicitors of the individual prosecutors. Further, all the prosecutions were managed for the county by a single barrister, who assisted the Attorney-General and left no opening for other members of the Bar. The counsel for one of the prisoners objected to this method, not only on the ground of its unfairness to the legal profession, but on the wider ground of the interests of justice. For it was inconsistent with the impartiality required from magistrates who committed prisoners, that they should go on to mix themselves up with the management of the prosecution; in many cases these magistrates served again as grand jurors in the proceedings against the prisoners. Such procedure, he argued ' was calculated to throw at least a strong suspicion on the fair administration of justice.' These protests, however, were silenced by the judges, and though the Attorney-General announced that he was willing that the counsel for the magistrates should retire, no change was made in the arrangements.

The Salisbury prisoners were under a further disadvantage peculiar, it is to be hoped, to that gaol. They were forbidden to see their attorney except in the presence of the gaoler or his servants. This rule seems to have been construed by the authorities in a manner that simplified considerably the task of the prosecution. The facts of the case of James Lush, condemned to death on two charges of extorting money in a mob, were made public by Hunt in a letter to the *Times*, 22nd January 1831. Lush was a very poor man, but when first committed he sent for an attorney and made a full confession. ' This confession, so confidentially made to his attorney (by an extraordinary rule of the gaol) the legal adviser was compelled to submit to the inspection of the gaoler, which paper he kept in his hands for several days and in all human probability, this document, or a copy of it, was either submitted to the inspection of the judge, or placed in the hands of the prosecutor, the Crown Solicitor, or the Attorney-General : when this man was called up for trial, such was his extreme poverty, that he could not raise a guinea to fee counsel, and he was left destitute, without legal advice or assistance.' The Attorney-General could only answer this charge in the House of Commons by declaring that he had no recollection of any such circumstance himself, and that no gentleman of the Bar would avail himself of information obtained in such a manner. Lush could not distinguish these niceties of honour, or understand why his confession should be examined and kept by the gaoler unless it was to be used against him, and it is not surprising that he thought himself betrayed. It is only fair to Lord Melbourne to add that when Hunt drew his attention to this iniquitous rule in Salisbury Gaol he had it abolished.

The cases tried were very similar to those at Winchester ; batch after batch of boys and men in the prime of life were brought up to the dock for a brief trial and sentence of exile. Such was the haste that in one case at least the prisoners appeared with the handcuffs still on their wrists, a circumstance which elicited a rebuke from the judge, and an excuse of overwork from the gaoler. Amongst the first cases eight prisoners, varying in age from seventeen to thirty, were sentenced to transportation for life for doing £500 worth of damage at Brasher's cloth mill at Wilton. Thirteen men were transported for seven years and one for fourteen years for breaking threshing machines on the day of the Pyt House affray. Mr. John Benett was satisfied with this tale of victims in addition to the man killed by the yeomanry, and refrained from prosecuting for the stones thrown at him. For this he took great credit in the House of Commons, and no doubt it was open to him to imitate Bingham Baring's friends, and to talk of that kind of outrage as ' murder.'

At Salisbury, as at Winchester, evidence about distress and wages was ruled out by the judges whenever possible ; thus when twelve men, nine of whom were afterwards transported for seven years, were being tried for breaking a threshing machine on the farm of a man named Ambrose Patience, the cross-examination of Patience, which aimed at eliciting facts about wages and distress, was stopped by the court on the ground that in a case of this sort such evidence was scarcely regular ; it was intimated, however, that the court would hear representations of this kind later. But some light was thrown incidentally in the course of the trials on the circumstances of the prisoners. Thus one of the Pyt House prisoners urged in his defence : ' My Lord, I found work very bad in my own parish for the last three years, and having a wife and three children to support I was glad to get work wherever I could get it. I had some work at a place four miles from my house.' He then described how on his way to work he was met by the mob and forced to join them. ' It is a hard case with me, my Lord ; I was glad to get work though I could earn only seven shillings per week, and it cost me a shilling a week for iron, so that I had only six shillings a week to support five persons.' Another prisoner, Mould of Hatch, was stated by Lord Arundel to be very poor : he had a wife and six children, of whom one or two had died of typhus since his committal. They had nothing to live on but what they got at Lord Arundel's house. The benevolent Lord Arundel, or the parish, must have supported the survivors indefinitely, for Mould was exiled for seven years. Barett again, another of these prisoners, was supporting himself, a wife, and a child on 5s. a week. The usual rate of wages in Wiltshire was 7s. a week.

Evidence about the instigation of the labourers by those in good circumstances was also ruled out, and much that would be interesting in the history of the riots has thus perished. When six men were being prosecuted for breaking a threshing machine on the farm of Mr. Judd at Newton Toney, counsel for the defence started a cross-examination of the prosecutor designed to show that certain landowners in the parish had instigated the labourers to the outrages, but he was stopped by Mr. Justice Alderson, who declared that such an inquiry was not material to the issue, which was the guilt or innocence of the prisoners. If the prisoners were found guilty these circumstances would be laid before the court in mitigation of punishment. However strong the mitigating circumstances in this case were, the punishment was certainly not mitigated, for all six men were sentenced to the maximum penalty of seven years' transportation. In a similar case in Whiteparish it came out in the evidence that Squire Bristowe had sent down buckets of strong beer, and that Squire Wynne, who was staying with Squire Bristowe, was present at the breaking of the machine. In the affair at Ambrose Patience's farm already mentioned, the defence of the prisoners was that Farmer Parham had offered them half a hogshead of cider if they would come and break his machine, whilst in another case three men were acquitted because one of the witnesses for the prosecution, a young brother of the farmer whose property had been destroyed, unexpectedly disclosed the fact that his brother had said to the mob : ' Act like men, go and break the machine, but don't go up to the house.'

The proportion of charges of extorting money was smaller at Salisbury than at Winchester : most of the indictments were for breaking machines only. In some instances the prosecution dropped the charge of robbery, thinking transportation for seven years a sufficient punishment for the offence. Three brothers were sentenced to death for taking half a crown : nobody received this sentence for a few coppers. In this case the three brothers, William, Thomas, and John Legg, aged twenty-eight, twenty-one, and eighteen, had gone at midnight to the kitchen door of the house of Mrs. Montgomery, wife of a J.P., and asked the manservant for money or beer. The man gave them half a crown, and they thanked him civilly and went away. A curious light is thrown on the relations between robbers and the robbed in the trial of six men for machine-breaking at West Grimstead : the mob of fifty persons asked the farmer for a sovereign, he promised to pay it next day, whereupon one of the mob, a man named Light who was his tenant, offered to pay the sovereign himself and to deduct it from the rent.

At Salisbury, as at Winchester, the fate of the victims depended largely on the character given to the prisoners by the local gentry. This was especially the case towards the end when justice began to tire, and a good many charges were dropped. Thus Charles Bourton was only imprisoned for three months for breaking a threshing machine, whilst John Perry was transported for seven years for the same offence. But then John Perry had been convicted seven or eight times for poaching.

In Wiltshire, as in Hampshire, the judges were particularly severe to those prisoners who were not agricultural labourers. A striking instance is worth quoting, not only as illustrating this special severity, but also because it shows that the judges when inflicting the maximum penalty of seven years' transportation for machine-breaking were well aware that it was tantamount to exile for life. Thomas Porter, aged eighteen, a shepherd, Henry Dicketts, aged nineteen, a bricklayer's labourer, Aaron Shepherd, aged forty (occupation not stated), James Stevens, aged twenty-five, an agricultural labourer, and George Burbage, aged twenty-four, also an agricultural labourer, were found guilty of machine-breaking at Mr. Blake's at Idmiston. Stevens and Burbage escaped with two years' and one year's imprisonment with hard labour, respectively, and the following homily from Mr. Justice Alderson to think over in prison: ' You are both thrashers and you might in the perversion of your understanding think that these machines are detrimental to you. Be assured that your labour cannot ultimately be hurt by the employment of these machines. If they are profitable to the farmer, they will also be profitable ultimately to the labourer, though they may for a time injure him. If they are not profitable to the farmer he will soon cease to employ them.' The shepherd boy of eighteen, the bricklayer's labourer of nineteen, and their companion of forty were reserved for a heavier penalty: ' As to you, Aaron Shepherd, I can give you no hope of remaining in this country. You Thomas Porter, are a shepherd, and you Henry Dicketts, are a bricklayer's labourer. You have nothing to do with threshing machines. They do not interfere with your labour, and you could not, even in the darkness of your ignorance, suppose that their destruction would do you any good. . . . I hope that your fate will be a warning to others. You will leave the country, all of you : you will see your friends and relations no more : for though you will be transported for seven years only, it is not likely that at the expiration of that term you will find yourselves in a situation to return. You will be in a distant land at the expiration of your sentence. The land which you have disgraced will see you no more : the friends with whom you are connected will be parted from you for ever in this world.'

Mr. Justice Alderson's methods received a good deal of attention in one of the Salisbury trials, known as the Looker case. Isaac Looker, a well-to-do farmer, was indicted for sending a threatening letter to John Rowland : ' Mr. Rowland, Haxford Farm, Hif you goes to sware against or a man in prisson, you have here farm burnt down to ground, and thy bluddy head chopt off.' Some evidence was produced to show that Isaac Looker had asserted in conversation that it was the magistrates and the soldiers, and not the mobs, who were the real breakers of the peace. But this did not amount to absolute proof that he had written the letter : to establish this conclusion the prosecution relied on the evidence of four witnesses ; the first had quarrelled with Looker, and had not seen his writing for four or five years ; the second denied that there had been any quarrel, but had not been in the habit of speaking to the prisoner for five or six years, or seen his writing during that time ; the third had not had ' much of a quarrel ' with him, but had not seen his writing since 1824 ; the fourth was the special constable who found in Looker's bureau, which was unlocked and stood in the kitchen where the family sat, a blank piece of paper that fitted on to the piece on which the letter was written. More witnesses were called for the defence than for the prosecution, and they included the vestry clerk of Wimborne, an ex-schoolmaster ; all of these witnesses had known Looker's writing recently, and all of them swore that the threatening letter was not in his writing. Mr. Justice Alderson summed up against the prisoner, the jury returned a verdict of guilty, and sentence of transportation for life was passed upon Looker in spite of his vehement protestations of innocence. ' I cannot attend to these asseverations,' said Mr. Justice Alderson, ' for we all know that a man who can be guilty of such an offence as that of which you have been convicted, will not hesitate to deny it as you now do. I would rather trust to such evidence as has been given in your case, than to the most solemn declarations even on the scaffold.'

The learned judge and the jury then retired for refreshment, when a curious development took place. Edward, son of Isaac Looker, aged eighteen years, came forward and declared that he had written the letter in question and other letters as well. He wrote a copy from memory, and the handwriting was precisely similar. He explained that he had written the letters without his father's knowledge and without a thought of the consequences, in order to help two cousins who were in gaol for machine-breaking. He had heard people say that ' it would get my cousins off if threatening letters were written.' He had let his father know in prison that he had written the letters, and had also told his father's solicitor. Edward Looker was subsequently tried and sentenced to seven years' transportation : Isaac's case was submitted to the Home Secretary for pardon.

Although, as we have said, the Government, or its representatives, grew rather more lenient towards the end of the
proceedings at Salisbury, it was evidently thought essential to produce some crime deserving actual death.   The
culprit in this case was Peter Withers, a young man of twenty-
three, married and with five children.   His character till the
time of the riots was exemplary.   He was committed on a
charge of riot, and briefed a lawyer to defend him for this
misdemeanour.   Just before the trial came on the charge
was changed, apparently by the Attorney-General, to the
capital charge of assaulting Oliver Calley Codrington with a
hammer.   His counsel was of course unprepared to defend
him on this charge, and, as he explained afterwards, ' it was
only by the humane kindness of the Attorney-General who
allowed him to look at his brief that he was aware of all the
facts to be alleged against his client.'   Withers himself seemed
equally unprepared ; when asked for his defence he said that
he would leave it to his counsel, as of course he had arranged
to do when the charge was one of misdemeanour only.

The incident occurred in an affray at Rockley near
Marlborough. Mr. Baskerville, J.P., rode up with some
special constables to a mob of forty or fifty men, Withers
amongst them, and bade them go home. They refused,
declaring that they did not care a damn for the magistrates.
Mr. Baskerville ordered Mr. Codrington, who was a special
constable, to arrest Withers. A general mêlée ensued, blows
were given and received, and Codrington was hit by a hammer
thrown by Withers. Withers' own version of the affair was
that Codrington attacked him without provocation in a
ferocious manner with a hunting whip, loaded with iron at
the end. Baskerville also struck him. He aimed his hammer
at Codrington and it missed. Codrington's horse then crushed
him against the wall, and he threw his hammer a second time
with better aim. There was nothing in the evidence of the
prosecution to discredit this version, and both Baskerville and
Codrington admitted that they might have struck him. Codrington's injuries were apparently more serious than Bingham
Baring's ; it was stated that he had been confined to bed for
two or three days, and to the house from Tuesday to Saturday,
and that he had a scar of one and a half inches on the right
side of his nose. No surgeon, however, appeared as a witness,
and the hammer was not produced in court. Withers was
found guilty and reserved, together with Lush, for execution.

The special correspondent of the *Times* who had been present at Winchester made an interesting comparison between the Hampshire and the Wiltshire labourers on trial (8th January 1831). The Wiltshire labourers he described as more athletic in appearance and more hardy in manner. ' The prisoners here turn to the witnesses against them with a bold and confident air: cross-examine them, and contradict their answers, with a confidence and a want of common courtesy, in terms of which comparatively few instances occurred in the neighbouring county.' In this behaviour the correspondent detected the signs of a very low state of moral intelligence.

When the time came for the last scene in court there was no trace of the bold demeanour which had impressed the *Times* correspondent during the conduct of the trials. For the people of Wiltshire, like the people of Hampshire, were stunned by the crash and ruin of this catastrophic vengeance. The two men sentenced to death were reprieved, but one hundred and fifty-four men and boys were sentenced to transportation, thirty-three of them for life, the rest for seven or fourteen years, with no prospect of ever returning to their homes. And Alderson and his brother judges in so punishing this wild fling of folly, or hope, or despair, were not passing sentence only on the men and boys before them : they were pronouncing a doom not less terrible on wives and mothers and children and babes in arms in every village on the Wiltshire Downs. One man begged to be allowed to take his child, eight months old, into exile, for its mother had died in childbirth, and it would be left without kith or kin. He was told by the judge that he should have remembered this earlier. The sentence of final separation on all these families and homes was received with a frenzy of consternation and grief, and the judges themselves were affected by the spectacle of these broken creatures in the dock and round the court, abandoned to the unchecked paroxysms of despair.[1] ' Such a total prostration of the mental faculties by fear,' wrote the *Times* correspondent, ' and such a terrible exhibition of anguish and despair, I never before witnessed in a Court of Justice.' ' Immediately on the conclusion of this sentence a number of women, who were seated in court behind the prisoners, set up a dreadful shriek of lamentation. Some of them rushed forward to shake hands with the prisoners,

---

[1] The scene is still vividly remembered by an old woman over ninety years of age with whom Mr. Hudson spoke.

and more than one voice was heard to exclaim, "Farewell, I shall never see you more." '

' The whole proceedings of this day in court were of the most afflicting and distressing nature. But the laceration of the feelings did not end with the proceedings in court. The car for the removal of the prisoners was at the back entrance to the court-house and was surrounded by a crowd of mothers, wives, sisters and children, anxiously waiting for a glance of their condemned relatives. The weeping and wailing of the different parties, as they pressed the hands of the convicts as they stepped into the car, was truly heartrending. We never saw so distressing a spectacle before, and trust that the restored tranquillity of the country will prevent us from ever seeing anything like it again.'

The historian may regret that these men do not pass out before him in a cold and splendid defiance. Their blind blow had been struck and it had been answered ; they had dreamt that their lot might be made less intolerable, and the governing class had crushed that daring fancy for ever with banishment and the breaking of their homes ; it only remained for them to accept their fate with a look of stone upon their faces and a curse of fire in their hearts. So had Muir and Palmer and many a political prisoner, victims of the tyrannies of Pitt and Dundas, of Castlereagh and Sidmouth, gone to their barbarous doom. So had the Lantenacs and the Gauvains alike gone to the guillotine. History likes to match such calm and unshaken bearing against the distempered justice of power. Here she is cheated of her spectacle. Outwardly it might seem a worse fate for men of education to be flung to the hulks with the coarsest of felons : for men whose lives had been comfortable to be thrust into the dirt and disorder of prisons. But political prisoners are martyrs, and martyrs are not the stuff for pity. However bitter their sufferings, they do not suffer alone : they are sustained by a Herculean comradeship of hopes and of ideas. The darkest cage is lighted by a ray from Paradise to men or women who believe that the night of their sufferings will bring a dawn less cold and sombre to mankind than the cold and sombre dawn of yesterday. But what ideas befriended the ploughboy or the shepherd torn from his rude home ? What vision had he of a nobler future for humanity ? To what dawn did he leave his wife or his mother, his child, his home, his friends, or his trampled race ? What robe of dream and hope and fancy was thrown over his exile or their hunger, his poignant hour of separation, or their ceaseless ache of poverty and cold

> 'to comfort the human want
> From the bosom of magical skies'?

The three judges who had restored respect for law and order in Wiltshire and Hampshire next proceeded to Dorchester, where a Special Commission to try the Dorsetshire rioters was opened on 11th January. The rising had been less serious in Dorset than in the two other counties, and there were only some fifty prisoners awaiting trial on charges of machine-breaking, extorting money and riot. The Government took no part in the prosecutions; for, as it was explained in a letter to Denman, 'the state of things is quite altered; great effect has been produced: the law has been clearly explained, and prosecutions go on without the least difficulty.'[1] Baron Vaughan and Mr. Justice Parke had given the charges at Winchester and Salisbury: it was now the turn of Mr. Justice Alderson, and in his opening survey of the social conditions of the time he covered a wide field. To the usual dissertation on the economics of machinery he added a special homily on the duties incumbent on the gentry, who were bidden to discourage and discountenance, and if necessary to prosecute, the dangerous publications that were doing such harm in rural districts. But their duties did not end here, and they were urged to go home and to educate their poorer neighbours and to improve their conditions. The improvement to be aimed at, however, was not material but moral. 'Poverty,' said Mr. Justice Alderson, 'is indeed, I fear, inseparable from the state of the human race, but poverty itself and the misery attendant on it, would no doubt be greatly mitigated if a spirit of prudence were more generally diffused among the people, and if they understood more fully and practised better their civil, moral and religious duties.'

The Dorsetshire labourers had unfortunately arrived at the precipitate conclusion that a spirit of prudence would not transform 7s. a week into a reasonable livelihood. They used no violence beyond breaking up the threshing machines. 'We don't intend to hurt the farmer,' they told the owner of one machine, 'but we are determined that the land shall come down, and the tithes, and we will have more wages.' When

[1] H. O. Papers, Disturbance Entry-Book, Letter of January 3, 1831.

money was taken it seems to have been demanded and received in an amicable spirit. The sums asked for were often very small. Sentence of death was pronounced on two men, Joseph Sheppard and George Legg, for taking 2s. from Farmer Christopher Morey at Buckland Newton. The mob asked for money, and the farmer offered them 1s. : they replied that they wanted 1s. 6d., and the farmer gave them 2s. Sheppard's character was very good, and it came out that he and the prosecutor had had a dispute about money some years before. He was transported, but not for life. Legg was declared by the prosecutor to have been 'saucy and impudent,' and to have 'talked rough and bobbish.' His character, however, was stated by many witnesses, including the clergyman, to be exemplary. He had five children whom he supported without parish help on 7s. a week : a cottage was given him but no fuel. Baron Vaughan was so much impressed by this evidence that he declared that he had never heard better testimony to character, and that he would recommend a less severe penalty than transportation. But Legg showed a lamentable want of discretion, for he interrupted the judge with these words : 'I would rather that your Lordship would put twenty-one years' transportation upon me than be placed in the condition of the prosecutor. I never said a word to him, that I declare.' Baron Vaughan sardonically remarked that he had not benefited himself by this observation.

The tendency to give less severe punishment, noticed in the closing trials at Salisbury, was more marked at Dorchester. Nine men were let off on recognisances and ten were not proceeded against : in the case of six of these ten the prosecutor, one Robert Bullen, who had been robbed of 4s. and 2s. 6d., refused to come forward. But enough sharp sentences were given to keep the labourers in submission for the future. One man was transported for life and eleven for seven years : fifteen were sentenced to various terms of imprisonment ; seven were acquitted. It was not surprising that the special correspondent of the *Times* complained that such meagre results scarcely justified the pomp and expense of a Special Commission. In the neighbouring county of Gloucester, where the country gentlemen carried out the work of retribution without help from headquarters, seven men were transported for fourteen years, twenty for seven years, and twenty-five were sentenced to terms of imprisonment ranging from six months to three years. All of these sentences were for breaking threshing machines.

The disturbances in Berks and Bucks had been considered serious enough to demand a Special Commission, and Sir James Alan Park, Sir William Bolland and Sir John Patteson were the judges appointed.   The first of the two Berkshire Commissions opened at Reading on 27th December.   The Earl of Abingdon, Lord-Lieutenant of the County, and Mr. Charles Dundas were the two local commissioners.   Mr. Dundas has figured already in these pages as chairman of the meeting at Speenhamland. One hundred and thirty-eight prisoners were awaiting trial at Reading : they were most of them young, only eighteen being forty or over.   The rest, with few exceptions, varied from seventeen to thirty-five in age, and must have lived all their lives under the Speenhamland system.

It is impossible to compare the accounts of the Special Commissions in Berks and Bucks with those in Hampshire and Wiltshire without noticing a difference in the treatment of the rioters.   The risings had been almost simultaneous, the offences were of the same character, and the Commissions sat at the same time.   The difference was apparent from the first, and on 1st January the *Times* published a leading article pleading for uniformity, and pointing out that the Berkshire Commission was ' a merciful contrast ' to that at Winchester. The cause is probably to be found in the dispositions and characters of the authorities responsible in the two cases.   The country gentlemen of Berkshire, represented by a man like Mr. Dundas, were more humane than the country gentlemen of Hampshire, represented by men like the Duke of Wellington and the Barings ; Mr. Gurney, the public prosecutor at Reading, was more lenient than Sir Thomas Denman, and the Reading judges were more kindly and considerate than the judges at Winchester.   Further, there had been in Berkshire little of the wild panic that swept over the country houses in Hampshire and Wiltshire.   The judges at Reading occasionally interjected questions on the prisoners' behalf, and in many cases they did not conceal their satisfaction at an acquittal. Further, they had a more delicate sense for the proprieties. Contrary to custom, they asked neither the Grand Jury nor the magistrates to dinner on the first day, being anxious, we are told, to free the administration of justice ' from the slightest appearance of partiality in the eyes of the lower classes.'   The Lord Chancellor and Lord Melbourne had been consulted and had approved.

It must not be supposed that Mr. Justice Park's theories of

life and social relationships differed from those of his brothers
at Winchester.   In his address to the Grand Jury he repudiated
with indignation the 'impudent and base slander . . . that
the upper ranks of society care little for the wants and
privations of the poor.   I deny this positively, upon a very
extensive means of knowledge upon subjects of this nature.
But every man can deny it who looks about him and sees the
vast institutions in every part of the kingdom for the relief
of the young and the old, the deaf and the lame, the blind,
the widow, the orphan——and every child of wretchedness
and woe.   There is not a calamity or distress incident to
humanity, either of body or of mind, that is not humbly
endeavoured to be mitigated or relieved, by the powerful and
the affluent, either of high or middling rank, in this our happy
land, which for its benevolence, charity, and boundless
humanity, has been the admiration of the world.'   The theory
that the rich kept the poor in a state of starvation and that
this was the cause of the disturbances, he declared later to
be entirely disproved by the conduct of one of the mobs in
destroying a threshing machine belonging to William Mount,
Esq., at Wasing, 'Mr. Mount having given away £100 no
longer ago than last winter to assist the lower orders during
that inclement season.'

A feature of the Reading Commission was the difficulty of
finding jurymen.   All farmers were challenged on behalf of
the prisoners, and matters were at a deadlock until the judges
ordered the bystanders to be impannelled.

The earlier cases were connected with the riots in Hungerford.   Property in an iron foundry had been destroyed, and
fifteen men were found guilty on this capital charge.   One
of the fifteen was William Oakley, who now paid the penalty
for his £5 and strong language.   But when the first cases were
over, Mr. Gurney began to drop the capital charge, and to
content himself, as a rule, with convictions for breaking
threshing machines.   One case revealed serious perjury on
one side or the other.   Thomas Goodfellow and Cornelius
Bennett were charged with breaking a threshing machine at
Matthew Batten's farm.   The prisoners produced four
witnesses, two labourers, a woman whose husband was in
prison for the riots, and John Gaiter, who described himself
as 'not quite a master bricklayer,' to prove that Matthew
Batten had encouraged the riots.   The first three witnesses
declared that Batten had asked the rioters to come and break

his machine in order to serve out his landlord and Mr. Ward, and had promised them victuals and £1. Batten and his son, on the other hand, swore that these statements were false. The prisoners were found guilty, with a recommendation to mercy which was disregarded. Goodfellow, who was found guilty of breaking other machines as well, was sentenced to fourteen, and Cornelius Bennett to seven years' transportation, The judge spoke of their scandalous attempt to blacken the character of a respectable farmer : ' it pleased God however that the atrocious attempt had failed.' It would be interesting to know what were the relations between Matthew Batten and his landlord.

On the last day of the trials Mr. Gurney announced that there would be no more prosecutions for felony, as enough had been done in the way of making examples. Some interesting cases of riot were tried. The most important riot had taken place as early as 19th November, and the hero of the proceedings was the Rev. Edward Cove, the venerable Vicar of Brimpton, one of the many parson magistrates. A mob had assembled in order to demand an increase of wages, and it was met by Mr. Cove and his posse of special constables. On occasions like this, Mr. Gurney remarked, we become sensible of the great advantages of our social order. Mr. Cove without more ado read the Riot Act ; the mob refused to disperse ; his special constables thereupon attacked them, and a general mêlée followed in which hard blows were given and taken. No one attempted to strike Mr. Cove himself, but one of his companions received from a rioter, whom he identified, a blow rivalling that given to Mr. Bingham Baring, which beat the crown of his hat in and drove the rim over his eyes : it was followed by other and more serious blows on his head and body. The counsel for the defence tried to show that it was distress that had caused the rioters to assemble, and he quoted a remark of the Chairman of Quarter Sessions that the poor were starved almost into insurrection ; but all evidence about wages was ruled out. The court were deeply impressed by this riot, and Mr. Justice Park announced that it had alarmed him and his fellow judges more ' than anything that had hitherto transpired in these proceedings.' ' Had one life been lost,' he continued, ' the lives of every individual of the mob would have been forfeited, and the law must have been carried into effect against those convicted.' As it was, nobody was condemned to death for his share in the affray, though the more violent, such as George Williams, alias 'Staffordshire Jack,' a 'desperate character,' received heavier penalties for machine-breaking in consequence.

Three men were reserved for execution : William Oakley, who was told that as a carpenter he had no business to mix himself up in these transactions ; Alfred Darling, a blacksmith by trade, who had been found guilty on several charges of demanding money ; and Winterbourne, who had taken part in the Hungerford affair in the magistrates' room, and had also acted as leader in some cases when a mob asked for money. In one instance the mob had been content with £1 instead of the £2 for which it had asked for breaking a threshing machine, Winterbourne remarking, ' we will take half price because he has stood like a man.'

Public opinion in Berkshire was horrified at the prospect of taking life. Petitions for mercy poured in from Reading, including one from ladies to the queen, from Newbury, from Hungerford, from Henley, and from other places. Two country gentlemen, Mr. J. B. Monck and Mr. Wheble, made every exertion to save the condemned men. They waited with petitions on Lord Melbourne, who heard them patiently for an hour. They obtained a reprieve for Oakley and for Darling, who were transported for life ; Winterbourne they could not save : he was hung on 11th January, praying to the last that his wife, who was dangerously ill of typhus, might die before she knew of his fate.

Fifty-six men were sentenced to transportation from Reading —twenty-three for life, sixteen for fourteen years, seventeen for seven years : thirty-six were sent to prison for various terms.

The same commissioners went on to Abingdon where proceedings opened on 6th January. Here there were only forty-seven prisoners, all but two of whom were agricultural labourers, most of them very young. The cases resembled those tried at Reading, but it is clear that the evidence of Mrs. Charlotte Slade, whose conduct we have already described, and her method of dealing with the rioters, made a great impression on Mr. Justice Park and his colleagues, and opened their eyes to the true perspective of the rhetorical language that had assumed such terrifying importance to other judges. One young labourer, Richard Kempster by name, who was found guilty of breaking a threshing machine, had carried a black-and-red flag in the mob, and when arrested had exclaimed. ' be damned if I don't wish it was a revolution, and that all was a fire together ' : it is easy to imagine the grave homily on the necessity of cutting such a man off for ever from his kind that these words would have provoked from the judges at Winchester.   Mr. Justice Park and his colleagues sentenced Kempster to twelve months' imprisonment.   At Abingdon only one man was sentenced to be transported ; Thomas Mackrell, an agricultural labourer of forty-three. Another, Henry Woolridge, had sentence of death commuted to eighteen months' imprisonment.   Thirty-five others were sent to prison for various terms.

The same three judges proceeded to Aylesbury to try the Buckinghamshire rioters.   The chief event in this county had been the destruction of paper-making machinery at Wycombe.   The Commission opened on 11th January : the Duke of Buckingham and Mr. Maurice Swabey were the local commissioners.   There were one hundred and thirty-six prisoners to be tried, almost all young and illiterate : only eighteen were forty years of age or over.   Forty-four men and boys were found guilty of the capital charge of destroying paper machinery.   Most of the other prisoners who were charged with breaking threshing machines were allowed to plead guilty and let off on their own recognisances, or else the charge was not pressed.   An exception was made in a case in which some members of a mob had been armed with guns. Three men who had carried guns were sent to transportation for seven years, and thirteen others involved were sent to prison for two years or eighteen months.   Several men were tried for rioting, and those who had combined a demand for increased wages with a request for the restoration of parish buns were sent to prison for six weeks.[1]   One more trial is worth notice, because it suggests that even in Buckinghamshire, where the general temper was more lenient, individuals who had made themselves obnoxious were singled out for special treatment. John Crook, a miller, was indicted with four others for riotously assembling and breaking a winnowing machine at Mr. Fryer's at Long Crendon.   As Crook was charged with a misdemeanour his counsel could address the jury, and we learn from his speech that Crook had been kept in prison since 2nd December, though £2000 had been offered in bail and many other prisoners had been allowed out.   The explanation, it was argued, was to be found in the fact that Crook had come into some property which qualified him to hold a gun licence and to kill game,

[1] See p. 268.

He was sentenced to three months' imprisonment without hard labour, and to pay a fine of £10.

Thirty-two men in all were sent to prison for the agricultural disturbances in addition to the three sentenced to transportation. Forty-two of those concerned in the breaking of paper-making machinery received sentence of death, but their punishment was commuted to life transportation for one, seven years' transportation for twenty-two, and imprisonment for various terms for the rest. Two men were reserved for execution. One, Thomas Blizzard, was thirty years old, with a wife and three children. His character was excellent. At the time of the riots he was a roundsman, receiving 1s. a day from the overseer's and 1s. 6d. a week from a farmer. He told his employer at Little Marlow that he would take a holiday to go machine-breaking, for he would endure imprisonment, or even transportation, rather than see his wife and children cry for bread. John Sarney, the other, was fifty-six years old and had a wife and six children : he kept a small beer-shop and his character was irreproachable. Petitions on behalf of the two men were signed extensively, and the sentence was commuted to transportation for life. The Aylesbury sentences seem lenient in comparison with those given at Salisbury and Winchester, but they did not seem lenient to the people in the district. ' Pen cannot describe,' wrote a *Times* correspondent, 'the heart-rending scene of despair, misery and want, prevailing at Flackwell-Heath, the residence of the families of the major part of the misguided men now incarcerated at Aylesbury.' The same correspondent tells of a benevolent Quaker, who had become rich as a maker of paper, helping these families by stealth.

The work of the Special Commissions was now over. Melbourne had explained in Parliament that they had been set up ' to expound the law ' and to bring home to the ignorant the gravity of their crimes against social order. In spite of the daily imposition of ferocious punishments on poachers and thieves, the poor apparently did not know in what letters of blood the code against rioting and discontent was composed. These three weeks had brought a lurid enlightenment into their dark homes. In the riots, as we have seen, the only man who had been killed was a rioter, killed according to the reports of the time by a yeomanry soldier, according to local tradition by a farmer, and for that offence he had been refused Christian burial.   On the other side, not a single person had been killed or seriously wounded.   For these riots, apart from the cases of arson, for which six men or boys were hung, aristocratic justice exacted three lives, and the transportation of four hundred and fifty-seven men and boys,[1] in addition to the imprisonment of about four hundred at home.   The shadow of this vengeance still darkens the minds of old men and women in the villages of Wiltshire, and eighty years have been too short a time to blot out its train of desolating memories.[2]   Nobody who does not realise what Mr. Hudson has described with his intimate touch, the effect on the imagination and the character of 'a life of simple unchanging action and of habits that are like instincts, of hard labour in sun and rain and wind from day to day,' can ever understand what the breaking of all the ties of life and home and memory meant to the exiles and to those from whose companionship they were then torn for ever.

We have said that one feature of the rising was the firing of stacks and ricks and barns.   This practice was widespread, and fires broke out even in counties where the organised rising made little progress.   Associations for the detection of incendiaries were formed at an early stage, and immense rewards were offered.   Yet not a single case of arson was tried before the Special Commissions, and the labourers kept

---

[1] Three boats carried the convicts, the *Eliza* and the *Proteus* to Van Diemen's Land, the *Eleanor* to New South Wales.   The list of the prisoners on board shows that they came from the following counties :—

Berks,	. 44	Hampshire,	100	Suffolk,	. 7
Bucks,	. 29	Hunts,	. 5	Sussex,	. 17
Dorset,	. 13	Kent, .	. 22	Wilts, .	. 151
Essex,	. 23	Norfolk,	. 11		
Gloucester, .	24	Oxford,	. 11	TOTAL, .	. 457

If this represents the total, some sentences of transportation must have been commuted for imprisonment ; possibly some rioters were sent later, for Mr. Potter MacQueen, in giving evidence before the Committee on Secondary Punishments, spoke of the six hundred able-bodied men who had been transported in conse-quence of being concerned in the Swing offences.—Report of Committee, p. 95. Four years later Lord John Russell, as Home Secretary, pardoned 264 of the convicts, in 1836 he pardoned 86 more, and in 1837 the survivors, mostly men sentenced for life or for fourteen years, were given pardons conditional on their 'continuing to reside in Australia for the remainder of their sentences.' No free passages back were granted, and Mr. Hudson states that very few, not more than one in five or six, ever returned.—*A Shepherd's Life*, p. 247.

[2] See Hudson, *Ibid.*

their secret well. Many of the governing class in the early days persuaded themselves that the labourers had no secret to keep, and that the fires were due to any one except the labourers, and to any cause except distress. Perhaps the wish was father to the thought, for as the *Times* observed, persons responsible for grinding the faces of their labourers preferred to think the outrages the work of strangers. Sometimes it was smugglers, suffering from the depression in their trade : sometimes it was foreigners : sometimes it was mysterious gentlemen in gigs, driving furiously about the country, led by Captain Swing, scattering fireballs and devastation. These were the fashionable theories in the House of Lords, although Richmond reminded his brother peers that there had been a flood of petitions representing the sufferings of the labourers from the very beginning of the year, and that the House of Lords had not thought it necessary to give them the slightest attention. Lord Camden ascribed the outrages to the French spirit, and argued that the country was enjoying ' what was undeniably a genial autumn.' The Duke of Wellington took the same view, denying that the troubles were due to distress : the most influential cause of disturbances was the example, ' and I will unhesitatingly say the bad and the mischievous example, afforded by the neighbouring States.' Eldon remarked that many of the prisoners taken in the riots were foreigners, a point on which Melbourne undeceived him. The speakers who regarded the disturbances in the south of England as the overflow of the Paris Revolution had no positive evidence to produce, but they had a piece of negative evidence which they thought conclusive. For if the labourers knew who were the incendiaries, they would surely have given information. In some cases a reward of £1000 with a free pardon for all except the actual author was waiting to be claimed, ' and yet not one of the miserable beings have availed themselves of the prospect of becoming rich.'

Some eleven cases of arson were tried at the Assizes in Essex, Kent, Sussex, and Surrey : all the prisoners were agricultural labourers and most of them were boys. Eight were convicted, often on very defective evidence, and six were executed. One of the eight, Thomas Goodman, a boy of eighteen, saved his life by declaring in prison that the idea had been put into his head by a lecture of Cobbett's. Two brothers of the name of Pakeman, nineteen and twenty years old, were convicted on the evidence of Bishop, another lad of eighteen, who had prompted them to set fire to a barn, and later turned king's evidence 'after a gentleman in the gaol had told him of the big reward.' This fire seems to have been a piece of bravado, as no doubt many others were, for Bishop remarked, as the three were sitting under a hedge after lighting the barn, 'who says we can't have a fire too, as well as them at Blean?' The two boys, who had never been taught to read or write, scandalised the public by displaying a painful indifference to the ministrations of the chaplain, and dying without receiving the sacrament.[1] A half-witted boy of fourteen, Richard Pennells, was tried at Lewes for setting fire to his master's haystack for a promise of sixpence from a man who was not discovered. His master, who prosecuted, remarked that he was 'dull of apprehension, but not so much as not to know right from wrong.' The boy, who had no counsel, offered no defence, and stood sobbing in the dock. The jury found him guilty, with a recommendation to mercy on account of his youth and imperfect understanding. Sentence of death was recorded, but he was told that his life would be spared.

These same Lewes Assizes, conducted by Mr. Justice Taunton, afforded a striking example of the comparative treatment of different crimes. Thomas Brown, a lad of seventeen, was charged with writing the following letter to Lord Sheffield, 'Please, my Lord, I dont wise to hurt you. This is the case al the world over. If you dont get rid of your foreign steward and farmer and bailiff in a few days time—less than a month— we will burn him up, and you along with him. My writing is bad, but my firing is good my Lord.' Lord Sheffield gave evidence as to the receipt of the letter : the prisoner, who had no counsel, was asked by the judge if he would like to put any questions, and he only replied that he hoped that his lordship would forgive him. The judge answered that his lordship had not the power, and sentenced Brown to transportation for life.[2] Later on in the same Assizes, Captain Winter, a man of sixty, captain of a coasting vessel, was tried for the murder of his wife, who had been killed in a most brutal manner. He had been hacking and wounding her for four hours at night, and she was last seen alive at half past two in the morning, naked and begging for mercy. Her

---

[1] See *Annual Register* and local papers.

[2] He was sent to Van Diemen's Land. It is only fair to Lord Sheffield to say that he applied in vain to Lord Melbourne for a mitigation of the life sentence. See Criminal Entry-Book, H. O. Papers.

body was covered with wounds. The man's defence was that he came home drunk, that he found his wife drunk, and that he had no knowledge of what followed. To the general surprise Captain Winter escaped with a verdict of manslaughter. 'The prisoner,' wrote the *Times* correspondent, 'is indebted for his life to the very merciful way in which Mr. Justice Taunton appeared to view the case, and the hint which he threw out to the jury, that the parties might have had a quarrel, in which case her death by the prisoner would amount to manslaughter only.'

When the disturbances began, the Duke of Wellington was Prime Minister, and Sir Robert Peel Home Secretary. But in November 1830 Wellington, who had made a last effort to rally the old Tories, sulking over his surrender on Catholic Emancipation, by some sudden thunder against Reform, had been beaten on the Civil List and resigned. Reform was inevitable, and with Reform the Whigs. Thus, towards the close of the year of the Revolution that drove Charles x. from France, Lord Grey became Prime Minister, to carry the measure which as Charles Grey, lieutenant of Charles Fox, he had proposed in the House of Commons in 1793, a few months after Louis xvi. had lost his head in the Revolution which had maddened and terrified the English aristocracy. Fortune had been sparing in her favours to this cold, proud, honourable and courageous man. She had shut him out from power for twenty-three years, waiting to make him Prime Minister until he was verging on seventy, and all the dash and ardour of youth had been chilled by disappointment and delay. But she had reserved her extreme of malice to the end, for it was her chief unkindness that having waited so long she did not wait a little longer. Grey, who had been forty-four years in public life, and forty-three in opposition, took office at the moment that the rising passed into Hampshire and Wiltshire, and thus his first act as Prime Minister was to summon his colleagues to a Cabinet meeting to discuss, not their plans for Parliamentary Reform, but the measures to be taken in this alarming emergency. After a lifetime of noble protest against war, intolerance, and repression, he found himself in the toils and snares of the consequences of a policy in which war, intolerance, and repression had been constant and conspicuous features. And those consequences were especially to be dreaded by such a man at such a time.

Grey became Prime Minister to carry Reform, and Reform was still enveloped to many minds in the wild fancies and terrors of a Jacobin past. To those who knew, conscious as they were of their own modest purposes and limited aim, that their accession to power boded to many violence, confusion, and the breaking up of the old ways and life of the State, it was maddening that these undiscerning peasants should choose this moment of all others for noise and riot. The struggle for Reform was certain to lead to strife, and it was hard that before they entered upon it England should already be in tumult from other causes. Moreover, Grey had to reckon with William IV. So long as he could remember, the Court had been the refuge of all that was base in English politics, and it was a question whether Liberal ideas had suffered more from the narrow and darkened mind of George III. or the mean and incorrigible perfidy of George IV. In comparison with his father, the new king had the wisdom of a Bentham or an Adam Smith ; in comparison with his brother, he had the generous and loyal heart of a Philip Sidney or a Falkland. But seen in any less flattering mirror, he was a very ordinary mortal, and Grey had known this jolly, drinking, sailor prince too long and too well to trust either his intellect or his character, under too fierce or too continuous a strain. These riots tried him severely. No sooner was William on his throne than the labourers came out of their dens, looking like those sansculottes whose shadows were never far from the imagination of the English upper classes. The king's support of Reform was no violent enthusiasm, and the slightest threat of disorder might disturb the uneasy equilibrium of his likes and fears. In the long run it depended on the will of this genial mediocrity—so strangely had Providence mixed caprice and design in this world of politics—whether or not Reform should be carried, and carried without bloodshed. Throughout these months then, the king, always at Melbourne's elbow, trying to tempt and push the Government into more drastic measures, was a very formidable enemy to the cause of moderation and of justice.

These influences were strong, and there was little to counteract them. For there was nobody in the world which Grey and Melbourne alike inhabited who could enter into the minds of the labourers. This is readily seen, if we glance at two men who were regarded as extreme Radicals in the House of Commons, Hobhouse and Burdett. Each of these men had served the cause of Reform in prison as well as in Parliament, and each with rather ridiculous associations; Hobhouse's imprisonment being connected with the ballad inspired by the malicious and disloyal wit of his friend and hero, Byron, and Burdett's with the ludicrous scene of his arrest, with his boy spelling out Magna Charta on his knee. It is difficult for those who have read Hobhouse's *Diaries* to divine what play of reason and feeling ever made him a Radical, but a Radical he was, an indefatigable critic of the old régime, and in particular of such abuses as flogging in the army. Burdett was a leader in the same causes. To these men, if to any, the conduct of the labourers might have seemed to call for sympathy rather than for violence. But if we turn to Hobhouse's *Diary* we see that he was never betrayed into a solitary expression of pity or concern for the scenes we have described, and as for Burdett, he was all for dragooning the discontented counties and placing them under martial law. And even Radnor, who as a friend of Cobbett was much less academic in his Radicalism, sat on the Wiltshire Commission without making any protest that has reached posterity.

All the circumstances then made it easy for Grey and his colleagues to slip into a policy of violence and repression. They breathed an atmosphere of panic, and they dreaded the recoil of that panic on their own schemes. Yet when all allowance is made for this insidious climate, when we remember that no man is so dangerous as the kind man haunted by the fear of seeming weak, at a moment when he thinks his power of doing good depends on his character for strength; when we remember, too, the tone of Society caught between scare and excitement, the bad inspiration of the Court, the malevolent influence of an alarmed Opposition, the absorbing interest of making a ministry, the game apart from the business of politics, it is still difficult to understand how men like Grey and Holland and Durham could ever have lent themselves to the cruelties of this savage retribution. When first there were rumours of the intention of the Government to put down the riots with severe measures, Cobbett wrote a passage in which he reviewed the characters of the chief ministers, Grey with his ' humane disposition,' Holland ' who never gave his consent to an act of cruelty,' Althorp ' who has never dipped his hand in blood,' Brougham ' who with all his half Scotch crotchets has at any rate no blood about him,' to show that the new ministers, unlike many of their Tory predecessors, might be trusted to be lenient and merciful. Two of these men, Grey and Holland, had made a noble stand against all the persecutions of which Tory Governments had been guilty, defending with passion men whose opinions they regarded with horror; if any record could justify confidence it was theirs. Unfortunately the politician who was made Home Secretary did not share in this past. The common talk at the time of Melbourne's appointment was that he was too lazy for his office; the real criticism should have been that he had taken the side of Castlereagh and Sidmouth in 1817. As Home Secretary he stopped short of the infamous measures he had then approved; he refused to employ spies, and the Habeas Corpus was not suspended. But nobody can follow the history of this rising, and the history of the class that made it, without recognising that the punishment which exiled these four hundred and fifty labourers is a stain, and an indelible stain, on the reputation of the Government that lives in history on the fame of the Reform Bill. It is difficult to believe that either Fox or Sheridan could have been parties to it. The chief shame attaches to Melbourne, who let the judges do their worst, and to Lansdowne, who sat beside the judges on the Salisbury bench, but the fact that the Prime Minister was immersed in the preparation of a reform, believed by his contemporaries to be a revolution, does not relieve him of his share of the odium, which is the due of Governments that are cruel to the weak, and careless of justice to the poor.

One effort was made, apart from the intercession of public opinion, to induce the Government to relax its rigours. When the panic had abated and the last echo of the riots had been stilled by this summary retribution, a motion was proposed in the House of Commons for a general amnesty. Unhappily the cause of the labourers was in the hands of Henry Hunt, a man whose wisdom was not equal to his courage, and whose egregious vanity demoralised and spoilt his natural eloquence. If those who were in close sympathy with his general aims could not tolerate his manners, it is not surprising that his advocacy was a doubtful recommendation in the unsympathetic atmosphere of the House of Commons. He was a man of passionate sincerity, and had already been twice in prison for his opinions, but the ruling class thinking itself on the brink of a social catastrophe, while very conscious of Hunt's defects, was in no mood to take a detached view of this virtue. The debate, which took place on the 8th of February 1831, reflects little credit on the House of Commons, and the division still less, for Hume was Hunt's only supporter. The chief speakers against the motion were Benett of Wiltshire, George Lamb, brother of Melbourne and Under-Secretary at the Home Office, and Denman, the Attorney-General. Lamb amused himself and the House with jests on the illiterate letter for writing which the boy Looker was then on the high seas, and Denman threw out a suggestion that Looker's father had had a share in the boy's guilt. Denman closed his speech by pouring scorn on those who talked sentimentality, and declaring that he would ever look back with pride on his part in the scenes of this memorable winter.

So far the Government had had it all their own way. But in their anxiety to show a resolute front and to reassure those who had suspected that a reform Government would encourage social disorder by weakness, Lord Grey and his colleagues were drawn into a scrape in which they burnt their fingers rather badly. They decided to prosecute two writers for inciting the labourers to rebel. The two writers were Richard Carlile and William Cobbett. Carlile was the natural prey for a Government in search of a victim. He had already spent six or seven years of his lion-hearted life in prison for publishing the writings of Paine and Hone : his wife, his sister, and his shopman had all paid a similar penalty for their association, voluntary or involuntary, with his public-spirited adventures. The document for which he stood in the dock at the Old Bailey early in January 1831 was an address to the agricultural labourers, praising them for what they had done, and reviewing their misfortunes in this sentence : ' The more tame you have grown, the more you have been oppressed and despised, the more you have been trampled on.' Carlile defended himself in a speech that lasted four hours and a half. The jury disagreed, but after several hours they united on a verdict of acquittal on the charge of bringing the Crown into contempt, and of guilty on the charge of addressing inflammatory language to the labouring classes. He was sentenced to imprisonment for two years, to pay a fine, and to find sureties.

Cobbett's trial was a more important event, for whereas Carlile was the Don Quixote of liberty of mind, Cobbett was a great political force, and his acquittal would give a very serious shock to the prestige of the Government that attacked him. The attention of the authorities had been called to Cobbett's speeches very early in the history of the riots, and the Home Office Papers show that appeals to the Government to prosecute Cobbett were the most common of all the recommendations and requests that poured into Whitehall from the country. Some of these letters were addressed to Sir Robert Peel, and one of them is endorsed with the draft of a reply : ' My dear Sir,—If you can give me the name of the person who heard Cobbett make use of the expression to which you refer you would probably enable me to render no small public service by the prosecution of Cobbett for sedition.—Very faithfully Yours, Robert Peel.'

In an evil moment for themselves, Peel's successors decided to take action, not indeed on his speeches, but on his articles in the *Political Register*. The character of those articles might perhaps be described as militant and uncompromising truth. They were inflammatory, because the truth was inflammatory. Nobody who knew the condition of the labourers could have found in them a single misstatement or exaggeration. The only question was whether it was in the public interest to publish them in a time of disturbance. From this point of view the position of the Government was seriously weakened by the fact that the *Times* had used language on this very subject which was not one whit less calculated to excite indignation against the rich, and the *Times*, though it was the organ of wealthy men, was in point of fact considerably cheaper to buy than the *Register*, the price of which Cobbett had raised to a shilling in the autumn of 1830. But this was not the only reason why the Government was in danger of exposing itself to a charge of malice in choosing Cobbett for a prosecution. The unrest in the southern counties had been due to a special set of economic causes, but there was unrest due to other causes in other parts of England. It was not the misery of ploughboys and labourers in Hampshire and Kent that had made Wellington and Peel decide that it was unsafe for the King to dine at the Guildhall in the winter of 1830 : the Political Unions, which struck such terror into the Court and the politicians, were not bred in the villages. There was a general and acute discontent with extravagant government, with swollen lists and the burden of sinecures, with the whole system of the control of the boroughs and its mockery of representation. Now in such a state of opinion every paper on the side of reform might be charged with spreading unrest. Statistics of sinecures, and

pensions, and the fat revenues of bishopricks, were scattered all
over England, and the facts published in every such sheet were
like sparks thrown about near a powder magazine.   The private
citizens who wrote to the Home Office in the winter of 1830
mentioned these papers almost as often as they mentioned
Cobbett's lectures.   Many of these papers were based on a
pamphlet written by Sir James Graham, First Lord of the
Admiralty in the very Government that prosecuted Cobbett.
One of the Barings complained in the House of Commons in
December 1830, that the official papers on offices and sinecures
which the Reform Government had itself presented to Parliament to satisfy public opinion of its sincerity in the cause of
retrenchment were the cause of mischief and danger.   At
such a time no writer, who wished to help the cause of reform,
could measure the effects of every sentence so nicely as to escape
the charge of exciting passion, and the Government was guilty
of an extraordinary piece of folly in attacking Cobbett for
conduct of which their own chief supporters were guilty every
time they put a pen to paper.

The trial took place in July 1831 at the Guildhall.   It was
the great triumph of Cobbett's life, as his earlier trial had been
his great humiliation.   There was very little of the lion in the
Cobbett who faltered before Vicary Gibbs in 1810 ; there was
very little of the lamb in the Cobbett who towered before
Denman in 1831.   And the court that witnessed his triumph
presented a strange scene.   The trial had excited intense
interest, and Cobbett said that every county in England was
represented in the company that broke, from time to time, into
storms of cheering.   The judge was Tenterden, the Chief
Justice, who, as a bitter enemy of reform, hated alike accusers
and accused.   Six members of the Cabinet, the Prime Minister
himself and the Lord Chancellor, Melbourne and Durham,
Palmerston and Goderich listened, from no choice of their own,
to the scathing speech in which Cobbett reviewed their conduct.
Benett of Pyt House was there, a spectre of vengeance from one
Commission, and the father of the boy Cook of Micheldever,
a shadow of death from another.   All the memories of those
terrible weeks seemed to gather together in the suspense of
that eager crowd watching this momentous encounter.

Denman, who prosecuted, employed a very different tone
towards Cobbett from the tone that Perceval had used at the
first of Cobbett's trials.   Perceval, when prosecuting Cobbett
for some articles on Ireland in the *Register* in 1803, asked the

jury with the patrician insolence of a class that held all the prizes of life, ' Gentlemen, who is Mr. Cobbett ? Is he a man writing purely from motives of patriotism ? *Quis homo hic est ? Quo patre natus ? ' * No counsel prosecuting Cobbett could open with this kind of rhetoric in 1831 : Denman preferred to describe him as ' one of the greatest masters of the English language.' Denman's speech was brief, and it was confined mainly to a paraphrase of certain of Cobbett's articles and to comments upon their effect.   It was no difficult task to pick out passages which set the riots in a very favourable light, and emphasised the undoubted fact that they had brought some improvement in the social conditions, and that nothing else had moved the heart or the fears of the ruling class.   But the speech was not long over before it became evident that Cobbett, like another great political defendant, though beginning as the accused, was to end as the accuser.   His reply to the charge of exciting the labourers to violence was immediate and annihilating. In December 1830, after the publication of the article for which he was now being tried, Brougham, as President of the Society for the Diffusion of Useful Knowledge, had asked and obtained Cobbett's leave to reprint his earlier ' Letter to the Luddites,' as the most likely means of turning the labourers from rioting and the breaking of machines.   There stood the Lord Chancellor in the witness-box, in answer to Cobbett's subpœna, to admit that crushing fact.   This was a thunderclap to Denman, who was quite ignorant of what Brougham had done, and, as we learn from Greville, he knew at once that his case was hopeless.   Cobbett passed rapidly from defence to attack.   Grey, Melbourne, Palmerston, Durham, and Goderich had all been subpœna'd in order to answer some very awkward questions as to the circumstances under which Thomas Goodman had been pardoned.   The Lord Chief Justice refused to allow the questions to be put, but at least these great Ministers had to listen as Cobbett told the story of those strange transactions, including a visit from a parson and magistrates to a ' man with a rope round his neck,' which resulted in Goodman's unexplained pardon and the publication of a statement purporting to come from him ascribing his conduct to the incitement at Cobbett's ' lacture.'   Cobbett destroyed any effect that Goodman's charge might have had by producing a declaration signed by one hundred and three persons present at the lecture —farmers, tradesmen, labourers, carpenters, and shoemakers— denying that Cobbett had made the statement ascribed to him in Goodman's confession, one of the signatories being the farmer whose barn Goodman had burnt. He then proceeded to contrast the treatment Goodman had received with the treatment received by others convicted of incendiarism, and piecing together all the evidence of the machinations of the magistrates, constructed a very formidable indictment to which Denman could only reply that he knew nothing of the matter, and that Cobbett was capable of entertaining the most absurd suspicions. On another question Denman found himself thrown on the defensive, for he was now confronted with his own misstatements in Parliament about Cook, and the affidavits of Cook's father present in court. Denman could only answer that till that day no one had contradicted him, though he could scarcely have been unaware that the House of Commons was not the place in which a Minister's statement about the age, occupation, pay, and conduct of an obscure boy was most likely to be challenged. Denman made a chastened reply, and the jury, after spending the night at the Guildhall, disagreed, six voting each way. Cobbett was a free man, for the Whigs, overwhelmed by the invective they had foolishly provoked, remembered, when too late, the wise saying of Maurice of Saxony about Charles v. : ' I have no cage big enough for such a bird,' and resisted all the King's invitations to repeat their rash adventure. To those who have made their melancholy way through the trials at Winchester and Salisbury, at which rude boys from the Hampshire villages and the Wiltshire Downs, about to be tossed across the sea, stood shelterless in the unpitying storm of question and insinuation and abuse, there is a certain grim satisfaction in reading this last chapter and watching Denman face to face, not with the broken excuses and appeals of ignorant and helpless peasants, but with a volleyed thunder that swept into space all his lawyer's artifice and skill. Justice plays strange tricks upon mankind, but who will say that she has not her inspirations ?

One more incident has to be recorded in the tale of suppression. The riots were over, but the fires continued. In the autumn of 1831 Melbourne, in a shameful moment, proposed a remedy borrowed from the evil practices which a Tory Parliament had consented at last to forbid. The setting of spring guns and man-traps, the common device of game preservers, had been made a misdemeanour in 1826 by an Act of which Suffield was the author. Melbourne now proposed to allow persons who obtained a license from two magistrates to protect their property by these means. The Bill passed the House of Lords, and the *Journals* record that it was introduced in the House of Commons, but there, let us hope from very horror at the thought of this moral relapse, silently it disappears.

When Grey met Parliament as Prime Minister he said that the Government recognised two duties : the duty of finding a remedy for the distress of the labourers, and the duty of repressing the riots with severity and firmness. We have seen how the riots were suppressed ; we have now to see what was done towards providing a remedy. This side of the picture is scarcely less melancholy than the other ; for when we turn to the debates in Parliament we see clearly how hopeless it was to expect any solution of an economic problem from the legislators of the time. Now, if ever, circumstances had forced the problem on the mind of Parliament, and in such an emergency as this men might be trusted to say seriously and sincerely what they had to suggest. Yet the debates are a mêlée of futile generalisations, overshadowed by the doctrine which Grey himself laid down that ' all matters respecting the amount of rent and the extent of farms would be much better regulated by the individuals who were immediately interested than by any Committee of their Lordships.' One peer got into trouble for blurting out the truth that the riots had raised wages ; another would curse machinery as vigorously as any labourer ; many blamed the past inattention of the House of Lords to the labourers' misery ; and one considered the first necessity of the moment was the impeachment of Wellington. Two men had actual and serious proposals to make. They were Lord King and Lord Suffield.

Both of these men are striking figures. King (1776-1833) was an economist who had startled the Government in 1811 by calling for the payments of his rents in the lawful coin of the realm. This dramatic manœuvre for discrediting paper money had been thwarted by Lord Stanhope, who, though in agreement with King on many subjects, strongly approved of paper money in England as he had approved of assignats in France. Lord Holland tells a story of how he twitted Stanhope with wanting to see history repeat itself, and how Stanhope answered with a chuckle : ' And if they take property from the drones and give it to the bees, where, my dear Citoyen, is the great harm of that ? ' King was always in a small minority and his signature was given, together with those of Albemarle, Thanet, and Holland, to the protest against establishing martial law in Ireland in 1801, which was written with such wounding directness that it was afterwards blackened out of the records of the House of Lords, on the motion of the infamous Lord Clare. But he was never in a smaller minority than he was on this occasion when he told his fellow landlords that the only remedy for the public distress was the abolition of the Corn Laws. Such a proposal stood no chance in the House of Lords or in the House of Commons. Grey declared that the abolition of the Corn Laws would lead to the destruction of the country, and though there were Free Traders among the Whigs, even nine years after this Melbourne described such a policy as ' the wildest and maddest scheme that has ever entered into the imagination of man to conceive.'

Suffield (1781-1835), the only other politician with a remedy, is an interesting and attractive character. Originally a Tory, and the son of Sir Harbord Harbord, who was not a man of very tender sensibilities, Suffield gradually felt his way towards Liberalism. He was too large-minded a man to be happy and at ease in an atmosphere where the ruling class flew instinctively in every crisis to measures of tyranny and repression. Peterloo completed his conversion. From that time he became a champion of the poor, a fierce critic of the Game Laws, and a strong advocate of prison reform. He is revealed in his diary and all the traditions of his life as a man of independence and great sincerity. Suffield's policy in this crisis was the policy of home colonisation, and its fate can best be described by means of extracts from a memoir prepared by R. M. Bacon, a Norwich journalist and publicist of importance, and printed privately in 1838, three years after Suffield had been killed by a fall from his horse. They give a far more intimate and graphic picture of the mind of the Government than the best reported debates in the records of Parliament.

We have seen in a previous chapter that there had been at this time a revival of the movement for restoring the land to the labourers. One of the chief supporters of this policy was R. M. Bacon, who, as editor of the *Norwich Mercury*, was in close touch with Suffield. Bacon set out an elaborate scheme of home colonisation, resembling in its main ideas the plan sketched by Arthur Young thirty years earlier, and this scheme Suffield took up with great enthusiasm. Its chief recommendation in his eyes was that it applied public money to establishing labourers with a property of their own, so that whereas, under the existing system, public money was used, in the form of subsidies from the rates, to depress wages, public money would be used under this scheme to raise them. For it was the object of the plan to make the labourers independent of the farmers, and to substitute the competition of employers for the competition of employed. No other scheme, Suffield used to maintain, promised any real relief. If rents and taxes were reduced the farmer would be able, but would not be compelled, to give better wages : if taxes on the labourers' necessaries were reduced, the labourers would be able to live on a smaller wage, and as long as they were scrambling for employment they were certain to be ground down to the minimum of subsistence. The only way to rescue them from this plight was to place them again in such a position that they were not absolutely dependent on the farmers. This the Government could do by purchasing land, at present waste, and compelling parishes, with the help of a public loan, to set up labourers upon it, and to build cottages with a fixed allotment of land.

Suffield's efforts to persuade the Government to take up this constructive policy began as soon as Grey came into office. His first letters to Bacon on the subject are written in November. The opposition, he says, is very strong, and Sturges Bourne and Lansdowne are both hostile. On 17th November he writes that a peer had told him that he had sat on an earlier committee on this subject with Sturges Bourne, as chairman, and that ' those who understood the subject best agreed with Malthus that vice and misery alone could *cure* the evil.' On 19th November he writes that he has had a conference with Brougham, with about the same success as his conference with Lansdowne and Sturges Bourne. On the 23rd he writes that he has been promised an interview at the Home Office ; on the 25th ' no invitation from Lord Melbourne ——the truth is he cannot find one moment of leisure. The Home Office is distracted by the numerous representations of imminent danger to property, if not to life, and applications for protection.' Later in the same day he writes that he has seen both Grey and Melbourne: ' I at once attacked Grey. I found him disposed to give every possible consideration to the matter. He himself has in Northumberland seen upon his own property the beneficent effects of my plan, namely of apportioning land to cottagers, but he foresaw innumerable difficulties.' A House of Lords Committee had been appointed on the Poor Laws at the instance of Lord Salisbury, and Suffield hoped to persuade this committee to report in favour of his scheme. He therefore pressed Grey to make a public statement of sympathy. Grey said ' he would intimate that Government would be disposed to carry into effect any measure of relief recommended by the Committee ; very pressed but would call Cabinet together to-morrow.' The interview with Melbourne was very different. ' Next I saw Lord Melbourne. " Oppressed as you are," said I, " I am willing to relieve you from a conference, but you must say something on Monday next and I fear you have not devoted much attention to the subject." " I understand it perfectly," he replied, " and that is the reason for my saying nothing about it." " How is this to be explained ? " " Because I consider it hopeless." " Oh, you think with Malthus that vice and misery are the only cure ? " " No," said Lord Melbourne, " but the evil is in numbers and the sort of competition that ensues." " Well then I have measures to propose which may meet this difficulty." " Of these," said Lord Melbourne, " I know nothing," and he turned away from me to a friend to enquire respecting outrages.' Suffield concludes on a melancholy note : ' The fact is, with the exception of a few individuals, the subject is deemed by the world a bore : every one who touches on it is a bore, and nothing but the strongest conviction of its importance to the country would induce me to subject myself to the indifference that I daily experience when I venture to intrude 'the matter on the attention of legislators.'

A fortnight later Suffield was very sanguine : ' Most satisfactory interview with Melbourne : thinks Lord Grey will do the job in the recess.' But the sky soon darkens again, and on the 27th Suffield writes strongly to Melbourne on the necessity of action, and he adds : ' Tranquillity being now restored, all the farmers are of course reducing their wages to that miserable rate that led to the recent disturbances.' Unhappily the last sentence had a significance which perhaps escaped Suffield. Believing as he did in his scheme, he thought that its necessity was proved by the relapse of wages on the restoration of tranquillity, but vice and misery-ridden politicians might regard the restoration of tranquillity as an argument for dropping the scheme. After this the first hopes fade away. There is strong opposition on the Select Committee to Suffield's views, and he is disappointed of the prompt report in favour of action which he had expected from it. The Government are indisposed to take action, and Suffield, growing sick and impatient of their slow clocks, warns Melbourne in June that he cannot defend them. Melbourne replies that such a measure could not be maturely considered or passed during the agitation over the Reform Bill. Later in the month there was a meeting between Suffield and Melbourne, of which unfortunately no record is preserved in the Memoir, with the result that Suffield declared in Parliament that the Government had a plan. In the autumn of 1831 an Act was placed on the Statute Book which was the merest mockery of all Suffield's hopes, empowering churchwardens or overseers to hire or lease, and under certain conditions to enclose, land up to a limit of fifty acres, for the employment of the poor. It is difficult to resist the belief that if the riots had lasted longer they might have forced the Government to accept the scheme, in the efficacy of which it had no faith, as the price of peace, and that the change in temperature recorded in Suffield's *Diary* after the middle of December marks the restoration of confidence at Whitehall.

So perished the last hope of reform and reparation for the poor. The labourers' revolt was ended; and four hundred and fifty men had spent their freedom in vain. Of these exiles we have one final glimpse; it is in a letter from the Governor of Van Diemen's Land to Lord Goderich: ' If, my Lord, the evidence, or conduct, of particular individuals, can be relied on as proof of the efficiency or non-efficiency of transportation, I am sure that a strong case indeed could be made out in its favour. I might instance the rioters who arrived by the *Eliza*, several of whom died almost immediately from disease, induced apparently by despair. A great many of them went about dejected and stupefied with care and grief, and their situation after assignment was not for a long time much less unhappy.' [1]

[1] Correspondence on Secondary Punishment, March 1834, p. 23.

CHAPTER XIII

CONCLUSION

A ROW of eighteenth-century houses, or a room of normal eighteenth-century furniture, or a characteristic piece of eighteenth-century literature, conveys at once a sense of satisfaction and completeness. The secret of this charm is not to be found in any special beauty or nobility of design or expression, but simply in an exquisite fitness. The eighteenth-century mind was a unity, an order; it was finished, and it was simple. All literature and art that really belong to the eighteenth century are the language of a little society of men and women who moved within one set of ideas; who understood each other; who were not tormented by any anxious or bewildering problems; who lived in comfort, and, above all things, in composure. The classics were their freemasonry. There was a standard for the mind, for the emotions, for the taste: there were no incongruities. When you have a society like this, you have what we roughly call a civilisation, and it leaves its character and canons in all its surroundings and its literature. Its definite ideas lend themselves readily to expression. A larger society seems an anarchy in contrast; just because of its escape into a greater world it seems powerless to stamp itself on wood or stone; it is condemned as an age of chaos and mutiny, with nothing to declare. In comparison with the dishevelled century that follows, the eighteenth century was neat, well dressed and nicely appointed. It had a religion, the religion of quiet common sense and contentment with a world that it found agreeable and encouraging; it had a style, the style of the elegant and polished English of Addison or Gibbon. Men who were not conscious of any strain or great emotion asked of their writers and their painters that they should observe in their art the equanimity and moderation that were desirable in life. They did not torture their minds with eager questions; there was no piercing curiosity or passionate love or hatred in their souls; they all breathed the same air of distinguished satisfaction and dignified self-control. English institutions suited them admirably ; a monarchy so reasonable nobody could mind ; Parliament was a convenient instrument for their wishes, and the English Church was the very thing to keep religion in its place. What this atmosphere could produce at its best was seen in Gibbon or in Reynolds ; and neither Gibbon nor Reynolds could lose themselves in a transport of the imagination. To pass from the eighteenth century to the Revolt, from Pope to Blake, or from Sheridan to Shelley, is to burst from this little hothouse of sheltered and nurtured elegance into an infinite wild garden of romance and mystery. For the eighteenth century such escape was impossible, and if any one fell into the fatal crime of enthusiasm, his frenzy took the form of Methodism, which was a more limited world than the world he had quitted.

The small class that enjoyed the monopoly of political power and social luxuries, round whose interests and pleasures the State revolved, consisted, down to the French war, of persons accustomed to travel, to find amusement and instruction in foreign galleries and French salons, and to study the fashions and changes of thought, and letters and religion, outside England ; of persons who liked to surround themselves with the refinements and the decorations of life, and to display their good taste in collecting old masters, or fine fragments of sculpture, or the scattered treasures of an ancient library. Perhaps at no time since the days when Isabella d'Este consoled herself for the calamities of her friends and relatives with the thought of the little Greek statues that were brought by these calamities into the market, has there been a class so keenly interested in the acquisition of beautiful workmanship, for the sake of the acquisition rather than for the sake of the renown of acquiring it. The eighteenth-century collectors bought with discernment as well as with liberality : they were not the slaves of a single rage or passion, and consequently they enriched the mansions of England with the achievements of various schools. Of course the eighteenth century had its own fashion in art, and no admiration is more unintelligible to modern taste than the admiration for Guercino and Guido Reni and the other seventeenth-century painters of Bologna. But the pictures that came across the Channel in such great numbers were not the products of one school, or indeed the products of one country. Dutch, Flemish, French, Italian, they all streamed into England, and the nation suddenly found itself, or rather its rulers, very rich in masterpieces. The importance of such a school of manners as this, with its knowledge of other worlds and other societies, its interest in literature and art, its cosmopolitan atmosphere, can only be truly estimated by those who remember the boorish habits of the country gentlemen of the earlier eighteenth century described by Fielding. With the French war this cosmopolitan atmosphere disappeared. Thenceforth the aristocracy were as insular in their prejudices as any of their countrymen, and Lord Holland, who preserved the larger traditions of his class, provoked suspicion and resentment by travelling in Spain during the Peninsular War.[1]

But if the art and literature of the eighteenth century show the predominance of a class that cultivated its taste outside England, and that regarded art and literature as mere ministers to the pleasure of a few,[2] they show also that that class had political power as well as social privileges. There is no art of the time that can be called national either in England or in France, but the art of eighteenth-century England bears a less distant relation to the English people than the art of eighteenth-century France to the people of France, just in proportion as the great English houses touched the English people more closely than Versailles touched the French. English art is less of mere decoration and less of mere imitation, for, though it is true that Chippendale, Sheraton, and the Adam brothers were all in one sense copying the furniture of other countries—Holland, China, France—they all preserved a certain English strain, and it was the flavour of the vernacular, so to speak, that saved their designs from the worst foreign extravagance. They were designing, indeed, for a class and not for a nation, but it was for a class that had never broken quite away from the life of the society that it controlled. The English aristocracy remained a race of country gentlemen. They never became mere loungers or triflers, kicking their heels about a Court and amusing themselves with tedious gallantries and intrigues. They threw themselves into country life and

---

[1] See a remarkable letter from Lord Dudley. 'He has already been enough on the Continent for any reasonable end, either of curiosity or instruction, and his availing himself so immediately of this opportunity to go to a foreign country again looks a little too much like distaste for his own.'—Letters to Ivy from the first Earl of Dudley, October 1808.

[2] See on this subject a very interesting article by Mr. I.. March Phillipps in the *Contemporary Review*, August 1911.

government, and they were happiest away from London.
The great swarms of guests that settled on such country seats
as Holkham were like gay and boisterous schoolboys compared
with the French nobles who had forgotten how to live in the
country, and were tired of living at Versailles. If anything
could exceed Grey's reluctance to leave his great house in
Northumberland for the excitements of Parliament, it was
Fox's reluctance to leave his little house in Surrey. The
taste for country pleasures and for country sports was never
lost, and its persistence explains the physical vitality of the
aristocracy. This was a social fact of great importance, for it
is health after all that wins half the battles of classes. No
quantity of Burgundy and Port could kill off a race that was
continually restoring its health by life in the open air ; it did
not matter that Squire Western generally spent the night under
the table if he generally spent the day in the saddle. This
inheritance of an open-air life is probably the reason that in
England, in contrast to France and Italy, good looks are more
often to be found in the aristocracy than in other classes of
society.

It was due to this physical vigour that the aristocracy,
corrupt and selfish though it was, never fell into the supreme
vice of moral decadence. The other European aristocracies
crumbled at once before Napoleon : the English aristocracy,
amidst all its blunders and errors, kept its character for
endurance and fortitude. Throughout that long struggle,
when Napoleon was strewing Europe with his triumphs and,
as Sheridan said, making kings the sentinels of his power,
England alone never broke a treaty or made a surrender at
his bidding. For ten years Pitt seems the one fixed point
among the rulers of Europe. It is not, of course, to be argued
that the ruling class showed more valour and determination
than any other class of Englishmen would have shown : the
empire-builders of the century, men of daring and enterprise on
distant frontiers, were not usually of the ruling class, and
Dr. Johnson once wrote an essay to explain why it was that
the English common soldier was the bravest of the common
soldiers of the world. The comparison is between the English
aristocracy and the other champions of law and order in the
great ordeal of this war, and in that comparison the English
aristocracy stands out in conspicuous eminence in a Europe
of shifting and melting governments.

The politics of a small class of privileged persons enjoying
an undisputed power might easily have degenerated into a

mere business of money-making and nothing else. There is plenty of this atmosphere in the eighteenth-century system : a study merely of the society memoirs of the age is enough to dissipate the fine old illusion that men of blood and breeding have a nice and fastidious sense about money. Just the opposite is the truth. Aristocracies have had their virtues, but the virtue of a magnificent disdain for money is not to be expected in a class which has for generations taken it as a matter of course that it should be maintained by the State. At no time in English history have sordid motives been so conspicuous in politics as during the days when power was most a monopoly of the aristocracy. No politicians have sacrificed so much of their time, ability, and principles to the pursuit of gain as the politicians of the age when poor men could only squeeze into politics by twos or threes in a generation, when the aristocracy put whole families into the House of Commons as a matter of course, and Burke boasted that the House of Lords was wholly, and the House of Commons was mainly, composed for the defence of hereditary property.

But the politics of the eighteenth century are not a mere scramble for place and power. An age which produced the two Pitts could not be called an age of mere avarice. An age which produced Burke and Fox and Grey could not be called an age of mere ambition. The politics of this little class are illuminated by the great and generous behaviour of individuals. If England was the only country where the ruling class made a stand against Napoleon, England was the only country where members of the ruling class were found to make a stand for the ideas of the Revolution. Perhaps the proudest boast that the English oligarchy can make is the boast that some of its members, nursed as they had been in a soft and feathered world of luxury and privilege, could look without dismay on what Burke called the strange, wild, nameless, enthusiastic thing established in the centre of Europe. The spectacle of Fox and Sheridan and Grey leading out their handful of Liberals night after night against the Treason and Sedition Bills, at a time when an avalanche of terror had overwhelmed the mind of England, when Pitt, Burke, and Dundas thought no malice too poisoned, Gillray and Rowlandson no deforming touch of the brush too brutal, when the upper classes thought they were going to lose their property, and the middle classes thought they were going to lose their religion, is one of the sublime spectacles of history. This quality of fearlessness in the defence of great causes is displayed in a fine succession of characters and incidents ; Chatham, whose courage in facing his country's dangers was not greater than his courage in blaming his country's crimes ; Burke, with his elaborate rage playing round the dazzling renown of a Rodney ; Fox, whose voice sounds like thunder coming over the mountains, hurled at the whole race of conquerors ; Holland, pleading almost alone for the abolition of capital punishment for stealing before a bench of bishops ; a man so little given to revolutionary sympathies as Fitzwilliam, leaving his lord-lieutenancy rather than condone the massacre of Peterloo. If moral courage is the power of combating and defying an enveloping atmosphere of prejudice, passion, and panic, a generation which was poor in most of the public virtues was, at least, conspicuously rich in one. Foreign policy, the treatment of Ireland, of India, of slaves, are beyond the scope of this book, but in glancing at the class whose treatment of the English poor has been the subject of our study, it is only just to record that in other regions of thought and conduct they bequeathed a great inheritance of moral and liberal ideas : a passion for justice between peoples, a sense for national freedom, a great body of principle by which to check, refine, and discipline the gross appetites of national ambition. Those ideas were the ideas of a minority, but they were expressed and defended with an eloquence and a power that have made them an important and a glorious part of English history. In all this development of liberal doctrine it is not fanciful to see the ennobling influence of the Greek writers on whom every eighteenth-century politician was bred and nourished.

Fox thought in the bad days of the war with the Revolution that his own age resembled the age of Cicero, and that Parliamentary government in England, undermined by the power of the Court, would disappear like liberty in republican Rome. There is a strange letter in which, condoling with Grey on his father's becoming a peer, he remarks that it matters the less because the House of Commons will soon cease to be of any importance. This prediction was falsified, and England never produced a Cæsar. There is, however, a real analogy in the social history of the two periods. The English ruling class corresponds to the Roman senatorial order, both classes claiming office on the same ground of family title, a Cavendish being as inevitable as a Claudius, and an Æmilius as a Gower. The *equites* were the second rank of the Roman social aristocracy, as the manufacturers or bankers were of the English. A Roman *eques* could pass into the senatorial order by holding the quæstorship ; an English manufacturer could pass into the governing class by buying an estate.   The English aristocracy, like the Roman, looked a little doubtfully on new-comers, and even a Cicero or a Canning might complain of the freezing welcome of the old nobles ; but it preferred to use rather than to exclude them.

In both societies the aristocracy regarded the poor in much the same spirit, as a problem of discipline and order, and passed on to posterity the same vague suggestion of squalor and turbulence.   Thus it comes that most people who think of the poor in the Roman Republic think only of the great corn largesses ; and most people who think of the poor in eighteenth-century England think only of the great system of relief from the rates.   Mr. Warde Fowler has shown how hard it is to find in the Roman writers any records of the poor.   So it is with the records of eighteenth-century England.   In both societies the obscurity which surrounded the poor in life has settled on their wrongs in history.   For one person who knows anything about so immense an event as the disappearance of the old English village society, there are a hundred who know everything about the fashionable scenes of high politics and high play, that formed the exciting world of the upper classes. The silence that shrouds these village revolutions was not quite unbroken, but the cry that disturbed it is like a noise that breaks for a moment on the night, and then dies away, only serving to make the stillness deeper and more solemn. The *Deserted Village* is known wherever the English language is spoken, but Goldsmith's critics have been apt to treat it, as Dr. Johnson treated it, as a beautiful piece of irrelevant pathos, and his picture of what was happening in England has been admired as a picture of what was happening in his discolouring dreams.   Macaulay connected that picture with reality in his ingenious theory, that England provided the village of the happy and smiling opening, and Ireland the village of the sombre and tragical end.   One enclosure has been described in literature, and described by a victim, John Clare, the Northamptonshire peasant, who drifted into a madhouse through a life of want and trouble.   Those who recall the discussions of the time, and the assumption of the upper classes that the only question that concerned the poor was the question whether enclosure increased employment, will be struck by the genuine emotion with which Clare dwells on the natural beauties of the village of his childhood, and his attachment to his home and its memories.   But Clare's day was brief and he has few readers.[1] In art the most undistinguished features of the most undistinguished members of the aristocracy dwell in the glowing colours of a Reynolds; the poor have no heirlooms, and there was no Millet to preserve the sorrow and despair of the homeless and dispossessed. So comfortably have the rich soothed to sleep the sensibilities of history. These debonair lords who smile at us from the family galleries do not grudge us our knowledge of the escapades at Brooks's or at White's in which they sowed their wild oats, but we fancy they are grateful for the poppy seeds of oblivion that have been scattered over the secrets of their estates. Happy the race that can so engage the world with its follies that it can secure repose for its crimes.

De Quincey has compared the blotting out of a colony of Alexander's in the remote and unknown confines of civilisation, to the disappearance of one of those starry bodies which, fixed in longitude and latitude for generations, are one night observed to be missing by some wandering telescope. ' The agonies of a perishing world have been going on, but all is bright and silent in the heavenly host.' So is it with the agonies of the poor. Wilberforce, in the midst of the scenes described in this volume, could declare, ' What blessings do we enjoy in this happy country ; I am reading ancient history, and the pictures it exhibits of the vices and the miseries of men fill me with mixed emotions of indignation, horror and gratitude.' Amid the great distress that followed Waterloo and peace, it was a commonplace of statesmen like Castlereagh and Canning that England was the only happy country in the world, and that so long as the monopoly of their little class was left untouched, her happiness would survive. That class has left bright and ample records of its life in literature, in art, in political traditions, in the display of great orations and debates, in memories of brilliant conversation and sparkling wit ; it has left dim and meagre records of the disinherited peasants that are the shadow of its wealth ; of the exiled labourers that are the shadow of its pleasures; of the villages sinking in poverty and crime and shame that are the shadow of its power and its pride.

---

[1] Helpstone was enclosed by an Act of 1809. Clare was then sixteen years old. His association with the old village life had been intimate, for he had tended geese and sheep on the common, and he had learnt the old country songs from the last village cowherd. His poem on Helpstone was published in 1820.

APPENDIX A (1)

The information about Parliamentary Proceedings in Appendix A is taken from the *Journals* of the House of Commons or of the House of Lords for the dates mentioned. The place where the Award is at present enrolled is given, where possible, under the heading ' Award.' A Return, asked for by Sir John Brunner, was printed February 15, 1904, of Inclosure Awards, deposited with Clerks of the Peace or of County Councils.

ARMLEY, LEEDS, YORKS.—ENCLOSURE ACT, 1793

AREA.—About 175 acres.

NATURE OF GROUND.—Waste Ground, called Armley Moor or Common.

PARLIAMENTARY PROCEEDINGS.—*February 21, 1793.*—Petition for enclosure from ' several of the Owners of Lands within the Manor and Township of Armley,' stating that this parcel of waste ground is, in its present state, incapable of improvement. Leave given, bill presented March 15.

March 28.—Petition against the bill from various owners and proprietors of Messuages, Cottages, Lands and Tenements who ' by virtue thereof, or otherwise, have an indisputable Right of Common upon the said Moor,' stating that ' they conceive that an Inclosure of the said Moor and Waste Ground would be productive of no Advantage to any of the Proprietors claiming a Right of Common thereon, but, on the contrary, would very materially injure and prejudice their respective Estates in the said Townships, by laying upon the said Township the Burthen of making, maintaining, and repairing the necessary new Roads, which must be set out to a considerable Extent over the said Moor and Waste Ground, and also by increasing the Poors Rate, inasmuch as the Petitioners conceive that the Inhabitants of the said Town of Armley, who are very numerous, and principally poor Manufacturers of broad Woollen Cloth, receive considerable Benefit and Advantage from the present open State of the said Moor and Waste Ground, particularly in having Tenters and Frames to stretch and dry their Cloth, Warps, and Wool, after it has been dyed, put up and fixed upon the said Moor and Waste Ground, which Privileges and Advantages have hitherto conduced to alleviate the Distresses and Hardships of the said poor Manufacturers in the said Township of Armley, and which, if the said Inclosure takes Place, they will be

totally deprived of and reduced to Poverty and Want.' The
Petition was ordered to be heard on second reading.

April 9.—Bill read a second time. House informed that
Petitioners declined to be heard on second reading. The Petition
was referred to the Committee.

April 17.—(1) Petition against the bill from John Taylor, giving
same reasons as last petition. (2) Petition from various master
manufacturers of broad woollen cloth in Armley against the bill,
stating that, as the Moor only contains about 160 Acres, inclosure
which involves division 'amongst so great a Number of Claimants
in small Allotments,' and also 'the heavy and unavoidable
Expenses of obtaining the Act, surveying, dividing, inclosing, and
improving' will confer little or no Benefit on the proprietors,
whereas it will certainly deprive the poor Manufacturers, who are
very numerous, of (1) the Privileges and Advantages of fixing their
Tenters, etc., 'which they and their Ancestors have hitherto
enjoyed'; and (2) 'of that Pasturage upon the said Common
which they have hitherto much depended upon.' Both Petitions to
be heard at Report stage ; (3) Petition against the bill from various
owners and proprietors who 'at the Instance of several other
Owners of Lands' signed a petition for inclosure, 'under an Idea,
that the Inclosure would meet with the Approbation of, and be
of general Utility to the Inhabitants of the said Town,' but now
finding that this idea was mistaken, and that Inclosure would be
of general disadvantage, ask that their names should be erased,
and that if the bill is brought in, they should be heard against it.
Petition referred to Committee. Petitioners to be heard, 'if
they think fit' ('they' ambiguous, might be Committee or Petitioners).

REPORT AND ENUMERATION OF CONSENTS.—*April* 29.—Wilberforce
reported from the Committee ; Standing Orders complied with,
Committee had considered the two petitions referred to them
(apparently they had not heard Counsel), and had found that the
Allegations of the Bill were true, and that the parties concerned had
given their consent '(except the Owners of Land of the Annual
Value of £172, 8s. 2d. who refused to sign the Bill ; and also,
except the Owners of Lands of the Annual Value of £35, 15s. 9d.,
who declared themselves neuter ; and that the Whole of the
Land entitled to Right of Common is of the Annual Value of
£901, 12s. 1d.).' There is nothing to suggest that the petitioners
against the bill were heard at this stage. The Bill passed Commons and Lords. Royal Assent, June 3, 1793.

MAIN FEATURES OF ACT.—(Private, 33 George III. c. 61.)

COMMISSIONERS.—One only. William Whitelock of Brotherton,
Yorks, Gentleman. He is also to act as surveyor. Vacancy to
be filled, if necessary, by 'the major part in value' of those
interested in the Common. An arbitrator is to be appointed by
the Recorder of Leeds.

PAYMENT TO COMMISSIONER.—£1, 11s. 6d. for each working day. As surveyor, his remuneration is to be settled by the Recorder of Leeds.

CLAIMS.—The Commissioner is to hear and to determine upon all claims, but if any one is dissatisfied the matter can be referred to the Arbitrator, whose decision is final. If the appeal is vexatious, the Arbitrator can award costs against the appellant. The Arbitrator's decision is final except in respect of matters of Title which can still be tried at law.

SYSTEM OF DIVISION—SPECIAL PROVISIONS:

Provisions for Lord of the Manor.—(1) The equivalent in value of one-sixteenth of the whole in lieu of his right in the soil.

(2) His other manorial rights to continue as before, including his mineral rights, but he is forbidden to 'enter into or damage any House, Garden, or Pleasure Ground' hereafter made on the Common, and if he damages property he must pay for satisfaction either a yearly rent of £3 an acre or part of an acre actually used and damaged, or else make such compensation as shall be awarded by two indifferent persons, one chosen by the Lord of the Manor, the other by the person who sustains the damage. If these two cannot agree, they must choose an Umpire whose decision is to be final.

(3) The Lord of the Manor is to have the use of a spring in the close belonging to Samuel Blackburn.

Provisions for Tithe Owners.—None.

Provisions for the Poor.—(1) Allotment to Cottagers of 8½ acres in six or more distinct and separate places, as near as possible to the Cottages on or adjoining the Common 'which shall for ever hereafter remain open and uninclosed, and shall be used and enjoyed by the Occupiers of the several Cottages or Dwelling Houses now or hereafter to be built within the said Township of Armley, for the setting up and using of Tenters, Stretchers for Warp, Wool Hedges,' etc., under the direction of the Minister, Chapel Wardens, and Overseers. No buildings are to be erected on this ground, and no rent paid for the use of it; no roads or paths may be made through it, and no buildings erected within 20 yards on the South or West.

(2) Allotment to the Poor.—2 acres, to be vested in the Minister, Chapel Wardens, and Overseers, and used for a Poor House, School House, and for the benefit of a School master. Until used for these purposes, the rent and profits are to go towards the Poor Assessment.

Allotment for Stone for roads, etc.—5 acres (for the making and repairing of highways and private roads).

Allotment of Residue.—To be divided out amongst the persons having right of common according to their several rights and interests, quantity, quality, and situation considered, provided 'that in case it shall be determined that the Owners of any Messuages or Cottages, or Scites of Messuages and Cottages, are entitled to Right of Common on the said Common or Waste Ground, then that the said Commissioner . . . shall award and allot such Parcels of the Common and Waste Ground to the Owners of such Messuages or Cottages, as have been erected for Sixty Years and upwards, unless the same shall have been erected upon the Scite of an ancient Messuage or Cottage, as to him . . . shall appear a fair Compensation for such Right,' and in making this allotment he is not to pay any regard to the value of these Messuages and Cottages one to another, except with reference to the Quantity of land.   If any allottee is dissatisfied with his share, he can appeal for arbitration to the Recorder of Leeds, whose decision is to be final, except in cases where the question concerns any Right of Common claimed 'for or in respect of any ancient Houses or Scites of Houses, Lands or Grounds,' when there may be an appeal at law, if notice is given within a specified time.   Allotments must be accepted within 6 months after award.   Failure to accept excludes allottee from all benefits. (Saving clause for infants, etc.).

INCROACHMENTS.—(1) Incroachments 60 years old and more to be treated as old inclosures with right of common, except such Incroachments as have been made by or for the Curate of Armley for the time being.   (2) Incroachments from 40 to 60 years old to remain with possessors but not to confer any right of common. (3) Incroachments made within 40 years to be deemed part of the Common to be divided, but to be allotted to present holders as part of their allotments.   But if they do not lie adjoining the in-croacher's ancient estates then the Commissioner can allot them to anyone, giving 'adequate Satisfaction for any Improvement' to the incroacher.   The above does not apply to two inclosures made by Stephen Todd, Esqr. and by Joseph Akeroyd which are to be allotted to them respectively under their present indentures of lease.

FENCING.—To be done by allottees under the Commissioner's directions.   *Exception.*—The allotment of 2 acres for the poor is to be fenced and enclosed at the expense of the other proprietors. If allottees refuse to fence, the Commissioner can do it for them and charge them, ultimately distraining.   To protect the young quickset, no sheep or lambs are to be depastured in allotments for 7 years, unless special fences are made, and no cattle, sheep or lambs are to graze in the roads and ways for 10 years.

EXPENSES.—To be paid by the proprietors in such proportion as the Commissioner decides.   The Commissioner's accounts are to be entered in a book, and produced when 5 proprietors require it. To meet expenses, allotments may be mortgaged in some cases, with consent of the Commissioner, up to 60s. an acre.

COMPENSATION TO OCCUPIERS.—All leases, as regards right of common and other rights on the waste ground for 21 years and under to be null and void, the lessor making such satisfaction to the lessee as the Commissioner thinks a fit equivalent.

ROADS.—Commissioners have full power to set out and stop up roads and footpaths.

POWER OF APPEAL.—To Quarter Sessions only, and not in cases where the Commissioner's or Arbitrator's decision is said to be final; or where some other provision is made, *e.g.* to Recorder of Leeds about allotments.

AWARD.—Not with Clerk of the Peace or of County Council or in Record Office.

APPENDIX A (2)

ASHELWORTH, GLOUCESTER.—ENCLOSURE ACT, 1797

AREA.—Not given in Act. Commonable Land of every kind stated in Petition (see below) as 310 Acres in all.

NATURE OF GROUND.—' Open and Common Fields, Meadows, and Pastures, Commonable and intermixed Lands, and a Tract of Waste Ground, being Part and Parcel of a Common called Corse Lawn,[1] and also a Plot, Piece, or Parcel of Land or Ground, on the Eastern Side of the said Parish,[2] adjoining to, and lately Part of the Parish of Hasfield . . . but now Part of the Parish of Ashelworth '.

PARLIAMENTARY PROCEEDINGS.—*February* 21, 1797.—Petition for enclosure from various owners of lands and estates. March 24, Bill read first time.

April 7, 1797.—Petition from various Landowners and Owners of Mease Places, against the bill, stating ' That there are only about 310 Acres of Commonable Land belonging to Land Owners of the said Parish, of which 148 Acres are Meadow Land, called the *Upper Ham*, lying in the Manor of *Hasfield*, the Right of Common upon which belongs exclusively to the Petitioners (and some others) as Owners of Fifty Five Mease Places within the said Parish, and the Petitioners are the Owners of Thirty-four of such Mease Places ; and that the Remainder of the said Commonable Land consists of a Common Meadow, called *Lonkergins Ham*, containing about eight Acres (upon which Six Persons have a Right of Common) and about 150 Acres of Waste Land, Part of a Tract of Land called Corse Lawn, upon which Waste Land all the Land Owners of the said Parish are entitled to a Right of Common ; and that the several Estates within the said Parish, lie very compact and convenient, and many of such Estates are exempt from the Payment of Great Tithes ; and that of the Remainder of such Estates the Great Tithes (except a Portion of which the Vicar was endowed) belong to Charles Hayward Esq., who is Lord of the Manor of Ashelworth, and Owner of an Estate

---

[1] Referred to below as ' A '.   [2] Referred to below as ' B '.

in the said Parish; and that there is no one Object in the Bill sufficient, under the Circumstances of the Case, to justify the enormous Expences which will attend the obtaining and carrying it into Execution, but that, on the Contrary, it is fraught with great Evil, and will be extremely injurious to the Petitioners,' and asking that the Petitioners may be permitted to examine Witnesses and to be heard by their Counsel against the bill.

Petitioners to be heard on Second reading.

April 10. — Second reading of bill.   House informed that Petitioners did not wish to be heard at that stage.   Bill committed. Petitioners to be heard when Bill reported if they think fit.

REPORT AND ENUMERATION OF CONSENTS.—*May* 3, 1797.—Mr. Lygon reported from the Committee that the Standing Orders were complied with ; that the allegations were true; and that the Parties concerned had consented to the satisfaction of the Committee '(except the Owners of Property assessed to the Land Tax at £11, 0s. 5d., and that the whole of the Property is assessed at £86, 14s. 10d.) and that no Person appeared before the Committee to oppose the Bill.' (Nothing about hearing Petitioners.) Bill passed both Houses with some amendments. In the House of Lords an amendment was made about referring the quarrel between the Vicar of Ashelworth and the Rector of Hasfield on the subject of tithes to arbitration. Royal Assent, June 6, 1797.

MAIN FEATURES OF ACT.—(Private, 37 George III. c. 108.)

COMMISSIONERS.—Three appointed. Richard Richardson of Bath : Francis Webb of Salisbury : Thomas Fulljames of Gloucester, Gentlemen. Two to be a quorum. Surveyor to be appointed by Commissioners. Vacancies, both Commissioners and Surveyors, to be filled up by remaining Commissioners from persons not interested. If they fail to fill up, 'the major part in value' of the Proprietors and Persons interested can do so.

PAYMENT TO COMMISSIONERS.—2 guineas each working day. Survey to be made, unless the existing one seems satisfactory and correct.

SPECIAL CLAUSES.—It is enacted ' That all Fields or Inclosures containing the Property of Two or more Persons within One Fence, and also all Inclosures containing the Property of One Person only, if the same be held by or under different Tenures or Interests, shall be considered as Commonable Land, and be divided and allotted accordingly.'

Also 'all Homesteads, Gardens, Orchards, old Inclosures, and other Lands and Grounds,' shall, with the consent of their pro- prietors or Trustees, ' be deemed and considered to be open and uninclosed Land for the Purpose of the Division and Allotment hereby intended,' provided that Charles Hayward has to get Bishop of Bristol's consent.

CLAIMS.—All claims to be delivered in writing at first and second Meeting, and no claim to be received after second Meeting, except for some special cause allowed by Commissioners. Commissioners to hold a subsequent meeting and give account in writing of what claims are admitted and rejected.

Persons whose claims are rejected can bring an action on a feigned issue against some other Proprietor. Verdict to be final and conclusive. If Plaintiff wins, Commissioners pay costs; if Defendant wins, Plaintiff pays. Action must be brought within a specified time (3 months).

Exceptions.—(1) If the Commissioners disallow the claim of the Dean and Chapter of Westminster to the Right of Soil in 'A,' then the Dean and Chapter may bring an action within 12 months against the Bishop of Bristol and Charles Hayward for ascertaining the rights of soil. Costs to be paid by losers.

(2) If the Commissioners allow the above claim, then the Bishop of Bristol or Charles Hayward can bring an action *mutatis mutandis.*

Also, If any dispute or difference arises between the Parties interested in the inclosure 'touching or concerning the respective Shares, Rights, and Interests which they or any of them shall claim' in the land to be inclosed, 'or touching and concerning the respective Shares and Proportions' which they ought to have, the Commissioners have power to examine and determine the same; their determination to be 'final, binding and conclusive upon and to all Parties.' Commissioners can on request of person who wins his point assess costs on person who loses it, and ultimately distrain on his goods.

Exception.—Commissioners to have no jurisdiction about Titles.

Tithe owners are to send in their claims with all particulars. Commissioners' determination to be final '(if the Parties in Dispute think proper and agree thereto)'; but not to affect power to try titles at law.

SYSTEM OF DIVISION—SPECIAL PROVISIONS:

Lord of the Manor.—(1) The Bishop of Bristol is Lord of the Manor of Ashelworth (except 'A' and 'B'), and Charles Hayward is his lessee. He is to have such part as Commissioners judge full compensation, to be 'not less than $\frac{1}{15}$' of the Waste Land to be inclosed.

(2) Dean and Chapter of Westminster and also the Bishop of Bristol claim Right of Soil in 'A,' whichever establishes his claim to have not less than $\frac{1}{15}$ of 'A.'

(3) John Parker Esq., is Lord of Manor of 'B': to have not less than $\frac{1}{15}$ of 'B'.

Tithe Owners.—Allotment to be made from land about to be inclosed for all tithes on all land (including present inclosures), as follows:—

Not less in value than One Fifth of Arable Land. Not less in value than One Ninth of Meadow or Pasture Ground, Homesteads, Gardens, Orchards and Woodlands. Where Tithes only partially due, full equivalent to be given.

The Vicar of Ashelworth and the Rector of Hasfield can have their disputed rights to tithes of ' B ' settled by Arbitration.

Owners of old inclosures who have not large enough allotments to pay their due proportion of the tithe allotments, are to pay a lump sum of money instead; *unless* the Commissioners deem it convenient to allot part of the old inclosures to the tithe owners instead; in which case the land so set out is to ' be deemed Part of the Lands to be divided, allotted, and inclosed by virtue of this Act.'

Full equivalent to the Vicar for his Glebe Lands and their right of Common.

For Stone, Gravel, etc.—From 2 to 3 acres; ' to be used and enjoyed in Common' by proprietors and inhabitants, ' for the Purpose only of getting Stone, Gravel, or other Materials for making and repairing the Roads and Ways within the said Parish.' Herbage of above to be allotted to whomsoever Commissioners direct, or for some general, parochial or other use.

To Proprietors of Cottages.—Every proprietor or owner of a cottage and land of the annual value of £4 or under is to have from ½ acre to 2 acres ' as they the said Commissioners shall think proper.'

Allotment of Residue.—Amongst the various persons interested according to their respective rights and interests. Allotments to be as near homestead or old inclosure as conveniently may be. If two or more persons with allotments of not more than 2 acres each want to have the same laid together in order to avoid the expence of inclosing, they are to give notice to the Commissioners, and the Commissioners are then to put these allotments together ' and in and by their Award to direct how and in what manner such small Allotments shall be cultivated, and in what Manner and Proportion, and with what Cattle the same shall be stocked, depastured and fed, during the Time the same shall lie open to each other,' and if at any time the Major part of proprietors of the small Allotments wish it, they are to be inclosed.

Award with full particulars of allotments and of orders and regulations for putting Act in execution to be drawn up, and to be ' binding and conclusive upon and to all Persons, to all Intents and Purposes whatsoever.'

Allotments to be of same tenure as property in virtue of which they are given. Allotments must be accepted within 6 months; if allottee fails to accept, the Commissioners can put in a salaried Bailiff or Receiver to manage allotment till allottee accepts, when any surplus profits are to be handed over to allottee. (Saving clause for infants, etc.).

FENCING.—To be done by respective allottees according to Commissioners' directions.

Exceptions.—(1) In the case of allotments to Trustees for parochial or charitable purposes, the Commissioners are to deduct a portion for these allottees' share of fencing and expenses. This deducted land is to be divided amongst other proprietors. The Commissioners do the fencing.

(2) Glebe and Tithe Allotments to be fenced by other proprietors, and the fences to be kept in repair for 7 years at expense of persons named by the Commissioners.

If an allottee fails to fence, his neighbour can complain to a J. P. (not interested) and obtain an order to do it and charge expenses on allottee, or else enter and receive rents.

If any allottee has an unfair share of fencing the Commissioners can equalise matters. No sheep or lambs to be kept in any inclosure for 7 years, unless special fences are made. No sheep or lambs ever to be kept in the roads.

EXPENSES.—Part of the Common or Waste Land to be sold to defray expenses. If the money so raised is not sufficient, 'the deficiency shall be paid, borne, and defrayed' by the various proprietors (excluding the Tithe owners and the Lords of the Manor for their respective allotments) in such proportion as the Commissioners direct.

Land may be mortgaged up to 40s. an acre.

Money advanced for Act to have 5 per cent. interest.

Commissioners must keep accounts, which must be open to inspection.

ROADS.—Commissioners to set out roads, ways and footpaths, all others to be stopped up. But no turnpike road to be interfered with.

COMPENSATION.—Leases at rack-rent to be void; owners paying or receiving such satisfaction as the Commissioners think right.

Compensation (under Commissioners' direction) to be paid by new allottee to former owner for timber, underwood, etc., or else former owner can enter and cut down, unless Commissioners direct that trees etc. are not to be cut.

ARRANGEMENTS BETWEEN ACT AND AWARD.—Commissioners to have full power to direct the course of husbandry.

POWER OF APPEAL.—To Quarter Sessions only, and not in cases 'where the Orders, Directions and Determinations of the said Commissioners are directed to be conclusive, binding and final.'

AWARD.—Date, August 24, 1798. With Clerk of Peace or of County Council, Gloucester.

APPENDIX A (3)

CHESHUNT.—ENCLOSURE ACT, 1799

AREA.—2741 Acres.

NATURE OF GROUND.—Common Fields and common Lammas meadows about 1555 acres; A common called Cheshunt Common about 1186 acres.

PARLIAMENTARY PROCEEDINGS.—*February 23*, 1799.—Petition for enclosure from Sir George William Prescott Bt. (Lord of the Manor) the Rev. Joseph Martin (Tithe owner), Oliver Cromwell, William Tatnall and others. Leave given. Bill read twice; committed April 25.

May 7, 1799.—Petition against the bill from various proprietors of Lands and Common Rights setting forth 'That a very great Proportion of such Open Fields and Commonable Lands are of so bad a Quality, as to be incapable of any Improvement equivalent to the Expenses of the Inclosure; and that the said Commons in their present State, are well fitted for the breeding of Sheep and Support of lean Stock, and that many of the Inhabitants of the said Parish, who, by reason of their Residence and Occupation of small Tenements, have Rights of Common, are enabled, by the lawful Enjoyment of such Common Rights, to support themselves and their Families; but, as almost all the said Commons lie at the extreme Edge of the Parish, and are subject to very numerous and extensive Common Rights, any Allotments of the said Commons to the lesser Commoners must be too small, and too distant from their Habitations, to be of any substantial Use to them, which Inconveniences are now prevented by the Use of general Herdsmen; and that the Inclosure of the said Open Fields and other Commonable Lands would be, in many other Respects highly injurious to the Rights and Interests of the Petitioners.' Petitioners to be heard before the Committee. All to have voices.

REPORT AND ENUMERATION OF CONSENTS.—*May 24.*—Mr. Baker reported from the Committee that they had heard Counsel for the Petitioners; that the allegations were true; that the Parties concerned had given their consent to the bill, and also to the changing of one of the Commissioners named therein '(except the Proprietors of 314 Acres and 19 Perches of Land, who refused to sign the Bill; and also, the Proprietors of 408 Acres, 3 Roods and 22 Perches who were neuter; and that the whole Property belonging to Persons interested in the Inclosure consists of 6930 Acres, or thereabouts).'

Bill passed both Houses. June 13, Royal Assent.

MAIN FEATURES OF ACT.—(Private, 39 George III. c. 75.)

COMMISSIONERS.—Three appointed.

(1) John Foakes of Gray's Inn, Gentleman representing the Lord of the Manor.

(2) Richard Davis of Lewknor, Oxford, Gentleman representing the Impropriator of the Great Tithes.

(3) Daniel Mumford, of Greville St., Hatton Gardens, Gentleman, representing the other Proprietors of Estates with Right of Common or a major part in value. Two to be a quorum. Vacancies to be filled up by the parties represented from persons not interested in the enclosure. Surveyor appointed, Henry Craster of Cheshunt.

PAYMENT.—Commissioners, Surveyor, and Clerk or Agent to Commissioners each to have 2 guineas a day for each working day.

CLAIMS.—All claims with particulars of tenure, etc., to be handed in at specified times; claimants must give such particulars ' as shall be necessary to describe such Claims with as much Precision as they can.' No claim to be received afterwards, unless for some special cause. Commissioners' determination on claims to be final and conclusive, if no objection is made. If objection is made, the objector can (1) try the matter at law on a feigned issue; or (2) submit the question to 2 arbitrators, the claimant naming one arbitrator, the objector naming the other. If the arbitrators disagree, they can name an umpire, whose decision is final and conclusive. Commissioners can award costs. Commissioners to have no jurisdiction over matters of title which can be tried at law.

SYSTEM OF DIVISION—SPECIAL PROVISIONS:

To Lords of the Manor.—(7 of them.)

(1) Sir G. W. Prescott of Cheshunt.

(2) Rev. J. Martin of the Manors of the Rectory of Cheshunt.

(3) Anne Shaw, widow, of the Manors of Andrews and Le Mott.

(4) Francis Morland of the Manors of Theobalds, Tongs, Clays, Clarks, Darey's, Cross-Brookes, and Cullens.

(5) Robert William Sax, and

(6) Mary Jane Sax, and

(7) Joseph Jackson, of the Manors of Beaumont and Perriers.

So much ' as shall in the Judgment of the said Commissioners be an adequate Compensation and Satisfaction' for their Rights and Interests.

Tithe Owners.—One-fifth of arable or tillage, and one-ninth of the other land to be divided which is subject to tithes.

Above to be divided between Impropriator of Great Tithes and Vicar.

For Glebe Lands, a full equivalent. If any owner of old inclosed land who has no land in the common fields, but possesses a Right of Common over Cheshunt Common, wishes it, part of his allotment can (with the tithe owner's consent) be set aside and given to the tithe owners, and his Land will be free of tithes for ever.

For Stone and Gravel, etc.—2 Acres, to be used in common by proprietors and tenants, for their own use and also for the roads.

For Cottagers.—An allotment of 100 Acres, exclusive of Roads, to be vested in the Lord of the Manor, the Vicar, Churchwardens, and Overseers, 'for the Use of the Occupiers of Houses or Cottages within the said Parish already having Right of Common, without more than One Rood of Land belonging to and used with the same as a Garden or Orchard, the Yearly Rent of which, at the Time of passing this Act, shall not exceed Six Pounds, without paying any thing for such Use.'

The number of the Houses with their rents and the number of cattle are to be described in the Award. No one else is to send cattle on to the 100 acres.

These cottagers are also to have the herbage of the 2-acre allotment for stone and gravel.

Allotment of Residue.—Amongst the various persons interested in proportion to their various rights and interests, Quantity, Quality, and Situation considered.

Small allotments may, on application of allottees, if Commissioners think proper, be laid together, and enjoyed in common under Commissioners' direction.

Each Copyholder of all the Manors is to have a separate and distinct allotment. If any allottee is dissatisfied with his allotment, he can send in a complaint to the Commissioners, who are to hear and determine the matter; their determination is to be final and conclusive.

The Award is to be final and conclusive. If any allottee fails to accept his allotment, or molests another in accepting, he is to be 'divested of all Right, Estate, and Interest whatsoever' in the Lands to be divided.

The tenure of the allotment to be that of the estate in virtue of which it is given.

INCROACHMENTS.—Not mentioned.

FENCING.—Not specifically mentioned, but from clauses *re* tithe owners, etc., must be done at allottee's expense.

Beasts, cattle, etc., not to be depastured on the new allotments for 7 years unless special fences made, or a proper person sent to look after cattle.

Tithe owners' allotments to be fenced, and fencing kept in repair for 7 years by the other proprietors.

The 100-acre allotment for cottagers to be fenced at the expense of the owners of the residue of the common. Mortgage up to £2 an acre allowed for expense of fencing.

EXPENSES.—To be borne by all owners and proprietors (except the Rector and the Vicar, in regard to their Glebe and Tythe Allotments) in proportion to their shares, at an equal pound rate to be fixed by the Commissioners. If allottees fail to pay, Commissioners can distrain or enter and receive rents, etc.

Commissioners must keep accounts which must be open to

inspection. If they receive more money than is needed, the surplus is to go to the Poor Rates.

COMPENSATION.—All rack-rent leases to be void, the owners giving the tenants 'reasonable Satisfaction'; but where it seems more equitable to the Commissioners, the allotment can be held by the tenant during his lease at a rent to the owner fixed by the Commissioners.

Satisfaction for crops and for ploughing, manuring and tilling to be given by new allottee.

ARRANGEMENTS BETWEEN ACT AND AWARD.—Commissioners to have full power to direct the course of husbandry.

ROADS.—Commissioners to have full power to set out and to stop up roads and footpaths (except that they are not to make them over 'Gardens, Orchards, Plantations, and other Private Grounds'), and if ancient footways or paths are stopped up, the owners of old inclosed land, for whose accommodation it is done, are to pay something towards the general expenses of the act.

POWER OF APPEAL.—To Quarter Sessions only, and not when Commissioners' or others' determination is said to be final and conclusive.

AWARD.—Enrolled at Westminster, February 27, 1806. Record Office.

MAIN FEATURES OF AWARD :—

	a.	r.	p.
Whole area divided out including roads, some old inclosures and homesteads given up to be allotted, ...	2,667	2	33

	a.	r.	p.
Tithe owners in various allotments including 106 acres for exonerating old inclosures, and $1\frac{3}{4}$ acre for Vicar's Glebe and Right of Common,	474	1	13
The Lord of the Manor (Sir G. B. Prescott) and the trustees of the late Lord of the Manor, including $38\frac{3}{4}$ acres or $\frac{1}{18}$ for manorial rights,	438	0	24
Mrs. Anne Shaw, ...	376	2	7
Oliver Cromwell, Esq., ...	107	3	29
Occupiers of Cottages, ...	100	0	0
Gravel Pits, ...	1	3	13

The remainder (excluding roads) is allotted amongst 213 allottees :—

From 50—100 acres	4		
From 30— 50 acres	3	Above 10 acres	23
From 10— 30 acres	16		
		From 1—10 acres	141
From $\frac{1}{2}$—1 acre	37		
From $\frac{1}{4}$—$\frac{1}{2}$ acre	8	Below 1 acre	49
Below $\frac{1}{4}$ acre	4		
			213

The Award shows that there must have been 86 owners of the 1555 acres of Open Fields and Lammas Meadows as 86 allottees receive allotments in lieu of land. Of these 86, 63 receive allotments of under 10 acres in lieu of their land. (13 from 5-10 acres, 37 from 1-5 acres, 13 below 1 acre.)

AMENDING ACT *re* the 100 Acres Allotment, 1813.

PARLIAMENTARY PROCEEDINGS.—*November* 6, 1813.—Petition from the Lord of the Manor, the Vicar, Churchwardens and Overseers for amending Act.

REPORT AND ENUMERATION OF CONSENTS.—*November* 20, 1813.—Reported that the parties concerned had consented except 9 Persons with right of common who refused, and 3 who were neuter; the total number of persons having right of common being 183.

MAIN FEATURES OF AMENDING ACT.—(Local and Personal, 54 George III. c. 2.)

NEW ARRANGEMENTS RESPECTING 100-ACRE ALLOTMENT.—The Commissioners had set out the 100 Acres for the use of certain occupiers, who were to be entitled to turn out on May 12 till February 2 either 1 Horse or 2 Cows or other Neat Cattle, or 7 Sheep; 'And whereas, partly owing to the great Extent of the said Parish of Cheshunt, and to the Distance at which the greater Part of the Cottages or Houses, mentioned in the Schedule to the said Award, are situated from the said Plot or Allotment of One hundred Acres, and partly to the Inability of most of the Occupiers of such Cottages or Houses to maintain or keep any Horses, Cows, or other Neat Cattle or Sheep, the Persons for whose Benefit and Advantage such Plot or Allotment of Land was intended, derive little if any Advantage therefrom; but the Herbage of such Plot or Allotment of Land is consumed by the Cattle of Persons having no Right to depasture the same'; it is enacted that the Trustees are to have power to let out the 100 Acres to one or more tenants for not more than 21 years, 'at the best and most improved yearly Rent or Rents that can at the Time be reasonably had and obtained for the same. The proceeds of the rents (when expenses are paid, see below) are to be divided among the occupiers of the houses and cottages mentioned in the Schedule.

EXPENSES.—The Allotment is to be mortgaged up to £500 for the expenses.

To repay the mortgage £50 is to be set aside from the rents yearly.

Interest at 5% on the sum borrowed is to be paid from the rents.

APPENDIX A (4)

CROYDON, SURREY.—ENCLOSURE ACT, 1797

AREA.—2950 acres.

NATURE OF GROUND.—Open and Common Fields, about 750 acres, Commons, Marshes, Heaths, Wastes and Commonable Woods, Lands, and Grounds about 2200 acres.

PARLIAMENTARY PROCEEDINGS.—*November 7*, 1796.—Petition for enclosure from Hon. Richard Walpole, John Cator, Esq., Richard Carew, Esq., John Brickwood, Esq., and others. Leave given; bill presented May 8, 1797; read twice and committed.

May 18, 1797.—(1) Petition against the bill from Richard Davis and others, as prejudicial to their rights and interests; (2) Petition against it from James Trecothick, Esq. Both petitions to be heard before Committee. May 26, Petition against the bill from Richard Davis and others stating 'that the said Bill goes to deprive the Inhabitants of the said Parish and the Poor thereof in particular, of certain ancient Rights and Immunities granted to them (as they have been informed) by some, or one, of the Predecessors of His present Majesty, and that the said Bill seems calculated to answer the Ends of certain Individuals.'

Petitioners to be heard when the Bill was reported.

June 7.—Petition of various inhabitants of Croydon against the bill; similar to last petition. To be heard when Bill reported.

REPORT AND ENUMERATION OF CONSENTS.—*June* 19.—Lord William Russell reported from the Committee, standing orders complied with, that the Petitions had been considered, allegations true; parties concerned had given their consent to the satisfaction of the Committee, '(except the Owners of 230 Acres 2 Roods and 25 Perches of Inclosed Land, and 67 Acres 1 Rood and 31 Perches of Common Field Land, who refused to sign the Bill; and also the Owners of 225 Acres 1 Rood and 34 Perches of Inclosed Land, and 7 Acres 3 Roods and 5 Perches of Common Field Land, who, on being applied to, returned no Answer; and that the Whole of the Land consists of 6316 Acres and 37 Perches of Inclosed Land, and 733 Acres 1 Rood and 39 Perches of Common Field Land, or thereabouts). . .'

The same day (June 19) petition from various Freeholders, Copyholders, Leaseholders and Inhabitant Householders of Croydon stating that the promoters of the bill have named Commissioners without consulting the persons interested 'at an open and public meeting,' and that since the Archbishop of Canterbury as Lord of the Soil of the Wastes has named one Commissioner (James Iles of Steyning, Gentleman) the other two Commissioners ought, 'in common Justice and Impartiality' to be nominated by the proprietors of lands and the Parish at large; and as they understand that the Tithe owners and other Proprietors wish John Foakes, named in the bill, to remain a Commissioner, asking leave to nominate as the third Thomas Penfold of Croydon, Gentleman. Lord William Russell proposed to recommit the bill in order to consider this petition, but obtained only 5 votes for his motion against 51.

The Bill passed Commons.

In the Lords a Petition was read July 4, 1797, against the Bill from the Freeholders, Copyholders, Leaseholders and Inhabitant-Freeholders of Croydon, praying their Lordships, 'To take their Case into their most serious Consideration.' Petition referred to Committee.

July 10, 1797.—Bill passed Lords in a House of 4 Peers. (Bishop of Bristol, Lords Walsingham, Kenyon, and Stewart of Garlies.)

[3 of these had been members of the Committee of 6 to whom the Bill was committed.]

Royal Assent, July 19.

MAIN FEATURES OF ACT.—(Private, 37 George III. c. 144.)

COMMISSIONERS.—Three appointed. (1) James Iles of Steyning, Sussex; (2) John Foakes of Gray's Inn; (3) Thomas Crawter of Cobham, Gentlemen.

The first represents the Archbishop of Canterbury, Lord of the Manor of Croydon, the other two represent the proprietors of estates with right of common (the Archbishop excluded) 'or the major part in value' (such value to be collected from the rentals in land tax assessments). Vacancies to be filled up by the parties represented. New Commissioners not to be interested in the inclosure. Two Surveyors appointed by name: vacancies to be filled up by Commissioners.

PAYMENT TO COMMISSIONERS.—2 guineas a day. Surveyors to be paid what the Commissioners think 'just and reasonable.'

CLAIMS.—To be delivered in at the meeting or meetings advertised for the purpose. None to be received after, except for some special cause. Claimants must send in claims 'in Writing under their Hands, or the Hands of their Agents, distinguishing in such Claims the Tenure of the Estates in respect whereof such Claims are made, and stating therein such further Particulars as shall be necessary to describe such Claims with Precision.' The Commissioners are to hold a meeting to hear and determine about claims, and if no objections are raised, then their determination is final and conclusive. If objections are raised, then any one person whose claim is disallowed, or any three persons who object to the allowance of some one else's claim, can proceed to trial at the Assizes on a feigned issue. The verdict of the trial is to be final. Due notice of trial must be given and the allotment suspended. The Commissioners cannot determine on questions of title which may still be tried at law.

SYSTEM OF DIVISION—SPECIAL PROVISIONS:

Provisions for Lord of the Manor.—The Archbishop of Canterbury is Lord of the Manor of Croydon and also of Waddon, and there are six other Lords whose manors lie either wholly or partly within the parish, *i.e.* (1) Robert Harris, Esq., of Bermondsey; (2) Richard Carew, Esq., of Norbury; (3) John Cator, Esq., of Bensham; (4) William Parker Hamond, Esq, of Haling; (5) James Trecothick, Esq., of Addington, otherwise Temple, who also claims for Bardolph and Bures. (6) The Warden and Poor of the Hospital of Holy Trinity (Whitgift Foundation) of Croham. Each of these 7 Lords is to have one-eighteenth of the Commons and Wastes lying within his Manor. But whereas James Trecothick claims some quit-rents in the Manor of Croydon, if he makes good his claim to the Commissioners, then the Archbishop's eighteenth is to be divided between James Trecothick and the Archbishop, and this is to be taken by James Trecothick as his whole share as Lord of a Manor. The Archbishop can also have part of Norwood Common in lieu of his due share of Norwood woodlands.

Manorial rights, save Right of Soil, continue as before.

Compensation for the timber in Norwood Woodlands is to be fixed by the Commissioners and paid by the allottees to the Archbishop.

Provision for Tithe Owners.—For Rectorial Tithes, such parcel or parcels as Commissioners judge to be full equivalent.

Whereas the Archbishop claims that Norwood Woodlands (295 acres) are exempt from all tithes, this claim is to be determined by the Commissioners or at law, and if not found good, another parcel to be set out as full equivalent.

But the tithe allotments in all are not to equal in value more than one-ninths of the Commons, marshes etc.

For Vicar's tithes over Norwood Common, an equivalent parcel of land.

Provisions for the Poor.—If the inhabitants of Croydon prove their claim to Rights of Common on Norwood Common, and in Norwood Commonable Woods to the satisfaction of the Commissioners, or before a Court (if it is tried at law) then the Commissioners are to set out from the Commons, Wastes, etc., as much land as they judge to be equivalent to such right, 'having particular Regard to the Accommodation of Houses and Cottages contiguous to the said Commons, etc.,' and this land is to remain common, for the use of the inhabitants of Croydon, subject to the right of getting gravel from it. Suppose, however, that the inhabitants' claim is not allowed, or if allowed does not equal 215 acres of common in value: even then the Commissioners are to set out 215 acres for the above purpose. These 215 acres are to be vested in the Vicar, Churchwardens, Overseers, and 6 Inhabitants chosen at a Vestry meeting. These trustees can inclose as much as a seventh part and let it on lease for 21 years.

They are to manage the common with regard to stint, etc., and to dispose of rents.

Allotment of Residue.—The open common fields, commons, marshes, etc., to be divided amongst the several persons 'according to their respective Rights and Interests,' due regard being paid to Quality, Quantity, and Situation, and the allotments being placed as near the Homesteads, etc., as is consistent with general convenience.

All houses erected 20 years and more before the Act, and the Sites of all such houses to be considered as ancient messuages entitled to right of common, with the exception of houses built on encroachments, the owners of which are to have whatever allotment the Commissioners think fair and reasonable.

The Commissioners are to give notice of a place where a schedule of allotments can be inspected and of a meeting where objections can be heard. The Commissioners are to hear complaints, but their determination is to be binding and conclusive on all parties.

When the award is drawn up 'the said Allotments, Partitions, Divisions, and Exchanges, and all Orders, and Directions, Penalties, Impositions, Regulations and Determinations so to be made as aforesaid, in and by such Award or Instrument, shall be, and are hereby declared to be final, binding and conclusive unto and upon all Persons interested in the said Division and Inclosure.' Persons who refuse to accept within an appointed time, or who molest others who accept, are 'divested of all Right of Possession, Right of Pasturage and Common, and all other Right, Estate and Interest whatsoever in the allotments.' Allotments are to be of the same tenure as the estates in right of which they are given. Copyhold allotments in the Manors of Croydon and Waddon can be enfranchised by the Commissioners at the request of the allottees, a part of such allotments being deducted and given to the Archbishop for compensation. Allotments may be laid together if the different owners wish it.

INCROACHMENTS.—Those made within 6 months not to count. Those of 20 years old and over to remain with present possessor, but not to confer right to an allotment.

Encroachments under 20 years old, (1) if the encroacher has a right to an allotment, then it shall be given to him as whole or part of that allotment (not reckoning the value of buildings and improvements); (2) if the allotment to which he has a right is unequal in value to the encroachment, or if he has no right to an allotment, he can pay the surplus or the whole price at the rate of £10 an acre; (3) if the encroacher cannot or will not purchase, the Commissioners are to allot him his encroachment for which he is to pay rent at the rate of 12s. an acre a year for ever, such rent being apportioned to whomever the Commissioners direct as part of their allotment.

Provisions are also made for giving encroachers allotments elsewhere instead, in certain cases.

FENCING.—To be done by allottees. If the proportion of fencing to be done by any allottee is unfair, the Commissioners have power to equalise it. *Exception.*—(1) The allotment to Rector for Tithes which is to be fenced at the expense of or by the person or persons whom the Commissioners appoint; (2) The allotments belonging to certain estates leased out at reserved rents by the Archbishop and by Trinity Hospital for 21 years, are to be fenced by the lessees; to compensate lessees new leases are to be allowed; (3) Allotments to Charity Estates (except Trinity Hospital) are to have a part deducted from them and be fenced by the Commissioners. If any proprietor refuses to fence, his neighbour can, on complaint to a J.P., obtain an order or an authorisation to enter, do the fencing, and take the rents till it is paid for.

Guard fences to protect the quickset are allowed.

Penalty for damaging fences from 40s. to £10. The owner of the damaged fence may give evidence. Half the penalty goes to the informer and half to the owner. But if the owner informs, the whole penalty goes to the Overseer.

Estates may be mortgaged up to 40s. an acre to meet expenses of fencing. Roads are not to be depastured for 10 years.

EXPENSES.—To meet all expenses (including the lawsuits on feigned issues) part of the Commons, Wastes, etc., are to be sold by public auction. Private sales are also authorised, but no one person may buy privately more than 2 acres; except that if James Trecothick, Esq., so wishes, the Commissioners are to sell him by private contract part of Addington Hills at what they judge a fair and reasonable price.

Any surplus is to be paid to the Highways or Poor Rates within 6 months after award. Commissioners are to keep Accounts, which must be open to Inspection.

Common Rights and Interests may be sold before the execution of the award by allottees except the Archbishop, the Vicar, Trinity Hospital, and Trustees for Charitable purposes.

COMPENSATION TO OCCUPIERS.—In the case of leases at rack-rent the Commissioners are to set out the allotment to the owner, but the owner is to pay fair compensation to the tenant for loss of right of common, either by lowering his rent or by paying him a gross sum of money as the Commissioners direct. *Exception.*— If the Commissioners think it a more equitable course they may allot the allotment to the tenant during his lease, and settle what extra rent he shall pay in respect of the owner's expense in fencing, etc.

Satisfaction for crops, ploughing, tilling, manuring, etc. is to be given in cases where the ground is allotted to a new possessor.

ROADS.—Commissioners have power to set out and shut up roads (turnpike roads excluded), footpaths, etc., but if they shut up a footpath through old inclosed land, the person for whose benefit it is shut is to pay such compensation as the Commissioners decide, the money going towards the Expenses of the Act.

POWER OF APPEAL.—To Quarter Sessions only, and not in cases, *e.g.* claims and allotment, where the Commissioners' decisions are final and conclusive or a provision for trial at law is made.

ARRANGEMENTS BETWEEN ACT AND AWARD.—As soon as the Act is passed the Commissioners are to have sole direction of the course of husbandry. *Exception.*—They are not to interfere with Thomas Wood and Peter Wood, Gentlemen, in their cultivation of such parts of the common fields of Waddon as are leased to them by the Archbishop. (Four years of the lease are still to run.)

AWARD.—Date, March 2, 1801. Clerk of Peace or of County Council, Surrey.

AMENDING ACT, 1803.—(Private, 43 George III. c. 53.)

Passed in response to a petition (February 16, 1803) from the Vicar, Churchwardens, Overseers, and other inhabitants of Croydon, stating that whereas the Commissioners have set out 237 acres 2 roods for the inhabitants of Croydon, instead of 215 acres, doubts have arisen as to whether this land is vested in trustees as was directed to be done with the 215 acres.

MAIN FEATURES.—The 237 acres 2 roods to be treated as the 215 acres. Land up to 5 acres to be sold to defray cost of this new Act; any surplus to go to Use and Benefit of Poor, any deficit to be made up by rents or sale of gravel.

NOTE ON RESULTS.—Third Report of Select Committee on Emigration, 1826-7, p. 369. Dr. Benjamin Wills stated that as the result of the loss of common rights suffered under the Bill, he had seen some 900 persons summoned for the Poor Rate. 'By the destruction of the common rights, and giving no remuneration to the poor man, a gentleman has taken an immense tract of it and converted it into a park: a person in the middling walk of life has bought an acre or two; and though this common in its original state was not so valuable as it has been made, yet the poor man should have been consulted in it; and the good that it was originally to him was of such a nature that, destroying that, has had an immense effect.'

APPENDIX A (5)

HAUTE HUNTRE, LINCS.—ENCLOSURE ACT, 1767

AREA.—22,000 Acres 'more or less.'

NATURE OF GROUND.—Haute Huntre, Eight Hundred or Holland Fen and other commonable places adjacent.

Owners and Proprietors of Houses and Toftsteads in the following 11 Parishes or Townships have Right of Common:— Boston West, Skirbeck Quarter, Wyberton, Frampton, Kirton, Algarkirke, Fosdyke, Sutterton, Wigtoft, Swineshead, and Brothertoft; and also in a place called Dog Dyke in the Parish of Billinghay.

PARLIAMENTARY PROCEEDINGS.—*December* 4, 1766.—Petition for enclosure from various owners and proprietors with right of common, asking that the fen shall be divided up into specific allotments for each Town. Leave given. Bill read first time, December 9.

March 4, 1767.—Long petition against the bill from (1) the Master, Fellows and Scholars of Trinity College, Cambridge, which College is Impropriator of the Great Tythes, and Patron of the Vicarage of Swineshead, (2) the Rev. John Shaw, Patron and Rector of Wyberton, (3) Zachary Chambers, Esq., Lord of the Manor of Swineshead, and others. The petition gave a history of the movement for enclosure. On August 26, 1766, a meeting of several gentlemen and others was held at the Angel Inn, Sleaford, at which a resolution was passed that a Plan or Survey of the fen with a return of the Houses etc., with Right of Common should be made before a bill was brought in. On October 16, 1766, a public meeting of several proprietors was held at Sleaford at which some of those present proposed to read a bill for dividing and inclosing the fen; the great majority however of those present objected to this course, and requested and insisted that as no Survey had been produced, nothing further should be done till the following spring, 'but notwithstanding the said Request, some few of the said Proprietors then present proposed that a Petition for the said Bill might then be signed; which Proposition being rejected by a considerable Majority, the said few Proprietors declared their Resolution to sign such a Petition, as soon as their then Meeting was broke up, without any Resolutions being concluded upon, or the Sentiments of the Majority of the Proprietors either entered down or paid any Regard to, and without making any Adjournment of the said Meeting; and that, soon after the said Meeting broke up, some of the Proprietors present at the said Meeting signed the Petition, in consequence of which the said Bill hath been brought in.' The petitioners also pointed out that the petition for enclosure was signed by very few proprietors except those in Boston West, and requested that no further measures should be taken till next session, and that meanwhile the Survey in question should be made, and suggested that the present bill was in many respects exceptionable, and asked to be heard by Counsel against the bill as it now stood. Petition to lie on table till second reading.

March 6, 1767.—Bill read second time and committed. Petition referred to Committee.

March 21.—Petition against the bill from Sir Charles Frederick, Knight of the Bath, sole owner of Brothertoft, where there are 51 Cottages or Toftsteads with right of common. Referred to Committee.

March 27.—Petition against the bill from Sir Gilbert Heathcote, Bart. and others; bill injurious to interests. Referred to Committee.

REPORT AND ENUMERATION OF CONSENTS.—*April* 29, 1767.—Lord Brownlow Bertie reported from the Committee; Committee had heard Counsel in favour of the first petition and considered the other two; that the Allegations of the Bill were true; and that the Parties concerned had given their consent to the Bill to the satisfaction of the Committee '(except 94 Persons with Right of Common and Property of the Annual Value of £3177, 2s. 6d. who refused, and except 53 Persons with Right of Common and Property of the Annual Value of £694, 10s. who could not be found, and except 40 Persons with Right of Common and Property of the Annual Value of £1310, 0s. 6d. who declared they were indifferent, and that the whole Number of Persons with Right of Common was 614, and the whole Property of the Annual Value of £23,347, 8s.).' Several amendments were made in the Bill and it was sent up to the Lords. In the Lords, petitions against it were received from Sir Gilbert Heathcote (May 7) and Samuel Reynardson, Esq. (May 14), both of which were referred to the Committee. Several amendments were made, including the insertion of a clause giving the Proprietors or Occupiers the same right of common over the Parish allotment as they already had over the whole. Royal Assent, June 29, 1767.

MAIN FEATURES OF ACT.—(Private, 7 George III. c. 112.)

COMMISSIONERS.—Five are to be appointed; they are to be chosen by eleven persons, each representing one of the eleven townships. These eleven persons are to be elected in each township by the owners and proprietors of Houses, Toftsteads, and Lands which formerly paid Dyke-reeve assessments; except in the case of Brothertoft, where Sir Charles Frederick, as sole owner and proprietor, nominates the person. No person interested in the inclosure is to be chosen as Commissioner, and in addition to the usual oath of acting 'without favour or affection' the Commissioners are required to take the following oath:—

' I, A. B., do swear, that I am neither Proprietor nor Occupier of, nor, to the best of my Knowledge, am I concerned as Guardian, Steward or Agent for any Proprietor of any Houses, Toftsteads, or Lands within any of the Parishes of' (names given) 'or for any Person to whom any Allotment is to be made by virtue of the said Act.'

Three Commissioners are a quorum. Vacancies are to be filled by the 11 persons elected as before. If they fail to do so, the remaining Commissioners can nominate. Survey to be made by persons appointed by the Commissioners, and number of present Houses and Toftsteads to be recorded except in Boston West and Brothertoft. Edward Draper of Boston, Gentleman, to be Clerk.

PAYMENT.—Commissioners each to have £210 and no more. Two guineas to be deducted for each day's absence.

CLAIMS.—Nothing is said about sending in claims, as the survey giving the Houses, etc., does instead. If any difference or dispute arise between parties interested in the division with respect to shares, rights, interests, and proportions, the Commissioners are to hear them, and their determination is to be binding and conclusive.

SYSTEM OF DIVISION—SPECIAL PROVISIONS:

To Lords of the Manor.—Zachary Chambers, Esq., is Lord of the Manor of Swineshead; Charles Anderson Pelham, Esq., is Lord of the Manor of Frampton. These two are intitled jointly to the soil of the fen, and Charles Anderson Pelham, Esq., is also intitled 'to the Brovage or Agistment' of 480 head of cattle on the fen every year.

(1) Zachary Chambers, Esq., is to have 120 Acres in one piece in a part called Brand End in lieu of his rights of soil and of all mines and quarries of what nature whatsoever.

(2) Charles Anderson Pelham, Esq., is to have 120 Acres in one piece, near Great Beets, for his rights of soil and of mines and quarries.[1]

Charles Anderson Pelham, Esq., is also to have in lieu of his right of Brovage a parcel of the same number of acres that were given by an Act of 9 James I. to the Lords of the Manor of Swineshead for Brovage.

Tithe Owners.—Not mentioned.

Allotment of Residue.—After part has been sold for expenses (see below) and after allotment to the Lords of the Manor, the residue is to be divided amongst the eleven townships and Dog Dyke in proportion and according to the number of Houses and Toftsteads in each parish. For Brothertoft and Dog Dyke there are special arrangements; in the ten remaining townships or parishes, the following method is to be pursued:—For each House or Tenement there must be 4 acres, and for each Toftstead 2 acres allowed; when this proportion has been set out, the remainder is to be shared out in proportion to the Dyke-reeve assessments before the passing of a recent drainage Act. Quantity, Quality, and Situation are to be considered. *Special provision.*—Boston West is to have the same proportion of fen as Frampton.

The share that each of the above ten townships receives is to be the common fen belonging to the township or parish, subject

---

[1] Note that the compensation to the Lords of the Manor added together comes to less than one ninety-first part of the soil.

to the same common rights as the present fen, and is to be contiguous to the township.

Brothertoft and Dog Dyke allotments.—The allotment for Brothertoft is to be half as many acres as are allotted to Boston West, and is to go to Sir Charles Frederick, sole owner and proprietor, and to be near Brothertoft.

The Allotment to Dog Dyke is to be calculated in reference to the share that Brothertoft receives. Each House or Toftstead in Dog Dyke is to have $\frac{2}{3}$ of the proportion that each House or Toftstead in Brothertoft is assigned. The Dog Dyke Allotment is to go to Earl Fitzwilliam, the sole owner, and is to be near the Earl's gardens.

If any half-year lands, and other inclosed lands, directed to be sold (see Expenses) remain unsold, these are to be sold and the leases are to be allotted to the parishes in such proportions as the Commissioners direct.

An award is to be drawn up and its provisions are binding and conclusive.

FENCING.—Each township's share is to be divided by an 8-feet wide ditch and a quick hedge, and guarded with a fence and rail $4\frac{1}{2}$ feet high, with double bars of fir or deal and with oak posts; the fence and the rail are to be nailed or mortified together. The Commissioners do this fencing out of the money raised for defraying the expenses of the Act, but each township is to keep up its fences according to the Commissioners' directions. The fences, etc., are to be made within 18 months.

Penalty for wilfully and maliciously cutting, breaking down, burning, demolishing, or destroying any division fence:

1st offence (before 2 J.P.'s), fine of £5 to £20, or from 1 to 3 months in House of Correction.

2nd offence (before 2 J.P.'s), fine of £10 to £40, or from 6 to 12 months in House of Correction.

3rd offence (before Quarter Sessions), transportation for 7 years as a felon.

EXPENSES.—To defray all expenses the Commissioners can—

(1) sell the Right of Acreage or Common upon certain specified half-year lands,[1] *e.g.* The Frith, Great Beets, Little Beets, the Mown Rakes, etc., to the owners and proprietors of these lands. If the owners refuse to buy or do not pay enough to cover the expenses of the Act, the Commissioners can—

(2) sell part of the Fen. In this case the first land to be sold is Coppin Sykes Plot, Ferry Corner Plot, Pepper Gowt Plot, and Brand End Plot; the next land, Gibbet Hills.

As Coppin Sykes Plot, etc., belong to the Commissioners of two Drainage Acts, the drainage Commissioners can as compensation

---

[1] *I.e.* lands over which there is right of common for half the year between Michaelmas and Lady Day or Lammas and Lady Day.

charge rates on the respective townships instead, and if any township refuses to pay, they can inclose a portion of its allotment, but not for tillage.

Penalty for taking turf or sod after Act.

Culprit can be tried before one J.P., and fined from 40s. to £10, or, if he or she fails to pay, be given hard labour in the House of Correction for 1 to 3 months, or till the penalty is paid. Notice of this penalty is to be fixed on Church and Chapel Doors and published in newspapers.

POWER OF APPEAL.—To Quarter Sessions only, and not in cases where the Commissioners' decisions are said to be final and conclusive.

AWARD.—Date, May 19, 1769. With Clerk of Peace or County Council, Lincoln.

From *Annual Register*, 1769, p. 116 (Chronicle for July 16):

'Holland Fen, in Lincolnshire, being to be inclosed by act of parliament, some desperate persons have been so incensed at what they called their right being taken from them, that in the dead of night they shot into the windows of several gentlemen whom they thought active in procuring the act for inclosure; but happily no person has been killed.'

AMENDING ACT, 1770.

PARLIAMENTARY PROCEEDINGS.—*January 25*, 1770.—Petition for an amending Act from the Commissioners who carried out the previous one; stating that 'the Posts and Rails for many Miles in the Division Fences, which have been erected pursuant to the Directions of the said Act, have been pulled down, and the greatest Part thereof destroyed, together with great Part of the Materials for completing the said Fencing,' and asking for leave. to take down the Fencing and to make wide ditches instead.

Leave given. Bill passed both Houses and received Royal Assent.

MAIN FEATURES OF AMENDING ACT.—(Private, 10 George III. c. 40.)

The Commissioners are empowered to take down the posts and rails, and to make ditches 10 feet wide and 5 feet deep as boundaries instead.

The Posts and Rails are to be sold, and the proceeds are to defray the expenses of this Act and the costs of the Commissioners. The Commissioners are to have a sum of £31, 10s. each as payment, with 2 guineas deducted for each day's absence.

Edward Draper, Clerk to the Commissioners, is to be repaid up to £1000, his costs in prosecuting fence-destroyers.

If any proprietor has already made ditches wide enough, he is to be repaid his proportion.

Any surplus is to be handed over to Drainage Commissioners.

NOTES:—

				Act.	Award.
Boston West division was enclosed in				1771	1772
Algarkirke cum Fosdyke			,,	1771	...
Frampton	,,	,,	,,	1784	...
Kirton	,,	,,	,,	1772	1773
Skirbeck	,,	,,	,,	1771	1772
Swineshead	,,	,,	,,	1773	1774
Sutterton	,,	,,	,,	1772	1773
Wigtoft	,,	,,	,,	1772	1773
Wyberton	,,	,,	,,	1789	...

APPENDIX A (6)

KNARESBOROUGH FOREST.—ENCLOSURE ACT, 1770

AREA.—About 20,000 acres.

NATURE OF GROUND.—Open, Commonable or Waste Lands.

PARLIAMENTARY PROCEEDINGS.—*February* 8, 1770.—Petition for enclosure from several freehold and copyhold tenants within the Forest; stating that the said tracts are of little advantage now, whereas it would be of public utility to have them divided into just allotments and enclosed. Leave given, bill presented, read twice, March 19; committed March 28. Petition against the bill from 'a very great Number of the Freeholders, and Customary or Copyhold Tenants having Right of Common,' stating that the bill contains provisions very injurious to the petitioners and others. Referred to the Committee.

REPORT AND ENUMERATION OF CONSENTS.—*May* 7, 1770.—Lord Strange reported from the Committee that the allegations of the bill were true, that no person had appeared before the Committee to oppose the bill, and that 'the Parties concerned had given their Consent' '(except the Proprietors of Land in the Seven Lower Constableries, assessed to the Land Tax at £47, 2s. 3d. per Annum, and the Proprietors of Land in the Four Higher Constableries assessed to the Land Tax at £118, 3s. 6¾d., and that the whole of the Assessment in the Seven Lower Constableries, and for Estates of several Persons adjoining, being within the District called the Forest, in virtue whereof Right of Common is enjoyed, amounts to £497, 1s. 4½d., and in the Four High Hamlets to £183, 9s. 8d.).'

The bill passed both Houses and received the Royal Assent on May 19.

MAIN FEATURES OF ACT.—(Private, 10 George III. c. 94.)

COMMISSIONERS.—Five appointed. William Hill of Tadcaster, Gentleman; Joseph Butter of Bowthorp, Surveyor; William Chippendale of Ripley, Surveyor; John Flintoff of Boroughbridge, Surveyor; Thomas Furness of Otley, Gentleman. Vacancies to be filled up by remaining Commissioners. Three are a quorum.

ARBITRATORS.—Nine appointed by name. Two can act. Vacancies to be filled up by Commissioners from barristers.

SURVEYORS.—Three named, two of them are also Commissioners. Vacancies to be filled up by Commissioners.

PAYMENT TO COMMISSIONERS, ARBITRATORS AND SURVEYORS.— Nothing stated.

CLAIMS.—All claims to be delivered in at the first, second or third meeting; claims must be in writing and must specify and contain 'an Account and Description of the Messuage or Messuages, antient Building or Buildings, and Lands' in respect of which the claim is made, and also the name or names of the person or persons in actual possession. For a month after the third meeting all claims are to be open to the inspection of other claimants. Failure to deliver in 'such Writing and Account as aforesaid' at the first three meetings debars the would-be claimant from all right to allotment, 'Infancy, Coverture, Lunacy, or any other general legal Impediment whatsoever of or in any such Person in anywise notwithstanding.'

If claims are duly made and no objection raised to them by any person, they are to be allowed finally and conclusively at the fourth meeting; and no right so allowed can be disputed afterwards. Supposing objections are made by any two other claimants or by any Commissioner present, then the matter is to be referred to two or more of the arbitrators whose decision is to be final and conclusive. If unreasonable, unjust, frivolous or vexatious claims or objections are made, the Arbitrators can assess the costs on the maker.

In deciding on claims, 40 years' enjoyment of commonage is to be considered to confer a right, when it is enjoyed in respect of owning ancient messuages, etc., whether situated within or without the limits of the Forest (save and except in respect of Commonage by Vicinage).

The quantity and the value of the lands in virtue of which claims are made, are to be adjudged by the Commissioners, and such judgment is to be final and conclusive, but no ancient Messuage or Building or Scite thereof is to be allowed at greater value than any other.

Disputes between landlords and tenants are to be referred to the Arbitrators, and their award is to be final and conclusive.

SYSTEM OF DIVISION—SPECIAL PROVISIONS:

Provisions for the Lord of the Manor (the King).—(1) One-tenth part of the whole, after allotments for Stone Quarries, watering places and roads have been deducted; 'the said Tenth Part to consist of a proportionable Share of the best and worst kind of Land as near as may be.'

(2) All incroachments made within 40 years, and held by persons not entitled to right of common ; but see Incroachments.

(3) The King's rights to Mines, Minerals, and Quarries (except Stone Quarries) are not to be prejudiced, but he or his lessee is to pay reasonable satisfaction for any damage done, such satisfaction to be determined by 2 or more J.P.'s, or, if the parties are still dissatisfied, by a Jury of 12.

Provisions for Tithe Owners.—Such portions as the Commissioners shall adjudge to be ' full Recompence and Satisfaction.'

For Stone Quarries, Watering Places, and Roads.—Such allotment as the Commissioners think requisite.

For Harrogate Stray.—' Whereas there are within the constableries of Bilton with Harrowgate and Beckwith with Rosset, or One of them, certain Wells or Springs of medicinal Waters, commonly called Harrowgate Spaws, to which during the Summer Season great Numbers of Persons constantly resort to receive the Benefit of the said Waters to the great Advantage and Emolument of Tradesmen, Farmers, and other Persons in that Neighbourhood, and the Persons resorting to the said Waters now have the Benefit of taking the Air upon the open Part of the said Constableries,' it is enacted that 200 acres of land near the said springs shall be set apart and left free and open for ever. The Freeholders and Copyholders within the said Constableries are to have right of pasture on these 200 acres, the stint being regulated by the Commissioners, and such right of common being taken as part of their respective allotments.

For the Poor.—None.

Allotment of Residue.—To be allotted to the Persons entitled to commonage ' in Proportion to the real Value of their several and respective Messuages, Lands, and Tenements ' in respect of which they are entitled. Quality and situation to be considered in settling the Quantum. Allotments must be accepted within six months after award (see also Fencing).

Award to be drawn up with all particulars, but nothing is specifically said about its being final. It is to be Evidence in Courts of Law.

Stone Quarries are to be vested in the landholders. Allotments to be of the same tenure as the property in virtue of which they are given. Timber is to belong to copyholders as if they were freeholders. Disputes arising in the execution of the Act, which do not affect the persons in general interested in the Inclosure, can, if all the Parties concerned in the particular dispute wish it, be referred to some other Arbitrator or Arbitrators not mentioned in the Act, and his or their decision is to be final.

Incroachments.—(1) Incroachments 40 years old and upwards, with all buildings thereon, to be absolute property of persons in possession ; but Copyhold.

(2) Incroachments made within 40 years.

(*a*) If incroachers are also owners who have a right of common, then the incroachments are to be given as their respective allotments (reckoning the value of the land only). If any particular incroachment is bigger than the allotment to which the incroacher is entitled, the surplus ground is to be treated as ordinary distributable ground.

(*b*) If incroachers are not entitled to right of common, then their incroachments, together with all the buildings on them, are to go to the King as Lord of the Manor; But whereas these incroachments 'consist chiefly of Buildings and Inclosures which have been erected and inclosed, or are held and enjoyed by poor Persons who have, by their own Industry and Labour, built and improved the same, or by Persons who have been at considerable Charges therein,' His Majesty is graciously pleased to grant Leases for 40 years in possession, 'to the End no Person whatsoever may be removed from or deprived of his, her, or their present Possessions.' These leases are to hold good even though not amounting to one-third of the improved annual value of the incroachments. After 40 years, full rents must be taken. *Exception* to (2 *b*).—Small incroachments made for Workhouses, for cottages of Poor chargeable to the Parish, or for Free Schools, are to be assigned to Trustees for benefit of the users.

In spite of above provisions any Incroachments which the Commissioners think fit can be set out for roads, ditches, or fences, etc.

FENCING.—In the paragraph about selling land for expenses it says that the Ring fences to be made by Commissioners, but elsewhere it says fencing to be done by allottees under Commissioners' directions. *Exception.*—Tithe allotments which are to be fenced by other proprietors, and certain other cases. If allottees do not fence, Commissioners do it for them and charge. If any persons think their allotments not worth fencing, then two or more of them whose allotments are contiguous can agree to leave them unenclosed, provided that within 12 months they set up a good stone wall or other substantial Fence between their allotments and those of others. They must keep this wall or fence in repair always.

No sheep or goats to be kept for 7 years in any Inclosure adjoining a boundary fence, unless a special wall or Pale-fence is provided.

EXPENSES.—To be defrayed by sale at auction of parcels of land. Any surplus to be distributed amongst allottees in proportion to allotments. But if a Majority in Value of the persons interested do not wish any land sold, they can signify the same in writing, and can deposit a sufficient sum of money for the purposes of the Act with the Commissioners, and then the provisions for sale cease. Mortgages, in certain cases up to 50s. an acre, to meet expenses are allowed.

ROADS.—In Award, Commissioners are to give orders for laying out roads, etc.

COMPENSATION TO OCCUPIERS.—None.

POWER OF APPEAL.—To Quarter Sessions only, and not in cases where decisions are said to be final and conclusive.

AWARD.—June 25, 1775.   Duchy of Lancaster.

AMENDING ACT, 1774.—(Private, 14 George III. c. 54.)

PARLIAMENTARY PROCEEDINGS.—*February* 21, 1774.—Petition from Sir Bellingham Graham, Bart., Walter Masterman, Esq., and others stating that the land to defray expenses is not yet sold, and asking for an amending Act to enable the Petitioners and others to pay their respective shares instead of the land being sold. Leave given and bill brought in.   March 23, 1774, Petition from Mary Denison of Leeds, widow, and her heirs, who had 'neglected to deliver her Claim of Common Right within the Time limited by the said Act, of which Neglect the Petitioners were not acquainted till after the Third Meeting of the Commissioners; soon after which the Petitioners caused a Claim to be made and delivered, but the said Commissioners refused to accept the same,' asking for relief.   Petition referred to the Committee, with instructions that they have power to make provision in the bill.

March 25.—Petition from several persons asking relief on same grounds as Ellen Oxley (see April 15 below).

Petition from various persons asking that their allotments may be near within their townships.

April 14.—Petition from Daniel Lascelles, Esq., Sir Savile Slingsby, Oliver Coghill, Esq., and the Rev. William Roundell stating that they sent in claims as owners of rights of common; that these claims were referred to the Arbitrators; and that 'it was discovered that Mistakes were made in the Description of such Tenements, or some Parts therof; and that, notwithstanding the said Errors arose merely from Inadvertency, and in no respect altered the Merits of the Petitioners' Claims, the Arbitrators did not think fit to permit the Petitioners to rectify the same,' but disallowed the claims.   The Petitioners ask for reconsideration.

April 15.—Petitions from Rev. Thomas Collins who through 'Inadvertency' had neglected to deliver in his claim of common right in respect of two Copyhold Messuages within the specified time, and from Francis Bedford, ditto, *re* copyhold close.

April 15.—Petition from Ellen Oxley and John Clarke, stating that they preferred claims of common rights to the Commissioners; that these claims were objected to and referred to the Arbitrators, who heard divers claims, several of which they disallowed; that as Ellen Oxley and John Clarke could not produce such evidence as was required by the Arbitrators in support of their claims, they withdrew them; that subsequently a Verdict was produced and read in evidence to the Arbitrators, by means of which similar claims were allowed.

Bill passed both Houses.   Royal Assent.

M<small>AIN</small> F<small>EATURES OF</small> A<small>MENDING</small> A<small>CT</small>.—(Private, 14 George III. c. 54.)
New Commissioner added, Richard Richardson (who was one of
the Surveyors under the former Act).

E<small>XPENSES</small>. — Commissioners can set out allotments without
abatement for sale to 48 persons named, and other allottees
who give notice. In the case of these allottees, the Commissioners
are to settle their quota of charges and assess them accordingly.

The Commissioners in rendering their account may charge one
guinea a day for loss of time, and 10s. a day for expenses.
The surveyors' charges must be 'reasonable and moderate.'
The Commissioners must give an account before they call for
payment, and the account is to be open to inspection at the
charge of 6d.

C<small>LAIMS</small>.—The claims of 32 persons named, which have been
disallowed or withdrawn (1) for want of evidence; (2) for
misnomers; (3) for failure to deliver in time, are to be recon-
sidered. Such claims must be delivered in at the first meeting,
and must not be greater than they were before. They can be
referred on appeal to the Arbitrators as before, but the appellant
must now give security for costs in case the appeal fails.

I<small>NCROACHMENTS</small>. — As some encroachments of over 40 years
standing are found to have no right of common (and so cannot
contribute their share to the Tithe Allotment), tithes can be
charged on these in the form of rent charges.

P<small>OWER OF</small> A<small>PPEAL</small>.—To Quarter Sessions in respect of the
Commissioners' accounts, if any person interested thinks any item
unreasonable, and no satisfactory explanation is forthcoming.

A<small>WARD</small> (for 2 Acts).—June 25, 1775. Duchy of Lancaster.

From the Award we learn as follows :—

Over 2751 Acres were sold to meet the expenses of the Act.

The King received 2344 acres.

The tithe owners received 4694 acres odd.

The remainder was divided amongst over 700 different persons
and bodies. The allottees' shares varied from as much as 1386
acres (Devisees of Sir John Ingelby, Bart.) down to a few perches.

The amount that went to trustees for the use of the poor,
including the various small incroachments (for schools, workhouses,
etc.), which were allowed to stand was about 32 acres.

N<small>OTES ON</small> A<small>FTER</small>-H<small>ISTORY</small>.—*Annals of Agriculture,* vol. xxvii.
p. 292.—In 1793 Arthur Young bought an estate in Knares-
borough Forest of about 4400 acres; 4000 acres of this was
waste land, let out at a rental of 6d. an acre; 2751 acres
of the estate were copyhold, and had been sold to pay the
expenses of inclosure. The rest had formed part of the King's
allotment, and was hired on a long lease. On the 400 acres of
cultivated land there were 3 farmhouses. The game of the
waste was let for £30 a year; peats dug from it produced £6 to
£8 a year, and Arthur Young calculated that one Scotch wether
could be supported per acre.

APPENDIX A (7)

LALEHAM.—ENCLOSURE ACT, 1774

AREA.—(From Award), 918 Acres.

NATURE OF GROUND.—'Several large and open Fields,' 'and likewise certain Wastes and Commons.'

PARLIAMENTARY PROCEEDINGS.—

First attempt, January 31, 1767.—Petition from Sir James Lowther, Lord of the Manor, and from ' divers owners' for enclosure of the open fields and commons, and also of 'a large Pasture called Laleham Burway.' Leave given, but bill dropped after first reading.

Second attempt, December 7, 1767.—Petition for enclosure from Sir James Lowther alone, on behalf of himself and others. Leave given ; bill prepared by Mr. Anthony Bacon and Mr. Fuller, read twice and committed (December 14) to Mr. Bacon, Mr. Jenkinson, Sir James Lowther, and others.

December 21, 1767.—Petition against the bill from various persons, being Owners, Proprietors and Occupiers entitled to Rights of Common, and also Owners of Cow Gates on Laleham Burway, setting forth 'that the Inclosure sought by the said Bill is contrary to the general Sense and Opinion of the Petitioners and others, who compose a Majority in Number of the Owners or Proprietors of, or Persons interested' in the Inclosure, and also stating that the meadow of Laleham Burway is not within the Manor of Laleham, but has been proved by a trial at law to be part of the Manor of Chertsey Beaumont. Petitioners to be heard on Report.

REPORT AND ENUMERATION OF CONSENTS.—*December* 21, 1767 (same day).—Mr. Anthony Bacon reported from the Committee that the Allegations of the Bill were true, and 'that the Parties concerned had given their Consent to the Bill, to the Satisfaction of the Committee (except the Proprietors of Estates, who are entitled to Right of Common in the said Manor, who are rated to the Poors Rate to the Amount of £8, 2s. 0d. per Annum ; and also the Proprietors of Estates, who are intitled to Right of Common in the said Manor, who are rated to the Poors Rate to the Amount of 15s. per Annum, who, being applied to, refused to sign the Bill, but declared they would not oppose the same ; and that the whole of the Estates, in the said Manor, are rated to the Poors Rate to the Amount of £27, 6s. 6d. or thereabouts ; and that the Proprietors of Eighty-six Cow Pastures or Farines, had refused to give their Consent to the said Bill ; and that the whole Number of Cow Pastures, or Farines, are 292½) ; and that no Person appeared before the Committee to oppose the said Bill.'

The consideration of the Report was put off several times ; February 25, 1768, a debate on the subject, resumed on February 29, with the result that the Bill was defeated.

Third Attempt, February 28, 1774.—Petition from various owners and occupiers for enclosure of Laleham and of Laleham Burway. Leave given.   Bill read first time March 18.

March 22.—Petition against the bill from various owners and proprietors of certain Messuages, Cottages, Farmsteads, Lands and Rights of Common, and also owners of Cattle gates on Laleham Burway, setting forth that the 'Bill is contrary to the general Sense and Opinion of the Petitioners and others, who compose a great Majority of the real Owners and Proprietors of, or Persons interested in, the Lands and Grounds intended to be inclosed : and that the Petitioners conceive that the said Bill, if passed into a Law, will in general be injurious to all the Petitioners, and in particular highly burthensome and oppressive to such of them who enjoy small and inconsiderable Rights and Interests therein.'   The Petition again pointed out that Laleham Burway was not in the Manor of Laleham, and that apart from that fact, 'Inclosure would render the Enjoyment thereof' inconvenient if not impracticable.   To be heard by Counsel on second reading.   On April 15 came another Petition from William Barwell, Esq., and other proprietors in and near Chertsey, opposing the enclosure of Laleham Burway as detrimental to the proprietors thereof and to the inhabitants in general of Chertsey, and suggesting that it is 'calculated only for the private Emolument of some One or few' of the proprietors. Petition to lie on table.

May 20.—Bill read a second time.   Both above Petitions read and Counsel against the Bill heard and several witnesses examined. Bill committed.

REPORT AND ENUMERATION OF CONSENTS.—*June* 7, 1774.—Mr. Norton reported from the Committee, that the allegations were true and that the parties concerned had consented '(except the Owners of 13 Houses intitled to Right of Common and the Proprietors of Lands rated to the Land Tax of £35, 4s. 6d. per Annum who refused to sign the Bill, and also except the Proprietors of Lands rated to the Land Tax at 9s. per Annum who could not be found ; and that the whole Number of Houses having Right of Common is 80, and the whole of the said Lands are rated to the Land Tax at £168, 2s. 6d. per Annum).'

'A Clause was offered to be added to the Bill, for giving an Appeal to Quarter Sessions,[1] and this was agreed to.   Other clauses to restrain the Commissioners from setting out a road over Laleham South Field and for saving the rights of tithe owners were also added.

The Bill passed both Houses and received the Royal Assent, June 22, 1774.

MAIN FEATURES OF ACT.—(Private, 14 George III. c. 114.)

[1] This referred to roads only, see Act.

COMMISSIONERS.—Three appointed:—Ralph Gowland, Esq., of Laleham; Thomas Jackman of Guildford; Henry Brumbridge of Thorpe.

Two a quorum. Vacancies to be filled by remaining Commissioners from persons not interested in allotments or division.

Surveyor or surveyors to be appointed by Commissioners.

PAYMENT.—Nothing stated.

A special clause enacting that they are to make the division and allotment on or before December 24, 1774, ' or as soon after as conveniently may be done.' [1]

CLAIMS.—All claims to be delivered in writing with particulars of right or title in respect of which claim is made at 1st or 2nd meeting. If any claim is objected to at 1st, 2nd, or 3rd meeting by another claimant then the Commissioners can hear and determine, and their determination is final and binding. *Exception.*— If a claimant refuses to refer the matter to the Commissioners, then he or she can bring an action at law against the objector on an issue to be settled if necessary by the officer of the Court. But if the claimant whose claim is objected to fails to bring the action, and still refuses to refer the question to the Commissioners, then (after 3 months) he loses all his rights.

There is also a clause ' for the better settling the Rights and Claims of all the said parties so interested and concerned as aforesaid ' by which it is enacted that in case any difference touching rights and claims arises between any of the parties so interested and concerned, the Commissioners have power to hear and finally determine the same, ' which Determination shall be binding and conclusive to all Parties.'

SYSTEM OF DIVISION—SPECIAL PROVISIONS :

Lord of the Manor (Sir James Lowther).—No special provision mentioned, but see Award.

Clause to say that the Lord of the Manor's rights are not to be prejudiced by the Act '(except such Common of Pasture, or other Rights of Common, as can or may be claimed by or belonging to him).'

Tithe Owners.—Nothing in the Act to affect any right or title to tithes.

Provision for the Poor.—Nothing mentioned, but see Award.

Allotment.—The Commissioners are to make the allotments amongst the several persons 'intitled to any Lands, Grounds, Right of Common or other Property,' in proportion to ' the real value of their several and respective Shares and Interests and Right of Common or other Property through and over the said Common Fields, or other the Premises to be allotted and divided.' Quantity, Quality and Convenience are to be considered. The Commissioners are to draw up an Award as soon as is convenient

---

[1] It took twenty-nine years.

after allotment, and 'the several Allotments, Partitions and Divisions so made' in and by the Award 'shall be and are hereby declared to be binding and conclusive unto and upon all and every the several Parties interested in the said open and common Fields, common Pastures, and commonable Lands.' Allotments must be accepted within 12 months after award. (Saving clause for infants, etc.) Failure to accept excludes allottee from all benefits in lands and estates allotted to any other person, and the Com missioners can appoint a Bailiff or rent receiver with full power to manage the allotment in question, any surplus of profits to go to the original allottee who has refused to accept—until he changes his mind and accepts it.

Allotments are to be of the same tenure as the estates for which they are claimed. The Herbage of the Lanes and Public Roads to be allotted to such person or persons as the Commissioners direct.

A special clause to exempt Laleham Burway from division.

INCROACHMENTS.—Not mentioned.

FENCING.—No instructions given; except that when an allotment abuts on the highway, the fences are to be kept up by the owner.

EXPENSES.—To be paid by the 'Owners and Proprietors and Persons interested of and in the said Lands and Grounds' in such proportion as the Commissioners decide. If persons refuse to pay, Commissioners can distrain or else enter on allotment and take rents. Allotments may be mortgaged up to 40s. an acre.

COMPENSATION TO OCCUPIERS AND OTHERS.—Leases at rack-rent 'shall cease and be totally extinguished' if Commissioners give notice; the owner giving such compensation to the tenant as the Commissioners direct.

Underwoods, hedges, shrubs, etc., are not to be grubbed up or destroyed before allotment without special permission from the Commissioners, but are to remain for the benefit of the allottee, the allottee paying the former owner such compensation as the Commissioners direct.

Also, If any land with woods, underwoods, hedges, shrubs, etc., is allotted to someone who does not already hold it, then the first owner may enter and fell, grub up and cut down the underwood, hedges, etc., and take them away, unless the same have been allotted by the Commissioners to the new owner.

POWER OF APPEAL.—Only with respect to roads, and then to Quarter Sessions only.

ARRANGEMENTS BETWEEN ACT AND AWARD.—Not mentioned.

AWARD.—Date, 1803. Record Office. During the 29 years between the Act and the Award 10 Commissioners were concerned, (A) Ralph Gowland, (B) Thomas Jackman, (C) Henry Brumbridge, (D) George Wheatley, (E) John Baynes Garforth,

(F) Sir Philip Jennings Clarke, (G) Richard Penn, (H) Sir William Gibbons (see Stanwell), (I) Thomas Chapman, (J) George Kinderley, as follows :—

C refused to act straight away. A then appointed D. B refused to sit in 1781. A and D appointed E. A died 1787. D and E appointed F. F died 1788. D and E appointed G. D died 1802. E and G were desirous of being discharged from acting further. H was 'duly appointed.' E and G refused to act. H appointed I and J. H, I and J gave the award.

Distribution of Land.—918 acres odd, exclusive of roads, were divided out as follows :—

	Acres.
Lord Lowther [1] (including 18½ for his rights of soil), .	626½
Six *other owners* (in shares varying from 68¼ to John Coggan, Martha his wife, to 16¼ to the Vicar, .	223¼
Twenty-three owners (in shares varying from 7½ acres, Messrs. Blackwell and Elson, to 16 perches John Goodwin,	51¼
Churchwardens and Overseers for the Poor (see below),	13
Gravel Pit, ...	4
	918

The destiny of the 13 acres vested in the Churchwardens and Overseers is described thus: they are 'for the use of the poor of Laleham, as a compensation for their loss of Common, the said 13 acres in lieu of the herbage of the roads the use of which by the poor was thought might be injurious to the young quick by the grazing of their cattle on the roads, and as the Majority of the Proprietors have agreed' to give up this 13 acres as an equivalent for the Herbage, the Herbage is given to the proprietors instead.

The Churchwardens and Overseers may do one of two things with the 13 acres plot, they may (1) lease it out for 21 years at 'the best and greatest rent' to a parishioner: (the plan shows the 13 acres to have been wedged in between Lord Lowther's fields), or (2) 'if they should think it more advantageous to the parish to raise a certain sum of money upon it for the Purpose of erecting a Workhouse' they may let it out for 60 years.

APPENDIX A (8)

Louth, Lincolnshire.—Enclosure Act, 1801

Area.—In Petition for Enclosure, about 1770 Acres.

| In Act | „ | „ | 1854 | „ |
| In Award | „ | „ | 1701 | „ |

Nature of Ground.—'Open Common Fields, Meadows, Pastures, and other Commonable Lands and Waste Grounds.'

---

[1] Sir James Lowther, afterwards Lord Lowther, who had originally petitioned for enclosure, had died in 1802. He was succeeded by his cousin, Wordsworth's patron.

Description from Eden, vol. ii. p. 395 (June 1795).—' Most of the land belonging to this town lies in 2 large common fields, which are fallowed and cropped alternately: in several parts of these common fields there are large tracts of waste land, upon which a great number of poor people summer each a cow, which in winter go at large in these fields. The Poor complain heavily of the farmers, saying, "That they encroach on their property"; and the farmers say, "That the Poor take the opportunity of eating their corn with their cattle." Tithes are here taken in kind.'

PARLIAMENTARY PROCEEDINGS.—*March* 11, 1801.—Petition for enclosure from various persons, owners, or interested in estates in Louth. Leave given. Bill read twice, and committed on June 5. Same day, Petition of various Freeholders and Proprietors of old inclosed land against the bill; setting forth that there are ' now more than 750 acres of old inclosed Meadows and Pasture Lands very contiguous to the Town; and that the Soil of these Open Fields is best adapted for Wheat and Beans, of which it produces excellent Crops alternately, and is in a very high State of Cultivation; and that there is no Waste Land, as the Commons are a very rich Pasture, which keep a large Quantity of Cattle, the Property of a great many industrious People, who have Common Rights, and are enabled by their Common Rights to maintain their Families, and increase the Population and Prosperity of the Town of Louth'; and asking the House either to reject the Bill ' or not to suffer that Part thereof to pass into a Law, which would compel the Petitioners to relinquish Part of their Old Inclosed Land against their Consent, but permit them to remain subject to the Tythes they have hitherto paid.' Petition referred to the Committee. All to have Voices.

REPORT AND ENUMERATION OF CONSENTS.—*June* 17, 1801.—Mr. Annesley reported from the Committee that the Standing Orders had been complied with; that the allegations were true; and that the parties concerned had consented ' (except the Proprietors of Messuages, Cottages and Toftsteads, having Right of Common of the Annual Value of £465, 10s. who refused to sign the Bill, and also except the Proprietors of Messuages, Cottages and Toftsteads having Right of Common of the Annual Value of £177, 15s. who were neuter; and that the Whole of the Property interested in the Inclosure is of the Annual Value of £1670, 12s.).' The Bill passed both Houses. Royal Assent, June 24, 1801.

MAIN FEATURES OF ACT.—(Local and Personal, 41 George III. c. 124.)

COMMISSIONERS.—Three appointed. (1) John Renshaw of Owthorpe, Notts, gentleman, on behalf of Tithe owners;
(2) Isaac Leatham of Barton-le-Street, Yorks, gentleman, on behalf of the majority in value of the proprietors of common fields,

meadows and commonable Lands and Waste Grounds (tithe owners excluded);

(3) John Parkinson of Asgarby, Lincs, gentleman, on behalf of the majority in value of the proprietors of ancient inclosures and of Common Right Houses and Toftsteads (tithe owners excluded).

Two to be a quorum. Vacancies to be filled by the party represented from persons 'not interested in the inclosure.'

Surveyor appointed by name. Vacancy to be filled by majority in value of all those interested.

PAYMENT TO COMMISSIONERS.—2 guineas each a day. Surveyor to be paid what Commissioners think fit.

CLAIMS.—All claims to be delivered in with full particulars at meetings held for the purpose; no claims to be received afterwards except for some special cause. Full notice of a meeting to examine claims to be given. Commissioners can determine on claims, but if any claimant is dissatisfied with their determination he or she can try the matter at law by bringing an action on a feigned issue against any person interested in the Lands. Jury's Verdict to be final. Defendant's costs to be borne by all or some of the persons interested, as the Commissioners determine. If no notice of such action is given, then the determination of the Commissioners on claims is final and conclusive. But the Commissioners are not to determine on questions of title which can be tried at law. Such suits are not to impede inclosure, and the allotment is to be set out to the person in possession. Claimants in respect of Messuages, Cottages, Tofts, or Toftsteads need not prove usage of Right of Common.

SYSTEM OF DIVISION—SPECIAL PROVISIONS:

The Lord of the Manor (*i.e.* The Warden and Six Assistants of the Town of Louth and Free School of King Edward the Sixth) to have one twentieth in value of the Waste Lands and other Lands which are not the separate Property of any Person or Persons; in particular a piece of Common called *Julian Bower* with the Trees on it is to be included as part of the Allotment.

Tithe Owners.—(1) The Worshipful Roger Kedington, M.A., Prebendary of the Prebendal of Louth in Lincoln, impropriator of the Rectory of Louth, and patron of Vicarage; (2) William Hutton, Esq., lessee of above for 3 Lives; (3) Rev. Wolley Jolland, Vicar of Louth, entitled to Vicarage House and Garden and also to a Right of Common, and to small Tythes.

(1) Allotments which Commissioners consider equal in value and a full Compensation for present unenclosed Glebe Lands and Rights of Common.

(2) Such pieces of the Lands and Grounds to be enclosed (of every kind) as shall equal in value $\frac{1}{5}$ part of all the open, arable and tillage land '(although the same may be occasionally used in Meadow or Pasture)' ' and which are not Waste Lands.'

(3) Such pieces of the Lands and Grounds to be enclosed as

shall, in Commissioners' judgment, equal in value all the Great and Small Tythes and other Ecclesiastical Dues on ancient Inclosed Arable and Tillage Lands.

(4) Such pieces of the Lands and Grounds to be enclosed as shall equal in value $\frac{1}{8}$ part of all the ancient enclosed Meadow and Pasture Lands, Grounds and Homesteads ' (not being Glebe Lands, consecrated Burying Grounds, or Orchards or Gardens),' and of the Near East Field, Far East Field, Great Roarings, Butter Closes, and all other open and commonable Meadow or Pasture Lands, Commons and Grounds to be inclosed which are subject to tithes and ecclesiastical dues.

Arrangements for Owners of Old Inclosures.—(See Petition on March 11, 1801). Owners of old Inclosures who have not sufficient allotments in the land to be inclosed, to contribute from them their proportion of the above Tithe allotments, can *either* have part of their old inclosures allotted instead (with their consent) *or* pay such gross sum of money towards the expenses of the Act as the Commissioners direct, whilst a portion of the land to be inclosed is given to the tithe owner.

After this Act the only Tithes which remain are those for Gardens and Orchards, and Tithes of Mills, Pigs, Poultry, Bees and Honey; also Surplice Fees, Easter Offering and Mortuaries are untouched.

For Repair of Roads.—Sufficient pieces or parcels to be vested in the Surveyor of Highways.

For Fairs.—A piece of ground called ' The Quarry ' is to be allotted to the Lords of the Manor for the holding of Fairs.

Provision for the Poor.—None.

Allotment of Residue.—Amongst the various persons interested with due regard to Quantity, Quality and Situation. No undue Preference to be shown. The open fields to be allotted to their present owners, unless the owners ask for allotment elsewhere.

If an allottee is dissatisfied with his allotment, the Commissioners must hear his complaints, but their determination is final till the Award is made.

The Award is to be drawn up and read over to the Proprietors and all the orders and directions, penalties, impositions, regulations and determinations of the Award are to be final, binding and conclusive on all parties.

If an allottee refuses to accept or molests anyone else who accepts, he or she must pay the penalties decided on by the Commissioners.

The tenure of allotments is to be the same as that of the estate in virtue of which they are claimed.

The grass on the road allotment is to be allotted to such person or persons as the Commissioners direct, or else be applied for some general, Parochial, or other use.

No person is to graze cattle, dig, cultivate or plant in any road or way under penalty of a fine of £3.

INCROACHMENTS.—Incroachments 20 years old and over are to stand.   Incroachments made within 20 years are to be treated as part of the Commons to be divided, but, if the Commissioners think it fit and convenient they can be allotted to the person in possession, without considering the value of erections or improvements (1) as the whole or part of his allotment; (2) as his allotment, the allottee paying such extra sum of money as the Commissioners think fit (this is supposing the allotment he is entitled to is less in value than the incroachment); (3) for such sum of money as the Commissioners think fit (this is supposing he is not entitled to any allotment).

But if the Commissioners do not think it fit and convenient to allot an incroachment to the person in possession, they may (1) sell it at public auction and apply the money to the purposes of the Act; (2) allot it to someone else, in which case a 'reasonable' sum of money is to be given to the dispossessed owner, the new allottee paying the whole or part of it.

FENCING.—To be done by the several proprietors as the Commissioners direct.

Exception.—(1) The Tithe Owners' allotments are to be fenced by the other proprietors.

(2) In the case of allotments to Churchwardens, Overseers or Colleges, Chantries, Charities, etc., the Commissioners are to fence, deducting such portion of the allotments as is equal to the expenses of fencing and to these allottees' share of the expenses of the Act.

The portion deducted is to be divided amongst the other Proprietors who have to pay the expenses.

If any allottee refuses to fence, the Commissioners can do it and charge the expenses on the allotment, appointing a Bailiff to receive rents and money.

EXPENSES.—The expenses of the Act are to be defrayed by all the Proprietors benefited in proportion to the value of their allotments, *except* the Lords of the Manor and the Tithe owners in respect of their special allotments, and except the holders in trust for public bodies.   (These last have had a portion deducted.   See Fencing.)

The cost of the survey of the land to be inclosed is to be borne by those interested in it, and the cost of the survey of the old inclosures by the proprietors of old inclosures.

Mortgages are allowed under certain conditions (except to Tithe owners) up to £4 an acre.

Commissioners are to keep accounts which must be open to inspection.   A penalty is specified for failure to keep them.   Money amounting to £50 is to be paid in to a Banker.

Proprietors (tithe owners excepted) can sell their Common Rights or allotments before the Award.

COMPENSATION.—(1) Leases at Rack Rent of any land to be inclosed, either alone or together with any Messuages, Cottages, Toftsteads, etc., to be void ; the proprietor paying the lessee such satisfaction as the Commissioners direct. *Exception.*—No lease of any Messuage, Cottage, Toftstead, Lands, Hereditaments or ancient Estate in respect of which allotment is made for Right of Common is to be void ; but the allotments made to these are to belong to the proprietors who must pay to the lessees such satisfaction as the Commissioners direct.

(2) Satisfaction (adjudged by the Commissioners) is to be given for standing crops by the new allottee, unless the owner of the crops likes to come and reap them.

Satisfaction is also to be given to the occupier for ploughing, tilling and manuring, but no Swarth 6 years old is to be ploughed till allotments are entered on.

(3) If any trees, shrubs, etc., go with the ground to a new proprietor, the old proprietor is to be paid their valuation (as judged by the Commissioners).

ARRANGEMENTS BETWEEN ACT AND AWARD.—The Commissioners are to have absolute power to determine the course of husbandry.

ROADS.—Commissioners to have power to set out and stop up roads and footpaths (turnpike roads excepted), but are to give notice in a local newspaper *re* public carriage roads, and any person who thinks himself or herself aggrieved can appeal to Quarter Sessions whose decision is final.

If an ancient road or path is shut up, the person for whose accommodation it is shut up may be required by the Commissioners to pay compensation either (1) to person or persons injured or (2) for general expenses of the Act.

POWER OF APPEAL.—To Quarter Sessions only, and not where Commissioners' determinations are said to be final.

AWARD.—Date, 1806. Record Office.

MAIN FEATURES OF AWARD :—

	a.	r.	p.
Whole Area divided out, ...	1701	3	21
Tithe Owners (various allotments), in all, .	584	3	6[1]
One of the tithe holders also receives, .	24	3	4
The Lords of the Manor, ...	109	2	4[2]
Lords of the Manor, as Guardians of the Free School, ...	69	3	19
Allotments for repairing roads, . .	2	0	3
For Fairs, ...	4	1	12
	795	1	8

[1] These allotments were fenced by the other proprietors and did not bear any of the expenses of the Act.

[2] Including 8 acres 1 rood 5 perches for rights of soil.

The remainder is divided out amongst 130 allottees :—

From 50—100 acres 4 ⎫
From 30— 50 acres 7 ⎪
From 10— 30 acres 10 ⎬ Above 10 acres 21
                  ⎯⎯ ⎪
                  21 ⎭

From 1—10 acres 42

From ½ acre—1 acre 22 ⎫
From ¼ acre—½ acre 10 ⎪
Below ¼ acre   35[1] ⎬ Below 1 acre   67
                   ⎯⎯ ⎪   ⎯⎯⎯
                   67 ⎭   130

The smallest allotments are, Ann Metcalf, Spinster, 14 perches, which she must fence on the N. and W. sides; Ann Hubbard, Widow, 15 perches, which she must fence on the S. and W. sides.

These, like the other small allotments, are in lieu of Right of Common and all other Interest.

APPENDIX A (9)

SIMPSON, BUCKS.—ENCLOSURE ACT, 1770

AREA.—Not specified anywhere. The annual value unenclosed is stated to be £773, so the acreage was probably over 1500.

NATURE OF GROUND.—Open and Common Fields, Lammas Grounds and Pastures.

PARLIAMENTARY PROCEEDINGS.—

First Attempt, December 13, 1762.—Petition from Walden Hanmer, Esq., Lord of the Manor, William Edge, Gentleman, and other owners and proprietors, stating that the holdings are at present intermixed and dispersed, that the land in its present state is in great measure incapable of Improvement, and that if it were divided and inclosed great Benefit would accrue, and asking for leave to bring in a Bill to enclose. Leave was given, and the Bill passed its second reading and was sent to Committee. On March 16, 1763, came a petition against it from John Goodman and Nicholas Lucas, Gentlemen, and other owners and proprietors against the bill, 'alleging that the Petitioners are Owners and Proprietors of Four Fifth Parts, and upwards, of the said Fields, Grounds, and Pastures, so intended to be inclosed, and of several Rights and Privileges incident thereto,' stating that the bill would be greatly detrimental to all of them and 'tend to the Ruin of many of them,' and asking to be heard by Counsel against the bill. Petition to be heard when the bill was reported.

---

[1] Nine of them women.

REPORT AND ENUMERATION OF CONSENTS.—*March 25, 1763.*—Mr. Lowndes reported from the Committee, that the allegations were true and that 'the Parties concerned had given their Consent to the Bill, to the Satisfaction of the Committee (except Michael Woodward, Nicholas Lucas, senior, Lewis Goodman, who, being asked to sign a Bill testifying their Consent, and whose Interest in the said Lands and Grounds amounts to £31 a Year, or thereabouts, but the Witness could not ascertain the Interest of the said Lewis Goodman and Thomas Goodman, said that they had no Objection to the Inclosure, but did not care to sign, and also except Luke Goodman and Edward Chad, whose Interest in the said Lands and Grounds is £16 a Year; Edward Chad said he was by no means for it, and Luke Goodman said, he would neither meddle nor make; and also except Joseph Etheridge, a Minor, whose Interest in the said Lands and Grounds is £38 a Year; and Mary Etheridge, his Guardian whose Interest in the said Lands and Grounds is £16 a Year, said, she never was for it, as being a Woman, and having nobody to look after her Fencing; and also except —— Loughton, John Goodman, and Son, whose Interest in the said Lands and Grounds is £24 a Year; John Goodman said, he would lose his Life before he would lose his Land; his Son said, he did not care to meddle; and also except John Goodman, who, being asked to sign a Bill, testifying his Consent, and whose Interest in the said Lands and Grounds is £55 a year, said he would not sign it; and except Sear Newman, whose Interest in the said Lands and Grounds amounts to £30 a Year, who said he had no Objection to it, but did not care to meddle or make, upon Account of his Father being so much against it; and it appeared to your Committee, by Articles of Agreement, dated the 31st Day of December, 1761, that the said John Goodman and Sear Newman did thereby consent and agree to an Inclosure of all the Open and Commonable Fields, Lands, Cow Pasture, and Fields, within the said Parish of Simpson, and to pay their respective Proportions of the Expence of an Act of Parliament; and other the necessary Expences attending the same; and also except John Newman, whose Interest in the said Lands and Grounds is £30 a Year, who said he would not sign it; and also except Nicholas Lucas the younger, whose Interest in the said Fields is £36 a Year, who said he had no Objection to sign, if the Cow Pasture had been left open; and also except Daniel Lucas, whose Interest in the said Lands and Grounds is £25 a Year, who refused signing; and also except George Wilkes, whose Interest in the said Lands and Grounds is £1, 10s. a Year, who said he had no Occasion to sign, because he had agreed with Mr. Hanmer for the Purchase of his Commons; and also except Richard Goodman, Edward Ashwell, for a Minor, Edward Cooke and John Fox, whose Interest in the said Lands and Grounds together amounts to £5, 10s. a Year, who were not applied to; and also except Sarah Hawes, Widow, who is lately dead; and also except George Stone, whose Interest in the said Lands and Grounds is £3 a Year, who was not applied to, because he had sold his Interest to Mr. Hanmer, who has consented to the Bill; and also except Six out of Eight of the Feoffees of Lands belonging to the Poor of Simpson, which Lands are of the yearly Value of £24; and also except the Feoffees of certain Charity Lands and Grounds, of the yearly Value of £16; William Cooper, one of the Feoffees, being asked to sign a Bill testifying his Consent, said he was against it; and that the yearly Value of the said Lands and Grounds, in the said Fields, Cow Pasture, Common Meadows, Lammas Grounds, and Waste Grounds, amounts to Seven Hundred Ninety-nine Pounds, Fifteen Shillings, or thereabouts;) . . . .'

After the Report was read, Counsel was heard for the Petitioners against the Bill, but the Bill was read a third time and sent up to the Lords.   March 29, it was read a second time, and a Petition against it from John Goodman, John Newman, Nicholas Lucas and others was received.   April 14, Lord St. John of Bletsoe reported it without amendments from the Committee, but it was defeated on its third reading.

Second Attempt, January 15, 1765.—Walden Hanmer, Esquire, the Rector, and others again petitioned for enclosure. Leave was given to bring in a bill, but nothing came of it.

Third Attempt, February 6, 1770.—Walden Hanmer, Esquire, and others again petitioned for enclosure. Leave was given, and a bill read twice and sent to Committee.

March 6, 1770.—' A Petition of the Major Part of the Owners and Proprietors' against the Bill, stating ' that the Petitioners are very well satisfied with the Situation and Convenience of their respective Lands and Properties in their present uninclosed State,' and that the Bill will do them great Injury.

REPORT AND ENUMERATION OF CONSENTS.—*March* 6, 1770 (same day).—Mr. Kynaston reported that the allegations were true, and that the Parties concerned had consented to the Bill 'to the Satisfaction of the Committee,' with the following exceptions— Five Persons with property of the annual value of £192, 10s.; Sear Numan, with property of annual value of £20, 15s., ' who said he must do as his Father would have him '; John Lucas the younger, with property of the annual value of 15s.; George Cross, ' who would not say any Thing,' with property of the annual value of £5; Elizabeth Mead, ' who said she should sell when inclosed,' with property of the annual value of £2, 10s.; and Five Persons, who said they would not oppose the Bill, with property of the annual value of £77, 10s. The annual value of ' the whole of the Estates in the said Fields intended to be inclosed ' was given as £773. The Bill passed the Commons and the Lords, where a petition against it was considered. It received the Royal Assent on March 29, 1770.

MAIN FEATURES OF ACT.—(Private, 10 George III. c. 42.)

COMMISSIONERS.—Three appointed. (1) The Rev. John Lord of Drayton Parslow, Clerk ; (2) Thomas Harrison of Stoney Stratford, Gentleman; (3) Francis Burton of Aynho, Northamptonshire, Gentleman. Two a quorum. Vacancies to be filled up by remaining Commissioner or Commissioners from persons 'not interested in the Division and Inclosure.' No particulars of payment.

A survey to be made by a surveyor nominated by Commissioners.

CLAIMS.—The Commissioners are 'to hear and finally determine' any differences about Interests and Rights.

SYSTEM OF DIVISION—SPECIAL PROVISIONS:

Provisions for Lord of the Manor.—None (as there seems to have been no common or waste ground concerned).

His manorial rights, right of common excepted, to go on as before.

Provisions for Tithe Owners.—The Rector to have (1) such parcels of Land as shall be a full equivalent of his glebe lands and common Right; (2) ⅟₇ part of all the rest, 'Quantity as well as Quality considered,' as full compensation for all Tithes.

In the case of old inclosures which have allotments, the Commissioners can give him either part of these or part of the owner's allotment in place of tithes, and in case of old inclosures, etc., which have no allotment, they remain subject to Tithes.

The Rector is exonerated from keeping a Bull and a Boar.

Provision for Gravel, Sand, etc.—See Allotment of Residue.

Provision for Poor.—None.

Allotment of Residue.—As soon as is convenient after the survey is made, the Commissioners are to set out and allot the land in proportion to the respective interests and right of common of the claimants, 'having a due Regard to the Situation and Convenience, as well as to the Quantity and Quality of the Lands and Grounds.' The award, which contains their decision, is to be final and conclusive.

Allotments must be accepted within 12 calendar months. Failure to accept excludes the allottee from all Benefits under the Act. (Saving clause for infants, etc.)

If material is needed for the roads, the surveyors may, under an order from two J. P.'s not interested in the inclosure, enter on any allotment and take it, except where the allotment is a garden, park, orchard paddock, wood, or ground planted with an avenue of trees for the ornament of any House.

INCROACHMENTS.—Not mentioned ; as no common.

FENCING.—To be done 'at the proper Costs and Charges' of the respective allottees, as directed by the Commissioners, except in the case of the Rector, whose allotment is to be fenced for him by the other proprietors, and whose fences, if they abut on a highway, are to be kept up by the other proprietors for 7 years. The fencing of all allotments must be carried out within 12 months after the Award, and if any person refuse to fence, the Commissioners, on complaint of a neighbour, can do the fencing and charge it to the recalcitrant owner, distraining on his goods, if necessary. If any one proprietor has more than his fair share of fencing to do, then the Commissioners can make the other proprietors pay something towards it. If any allotment abuts on a common field, fencing is not compulsory.

EXPENSES.—These are to be paid by the Owners and Proprietors 'by an equal Pound Rate according to the Value of the Lands and Grounds each Person shall have allotted to him.' Proprietors are allowed to mortgage their allotments up to 40s. an acre in order to meet expenses.

COMPENSATION TO OCCUPIERS.—All rack-rent leases are to be null and void, the owners making such satisfaction to the tenants as the Commissioners think reasonable.

ROADS.—Commissioners to have full power to set out and shut up roads, footpaths, etc.

POWER OF APPEAL.—To Quarter Sessions only ; and not in cases where the Commissioners' decisions are final and conclusive, as, *e.g.*, on claims and allotments.

ARRANGEMENTS BETWEEN ACT AND AWARD.—Directly the Act is passed, till the allotments are made, the Commissioners are to have 'the sole, intire and absolute Management, Order and Direction' of all the land with regard to cultivation, flocks, etc., any usage to the contrary notwithstanding.

AWARD.—Bucks, with Clerk of the Peace or Clerk of the Council. Date, April 26, 1771.

APPENDIX A (10)

STANWELL.—ENCLOSURE ACT, 1789

AREA.—According to Act 'by Estimation about 3000 Acres,' but Award gives 2126 Acres only.

NATURE OF GROUND.—'Large open fields, Arable and Meadow Grounds, and Lammas Lands, about 1621 acres, and also several Commons, Moors and Waste Lands,' about 505 acres (unstinted).

PARLIAMENTARY PROCEEDINGS.—

First Attempt, December 12, 1766.—Petition for Enclosure from the Lord of the Manor, the Impropriator of the Great Tythes, the Vicar, and the most considerable Proprietors. Leave given. Bill read first time, January 27, 1767.

February 18, 1767.—Petition against the bill from various

'Owners or Occupiers of Cottages or Tenements in the parish of Stanwell,' setting forth 'that the Petitioners in Right of their said Cottages and Tenements are severally intitled to Common of Pasture for their Cattle and Sheep upon all the said Commons, Moors, and Waste Lands, at all Times of the Year, except for Sheep, without any Stint whatsoever, as also a Right of intercommoning their Cattle and Sheep, with those of the Tenants of divers other Manors, at all Times in the Year, upon the large Common called *Hounslow Heath*: and the Petitioners in the Rights aforesaid, are also intitled to and do enjoy Common of Turbary on the said Commons and Heath, and that the Lord of the Manor of Stanwell lately caused part of the said Moors within the said Parish, to be fenced in, and inclosed with Pales for his own sole and separate Use, without the Consent of the Petitioners and other Persons intitled to a Right of Common therein, which said Pales have been since pulled down by several of the Petitioners and others, against whom several Actions have been commenced by the Lord of the said Manor, in order to try the Petitioners' said Right of Common therein, all which Actions are now depending; and that the Petitioners apprehend, and believe, in case the said Bill should pass into a Law, the Legality of the Petitioners' said Rights will be left to the Determination of Commissioners unqualified to judge of the same: and that in case the Petitioners' said Rights should be allowed by such Commissioners, that no adequate Compensation in Land will or can be awarded to the Petitioners for the same: and that the dividing and inclosing the said Commons, Moors, and Waste Lands within the said Parish, will greatly injure and distress many. . . .' Another petition was presented on the same day from George Richard Carter, Esq., Samuel Clark, Esq., Jervoise Clark, Esq., John Bullock, Esq., and several others, being owners and proprietors of Farms and Lands in the parish of Stanwell, setting forth that the Petitioners, as also the Owners of near 100 Cottages or Tenements within the said Parish, and their respective Tenants are entitled to right of pasture as in the petition given above, and stating that inclosing will be attended with great inconvenience.

On February 26 came yet another petition from owners and occupiers in the parishes of Harmondsworth, Harlington, Cranford, Heston, Isleworth, Twickenham, Teddington, Hampton, Hanworth, Feltham, and East Bedfont in Middlesex, setting forth that the Commons and Waste Lands in the parish of Stanwell were part of Hounslow Heath, over which the petitioners had right of pasture, and stating that if the part of the Heath in Stanwell parish were inclosed it would be very injurious to all the owners and occupiers in the parish of Stanwell, except to the Lord of the Manor, and would also be prejudicial to the petitioners.

All these petitions were ordered to lie on the table till the second reading, which took place on February 26. Counsel was heard for and against the Bill; the motion that the Bill should be

committed was defeated by 34 to 17 votes, and thus the farmers
were able to parade along Pall Mall with cockades in their hats.[1]

Second Attempt, February 20, 1789.—Petition from the Lord
of the Manor (Sir William Gibbons), the Vicar and others
for enclosure. Leave given. Bill read twice.

REPORT AND ENUMERATION OF CONSENTS.—*March* 30, 1789.
—Sir William Lemon reported from the Committee that the
Standing Orders had been complied with ; that the allegations
were true, and that the parties concerned had given their consent
' (except the Proprietors of Estates of the Annual Value of £164,
14s. or thereabouts who refused to sign the Bill, and also except
the Proprietors of £220, 5s. 8d. per Annum or thereabouts who
did not chuse to sign the Bill, but made no Objection to the
Inclosure, and also except some small Proprietors of about £76
per Annum who could not be found, and that the whole Property
belonging to Persons interested in the Inclosure amounts to
£2,929, 5s. 4d. per annum or thereabouts).' Bill passed both
Houses. Royal Assent, May 19, 1789.

MAIN FEATURES OF ACT.—(Private, 29 George III. c. 15.)

COMMISSIONERS.—Edward Hare of Castor, Northampton, Gentleman ; William Young of Chancery Lane, Gentleman ; Richard
Davis of Lewknor, Oxford, Gentleman. Two a quorum. Vacancies
to be filled by remaining Commissioners from persons not interested
in the Inclosure.

SURVEYOR.—One named. Vacancy to be filled by Commissioners.

PAYMENT TO COMMISSIONERS.—£2, 2s. for each working day.
Nothing about Surveyor's pay.

Special clause that certain Surveys already made may be
used.

CLAIMS.—All claims about Right of Common ' and all Differences
and Disputes which shall arise between the Parties interested, or
claiming to be interested in the said intended Division and
Inclosure, or any of them concerning their respective Rights,
Shares, and Interests in the said open Fields, arable and meadow
Grounds, and Lammas Lands, Commons, Moors, and Waste
Grounds, or their respective Allotments, Shares and Proportions
which they, or any of them ought to have' in the division, are to
be heard and determined by the Commissioners. This determination is to be binding and conclusive on all parties ; except with
regard to matters of Title which can be tried at law.

SYSTEM OF DIVISION—SPECIAL PROVISIONS :

(1) *Lords of the Manor* (Sir William Gibbons, Thomas Somers
Cocks, Esq, and Thomas Graham, Esq.).—One sixteenth part of
the residue of the Moors and Waste Lands, when roads and allotment for gravel have been deducted.

---

[1] See p. 55.

(2) *Tithe Owners.*—Not to be prejudiced by the Act. Land still to be liable to tithes as before.

(3) *Gravel Pits.*—For roads and for use of inhabitants ; not more than 3 acres.

(4) *Provision for Poor.*—Such parcel as the Commissioners think proper ('not exceeding in the whole 30 Acres'). To be vested in the Lords of the Manor, the Vicar, Churchwardens, and Overseers, and to be let out, and the rents and profits thereof to be given for the benefit of such occupiers and inhabitants as do not receive parish relief, or occupy lands and tenements of more than £5 a year, or receive any allotment under the Act.

Allotment of Residue.—The land to be divided among the various persons interested 'in proportion and according (Quantity, Quality and Situation considered) to their several and respective Shares, Rights, and Interests therein.' If the Commissioners think that any of the allotments in the common fields are too small to be worth enclosing they may lay such proprietors' allotments together.

Certain principles to be followed.—Owners of cottage commons who are also proprietors of lands in the open fields are to have their allotment in virtue of their Right of Common added to the other allotment to which they are entitled.

Owners of cottage commons who do not possess land in the open fields as well, are to have their allotments put all together for a cow common, with such stint as the Commissioners decide. But if they wish for separate allotments they may have them.

Allotments must be accepted within six months after award. Failure to accept excludes allottee from all 'Benefit Advantage' by this Act, and also from all estate right or interest in any other allotment. (Saving clause for infants, etc.)

The award is to be drawn up; 'and the Award, and all Orders, Directions, Regulations, and Determinations therein contained, and thereby declared, shall be binding and conclusive to and upon all Persons whomsoever.' Tenure of allotments to be that of estates in virtue of which they are granted. Copyhold allotments can be enfranchised if wished, the Commissioners deducting a certain amount as compensation for Lord of the Manor. Allottees lose all Right of Common on any common in adjoining parishes.

INCROACHMENTS.—Not mentioned in Act.

EXCHANGES.—Allowed (as always). Also former exchanges can be confirmed by the Commissioners 'notwithstanding any legal or natural Incapacity of any Proprietor or Owner having made any such Exchanges.'

FENCING.—To be done by allottees. If any person has an undue proportion Commissioners have power to equalise.

Exceptions.—(1) Fences of cow common allotment for those who have Cottage Common only (see above), which are to be made and kept in repair by the other proprietors; but if these allottees choose to have separate allotments they must fence them themselves.

(2) Allotment for the Poor (30 acres).—To be fenced by other proprietors.

(3) Allotments to charities, ditto.

If any allottee refuses to fence or keep fences in repair his neighbour can complain to a J.P. 'not interested' in the inclosure, and the J.P. can either make an order, or else empower the complainant to enter and carry the work out at the charge of the owner.

EXPENSES.—Part of the Commons and Wastes to be sold by auction to cover expenses. Any surplus to be laid out by Commissioners on some lasting improvements; any deficit to be made up by proprietors as Commissioners direct.

Commissioners are to keep accounts which must be open to inspection.

To meet expenses allotments may be mortgaged up to 40s. an acre.

COMPENSATION TO OCCUPIERS.—Leases at rack or extended rents of any of the land to be inclosed by this Act to be void, owners paying tenants such compensation as Commissioners direct. Satisfaction is also to be given for standing crops, for ploughing, manuring, and tilling.

ARRANGEMENTS BETWEEN THE ACT AND AWARD.—The Commissioners are to direct the course of husbandry 'as well with respect to the Stocking as to the Plowing, Tilling, Cropping, Sowing, and Laying down the same.'

ROADS.—Full power to set out roads and footpaths and to shut up others. Turnpike roads excluded.

POWER OF APPEAL.—None.

AWARD.—Record Office.

From the Award we learn as follows :—

14 parcels of land, containing in all over 123 acres were sold to cover expenses for £2512.

31½ acres are allotted to the Lords of the Manor (Sir William Gibbons, Thomas Somers Cocks, and Thomas Graham) in lieu of their rights as Lords of the Soil.

490 acres to Sir William Gibbons in trust for himself and the other Lords of the Manor in lieu of all other claims (freehold lands, rights of common, etc.).

69 acres to the mortgagees of the late Sir J. Gibbons.

6 acres to the Trustees of the late Sir J. Gibbons.

400 acres to Edmund Hill, Esq. (who also bought 117 acres of the land sold to defray costs).

100 acres to Henry Bullock, Esq.

72 acres to Thomas Hankey, Esq.

45 acres to Jervoise Clark Jervoise, Esq.

Allotments of from 20 to 40 acres to eleven other allottees.

Allotments of from 10 to 20 acres to twelve allottees.

Allotments of from 12 perches to 9 acres to seventy-nine allottees.

Twenty-four of these smaller allotments (including six of less than 2 acres) are given in lieu of open field property; the remaining fifty-five are given in compensation for common rights of some sort or other.

Sixty-six cottages appear as entitling their owners to compensation.[1] Of these 66, 16 belong to Henry Bullock and 8 to Sir William Gibbons, and the remaining 42 to 38 different owners. The allotments to cottages vary from a quarter of an acre (John Merrick) to over an acre (Anne Higgs). The owners of cottage commons only had their allotments separately and not in common.

APPENDIX A (11)

WAKEFIELD, YORKS.—ENCLOSURE ACT, 1793

AREA.—2300 acres 'or thereabouts.'

NATURE OF GROUND.—Open Common Fields, Ings, Commons, Waste Grounds, within the townships of Wakefield, Stanley, Wrenthorpe, Alverthorpe, and Thornes.

PARLIAMENTARY PROCEEDINGS.—*January 23, 1793.*—Petition from several owners and proprietors for enclosure. Leave given to prepare bill. January 28, Wilberforce presented it; February 18, it was committed to Wilberforce, Duncombe and others.

February 28.—Petition against the bill from the Earl of Strafford, stating that the bill will greatly affect and prejudice his property. Petition referred to Committee.

Same day, Petition against the bill from several Persons, being Owners of Estates and Occupiers of Houses in the Town and Parish of Wakefield. 'Setting forth, That, if the said Bill should pass into a Law, as it now stands, the same will greatly affect and prejudice the Estates and Property of the Petitioners, (viz.), their being deprived of the Benefit they now receive from the Pasturage of the Ings, from the 12th of August to the 5th of April, and for which they cannot receive any Compensation adequate thereto, as well as the Restrictions which exclude the Inhabitants from erecting Buildings on Land that may be allotted to them for Twenty, Forty, and Sixty Years, on different Parts of Westgate Common, as specified in the said Bill.' This petition also was referred to the Committee.

REPORT AND ENUMERATION OF CONSENTS.—*March* 12.—Wilberforce reported from the Committee that the Standing Orders had

---

[1] See Petition, p. 379, where nearly a hundred are said to do so.

been complied with, that they had considered the first Petition (Lord Strafford's), (no one had appeared to be heard on behalf of the second Petition), that they found the allegations of the Bill true, that 'the Parties concerned' had given their consent to the Bill, and also to adding one Commissioner to the three named in the Bill '(except the Owners of Estates whose Property in the Lands and Grounds to be divided and inclosed is assessed to the Land Tax at £5 per Annum or thereabouts, who refused to sign the Bill; and also, except the Owners of Estates whose Property in the said Lands and Grounds is assessed to the Land Tax at about £51 per Annum, who have either declared themselves perfectly indifferent about the Inclosure, or not given any Answer to the Application made to them respecting it; and that the whole Property belonging to Persons interested in the Inclosure is assessed to the Land Tax at £432 per Annum, or thereabouts . . .).'

Bill passed Commons and Lords. March 28, Royal Assent.

MAIN FEATURES OF ACT.—(Private, 33 George III. c. 11.)

COMMISSIONERS.—Four appointed. (1) Richard Clark of Rothwell Haigh, Gentleman; (2) John Renshaw of Owthorp, Notts, Gentleman; (3) John Sharp of Gildersome, Yorks, Gentleman; (4) William Whitelock of Brotherton, Yorks, Gentleman; the first representing the Duke of Leeds, the second the Earl of Strafford (no doubt this was the Commissioner added in Committee), and the other two representing the Majority in Value of the Persons interested. Any vacancy to be filled up by the party represented, and new Commissioners to be 'not interested in the said Inclosure.' Three to be a quorum. In case of dispute and equal division of opinion amongst the Commissioners, an Umpire is appointed (Isaac Leatham of Barton, Gentleman); the decision of Commissioners and Umpire to be final and conclusive.

PAYMENT TO COMMISSIONERS.—2 guineas each for each working day. The Surveyors (2 appointed) to be paid as Commissioners think fit.

CLAIMS.—All claims with full particulars of the nature and tenure of the property on behalf of which the claim is made are to be handed in at the 1st or 2nd meeting of the Commissioners; no claim is to be received later except for some special cause; and the determination of the Commissioners as to the various claims is to be binding and final. There are, however, three exceptions to the above, (1) Persons claiming in virtue of Messuages and Tofts need not prove usage of common; (2) Any Person who is dissatisfied with regard to his own or some one else's claim, may give notice in writing, and the Commissioners are then to take Counsel's opinion on the matter. The Commissioners are to choose the Counsel, who is to be 'not interested in the Premises.' The Commissioners may also on their own responsibility take Counsel's opinion at any time they think proper; Counsel's opinion is to be final. The costs are to be paid by the party against whom the dispute is determined, or otherwise as the Commissioners decide; (3) The Earl of Strafford is exempted from specifying particulars of Tenure in making his claim, for there are disputes on this subject between the Duke and the Earl, 'which Matters in Difference the said Duke and Earl have not agreed to submit to the Consideration or Determination of the said Commissioners.' The Commissioners need not specify the tenure of the Earl's share in making their award, and if the Duke and Earl go to law about their dispute and the matter is settled in a Court of Equity, then the Commissioners are to make a second special Award for them.

SYSTEM OF DIVISION—SPECIAL PROVISIONS:

Provisions for the Lord of the Manor—'the Most Noble Francis, Duke of Leeds.'—

(1) Such part of the Commons and Waste Grounds as is 'equal in Value to One full Sixteenth Part thereof in lieu of and as a sufficient Recompence for his Right to the Soil of the said Commons and Waste Grounds, and for his Consent to the Division and Inclosure thereof;

(2) An allotment of the Commons and Waste Grounds to be (in the judgment of the Commissioners) a fair compensation for his Coney Warrens which are to be destroyed;

(3) An allotment equal in value (in the judgment of the Commissioners) to £40 a year as compensation for the reserved Rents he has been receiving from persons who have made incroachments during the last 20 years;

(4) An allotment or allotments of not more than 5 acres in the whole, to be awarded in such place as the Duke or his Agents appoint, close to one of his stone quarries, as compensation for the right given by the Act to other allottees of the Common of getting stone on their allotments;

(5) The value of all the timber on allotments from the common is to be assessed by the Commissioners, and paid by the respective allottees to the Duke. If they refuse to pay, the Duke may come and cut down the timber 'without making any Allowance or Satisfaction whatsoever to the Person or Persons to whom any such Allotment shall belong, for any Injury to be done thereby';

(6) The Duke's power to work Mines and to get all Minerals is not to be interfered with by anything in this Act but the 'Owners or Proprietors of the Ground wherein such Pits or Soughs shall be made, driven, or worked, or such Engines, Machines or Buildings erected, or such Coals or Rubbish laid, or such Ways, Roads or Passages made and used,' are to have a 'reasonable Satisfaction for Damages.' The payment of the reasonable Satisfaction however is not to fall on the Duke, but on all the allottees of the Commons and Waste Grounds who are to meet together in the Moot Hall and appoint a salaried officer to settle the damages and

collect the money by a rate raised according to the Poor Rate of the previous year. If the claimant and the officer fail to agree, arbitrators, and ultimately an umpire, can be appointed.

Provisions for Tithe Owners.—A fair allotment is to be given to the Vicar in compensation for his small Tythes. In cases where the allottees have not enough land to contribute their due share to the tithe allotment, they have to pay a yearly sum instead.

For Stone and Gravel, etc.—Suitable allotments for stone and gravel, etc., to be made 'for the Use and Benefit' of all allottees 'for the Purpose of getting Stone, Sand, Gravel, or other Materials for making and repairing of the public Roads and Drains'; but these allotments are not to include any of the Duke's or of his tenants' stone quarries.

Provision for the Poor.—None.

Allotment of Residue.—(1) The open fields are to be divided out amongst the present proprietors in proportion to their present value and with regard to convenience; unless any owner of open-field land specially asks for an allotment elsewhere; (2) The owners of Ings are to have Ings allotted to them, unless they wish for land elsewhere; (3) The Commons and Waste grounds are first to have the various allotments to the Lord of the Manor and the Vicar specified above, and also the allotment for Stone and Gravel for roads deducted from them, and then the residue is to be allotted 'among the several Persons (considering the said Duke of Leeds as one) having Right of Common in or upon the said Commons and Waste Grounds' in the following fashion; one half is to be divided among the Owners or Proprietors of Messuages, Cottages or Tofts with Right of Common, according to their several Rights and Interests; the other half, together with the rest and residue of Land to be divided, is to be allotted among the Owners or Proprietors of open common fields, Ings, and old inclosed Lands according to their several rights and interests 'without any undue Preference whatsoever.' The Commissioners are also directed to pay due regard to situation and to putting the different allotments of the same person together. Allotments are to be of the same tenure, *i.e.* freehold or copyhold, as the holdings in respect of which they are claimed, but no fines are to be taken on account of the allotment.

With respect to the allottees of allotments on Westgate Moor, a special clause (see petition on January 23) is inserted. They are forbidden to put up any House, Building or Erection of any kind on one part for 20, on another for 40, on another for 60, years, unless the Duke consents, the object being 'thereby the more advantageously to enable the said Duke, his Heirs and Assigns, to work his Colliery in and upon the same Moor.'

The award, with full particulars of allotments, etc., is to be drawn up and is to be 'final, binding, and conclusive upon all Parties and Persons interested therein.'

If any person (being Guardian, etc., tenant in tail or for life of lessee, etc.) fails to accept and fence, then Commissioners can do it for him and charge; if he still refuses, Commissioners can lease allotment out and take rent till Expenses are paid.

INCROACHMENTS.—Incroachments 20 years old are to stand; those made within 20 years are to be treated as part of the Commons to be divided, but they are, if the Commissioners think it fit and convenient, to be allotted to the person in possession without considering the value of erections and improvements. Three contingencies for allotment to the person in possession are provided for;—(1) if he is entitled to an allotment, his incroachment is to be treated as part or the whole of his allotment;

(2) If his incroachment is of greater value than the allotment he is entitled to, then he is to pay whatever extra sum of money the Commissioners judge right;

(3) If he is not entitled to any allotment at all, then he has to pay the price set on his incroachment by the Commissioners.

If the Commissioners do not allot an incroachment to the person in possession, they may sell it at public auction and apply the money to the purposes of the Act, or they may allot it to someone not in possession, in which case a 'reasonable' sum of money is to be given to the dispossessed owner, the new allottee paying the whole or part of it.

The above provisions apply to the ordinary incroachers; the Duke has special arrangements. If he has made any new incroachments during the last 20 years in addition to any older incroachments, these new incroachments are to be valued by the Commissioners, and the Duke is to have them either as part of his allotment or for a money payment, as he chooses; also 'whereas the Tenants of the said Duke of Leeds of the Collieries on the said Commons and Waste Lands . . . . have from Time to Time erected Fire Engines, Messuages, Dwelling Houses, Cottages and other Buildings upon the said Commons and Waste Lands, and made several other Conveniences thereon for the Use and Accommodation of the said Collieries, and the Persons managing and working the same, a great Part of which have been erected and made within the last Twenty Years,' these are not to be treated like other incroachments, but are to 'be and continue the absolute Property of the said Duke of Leeds, his Heirs and Assigns, in as full and ample Manner' as if the erections had been made more than 20 years before.

FENCING.—All allotments are to be fenced at the expense of their several proprietors 'in such Manner, Shares and Proportions as the said Commissioners shall . . . direct' with the following exceptions—(1) the Vicar's allotment for small Tithes is to be fenced by the other proprietors; (2) the allotments to Hospitals, Schools, and other public Charities are to have a certain proportion deducted from them to cover the cost of fencing. Allottees who refuse to fence can be summoned before a J.P. by their neighbours, and the J.P. (who is not to be interested in the Enclosure) can make an order compelling them to fence.

To protect the new hedges, it is ordered that no sheep or lambs are to be turned out in any allotment for 7 years, unless the allottee makes special provision to protect his neighbour's young quickset, and no beasts, cattle or horses are to be turned into any roads or lanes where there is a new-growing fence.

EXPENSES.—Part of the Commons and Waste Grounds is to be sold to cover the expences; if the proceeds do not cover the costs the residue is to be paid by the allottees in proportion to their shares, and any surplus is to be divided among them. But Hospitals, Schools, and Public Charities are exempted from this payment, a portion of their allotments, in fact, having been already deducted in order to pay their share of Expenses. The Commissioners are to keep an account of Expenses, which is to be open to inspection. The owners of Ings are to pay a sum of money in return for the extinction of the right of Eatage (referred to by the Petitioners) on their land from August 12 to April 5; and this money is to be applied for the purposes of the Act.

If allottees find the expenses of the Act and of fencing more than they can meet, they are allowed (with the consent of the Commissioners) to mortgage their allotments up to 40s. an acre. If they dislike this prospect, they are empowered by the Act, at any time before the execution of the Award, to sell their rights to allotment in respect of any common right.

COMPENSATION TO OCCUPIERS.—Occupiers are to pay a higher rent in return for the loss of the use of common rights. The clause runs as follows :—' That the several Persons who hold any Lands or other Estates, to which a Right of Common upon the said Commons and Waste Grounds is appurtenant or belonging, or any Part of the said Open Common Fields or Inclosures, by virtue of any Lease, of which a longer Term than One Year is unexpired, shall and are hereby required to pay to their respective Landlords such Increase of Rent towards the Expences such Landlords will be respectively put to in Consequence of this Act, as the said Commissioners shall judge reasonable, and shall by Writing under their Hands direct or appoint, having Regard to the Duration of such respective Leases, and to the probable Benefit which will accrue to such respective Lessees by Reason of the said Inclosure.'

ROADS.—Commissioners to have full power to set out and shut up roads and footpaths (turnpike roads excepted).

POWER OF APPEAL.—To Quarter Sessions only, and not in any cases where the Commissioners' decisions are final, binding, or conclusive, as they are, e.g. on claims (except the Earl of Strafford's) and on allotments.

AWARD.—Not with Clerks of Peace or of County Council, or in Record Office.

APPENDIX A (12)

WINFRITH NEWBURGH, DORSET.—ENCLOSURE ACT, 1768

AREA.—2254 Acres or thereabouts.

NATURE OF GROUND. — Common Fields, Meadow Grounds, Sheep Downs, Commons, Common Heaths, and other Waste Grounds.

(In Report, Common Arable Fields and Common Meadows= 1218 acres.)

PARLIAMENTARY PROCEEDINGS.—*December* 1, 1767.—Petition for enclosure from Edward Weld, Esq., George Clavell, Esq., Benjamin Thornton, Clerk, William Weston, Clerk, John Felton, Gentleman, and others. Leave given; bill read twice and committed on December 11 to a Committee of 42 members in addition to the members for Dorset, Somerset, Devon and Cornwall. All to have Voices. January 25, 1768, Petition from persons being Freeholders, Proprietors of Estates or otherwise interested, against the bill stating 'that if the said Bill should pass into a Law the Estates of the Petitioners and others in the said Parish will be greatly injured, and several of them must be totally ruined thereby; and that some of the Petitioners, by Threats and Menaces, were prevailed upon to sign the Petition for the said Bill; but upon Recollection, and considering the impending Ruin they shall be subject to by the Inclosure, beg Leave now to have Liberty to retract from their seeming Acquiescence in the said Petition,' and ask to be heard by Counsel against the Bill. Petition referred to the Committee.

January 29, 1768.—Mr. Bond reported from the Committee that there was an erasure in the prayer of the said Petition and asked for instructions. A fresh Committee of 36 members (many of whom were also members of the other Committee) was appointed to examine into the question of how the erasure was made, and whether it was previous or subsequent to the signing. This Committee was ordered to report to the House, but there is no record of its report.

REPORT AND ENUMERATION OF CONSENTS.— *February* 2, 1768.—Mr. Bond reported from the Committee that the allegations were true, and that the ' Parties concerned ' had given their consent ' (except Four Persons who could not be found whose Property in the Common Meadows to be inclosed amounts to Five Acres, Three Roods, Twenty Three Perches and a half; and also except Four other Persons who, when applied to for their Consent to the Bill, refused to sign, though they declared they had no Objection, and whose Property in the Common Meadows to be inclosed amounts to Four Acres, One Rood, Thirty Eight Perches; and also except Six Persons whose Property in the Common Arable Fields and Common Meadows to be inclosed mounts to One hundred and

twenty two Acres, Thirty Three Perches, who refused to sign the
Bill; and also, except Three Persons, whose Property in the
Common Arable Fields and Common Meadows, to be inclosed,
amounts to One hundred and seven Acres, Twenty Three Perches,
who hold under Copies of Court Roll, granted on Condition that
they would join in any Act or Deed for the dividing and inclosing
the said Common Fields, and Meadows, and other Commonable
Lands within the said Manor, when thereto requested by the
Lord of the said Manor; and that the whole Number of Acres in
the said Common Arable Fields and Common Meadows is One
thousand, Two hundred and eighteen, Twenty Eight Perches and
a half, and that the Rector of Winfrith Newburgh and Vicar of
Campden, who are intitled to all the Great and Small Tithes
arising out of the said Common Arable Fields and Common
Meadows have consented thereto).'

February 2, 1768 (same day).—Another Petition against the bill
from Freeholders, Proprietors and Persons otherwise interested
stating that the Inclosure is 'contrary to the general Sense of the
Persons interested therein,' and will be 'injurious to the Property
of the Petitioners and others, the smaller Landholders within the
said Parish, some of whom must, in the Petitioners' Judgment, be
totally ruined thereby.' Petitioners to be heard when Report
considered.

February 3, 1768.—Report considered. House informed that
no Counsel attended. Report read. Clause added settling the
expenses to be paid by Copyholders and Lessees for Lives. Bill
sent to Lords. February 9, Committed. Same day, Petition against
it from various persons as 'contrary to the general Sense of the
Persons interested therein.' Referred to Committee. February 12,
Lord Delamer reported from the Committee without amendment.
February 24, Royal Assent.

MAIN FEATURES OF ACT.—(Private, 8 George III. c. 18.)

COMMISSIONERS.—Seven appointed. (1) John Bond, Esq., of
Grange; (2) David Robert Mitchell, Esq., of Dewlish; (3)
Nathaniel Bond, Esq., of West Lulworth; (4) Thomas Williams,
Esq., of Herringstone; (5) William Churchill, Esq., of Dorchester;
(6) George Lillington of Burngate, Gentleman; (7) Joseph
Garland of Chaldon, Gentleman; all of Dorset.

Sometimes 3, sometimes 4 a quorum. Vacancies to be filled up
by remaining Commissioners from persons not interested in the
land to be inclosed.

Survey to be made if Commissioners 'shall think the same
necessary.'

PAYMENT.—Nothing stated.

CLAIMS.—Commissioners to examine into and determine on all
claims; and 'in case any Difference or Dispute shall arise between
all or any of the Parties interested in the said Division and

Inclosure, with respect to the Premises, or any Matter or Thing herein contained or consequent thereon, or in relation thereunto, the same shall be adjusted and finally determined between the said Parties, and every of them, by the said Commissioners, or any Three or more of them.' Commissioners can examine witnesses on oath, ' and the Determinations of the said Commissioners, or any Three or more of them therein, shall be binding and conclusive to all and every the said Parties. . . .'

SYSTEM OF DIVISION—SPECIAL PROVISIONS :

Lords of the Manor (Edward Weld, Esq., of Winfrith Newburgh ; George Clavell, Esq., of Langcotts and East Fossell).—No special provision for allotment. Their Manorial Rights are not to be prejudiced by Act except as regards ' the Mines, Delves, and Quarries lying within and under such Parts, Shares, and Proportions of the said Common Fields, Meadow Grounds, Sheep Downs, Commons, Common Heaths and other Waste Grounds, as shall or may be allotted and assigned to the several other Freeholders and Owners of Lands ' within these Manors ' or to any Person or Persons not having any Lands within the said In-Parish or Manors, or within the Precincts thereof as aforesaid, in Lieu of or as an Equivalent for such Right or Claim as aforesaid ; and other than and except such Common of Pasture and other Common Rights as can or may be claimed by or belonging to the Lord or Lords of the said Manors in and upon the Premises so intended to be divided and inclosed as aforesaid.'

Tithe Owners.—Tithe owners to have the same rights to Tithes over the land about to be inclosed as they have over the lands already inclosed.

If arable land is converted to pasture on inclosure (for Dairy Cows or Black Cattle) then allottees shall pay an annual 3s. an acre to tithe owners as compensation for corn tithes. Allotments given in virtue of estates which are Cistertian Lands, are to be deemed Cistertian Lands too, *i.e.* to have same exemption from tithes, but any Cistertian Lands which are allotted are to be under the same obligations for tithes as the estates in virtue of which they are allotted.

Provision for the Poor.—None.

Provision for Fuel Allotment.—Commissioners are to ascertain and determine all Rights of Common over the land to be enclosed, and are then to set out such part or parts ' as shall appear to them to be sufficient, and to be conveniently situate for the preserving and raising Furze, Turf, or other Fuel, for the Use of the several Persons ' who shall appear to the Commissioners to be intitled to a Right of Common.

Allotment of Residue. — Amongst all persons who appear to the Commissioners to be intitled to a Right of Common, or to have or be intitled to any other Property in the said Common Fields, etc., in such proportions as the Commissioners judge right 'without giving any undue Preference,' and with due regard to Quality, Quantity, and Situation.

But the following Rules are to be observed with regard to proportions :—

(1) Common Fields and Sheep Downs are to be divided ‘by and according to the Parts and Proportions of the Arable Lands lying in the said Common Fields, where the said Parties respectively now are, or, at the Time of such Allotments so as aforesaid to be made shall be intitled to.’

(2) Meadow Grounds, Commons, Common Heaths, and other Waste Grounds to be divided ‘according to the Sum or Sums of money which the said Parties and each of them now stand charged with towards the Relief of the Poor of the said Parish’ in respect of their lands which have right of common.

Special Clause.—In case it appears to the Commissioners that any persons who have no land, nevertheless have a right of common, then the Commissioners can allot such person such part of the land to be inclosed as they think an equivalent for such right of common. In order to prevent all Differences and Disputes, the Commissioners are to draw up an Award, and this Award shall be binding and conclusive to all and every Person and Persons interested. Failure to accept within 6 months excludes allottee from all benefit and advantage of this Act, and also ‘from any Estate, Interest or Right of Common, or other Property whatsoever’ in any other allotment.   (Saving clause for infants, etc.)

INCROACHMENTS.—Not mentioned.

FENCING, etc.—To be done by allottees in such proportions as Commissioners direct.   Such directions to be put in award, and to be final and binding.   Fences to be made within 12 months, or some other convenient space of time.

If an allottee fails to fence, his neighbour can complain to a J.P. (not interested in the inclosure), who can authorise complainant to do it, and either charge defaulter or to enter on premises and receive rents till expenses paid.   *Exception.*—Allotment of Copyholders and leaseholders for one or more lives are to be fenced partly by the Lord of the Manor and partly by the allottees in such proportion as the Commissioners (or 4 of them) direct.

EXPENSES.—(1) Expenses of obtaining and passing the Act to be borne by the Lords of the Manor.

(2) Expenses of carrying out the Act (survey, allotment, Commissioners' charges, etc.) to be borne by the several allottees in proportion to the Quantity of Land allotted to them, or otherwise as Commissioners direct.   *Exception.*—Tithe owners' share to be borne by the Lords of the Manor.   Commissioners can distrain for payment.

Trustees, Tenants in Tail or for Life may mortgage up to 40s. an acre.

COMPENSATION.—Leases and agreements at Rack Rent to be void, owners making such compensation to Lessees as Commissioners judge right.

ROADS.—Commissioners have power to set out and shut up roads and footpaths.

POWER OF APPEAL.—To Quarter Sessions only, and not when Commissioners' determination said to be final.

AWARD.—August 17, 1771. With Dorset Clerk of Peace or of County Council.

APPENDIX A (13)

QUAINTON.—ATTEMPTED ENCLOSURE, 1801

PARLIAMENTARY PROCEEDINGS.—*March* 20, 1801.—Petition for enclosures from 'several persons.' Leave given. Earl Temple, Sir William Young, and Mr. Praed to prepare bill.

April 2.—Bill read first time.

April 13.—Petition from various proprietors of Lands, Common Rights, and other Hereditaments against the bill, stating that enclosure ' would be attended with an Expence to the Proprietors far exceeding any Improvement to be derived therefrom.' Ordered to be heard on second reading.

April 15.—Bill read second time. Petitioners declined to be heard. Bill committed to Mr. Praed, Earl Temple, etc.

April 21.—Petition against the bill from various proprietors stating 'that the Proprietors of the said Commonable Lands are very numerous, and the Shares or Properties belonging to most of them are so small that the proposed Division and Inclosure would be attended with an Expence far exceeding any Improvement to be derived therefrom; and that a great Majority in Number of the said Proprietors dissent to the said Bill, and the Proprietors of more than One-third, and very nearly One-half Part in Value, of the Lands to be inclosed, also dissent thereto; and that many of the Clauses and Provisions in the said Bill are also highly injurious' to the petitioners.

Referred to the Committee. All to have voices.

REPORT AND ENUMERATION OF CONSENTS.—*June* 12.—Mr. Praed reported from the Committee that the Standing Orders had been complied with, that the allegations were true, and that the Parties concerned had given their consent (except the owners of Estates assessed to the Land Tax at £39, 12s. 6¼d. who refused to sign the bill, and the owners of Estates assessed at £3, 10s. 0d. who were neuter; and that the whole of the Estates ' interested' were assessed at £246, 8s. 6d.).

Same day.—Petition against the bill from Richard Wood on behalf of himself and other proprietors who were parties to the former petition, Richard Wood being the only one left in London, setting forth 'that the said Bill proposes to inclose only a Part of the said Parish of Quainton, consisting of 3 open Arable Fields, and about 280 Acres of Commonable Land, lying dispersedly in, or adjoining to the said Open Fields, the rest of the said Parish being Old inclosed Lands'; that the agent for the bill had given the Committee a statement (1) of the names of the persons interested; (2) of the amount at which these persons were assessed to the Land Tax for their property throughout the parish, according to which statement it appeared, first, that of the 34 persons interested, 'not being Cottagers,' 8 assented, 4 were neuter, and 22 dissented; but that, second, as stated in terms of Land Tax Assessment, £203, 5s. 11¾d. assented, and £39, 12s. 6¼d. dissented; that this statement was wrong inasmuch as the proprietors of old inclosed lands had in respect of old inclosures no rights over the commonable lands, and that therefore no old inclosed land could rank as property 'interested' in the inclosure. The petitioners gave the following enumeration of Consents as the correct one; whole quantity of land in the Open Fields, 'in respect of which only a Right of Common could be claimed,' 42¼ yard lands :—

Land belonging to those who assented,   21¾ yard lands
    ,,   ,,   dissented,   19½   ,,
    ,,   ,,   were neutral,   1   yard land
or in terms of annual value—

Assenting,	. . . . . .	£406	10	0
Dissenting,	. . . . .	370	0	0
Neutral,	. . . . . .	37	0	0

The petitioners further stated that their Counsel had offered to call witnesses before the Committee to prove the above facts; that the agent for the bill had retorted that old inclosed lands had a right in the Commons, although he did not pretend that such right had ever been enjoyed, or produce any witness to show that it had ever been claimed, but supported his claim by quoting a clause in the bill by which it was proposed that the Rector's Tithes for the old inclosures as well as the new should be commuted for an allotment of land; and that the Committee refused to hear the evidence tendered by the petitioners' Counsel. This Petition was referred to the Committee to whom the bill was recommitted, and the bill was dropped.

APPENDIX A (14)

Subsequent History of King's Sedgmoor

In 1775, Mr. Allen, Member of Parliament for Bridgwater, tried to get an enclosure bill passed. 'Sanguine of success, and highly impressed with the idea of its importance, he purchased a large number of rights, and having obtained a signature of consents, went to Parliament; but not having interest enough in the House to stem the torrent of opposition, all his delusive prospects of profit vanished, and he found himself left in a small but respectable minority.'[1] No further attempt was made till 1788, when a meeting to consider the propriety of draining and dividing the moor, was held at Wells. 'At this meeting Sir Philip Hales presided; and after much abuse and opposition from the lower order of commoners, who openly threatened destruction to those who supported such a measure, the meeting was dissolved without coming to any final determination.

'The leading idea was, however, afterwards pursued, with great assiduity, by Sir Philip, and his agent Mr. Symes of Stowey; and by their persevering industry, and good management,'[2] application was again made to Parliament in 1791.

PARLIAMENTARY PROCEEDINGS.—*February* 18, 1791.—Petition from several Owners and Proprietors for a bill to drain and divide the tract of waste ground of about 18,000 acres called King's Sedgmoor. Petitioners point out that the moor is liable to be overflowed, 'and thereby the same is not only less serviceable and useful to the Commoners, but also, by reason of the Vapours and Exhalations which arise from thence, the Air of the circumjacent Country is rendered less salubrious'; also that it would be 'beneficial, as well to the wholesomeness of the neighbouring Country as also to the Profitableness of the Pasturage of the said Moor' if it were drained and divided into Parochial or other large allotments. The House was also informed that the expense of the undertaking was not proposed to be levied by Tolls or Duties upon the Parties interested.

Leave given. Mr. Philips and Sir John Trevelyan to prepare. February 28. Bill committed to Mr. Philips, Mr. Templar, etc.

REPORT AND ENUMERATION OF CONSENTS.—*March* 7.—Mr. Philips reported that the Standing Orders had been complied with, that the allegations were true, and that the parties concerned had consented '(except the Owners of 107 Rights on the said Moor, who declared themselves neuter in respect to the Bill; and also except the Owners of 84 Rights, who declared themselves against the Bill; and that the whole of the Rights on the said Moor consist of 1740, or thereabouts; and that no Person appeared before the Committee to oppose the Bill).'

The Bill passed Commons, March 9; Lords, April 15. Royal Assent, May 13.

Billingsley, after describing the attempts to enclose Sedgmoor, remarks (p. 192): 'I have been thus particular in stating the progress of this business merely to show the impropriety of calling public meetings with a view of gaining signatures of consent or

---

[1] Billingsley's *Somerset*, p. 191.   [2] *Ibid.*, pp. 191-2.

taking the sense of the proprietors in that way. At all publick meetings of this nature which I ever attended noise and clamour have silenced sound sense and argument. A party generally attends with a professed desire to oppose, and truth and propriety have a host of foes to combat. Whoever therefore has an object of this kind in view let him acquire consent by *private application* ; for I have frequently seen the good effects thereof manifested by the irresistible influence of truth when coolly and quietly administered ; and it has frequently happened that men hostile to your scheme have by dispassionate argument not only changed their sentiment but become warm partisans in that cause which at first they meant to oppose.'

The task of Sir Philip and Mr. Symes in acquiring consents by the cool and quiet administration of truth must have been considerably lightened by the fact that Parliament anticipated the Commissioners with extraordinary accuracy in disregarding 55% of the claims. The Commissioners, says Billingsley, investigated 4063 claims, of which only 1798 were allowed. The Parliamentary Committee had asserted that there were 1740 rights, 'or thereabouts.'

The Act for draining and dividing King's Sedgmoor is not, so far as we have been able to discover, amongst the printed Statutes.

Particulars of the expenses are given by Billingsley (p. 196), who estimates the area at 12,000 acres :—

	£	s.	d.
To act of parliament and all other incidental expenses,	1,628	15	0
Interest of money borrowed,	3,239	4	11
Commissioners,	4,314	7	8
Clerk,	1,215	19	0
Surveyor,	908	12	6
Printers,	362	6	3
Petty expenses,	575	11	1
Land purchased,	2,801	4	11
Drains, sluices, bridges and roads,	15,418	2	8
Awards and incidentals,	1,160	0	8
	£31,624	4	8

About 700 acres were sold to discharge the expenses.

The drainage and division into parochial allotments was a preliminary to enclosure of the different parochial shares, which was of course made easier by the fact that 55% of the claims had already been disallowed. In the years 1796, '97, and '98, fourteen Enclosure Acts for the different parishes were passed.

(Butleigh and Woollavington, 1796. Aller, Ashcott, Compton Dundon, Higham, Othery, Moorlinch, Somerton, Street, and Weston Zoyland, 1797. Bridgwater, Chedjoy, and Midellzoy, 1798.)

Billingsley estimated that the total cost of subdividing parochial allotments would be £28,000.

He also estimated that the value of the land rose from 10s. to 35s. an acre.

APPENDIX B

BEDFORDSHIRE.—CLOPSHILL, 1795.[1]

FAMILY OF SIX PERSONS.

Expences by the Week—		£	s.	d.
Bread, flour, or oatmeal	. . .	0	7	6
Yeast and salt, .	. . .	0	0	3
Thread and worsted, .	. . .	0	0	2
Bacon or other meat,	. . .	0	1	6
Tea, sugar, and butter,	. . .	0	0	10½
Soap, . . .	. . .	0	0	5
Candles, . . .	. . .	0	0	5
Beer, . . .	. . .	0	0	7
Total of the Week,	. . .	£0	11	8½
Amount per Annum,	. . .	£30	8	10
Rent, . . .	. . .	1	10	0
Wood, . . .	. . .	1	12	6
Cloaths, . . .	. . .	2	2	0
Sickness, . . .	. . .	0	5	0
Total Expences per Annum,	.	£35	18	4
Earning per Week—				
The man, . . .	. . .	£0	7	6
The woman, . .	. . .	0	1	6
The children, . .	. . .	0	4	0
Total of the Week,	. . .	£0	13	0
Total Earnings per Annum,	.	£33	16	0

N.B.—'The Harvest earnings not included: they go a great way towards making up the deficiency.'

DORSET.—SHERBORNE, 1789.[2]

FAMILY OF FIVE PERSONS.

Expences per Week—		£	s.	d.
Bread, . . .	. . .	0	3	0
Salt, . . .	. . .	0	0	1½
Meat, . . .	. . .	0	0	8
	Carry forward, .	0	3	9½

Eden, vol. iii. p. cccxxxix.   [2] Davies, p. 152.

Expences per Week—continued.

	£	s.	d.
Brought forward, .	0	3	9½
Tea, etc., ...	0	0	2
Cheese, ...	0	0	7
Milk, ...	0	0	4
Soap, ...	0	0	2½
Candles, ...	0	0	6
Thread, etc., ...	0	0	1
Total, ...	£0	5	8
Amount per Annum, . . .	£14	14	8
Rent, ...	2	0	0
Fuel, ...	3	18	0
Clothes, etc., ...	1	0	0
Total Expences per Annum, .	£21	12	8

Earnings per Week—

	£	s.	d.
The man, ...	£0	6	0
The woman, ...	0	2	6
Total, ...	£0	8	6
Total Earnings per Annum, .	£22	2	0

HAMPSHIRE.—LONG PARISH, 1789.[2]
FAMILY OF SIX PERSONS.

Expences per Week—

	£	s.	d.
Bread or Flour, ...	0	5	0
Yeast and Salt,. . . .	0	0	3
Bacon or other Meat, . .	0	1	0
Tea, Sugar, and Butter, . .	0	0	6
Cheese, ...	0	0	5
Soap, Starch, and Blue, . .	0	0	2
Candles.	0	0	2
Thread, Thrum, and Worsted, .	0	0	3
Total, ...	£0	7	9
Amount per Annum, . . .	£20	3	0
Rent, Fuel ('both very high and scarce') Clothes, Lying-in, etc., .	7	0	0
Total Expences per Annum, .	£27	3	0

Earnings per Week—

	£	s.	d.
The man, ...	£0	8	0
The woman, ...	0	1	0
Total, ...	£0	9	0
Total Earnings per Annum, .	£23	8	0

[1] Davies puts 1½d., but this is probably a slip.   [2] Davies, p. 166.

Herts.—Hinksworth, 1795.[1]

Family of Six Persons.

Expences by the Week—

	£	s.	d.
Bread, flour, or oatmeal, . . .	0	10	5
Heating the oven, ...	0	0	4
Yeast and salt, ...	0	0	4
Bacon or pork, ...	0	3	4
Tea, sugar, and butter, . . .	0	1	$9\frac{1}{2}$
Soap, ...	0	0	5
Cheese, ...	0	0	$7\frac{1}{2}$
Candles, ...	0	0	4
Small beer, ...	0	0	$6\frac{3}{4}$
Milk, ...	0	0	4
Potatoes, ...	0	1	3
Thread and worsted, ...	0	0	4
Total of the Week, . . .	£1	0	$0\frac{1}{2}$
Amount per Annum, . . .	£52	2	2
Rent, ...	2	0	0
Cloaths, ...	6	5	10
Fuel, coal, wood, etc., . . .	3	15	3
Births and burials, ...	1	3	6
Total Expences per Annum, .	£65	6	9

Earnings per Week—

	£	s.	d.
The man, ...	£0	9	$2\frac{3}{4}$
The woman, ...	0	1	6
The children, ...	0	4	8
Total of the Week, . . .	£0	15	$4\frac{3}{4}$
Total Earnings per Annum, .	£40	0	7

Northamptonshire.—Castor, 1794.[2]

Family of Six Persons.

Expences per Week—

	£	s.	d.
Bread and Flour, ...	0	4	3
Salt, ...	0	0	1
Meat, ...	0	1	6
Tea, Sugar, and Butter, . .	0	1	1
Cheese (sometimes), . . .	0	0	5
Soap $\frac{1}{4}$ lb., Starch, etc., . .	0	0	$2\frac{1}{2}$
Candles $\frac{1}{2}$ lb., Thread, etc., . .	0	0	6
Total, .	£0	8	$0\frac{1}{2}$

[1] Eden, vol. iii. p. cccxlii.   [2] Davies, p. 176.

	£	s.	d.
Amount per Annum, . . .	20	18	2
Rent, ...	1	15	0
Fuel and coals, ...	1	10	0
Clothing, ...	2	15	0
Lying-in, loss of time, etc., . .	1	10	0
Total Expenses per Annum, .	£28	8	2

Earnings per Week—

	£	s.	d.
The man, ...	£0	7	6
The woman, ...	0	0	10
The children, ...	0	0	4
Total, ...	£0	8	8
Total Earnings per Annum, .	£22	10	8

N.B.—To the earnings may be added what is got by gleaning.

NORFOLK.—DISS, 1793.[1]
FAMILY OF SIX PERSONS.

Expences by the Week—

	£	s.	d.
Bread, flour or oatmeal, . . .	0	4	$7\frac{1}{2}$
Yeast and salt, ...	0	0	2
Bacon or other meat, . . .	0	0	3
Tea, sugar, and butter, . . .	0	0	$9\frac{1}{4}$
Soap, ...	0	0	$2\frac{1}{4}$
Candles, ...	0	0	3
Cheese, ...	0	0	$5\frac{1}{2}$
Milk, ...	0	0	6
Potatoes, ...	0	0	6
Thread and worsted, . . .	0	0	2
Total per Week, . . .	£0	7	$10\frac{1}{2}$
Total per Annum, ...	£20	9	6
Rent, ...	3	3	0
Fuel, ...	1	4	0
Cloaths, ...	2	3	0
Births, burials, sickness, . .	0	10	0
Total Expenses per Annum, .	£27	9	6

Earnings per Week—

	£	s.	d.
The Man, ...	£0	9	0
The Woman, ...	0	1	0
The Children, ...	0	1	6
Total, ...	£0	11	6
Total Earnings per Annum, .	£29	18	0

N.B.—In 1795 the earnings of this family were the same but their expenses had risen to £36, 11s. 4d. On bread they spent 8s. a week instead of 4s. $7\frac{1}{2}$d.

[1] Eden, vol. iii. p. cccxlvi.

CHIEF AUTHORITIES

Journals of House of Commons for period.
Journals of House of Lords for period.
Reports of Parliamentary Debates for period in *Parliamentary Register, Parliamentary History, Senator* and *Parliamentary Debates.*
Statutes, Public and Private for period.
Enclosure Awards in Record Office or Duchy of Lancaster.
Home Office Papers in Record Office.
Parliamentary Papers for period; specially—

FOR ENCLOSURES—
    Report from Select Committee on Standing Orders relating to Private Bills, 1775.
    Report from Select Committee on Waste Lands. Ordered to be printed December 23, 1795.
    Report from Select Committee on Waste Lands, 1797.
    Report from Select Committee on Means of Facilitating Inclosure, 1800. (Deals specially with Expense).
    Report from Select Committee on Constitution of Select Committees on Private Bills, 1825.
    Report from Select Committee on Commons Inclosure, 1844.

FOR POOR LAWS—
    Report from Select Committee on Poor Laws, 1817.
    Report from Lords Committee on Poor Laws, 1818.
    Report from Select Committee on Poor Laws, 1819.
    Report from Select Committee on Relief of Able-Bodied from the Poor Rate, 1828.
    Report from Lords on Poor Law, 1828.
    Documents in possession of Poor Law Commissioners, 1833.
    Report of Poor Laws Commissioners, 1834.

FOR GAME LAWS, CRIME, AND PUNISHMENT—
    Report from Select Committee on Game Laws, 1823.
    Report from Lords Committee on Game Laws, 1828.
    Report from Select Committee on Criminal Commitments and Convictions, 1827.
    Report from Select Committee on Criminal Commitments and Convictions, 1828.
    Return of Convictions under the Game Laws from 1827-30.
    Report from Select Committee on Secondary Punishments, 1831.

Report from Select Committee on Secondary Punishments,
   1832.
Report from Select Committee on Transportation, 1838.

FOR OTHER SOCIAL QUESTIONS—
   Report from Select Committee on Agricultural Distress, 1821.
   Report from Select Committee on Labourers' Wages, 1824.
   Reports from Select Committee on Emigration, 1826-7.
   Report from Select Committee on Agriculture, 1833.
   Report from Select Committee on Allotment System, 1843.

Publications of Board of Agriculture.
General Report on Enclosures, 1808.
Report on the Agricultural State of the Kingdom, 1816.
Agricultural Surveys of different Counties, by various writers,
   alluded to in text as *Bedford Report, Middlesex Report*, etc.

Annual Register for period.
Annals of Agriculture, 1784-1815 (46 vols.).
Cobbett's *Political Register*, 1802-35.
The Tribune (mainly Thelwall's lectures), 1795-6.
Reports of the Society for Bettering the Condition and Improving
   the Comforts of the Poor, (5 vols.), 1795-1808.
Ruggles, Thomas, *History of the Poor*, 1793 (published first in
   Annals of Agriculture).
Davies, David, *The Case of Labourers in Husbandry stated and
   considered*, 1795.
Eden, Sir Frederic Morton, *The State of the Poor or An History
   of the Labouring Classes in England*, 1797.
The Works of Arthur Young, William Marshall, and other
   contemporary writers on agriculture and enclosures; see
   list in Hasbach, *History of the English Agricultural Labourer.*
Cobbett's *Works.*
Dunkin's *History of Oxfordshire.*
Carlisle Papers, Historical MSS. Commission.
Memoir of Lord Suffield, by R. M. Bacon, 1838.
Life of Sir Samuel Romilly, 1842.

MODERN AUTHORITIES

Babeau, A., *Le Village sous l'ancien Régime.*
Cunningham, W., *The Growth of English Industry and Commerce.*
Curtler, W. H. R., *A Short History of English Agriculture.*
Eversley, Lord, *Commons, Forests, and Footpaths.*
Hasbach, Wilhelm, *History of the English Agricultural Labourer.*
Hirst, F. W., and Redlich, J., *Local Government in England,*
Hobson, J. A., *The Industrial System.*
Hudson, W. H., *A Shepherd's Life.*
Jenks, E., *Outlines of Local Government.*

Johnson, A. H., *The Disappearance of the Small Landowner.*

Kovalewsky, M., *La France Économique et Sociale à la Veille de la Révolution.*

Levy, H., *Large and Small Holdings.*

Mantoux, P., *La Révolution Industrielle.*

Porritt, E., *The Unreformed House of Commons.*

Prothero, R., *Pioneers and Progress of English Farming.*

Scrutton, T. E., *Commons and Common Fields.*

Slater, G., *The English Peasantry and the Enclosure of Common Fields.*

Smart, W., *Economic Annals of the Nineteenth Century.*

De Tocqueville, *L'ancien Régime.*

Vinogradoff, P., *The Growth of the Manor.*

Webb, S. and B., *English Local Government.—The Parish and the County.*

—— —— *English Local Government.—The Manor and the Borough.*

INDEX

ABEL, Mr., 248 f.
Abingdon, 267; Special Commission at, 305 f.
Abingdon, Lord, and Otmoor, 88, 91; on Special Commission, 302.
Abree, Margaret and Thomas, 109 *n*.
Adam, the brothers, 327.
Addington, H. *See* Sidmouth.
—— Stephen, 31, 44.
Addington Hills, 48.
Addison, 325.
Aglionby, Mr., M.P., 53.
Agriculture, and enclosure, 36; during French war, 166 ff.; Brougham on, 171.
Aix, Archbishop of, 217.
Albemarle, Lord, 321.
Aldeborough, 9.
Alderson, Mr. Justice, on Special Commissions, 272, 275, 277, 278, 281, 290, 293, 295, 298, 300; and Looker case, 295 f.
Allotments, and enclosure, 84 ff.; experiments, 154 ff.; hostility of farmers to, 159 f.; M. Chateauvieux on, 232 f.; Suffield's scheme in 1830, 322 ff.
Almack's, 68, 70.
Althorp, Lord, 190, 202, 288; Cobbett on, 313.
America, farmers in, 212; Cobbett in, 235.
Amnesty Debate, 314.
Andover, 260, 280, 285.
Appeal, against enclosure award, 59 f.
Arbuthnot, J., 37, 81.
Aristocracy, contrast between English and French, 1 ff.; control over all English institutions, 7 ff.; Burke on, 24 f.; characteristics, Chapter xiii.
Armley (enclosure), 51, 59, 60, and Appendix A (1).
Arson, in 1830, 243 ff., 268 f.; penalties for, 273; trials for, 309 f.
Artaxerxes, 70.
Arthur, Sir George (Governor of Van Diemen's Land), 205, 324.
Arundel, 256.

Arundel, Lord, 261, 293.
Ash, 183.
Ashbury (enclosure), 43 *n*
Ashelworth (enclosure), 46, 50 59, 98, and Appendix A (2).
Astley, Sir E., 71.
Aston, Tirrold, 263.
Atkins, Elizabeth, 102.
Attorney-General. *See* Denman.
Aunalls, James, 285.
Austen, Jane, 214.
Avington, 258, 265.
Award, enclosure, 60.
Aylesbury, 132; riots in 1795, 121, Special Commission, 275, 306 f.
Azay le Rideau, 3.

BABEAU, M., 1, 215, 223.
Bacon, R. M., 321.
Bagehot, W., 36.
Bagshot Heath, 40.
Bailiffs, 160, 213.
Baily, Mr., 97 *n*.
Baker, Mr., M.P., and Settlement, 153.
Bakewell, 36.
Bamford, S., 213, 238.
Bampfylde, Copleston Warre, 65.
Barett, 293.
Baring, Bingham, 292, 304; and Cook, 286; and Deacle case, 278, 287.
—— Sir Thomas, 187, 192, 284.
Barings, the, 243, 288, 302, 317.
Barkham, 82.
Barnes, 277.
—— Common, 31.
Barré, Colonel, 219.
Barton Stacey, 284, 285.
Basingstoke, 162 *n*., 289.
Baskerville, Mr., J.P , 297
Bath, 121, 127, 130 *n*., 190 *n*.
Bathurst, Lord, 56.
Batten, Matthew, 303.
Battersea, 30.
Battle, 248, 250, 253, 255, 256.
Beaconsfield, 135.
Beckett (the gaoler), 277.
Beckley, 88 f., 91.